Lecture Notes in Artificial Intelligence   1760

Subseries of Lecture Notes in Computer Science
Edited by J. G. Carbonell and J. Siekmann

Lecture Notes in Computer Science
Edited by G. Goos, J. Hartmanis and J. van Leeuwen

Springer
Berlin
Heidelberg
New York
Barcelona
Hong Kong
London
Milan
Paris
Singapore
Tokyo

John-Jules Ch. Meyer
Pierre-Yves Schobbens (Eds.)

Formal Models
of Agents

ESPRIT Project ModelAge Final Workshop
Selected Papers

Springer

Series Editors

Jaime G. Carbonell, Carnegie Mellon University, Pittsburgh, PA, USA
Jörg Siekmann, University of Saarland, Saarbrücken, Germany

Volume Editors

John-Jules Ch. Meyer
Utrecht University, Department of Computer Science
Padualaan 14, De Uithof, 3508 TB Utrecht, The Netherlands
E-mail: jj@cs.uu.nl

Pierre-Yves Schobbens
Institut d'Informatique
Rue Grandgagnage 21, 5000 Namur, Belgium
E-mail: pys@info.fundp.ac.be

Cataloging-in-Publication data applied for

Die Deutsche Bibliothek - CIP-Einheitsaufnahme

Formal models of agents : ESPRIT project ModelAge final workshop ; selected papers/
John-Jules Ch. Meyer ; Pierre-Yves Schobbens (ed.). - Berlin ; Heidelberg ;
New York ; Barcelona ; Hong Kong ; London ; Milan ; Paris ; Singapore ;
Tokyo : Springer, 2000
  (Lecture notes in computer science ; Vol. 1760 : Lecture notes in
  artificial intelligence)
  ISBN 3-540-67027-0

CR Subject Classification (1998): I.2.11, C.2.4, D.2, F.3, I.2

ISBN 3-540-67027-0 Springer-Verlag Berlin Heidelberg New York

© Springer-Verlag Berlin Heidelberg 2000
Printed in Germany

Typesetting: Camera-ready by author
SPIN 10719643   06/3142 – 5 4 3 2 1 0   Printed on acid-free paper

Preface

This volume contains a number of revised papers that were selected from papers presented at the last ModelAge workshop held in Certosa di Pertignano (Italy) in 1997, organised by the Institute of Psychology of the Italian CNR (IP-CNR), Division of Artificial Intelligence, Cognitive Modeling and Interaction. The organisation chair was held by Amedeo Cesta. The workshop, and indeed the ModelAge project as a whole, aimed to bring together a number of researchers stemming from different disciplines to discuss formal models of agency from different perspectives. These disciplines included artificial intelligence, software engineering, applied logic, databases, and organisation theory. The field of intelligent agents has become an important research area within these disciplines, and in the workshop as in the present volume the concept of agency is thus considered from a multi-disciplinary perspective.

In the introductory chapter of this volume more can be found on the area of intelligent agents as well as on the topic of formal models of these. We furthermore provide some key references, so that the reader can better appreciate the position of the present volume within the literature on agent technology. Moreover, we briefly describe the ModelAge project which was an ESPRIT-funded Basic Research Working Group dedicated to the study of formal models of agents, and one may find the details of the organisation of the workshop here. Finally in this chapter we give a detailed overview of the contents of this book from which we hope you will get an impression of the deliberately multi-disciplinary approach that is taken.

Finally, we would like to take this opportunity to thank all the persons involved in the realisation of this book: authors, PC members, additional reviewers, the organisers and audience of the ModelAge workshop, and the people from Springer-Verlag.

November 1999

John-Jules Meyer
Pierre-Yves Schobbens

Table of Contents

Formal Models of Agents:
An Introduction

John-Jules Ch. Meyer[1] and Pierre-Yves Schobbens[2]

[1] Intelligent Systems Group, Dept. of Computer Science, Utrecht University, P.O.
Box 80089, 3508 TB, Utrecht, The Netherlands, jj@cs.ruu.nl
[2] Institut d'Informatique, Fac. Univ. Notre-Dame de la Paix, Rue Grandgagnage 21,
B-5000 Namur, Belgium

1 Intelligent Agents

Although in philosophical literature the notion of an agent as a cognitive subject
has been around for a long time, in the last decade or so the area of 'Intelligent
Agents' has also become a major area of research within artificial intelligence
and computer science, an area with a big promise as there are a myriad of possible applications (see e.g. [4]). As might be expected, within the latter areas the
concept of an agent generally has a more technical meaning, although there is no
general consensus on its definition. But mostly by an agent is meant a (software
or hardware) entity that has some degree of *autonomy*, which typically comes
down to displaying reactive and/or proactive behaviour (that is to say that the
agent is capable of reacting to its environment and taking initiative, independent
of the user, respectively), might possess reasoning and learning capabilities, and
is able to communicate in some intelligent way with other agents. Sometimes
agents are ascribed 'mental attributes' such as a mental state comprising *knowledge, belief,* Whether these mental attributes are merely metaphorical (i.e. a
convenient means of describing agents) or 'real' in the sense that these artificial
agents possess some 'truly cognitive' capabilities like human or, to a lesser extent, animal agents do, is of course a matter of philosophical debate but also a
question depending to a large extent on the application one has in mind.

One view of agents that is very 'computational' is that of viewing agents
as the next step in programming as a successor of the popular object-oriented
programming paradigm. Although objects already display some form of 'autonomy' in the sense that they have their own datatypes and methods which can
be called by other objects, agents are rather to be considered as 'subjects', possessing their own ontology (signature), their own knowledge / beliefs about their
environment (possibly including themselves if they have reflective capabilities)
and their own goals to achieve. Moreover, communicating is much less a matter
of just invoking a method of another agent, but rather asking questions to other
agents which these other agents may (or may not) handle in their own way.

Of course, these matters can also be viewed from a more cognitive perspective. (Some researchers like to include human agents into their conception of
an agent, and consider 'mixed' systems of human and artificial agents.) One can

then look at agents at the 'micro' level: their internal make-up, possibly described in terms of mental states (comprising knowledge, beliefs, intentions, etc.), and at the 'macro' level: external and 'social' behaviour (including communication, co-ordination, co-operation).

It is important to stress that the area of intelligent agents is truly multidisciplinary. Clearly the area has a big overlap with contemporary AI. Some feel that agent-based systems are the next generation of the information-based and knowledge-based (expert) systems from the 80's. In any case one can readily agree that agent systems are a new generation of intelligent systems, and as such part of the AI research programme. As we saw above agent-oriented programming can also be viewed as a new programming paradigm in computer science, more in general. And, as we have also briefly mentioned, traditionally there are influences from (analytical) philosophy. Many writings by (mostly 20th century) philosophers on the nature of 'action' are relevant for the field of 'intelligent agents'. Finally, also cognitive and social scientists show a great interest in agents, in particular systems in which multiple agents are present, the so-called *multi-agent systems (MAS)*. Their interest includes how agent societies develop and employ norms to govern / constrain their behaviour.

There has arisen a great deal of literature on the topic of intelligent agents. Many papers deal with the practical issue of designing and building them for particular applications such as agents for assisting users of the internet. See, for example, the Proceedings of the Autonomous Agents and PAAM (Practical Application of Intelligent Agents and Multi-Agent Technology) Conferences, where many researchers exchange their views on how to address these applications. More theoretical are the MAAMAW (e.g. [1]) and ICMAS conferences on Multi-Agent Systems (e.g. [2]), and particularly the series of books entitled "Intelligent Agents" in the Springer Lecture Notes in AI [8, 10, 9, 7, 5], based on the proceedings of the ATAL workshops ("Agent Theories, Architectures, and Languages").

2 Formal Models

Formal models are a tool to arrive at unambiguous and precise meanings of concepts. They may comprise a well-defined language with a precise, mathematical semantics in terms of set theory, for example. Also one may think of some axiomatic system (logic) that lays down the exact meanings of the terms of the logic by postulates / axioms. Since the field of agents is 'exploding' in many directions, it seems very reasonable to strive for a (common) formal model on which there is some consensus among the various researchers (stemming from different disciplines).

However, the need for formal models goes beyond the mere understanding of the subject of intelligent agents (although of course this is very important, too)! As with traditional software, in order to design and implement agent systems it would be very advantageous to have some formal means of describing and specifying the behaviour of these systems. For this reason, too, formal models of agency are called for. One might, for instance, think of a logical calculus with a well-defined semantics that describes the agent's (mental and social) attitudes. To do justice to the idea of multidisciplinarity of agents and agent research as we have discussed above it is important to view agents from several perspectives which will naturally lead to the use of formal models of different nature. To treat the different aspects of agency adequately it appeared that many theories have to be considered and combined: from the theory of reasoning about actions and change (a well-known area in AI) to the theory of norms (dealing with the social attitudes of agents), from database theory and the theory of concurrent computation to principles of software engineering.

We must mention here the well-known BDI model proposed by Rao & Georgeff [6] which has been very influential. The model is based on (branching time) temporal logic (CTL*). Agent behaviour is modelled by tree-like structures, where each path through such a tree represents a possible 'life' of the agent. The basic logic containing temporal modalities such as "along every path in the future there is some point where" is augmented by means of 'BDI'-modalities, viz. a belief operator BEL, a desire operator GOAL and an intention operator INTEND. Thus in this model one is able to express how the beliefs, desires and intentions of an agent evolve over time (or rather over possible time lines). Formally, Rao & Georgeff's BDI-model is a formal (modal) logic with a Kripke-style semantics and a logical calculus. Rao & Georgeff were especially interested in the relationship between the BDI modalities. In their paper they discuss several such possible relations such as Belief-Goal compatibility and Goal-Intention compatibility. The former expresses that agents believe that their goals are obtainable in some future, while the latter states that the agents' intentions should be goals. Rao & Georgeff and other researchers have used their model as an inspiration for their work on the realisation of agents. The BDI model have thus given rise to BDI architectures where the elements of belief bases, goal bases and plan libraries are central. Although these have been applied quite successfully, an as yet ongoing frustration among agent researchers is the gap between the formal (BDI) model and the (BDI-based) architectures in the sense that one would like to use the former to specify the latter formally and prove formal properties about these. But as yet this is not shown to be possible, as the 'distance' between the two 'worlds' is too great. Within the ModelAge project some work has been done to give an alternative for the 'classical' BDI logic where the basic logic is a logic of action (viz. dynamic logic) rather than a temporal logic [3]. It appears that in this way the gap can be made smaller, but a formal specification of a concrete agent in this logic is still a much wanted *desideratum*.

3 The ModelAge project

The ModelAge project was an ESPRIT-funded Basic Research Working Group (ESPRIT III BRWG 8319) intended to study formal models of (co-operating) intelligent agents by means of an multi-disciplinary approach. It ran from 1994 through 1997. The official title of the project was "A Common Formal Model of Cooperating Intelligent Agents". The project grew out of the realisation that the field of 'intelligent agents' was expanding rapidly within several (almost) disjoint communities with their own set of concepts, techniques and objectives, and that some kind of 'co-ordination' was necessary. In the project researchers participated from the areas of requirements engineering, organisational models, software design, concurrency theory, distributed artificial intelligence and (federative) databases.

The consortium consisted of groups from Namur, London (Imperial College), Keele, Lisbon, Oslo, Rotterdam, Utrecht / Amsterdam, Rome, Sophia-Antipolis (INRIA), Aachen and Braunschweig. The project had special interest groups on defeasibility and agent modalities, logics and models of action, interaction in organizations, software development process, business and legal applications, and on diagnostics, repair and reconfiguration. Apart from meetings of these special interest groups there have been four workshops of the project as a whole, of which the last one was advertised in a broader context with both PC members and presenters (and audience) outside the ModelAge project.

Although originally the objective of the project was to obtain *a common formal model of agency* using the expertise from the diverse fields above, this soon proved to be somewhat too ambitious. However, it is clear that by bringing experts together from the above fields in general meetings and workshops as well as in special interest groups the project addressed the various 'faces' of agency and succeeded to stimulate cross-fertilisation among these various fields, and in this way has been very successful and stimulating!

4 About This Book

4.1 The workshop

The present book is the result of the work done within the ModelAge project (complemented with some related work done outside the project), and in particular that of the last ModelAge Workshop held in Certosa di Pontignano in Italy in 1997, and organised by the Institute of Psychology of the Italian CNR (IP-CNR). Amedeo Cesta acted as the Organisation chair. The papers have been reviewed by an international programme committee in which also well-known researchers outside the ModelAge project had been invited, assisted by a number of additional reviewers. Although the book is not intended to be a complete survey of the work accomplished in the ModelAge project, it nevertheless reflects the interdisciplinary nature of the project very well.

The PC consisted of C. Castelfranchi (CNR, Rome), A. Cesta (CNR, Rome), R. Dieng (INRIA, Sophia-Antipolis), E. Dubois (Univ. Namur), J. Fiadeiro (Univ. Lisbon), A. Jones (Univ. Oslo), H. Levesque (Univ. Toronto), J. Mylopoulos (Univ. Toronto), J.-J. Ch. Meyer (Univ. Utrecht), W. Nejdl (Univ. Hannover), M. Ryan (Univ. Birmingham), G. Saake (Univ. Magdeburg), P.-Y. Schobbens (Univ. Namur, Programme Chair), K. Segerberg (Univ. Uppsala), Y.-H. Tan (Univ. Rotterdam), R. Wieringa (Vrije Univ. Amsterdam). The papers are selected from the papers presented at the workshop, which in turn were selected on the basis of three independent evaluations by PC members.

Furthermore, the following persons served as additional reviewers: D. d'Aloisi, G. Brewka, J. Carmo, H. Coelho, S. Conrad, R. Conte, M. Deen, F.M. Dionisio, Ph. Du Bois, V. Englebert, R. Falcone, A. Finkelstein, M. Gertz, S. Guerra, W. van der Hoek, J.-M. Jacquet, U. Lipeck, G.-J. Lokhorst, A. Lomuscio, M. Miceli, C. Paredes, M. Petit, H. Prakken, A.S. Rao, J.-F. Raskin, J. Scheerder, A. Sernadas, A. Sloman, L. van der Torre, C. Türker, I. Wright, J.-M. Zeippen.

4.2 Description of the papers

We now give a short description of the papers in this volume from which the multi-disciplinarity of the subject of agent modelling and the ModelAge project itself becomes apparent.

The paper by Stanislaw Ambroszkiewicz and Jan Komar considers rational behaviour of agents from a game-theoretic perspective. The desire component of a BDI-agent (as we have seen above) is represented as the agent's goal to maximize utility. The complete agent model comprises five parts dealing with perception, knowledge / belief, rational behaviour, the reasoning process, and intention.

Frances Brazier *et al.* present a generic model for the internal dynamic behaviour of a BDI agent. For this they employ the compositional multi-agent modelling framework DESIRE. Since DESIRE is aimed at the actual implementation of agent systems, this paper provides a first step of bridging the above mentioned gap between formal agent models (such as the BDI model) and implementations.

The contribution of John Bell and Zhisheng Huang deals with an important informational attitude of agents, viz. that of coping with their beliefs in situations where new information becomes available all the time. They propose an approach to belief revision using hierarchies of belief in order to cater for the difference in reliance of beliefs. These belief hierarchies themselves are dynamic in the sense that they (may) change over time.

In the paper of Stefan Conrad *et al.* the notion of an agent is viewed as a further development of the notion of an object in object-oriented programming. It is used to model the dynamics of information systems more adequately than traditional approaches. First steps towards an agent-oriented specification framework for this purpose are taken by employing an extended temporal logic.

Rosaria Conte *et al.* discuss in their paper some basic limitations of the use of game theory for modelling autonomous agents and multi-agent systems. In particular they show that Prisoners' Dilemma games fall short for modelling truly cooperative behaviour. In order to get an adequate theory for cooperation it is therefore proposed to also include elements from AI, in particular a theory of action and planning.

In their paper Enrico Denti and Andrea Omicini consider the communication and coordination aspects of multi-agent systems (MAS) from a computer science point of view. They provide a flexible coordination model based on an extensible coordination medium for a MAS. It is shown how a MAS can be designed around the communication abstraction behaviour.

Frank Dignum also addresses the issue of communication between agents, but focuses on the distinctions between 'global' and 'private' views on communication. In the former the MAS is seen as one big system, whereas in the latter view each action is ascribed to an individual agent having control over that action. The consequences of the two views for agent communication and the agent's degree of autonomy are investigated, and a sketch of a formalisation of the model in a multi-modal logic is provided.

Carlos Duarte looks in his paper at communication as well. He proposes a logical and, more specifically, a proof-theoretical foundation of the well-known actor model, which might be considered as an early computational model of a MAS, where the focus is on (rather low-level) communication. His work aims at the specification and verification of such actor systems.

The paper of Barbara Dunin-Keplicz and Anna Radzikowska use techniques from theoretical computer science to consider a typical AI problem that is relevant voor describing intelligent agents, viz. reasoning about (nondeterministic) actions with typical effects. They employ the KARO logic developed in the ModelAge project [3] for reasoning about actions / scenarios and add on top of this preferential models which are known from the area of common-sense (nonmonotonic) reasoning.

Agents typically function in a dynamic environment where circumstances change. Bruno Errico addresses the problem of describing the dynamics of an agent's mental attitudes, that is how these attitudes change as the environment changes. The attitudes studied concern the agent's beliefs and goals. His proposal is based on a well-known (within the area of AI) first-order formalism for reasoning about actions, viz. that of the situation calculus.

Fröhlich et al. treat an application of agent systems for the diagnosis of distributed technical systems such as computer networks. An agent is assigned to each subsystem. The system is implemented by means of the concepts of vivid agents (a software-controlled system whose state is represented by a knowledge base, and whose behaviour is represented by action / reaction rules) and extended logic programming.

In John-Jules Meyer & Patrick Doherty's contribution a new approach is set out for reasoning about actions. This is an infamous area in AI where there are problems like the frame, qualification and the ramification problem having to deal with the effects and particularly the non-effects of actions performed by some agent. While most proposed solutions regard the rather abstract level of logical theories on possible scenarios, here a solution is sought on the more concrete and computational level of the semantics (behaviour) of the actions themselves.

Another view of agents is given by Henry Prakken: agents engaged in a dispute using argumentations to come to an agreement. Argumentations might be defeasible in the sense that when more information becomes available different arguments may 'win'. In this paper a dialectical proof theory is proposed for defeasible argumentation in a setting in which also the priorities that determine which arguments are defeated themselves are subject to debate (argumentation) and thus are defeasible.

In the contribution of Leon van der Torre *et al.* we encounter yet another aspect of agent systems. In societies of agents (whether they consist of human or artificial agents) norms play an important role to regulate their behaviour. Traditionally (some of) these aspects are described by deontic logic in which one can reason about norms. In the present paper the authors argue that in order to also reason *with* norms to draw conclusions of how norms affect the agents' behaviour one needs to include elements from the theory of diagnostic reasoning and qualitative decision theory.

More about normative reasoning can be found in the article by Leon van der Torre and Yao-Hua Tan. Here a new kind of deontic logic (so-called contextual deontic logic) is proposed in which one can express that something is obligatory under some conditions *unless* something else is the case. The logic thus comprises an interesting amalgam of ideas from deontic logic and defeasible (default) reasoning. Contextual deontic logic is shown to be useful for treating so-called contrary-to-duty obligations, which occur widely in practical situations involving norms.

References

1. M. Boman & W. Van de Velde, *Multi-Agent Rationality, Proc. MAAMAW'97*, LNAI 1237, Springer, Berlin, 1997.
2. Y. Demazeau (ed.), Proc. of the Third Int. Conf. on Multi-Agent Systems, IEEE Computer Society, Los Alamitos, CA, 1998
3. W. van der Hoek, B. van Linder & J.-J. Ch. Meyer, An Integrated Modal Approach to Rational Agents, in: M. Wooldridge & A. Rao (eds.), *Foundations of Rational Agency*, Applied Logic Series 14, Kluwer, Dordrecht, 1998, pp. 133-168.
4. N.R. Jennings & M.J. Wooldridge, *Agent technology: Foundations, Applications, and Markets*, Springer, Berlin, 1997.
5. J.P. Müller, M.P. Singh & A.S. Rao (eds.), *Intelligent Agents V (Agent Theories, Architectures, and Languages)*, LNAI 1555, Springer, Berlin, 1999.
6. A.S. Rao & M.P. Georgeff, Modeling rational agents within a BDI-architecture, in *Proceedings of the Second International Conference on Principles of Knowledge Representation and Reasoning (KR'91)* (J. Allen, R. Fikes & E. Sandewall, eds.), Morgan Kaufmann, 1991, pp. 473–484.
7. M.P. Singh, A. Rao & M.J. Wooldridge (eds.), *Intelligent Agents IV*, LNAI 1365, Springer, Berlin, 1998.
8. M.J. Wooldridge & N.R. Jennings (eds.), *Intelligent Agents*, Springer, Berlin, 1995.
9. M. Wooldridge, J.P. Müller & N.R. Jennings (eds.), *Intelligent Agents III*, Springer, Berlin, 1997.
10. M. Wooldridge, J.P. Müller & M. Tambe (eds.), *Intelligent Agents Volume II – Agent Theories, Architectures, and Languages*, LNAI 1037, Springer, Berlin, 1996.

A Model of BDI–Agent in Game–Theoretic Framework*

Stanisław Ambroszkiewicz and Jan Komar

Institute of Computer Science, Polish Academy of Sciences
PL-01-237 Warsaw, ul. Ordona 21, Poland
sambrosz@ipipan.waw.pl
http://www.ipipan.waw.pl/mas/

Abstract. A model of BDI–agent in game–theoretic framework is presented. The desire is represented as agent's goal to achieve a maximum level of utility. A reasoning process based on agent's rational behavior is proposed. This process determines agent's intention. It is also shown how to use the backward induction consistently with the assumption of the common knowledge of rationality.

1 Introduction

We are going to discuss the following problem:

How does a rational agent use its knowledge in decision making ?

Since the problem is general, we put it in a game–theoretic framework. In the theory of games, agent's rationality is understood as a way of maximizing the utility of the agent relatively to its knowledge. The knowledge may concern the game that is to be played as well as the agents participating in a play.

The main task of the paper is to model BDI-agent that is supposed to *live* in the world of dynamic games. Agent's belief is identified with the knowledge about the game and about other agents together with a probability distribution.

The desire is represented as agent's goal to achieve a maximum level of its utility.

The intentions are determined by some methods that realize this level of utility. These methods are called *rational behaviors*. Bayesian behavior, that consists in maximizing the expected utility, may serve as the classical example of rational behavior considered in decision theory.

Let us suppose that agent j is characterized by the following belief B_j, desire D_j, and rational behavior Rb_j. Thus, according to the rational behavior, agent j considers some of its actions as not optimum, relatively to B_j, D_j. The actions that are not optimum are removed, so that the initial game is reduced; whereas the optimum actions may be regarded as temporal, partial, and individual intentions of agent j in the reasoning process.

---

* Our thanks are due to four anonymous referees for important remarks and suggestions. The work was supported by KBN Grant 8T11C 03110

J.-J. Ch. Meyer, P.-Y. Schobbens (Eds.): Formal Methods of Agents, LNAI 1760, pp. 8–19, 1999.

Now, let us suppose that agent i knows the characteristics (B_j, D_j, Rb_j) of agent j. Knowing this, agent i can reconstruct the reasoning process of agent j, and gets to know, in this way, the optimum actions of agent j, so that also the fact that the initial game has been reduced. Knowing that, agent i will use this reduced game as a basis to compute its own optimum actions. These optimum actions may be considered as temporal, partial, and individual intention of agent i in its reasoning process.

We may suppose that agent j knows the agent i's characteristics and the fact that agent i knows its own characteristics, i.e. (B_j, D_j, Rb_j). Then, agent j could compute its new knowledge about the game and on the basis of this knowledge its new more complete intention.

Let us note that since no new event occurs, these changes of knowledge and intention have nothing to do with revision and updating. It seems that these changes should be called knowledge and intention *evolution* in the reasoning process.

We can not model knowledge evolution in the formalism of Halpern et al. [6], because there the agents are supposed to be omniscient (i.e. the perfect reasoners), so that all changes are already incorporated in the knowledge.

As to the formalism introduced by Rao and Georgeff [10], the three notions of belief, desire, and intention are defined independently there. So that it seems that agent's intention are considered there as a final result of reasoning process, however without giving any reference to a construction of the process.

The main idea of our paper is that rational behavior may be used to construct such reasoning process. For this purpose we divide agent's knowledge into several hierarchical types. We distinguish a special type of knowledge, called *ground type*. This ground type knowledge is exactly the knowledge on which a rational behavior depends, i.e. the agent's action taking is directly dependent on this type of knowledge. It is natural to assume that the ground type forms a small part of all possible knowledge of the agent. Of course, the agent should be interested in having this ground knowledge as precise as possible. So that the agent tries to find transformations (logical rules) that transform all its knowledge into ground knowledge making it in this way more exact.

The process of reasoning is defined as a transformation that conveys the knowledge from higher types, in the hierarchy, into the lower types and finally into the ground type.

The final ground knowledge is the basis for determining the final intention.

Similar ideas of knowledge transformations may be found in [7], [13], [14] where a special kind of agent rationality is considered, namely Bayesian rationality. However, the idea of the ground type is not distinguished explicitly there. Moreover, in all the above papers only, a so called, static case is considered, that is, agents take actions only once. The dynamic case, where the agents take actions many times, is much more complex and causes a number of serious problems. One of them is the paradox, see [3], concerning backward induction, (i.e. a natural planning method), and common knowledge of the rationality of agents. Since these two notions are necessary for planning and reasoning about future, it is impossible to investigate seriously the dynamic multi–agent systems without an explanation of the reasons that cause the paradox.

In order to present briefly the paradox, let us consider the following two person game in extensive form. More details can be found in [11,3].

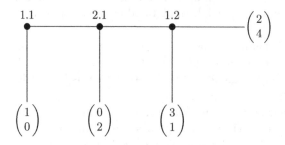

The first move of the game belongs to agent 1. At node 1.1 the agent can either continue the game (move *right*) or end the game (move *down*) with the payoffs: 1 dollar for agent 1, and 0 for agent 2. If agent 1 decides to continue the game, then agent 2 finds itself at decision node 2.1 and has to choose between *right* and *down*. If agent 2 chooses down then the game ends with the payoffs: 0 for agent 1, and 2 dollars for agent 2. And so on.

The backward induction with the assumption of common knowledge of agent rationality gives $\begin{pmatrix} 1 \\ 0 \end{pmatrix}$ as the solution of the game. The reason is as follows. At node 1.2 the agent 1, acting rationally, takes move *down*. Knowing this, agent 2 at node 2.1 also chooses *down* as the only rational move. So that knowing these both facts, agent 1 at node 1.1, chooses as optimum the move *down*.

However, let us consider again agent 2 at node 2.1. According to the backward induction and the assumption of common knowledge of rationality, agent 2 should never find itself at the decision node 2.1. If agent 2, in spite of this, does find itself at node 2.1, this means that the agent 1 has behaved irrationally at node 1.1 choosing *right* instead of *down*. This contradicts the assumption of the common knowledge of rationality.

It seems that the reason of the paradox is that agent, say i, can not have knowledge about future knowledge of another agent's (say j) knowledge at some future state of the world. If the agent did have such knowledge and this knowledge were true, then this would violate the causality principle. The explanation is simple: knowing that agent i had such knowledge, agent j would take some actions, that would make this future knowledge or this future state of the world impossible.

In the paper we present:

- a construction of reasoning process that determines agent's intention,
- how to convey the dynamic case into so called *one–shot* case where each agent takes action at most once,
- an explanation of the paradox.

These items above will allow to use the backward induction consistently with the assumption of the common knowledge of rationality.

2   Dynamic System

The dynamic system is supposed to be a world in which the agents *live*. It consists of:

- the set of global states denoted by Ω, with the distinguished state, say ω^0, being the initial state,
- enumeration of agent's sites denoted by the set $N = \{1, 2, 3, \ \ldots \ , n\}$,
- for each site $i \in N$, there is the set of actions A_i from which an agent, occupying the site i, may take one action at any (discrete) moment of time,
- transition function $\Phi : \Omega \times \prod_{i \in N} A_i \to \Omega$, determining the next global state of the system given the current state of the system and the actions taken by the agents,
- the duration of the system, say T, being a natural number.

We assume that the time is discrete and the system is synchronous, i.e. at any moment of time t, the agents take actions simultaneously, so that if the system state is ω and the agents take actions $a_1, a_2, \ \ldots \ , a_n$ respectively, then at time $t + 1$ the global state of the system is moved to $\omega' \overset{df}{=} \Phi(\omega, a_1, a_2, \ \ldots \ , a_n)$ according to the transition function.

Let us introduce some useful notations. Let $A \overset{df}{=} \prod_{i \in N} A_i$. Let $a^t \in A$, $a^t = (a_1^t, a_2^t, \ \ldots \ , a_n^t)$, denote the actions taken by the agents at time t. Let $(\omega^0, a^0, a^1, a^2, \ \ldots \ , a^{t-1})$ be called t-run of the system, or a possible history by the time t. It is clear that each t- run determines the global states of the system at times: 1, 2, $\ldots$, t.

Let $\Re$ be the the set of all T-runs.

Let $r(t) \overset{df}{=} \omega^t$ denote the global state of the system at time t determined by run r.

Let $r(i, t) \overset{df}{=} a_i^t$ denotes the action taken by the agent i at time t in the run r.

For $r = (\omega^0, a^0, a^1, a^2, \ \ldots \ , a^T) \in \Re$ and $t \leq T$, let $(r, t) \overset{df}{=} (\omega^0, a^0, a^1, a^2, \ \ldots \ , a^{t-1})$. Let (r, t) be called a situation at time t. Let S denote the set of all possible situations at times : 1,2, $\ldots$, T.

The dynamic system defined above is abstract and, in fact, describes only relations between the system states and actions of the agents. Similar dynamic systems are considered in the theory of distributed systems, see [8,9].

3   Agent Model

Let us stress that there are only agent sites in the dynamic system, so that it is up to a designer of a MAS to put into these sites specific agent architectures.

We are going to outline some aspects of abstract model of an agent that may occupy the site i in the dynamic system.

We distinguish the following five basic parts of this model: (1) Perception, (2) Desire, (3) Knowledge and belief, (4) Rational behavior, (5) Reasoning process, (6) Intention.

3.1   Perception

It is natural that an agent perceives more or less the world in which it lives. Since the world is a dynamic system, the complete information about the world is contained in the current global state of the system. Hence, agent perception should consist in partial information about this global state. What agent perceives constitutes its local world with its local states. Formally, let Q_i denote the set of local states of agent i. Then, agent i's perception is defined as the function $J_i : \Omega \to Q_i$ with the following interpretation. If the current global state is ω, then agent i perceives $q_i \overset{df}{=} J_i(\omega)$ as its local state, i.e. q_i is the current state of the (local world of) agent i. Hence, agent i knows only that the true global state of the system belongs to the set

$$J_i^{-1}(q_i) \overset{df}{=} \{\omega \in \Omega : \quad J_i(\omega) = q_i\}$$

Since each T–run r determines global states of the system at times $t = 0, 1, 2, \ldots, T$, say $\omega^0, \omega^1, \ldots, \omega^T$, let

$$J_i(r) \overset{df}{=} (J_i(\omega^0), J_i(\omega^1), \ldots, J_i(\omega^T))$$

denote the sequence of agent i's local states for run r. Let us notice that $J_i(r)$ is the perception record of agent i in the run r.

3.2   Desire

The desire of agent i is expressed by aspiration level, denoted by a real number α_i, and utility function u_i defined on its perception records, i.e. sequences of local states from time $t = 1$ to $t = T$. Formally

$$u_i : Q_i^T \to R,$$

where R is the set of real numbers.

Agent's desire is to find itself in the local states: $q_i^1, q_i^2, \ldots, q_i^T$, (state q_i^t at time t), such that

$$u_i(q_i^1, q_i^2, \ldots, q_i^T) \geq \alpha_i.$$

We assume that any agent remembers all his previous local states, so that the agent can calculate its utility. This implies that the agents know the global time; in game theory it is called *perfect recall*. We may drop this assumption, however then the notations become cumbersome.

3.3   Rational Behavior

If agent wants to maximize its utility, then its behavior leading to this maximization is called *rational* in game theory. Since there are several kinds of rational behavior, like Bayesian, risk aversion, or gambler behavior (see [2]), we introduce a general form of agent's behavior that leads the agent to satisfy its desire. In order to define agent behavior, we must define agent decision problems.

Primitive decision problem of agent i, (pdp_i for short), is the following

$$pdp_i \overset{df}{=} (A_i, (\mu_{a_i})_{a_i \in A_i}),$$

where μ_{a_i} is a probability distribution on the set of the real numbers.

The interpretation is following: if agent i has to deal with primitive decision problem pdp_i and takes action a_i then the probability that its utility will be x is equal to $\mu_{a_i}(x)$. So that in this case the agent is not sure about the result of its action.

Let PDP_i be the set of all pdp_i. Behavior of agent i is defined as Rb_i : $PDP_i \to 2^{A_i}$, with the following interpretation. If agent i's behavior is Rb_i, and the agent has to deal with pdp_i, then the agent considers the actions from the set $Rb_i(pdp_i) \subseteq A_i$ as optimal, i.e. satisfying its desire. Usually the desire attributes of the agent, α_i and u_i, are taken as the parameters of behavior Rb_i.

As an example of rational agent behavior, we may consider so called Bayesian behavior defined as follows: $Rb_i(A_i, (\mu_{a_i})_{a_i \in A_i})$ is the set of all actions a_i that maximize the expected utility

$$\sum_{x \in R} x \cdot \mu_{a_i}(x)$$

Sometimes an agent knows only that its primitive decision problem belongs to some set S, then it is natural to consider as optimum any action from the set:

$$A'_i = \bigcup_{pdp_i \in S} Rb_i(pdp_i).$$

Agent's behavior should reflect agent's desire to achieve its goal, see [2]. Since agent's behavior depends directly on the primitive decision problems, it is clear that all agent's knowledge and reasoning resources should be used to determine the pdp_i.

3.4   Knowledge and Belief

It is supposed that agent's perception function, agent's desire, and rational behavior can not be changed over time. However, agent's knowledge and belief is a subject of change.

At any moment of time t, agent i has knowledge about what T–runs are possible. Let the set of possible, according to agent i, T–runs be denoted by $\Re_i^t$. Agent may consider some T–runs as more or less probable, so that we must introduce the notion of agent belief at time t, denoted by Bel_i^t. It is a probability distribution on $\Re_i^t$.

Let $\Delta\Re_i^t$ denote the set of all probability distributions defined on $\Re_i^t$.

Let $(\Re_i^t, Bel_i^t)$ constitute agent i's *ground knowledge* at time t.

It should be clear that each $(\Re_i^t, Bel_i^t)$ determines unique

$pdp_i \overset{df}{=} (A_i, (\mu_{a_i})_{a_i \in A_i})$ in the following way:

Let $Z(a_i, x) \overset{df}{=} \{r \in \Re_i^t : \; r(i, t) = a_i \; \& \; u_i(J_i(r)) = x\}$, then

$$\mu_{a_i}(x) \overset{df}{=} \sum_{r \in Z(a_i, x)} Bel_i^t(r),$$

for the definition of $r(i, t)$, see Section 2, and for $J_i(r)$, see Section 3.1. So that we will somewhat abuse the notations writing $Rb_i(\Re_i^t, Bel_i^t)$ instead of $Rb_i(pdp_i)$.

Let

$$char_i^t \overset{df}{=} (\Re_i^t, Bel_i^t; J_i; u_i, \alpha_i, Rb_i)$$

denote a possible characteristics of agent i at time t. In fact, it consists of agent ground knowledge, perception, desire, and rational behavior. Let $CHAR_i^t$ denote the set of all such possible characteristics.

Now we are going to define a representation of mutual knowledge, i.e. knowledge about other agents and their knowledge. Let for any sequence $i, j_1, \dots, j_k$ (of elements from the set N),

$$\mathbf{K}_{i,j_1, \dots, j_k}^t \text{ be a subset of } CHAR_{j_k}^t$$

The meaning of the introduced notation is the following:

– *at time t agent i knows that agent j_1 knows that ... that agent j_k's characteristics belongs to the set $\mathbf{K}_{i,j_1, \dots, j_k}^t$.*

Let us see that the following sequence

$$(\mathbf{K}_i^t, \; (\mathbf{K}_{i,j_1}^t)_{j_1 \in N}, \; (\mathbf{K}_{i,j_1,j_2}^t)_{j_1,j_2 \in N}, \; \dots)$$

represents a tree, that is, $\mathbf{K}_i^t$ is the root of the tree and it is a characteristics of agent i, $(\mathbf{K}_{i,j_1}^t)_{j_1 \in N}$ is the collection of nodes at level 1, $(\mathbf{K}_{i,j_1,j_2}^t)_{j_1,j_2 \in N}$ is the collection of nodes at level 2, and so on. Hence, the tree is a representation of *mutual knowledge of agent i*. Of course we should put some restrictions on the sets $\mathbf{K}_{i \dots j}^t$, like that agent i can not know more about agent j's knowledge than agent j itself, and so on.

Let us note that this knowledge representation may be constructed in the way that is consistent with the standard notion of knowledge, see for example Halpern et al. [6].

The notion of mutual knowledge is weaker than the notion of common knowledge (for details see [6]), however it is enough for our purpose, because we will consider the trees with finite branches.

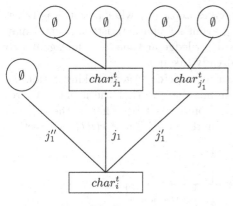

Fig. 1

In the figure we put for simplicity that $\mathbf{K}_i^t = \{char_i^t\}$ and $\mathbf{K}_{i,j_1}^t = \{char_{j_1}^t\}$, and $\mathbf{K}_{i,j_1'}^t = \{char_{j_1'}^t\}$. The rest components of the mutual knowledge are empty sets and denote that agent i has no knowledge about the agent j_1'', and no knowledge about what agents j_1, j_1' know about other agents. Similar representation of mutual knowledge is applied in Recursive Modeling Method, see [7].

There is also another representation of mutual knowledge that is much more simple to grasp, however is hard to use in applications. It may be called *generic representation* , and is constructed in the following way. Let $\mathcal{K}_i$ denote the type of agent i's knowledge, that will be defined below. Canonical form of an object of type $\mathcal{K}_i$ is

$$(char_i; \mathcal{G}_{ij}, j \in N)$$

where N is the set of all agents and $\mathcal{G}_{ij}$ is subset (may be empty) of objects of type $\mathcal{K}_j$.

Let us note that this construction is recursive and for practical reasons should not be nested ad infinitum.

3.5   Reasoning Process

Agent's reasoning should focus on reducing as much as possible the set of runs $\Re_i^t$ and determining belief Bel_i^t. These two constitute agent ground knowledge. A schema of such reasoning process is presented below as Fig. 2. Transformations are shown there as arrows.

From perception to $\Re_i^t$. This transformation is natural. Agent i perceiving q_i^t, knows that the true global state belongs to the set $J_i^{-1}(q_i^t)$. Hence the transformation consists in removing from the set $\Re_i^t$ those runs that determine the global states at time t not consistent with the local state q_i^t, i.e. such runs r for which $J_i(r(t)) \neq q_i^t$, for the definition of $r(t)$ see Section 2.

From perception to mutual knowledge. Agent i, knowing perception function (mechanism), of other agent j, can deduce roughly what agent j does perceive. For details see the next transformation. It is also the case of famous *three* *wise men puzzle* , see [8,9]. If agent perceives at time t what action was taken by agent j at time $t-1$, then, knowing agent's j characteristics, agent i may deduce what should be agent j's ground knowledge at time $t-1$ for agent j to take the action which the agent j has already taken.

From characteristics to revised characteristics. Agent, taking action a_i^t, makes in this way some T–runs to be impossible. So that the agent must remove these impossible (inconsistent) runs from the set $\Re_i^t$. That is, the run r is consistent with action a_i^t if $r(i,t) = a_i^t$, (for the definition of $r(i,t)$, see Section 2).

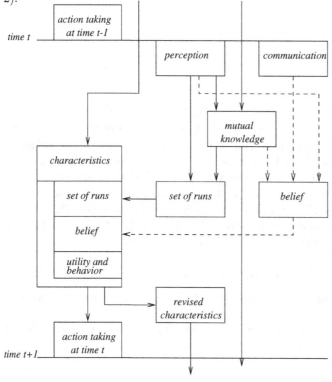

Fig. 2. Dynamic structure of knowledge and transformations: time from t to $t+1$.

Doted vectors denote the transformations that are not still constructed; they concern mainly the revision of belief Bel_i^t.

From Mutual Knowledge to $\Re_i^t$. This transformation deserves more attention. First let us consider so called *one–shot case* , where $T = 1$, i.e. the agents take action only once. Later on we will show how the dynamic case can be transformed into the one–shot case.

Let us note that for $T = 1$: $\Re = \Omega \times A$. So that T–runs are of the following form (ω, a).

Let us consider agent j's point of view. Since ω^0 is the inital global state of the system, according to its perception J_j, agent j knows that the true global state belongs to the set $J_j^{-1} J_j(\omega^0)$. Hence, agent j reduces $\Re$ to the set

$$\Re_j^0 \stackrel{df}{=} \{(\omega, a): \ J_j(\omega) = J_j(\omega^0) \& a \in A\}$$

of the runs that are consistent with its perception.

Since agent j's belief is a subject of change during its reasoning process, initially agent j considers all beliefs from the set $\Delta\Re_j^0$. Hence, agent j, according to its behavior Rb_j, regards as optimal actions from the set

$$A_j^0 \stackrel{df}{=} \bigcup_{Bel_j \in \Delta\Re_j^0} Rb_j(\Re_j^0, Bel_j)$$

Now let us consider agent i's point of view. Suppose that agent i knows the agent j's characteristics, however without Bel_j^0, what seems to be reasonable since the belief is a subject of change. So that agent i's mutual knowledge is

$$\mathbf{K}_{i,j}^0 = \{(\Re_j^0, *; J_j; u_j, \alpha_j, Rb_j)\}$$

where the star $*$ denotes that Bel_j^0 is unknown.

According to its perception, agent i knows that possible runs belong to the set

$$\Re_i^0 \stackrel{df}{=} \{(\omega, a): \ J_i(\omega) = J_i(\omega^0) \ \& \ a \in A\}$$

Since agent i knows agent j perception mechanism J_j, it knows only that

$$\Re_j^0 \text{ is a subset of the set} \bigcup_{(\omega, a) \in \Re_i^0} \{(\omega', a): \ J_j(\omega') = J_j(\omega)\}$$

Let the set at the right side of the inclusion be denoted by $\Re_{ij}^0$; the meaning is that agent i knows that agent j knows that the true state of the world belongs to this set. This is the standard definition, for details see for example Aumann [3,4]. Agent i considers all runs $r = (\omega, a) \in \Re_i^0$ as possible, so that if agent i assumes that ω was the true state, then according to agent i, agent j would know that this state belongs to the set $J_j^{-1} J_j(\omega)$.

Agent i is able to reconstruct the reasoning of agent j, so that agent i knows that

$$A_j^0 \text{ is a subset of the set} \bigcup_{Bel_j \in \Delta\Re_{ij}^0} Rb_j(\Re_{ij}^0, Bel_j)$$

Let the set on the right side of the inclusion be denoted as A_{ij}^0. This denotes that agent i knows that agent j's optimum actions belong to A_{ij}^0.

On the basis of this reasoning agent i reduces the set of possible runs to the set of all $(\omega, a_1, \ \ldots \ , a_j, \ \ldots \ a_n) \in \Re_i^0$ such that $a_j \in A_{ij}^0$.

In this way we have described transformation of knowledge $\mathbf{K}_{i,j}^0$ into $\mathbf{K}_i^0$, i.e. ground knowledge of agent i. In similar way we can define the transformations from $\mathbf{K}_{i,j_1,j_2}^0$ into $\mathbf{K}_{i,j_1}^0$ and generally from $\mathbf{K}_{i,j_1, \ \ldots \ j_k}^0$ into $\mathbf{K}_{i,j_1, \ \ldots \ j_{k-1}}^0$. Hence, starting with the highest nodes of the mutual knowledge tree (see Fig 2.) we can reduce this agent i's mutual knowledge to the root of the tree, i.e. to agent i's ground knowledge.

The idea how to convey the dynamic case where $T > 1$ is simple and uses so called *agent normal form of extensive game* introduced by Selten [12]. In order to make the presentation clear, let us assume that the agents perception is such that they know exactly the current global state of the system.

First we split agent i's site into the sites (s, i) where s is a situation from the set S of all situations, defined in Section 2. In each site (s, i) we put a copy of agent i denoted as agent si. New agent si has the same set of possible actions as the agent i, namely A_i, and is responsible to take at most one action say a_{si} from the set A_i in situation s. The perception, desire, and rational behavior of agent si are the same as the ones of agent i, and this fact is common knowledge between all the agents si, for fixed i and all $s \in S$.

This leads to the case where, at each agent site (s, i), action is taken at most once, i.e. when situation s takes place. Of course, some situations never occur.

Let us suppose that each agent si takes action $a_{si} \in A_i$. Then this determines some T–run (say r) of the system. This run, in turn, determines the sequence of global states of the system, and finally it gives the common utility $u_i(J_i(r))$ for each agent si for fixed i and all $s \in S$.

In this way the dynamic case may be transformed into one–shot case.

3.6   Intentions

Let us note that the transformation into *agent normal form* can be applied in any situation at any time of the dynamic system. So that any agent i can compute its own final ground knowledge at time t.

Once the final ground knowledge of agent i is computed, let it be $(\Re_i^t, Bel_i^t)$, agent i's final intention, concerning its decision of taking action at time t, is given by the set $Rb_i(\Re_i^t, Bel_i^t)$, meaning that agent i regards any action from this set as an optimum one.

4   Explanation of the Paradox

The transformation of a dynamic system into a game in normal form presented above allows to overcome the paradox concerning mutual knowledge and *backward induction* .

Coming back to the example, see Fig. 1, let us see that any agent performs its reasoning before the play starts, so that the agent can not consider itself nor other agents in some situations in a possible future.

After the transformation, there is no temporal, causal relations between nodes: 1.1, 2.1, and 1.2. So that we have three agents: agent 1.1, agent 2.1, and agent 1.2. Agents 1.1, and agent 1.2 share the same outcome, and the same utility. The agents exist at the same time in the same world, so that they can reason consistently about knowledge and rationality of the other agents. So that the backward induction (now rather iterated elimination of dominated actions) may be performed now equivalently on the game in normal form, where there are no reasons for a contradiction with the assumption of the common knowledge of agents' rationality.

5 Conclusion

In the reasoning process presented above, the transformations, that concern the revision of belief Bel_i^t, are missed. Also the communication, coordination between agents is not included there. So that the agent's intentions are individual and concern only individual actions of the agent. Hence, it is still a lot to be done in the modeling BDI–agents in the game–theoretic framework.

References

1. S. Ambroszkiewicz, "Knowledge and best responses in games," Annals of Operations Research, Vol. **51**, 63–71 (1994).
2. S. Ambroszkiewicz, "Knowledge and Behavior in Multiagent Systems: one–shot case," extended abstract in Proc. First International Conference on Multiagent Systems, June 12–14, 1995, San Francisco, California, full version as ICS PAS Reports No.**770**. 1995
3. R. J. Aumann, "Backward induction and common knowledge of rationality," Annals of Statistics , **4**, 6, pp. 1236–1239, 1976.
4. R. J. Aumann, "Agreeing to disagree," Games and Economic Behavior , **8**, pp. 6–19, 1995.
5. R. Fagin, J. Halpern and M.Y. Vardi, "A model-theoretic analysis of knowledge" J. ACM Vol. **38**, No. 2, pp. 382–428 (1991).
6. R. Fagin, J.Y. Halpern, Y.O. Moses, and M.Y. Vardi, Reasoning about Knowledge , The MIT Press, Cambridge Massachusetts, 1995.
7. P. J. Gmytrasiewicz, and E. H. Durfee, "A rigorous, operational formalization of recursive modeling," in Proc. First International Conference on Multiagent Systems, June 12–14, 1995, San Francisco, California, pp. 125–132.
8. J.Y. Halpern, and R. Fagin, Modeling knowledge and action in distributed systems. Distributed Computing **3**, 159–177, 1989.
9. J.Y. Halpern and Y.O. Moses, "Knowledge and common knowledge in a distributed environment," J. ACM **37**(3), 549–587, 1990.
10. A.S. Rao and M.P. Georgeff, "Modeling rational agents within a BDI– architecture," In J. Allen, R. Fikes, and B. Nebel, editors, Proc. KR& R-1991 .
11. P.J. Reny, "Common Belief and the Theory of Games with Perfect Information. Journal of Economic Theory," Journal of Economic Theory **59**, 257–274 (1993).
12. R. Selten, "Reexamination of the perfectness concept for equilibrium points in extensive games," International Journal of Game Theory   **4**, 25–55 (1975).
13. J. S. Sichman and Y. Demazeau, "Exploiting social reasoning to deal with agency level inconsistency," In Proc. First International Conference on Multiagent Systems, June 12–14, 1995, San Francisco, California.
14. W. Stirling, "Multi Agent Coordinated Decision–Making Using Epistemic Utility Theory," In C. Castelfranchi and E. Werner (Eds.) Artificial Social Systems,   Springer LNAI 830, 164–183, 1994.
15. M. Wooldridge and N.R. Jennings, "Agent Theories, Architectures, and Languages: A Survey," in Springer LNAI Vol. 890, 1–32, 1995.

Dynamic Belief Hierarchies

John Bell and Zhisheng Huang

Applied Logic Group, Computer Science Department
Queen Mary and Westfield College
University of London, London E1 4NS, UK
{jb, huang}@dcs.qmw.ac.uk

Abstract. Typically some of an agent's beliefs are more reliable than others. Consequently we give a hierarchical definition of belief, according to which an agent's beliefs form a coherent hierarchy and new beliefs are defined with reference to it. We then show how preferential entailment can be used to formalize the persistence and revision of belief hierarchies, and discuss the the relationship between our theory and the AGM theory of belief revision.

1 Introduction

Consider the following episode:

On January 14, 1997, Zhisheng was travelling by train from Rome to Siena in order to participate in a workshop on agent modelling. He had to change trains at Chiusi, so on arrival at the station he hurried to discover the platform number of the next train departing for Siena. According to the published timetable the next train would depart from platform one at 19:34, so he believed that this would be the case. Consequently he was very surprised when the electronic departures board in the station hall showed that the next train for Siena would depart from platform two. He considered that the information on the board was more reliable than that on the timetable, as it was more recent and more easily updated. So he dropped the belief that the train would depart from platform one in favour of the belief that it would depart from platform two. In order to be sure, he asked the man at the information desk and was assured that the next train for Siena would indeed depart from platform two. Zhisheng considered this to be the most reliable information so far. So he continued to believe that the train would depart from platform two despite the fact that at about 19:15 a train labelled "Chiusi - Siena" arrived at platform one. By 19:28 there was still no sign of a train on platform two, so he started to have doubts. Fortunately there was a signalman on platform three, so Zhisheng hurried over and asked him. The signalman told him that the next train for Siena was the one now on platform one. Zhisheng considered that the signalman was in a better position to know than the man at the information desk. So he revised his

J.-J. Ch. Meyer, P.-Y. Schobbens (Eds.): Formal Methods of Agents, LNAI 1760, pp. 20–35, 1999.
© Springer-Verlag Berlin Heidelberg 1999

beliefs again and hurriedly boarded the train on platform one. At 19:34
the train pulled out and, happily, it arrived at Siena in due course.

In this paper we aim to model reasoning of this kind. In order to do so we
introduce the notion of a *belief hierarchy*. At any point in time an agent has a
set of beliefs, a *belief set*, and considers some of these beliefs to be more reliable
than, or *preferable to*, others. For example, Zhisheng considered the platform
number given on the departures board to be more reliable than the one given in
the published timetable. The agent's preferences define a *preference ordering* on
the agent's belief set. Typically the preference ordering is partial. For example,
Zhisheng believed that the timetable showed that the next train for Siena would
depart from platform one, and he believed that the departures board showed
that the next train for Siena would depart from platform two. Since both beliefs
were based on his own observations, he considered them to be equally reliable;
that is, he regarded them *indierently*. At any point in time the agent's beliefs
and preferences among them form the agent's belief hierarchy at that point in
time.

Typically the agent's belief hierarchy is *dynamic*; as time progresses the
agent's beliefs and the preferences among them change. For example, Zhisheng
initially believed that the next train for Siena would depart from platform one,
however, after looking at the departures board, he believed instead that the
train would depart from platform two. However, the belief hierarchies of rational agents tend to exhibit a certain *stability*. For example, Zhisheng did not
reconsider his beliefs about what he had observed. The agent's beliefs and the
preferences among them thus *persist* by default. Indeed, the belief hierarchies of
rational agents tend to be *upwardly stable*; that is, the higher the belief in the
hierarchy, the more it tends to remain in and maintain its relative position in it.
For example, Zhisheng's beliefs about what he had observed were more stable
than his beliefs about which platform the next train for Siena would depart from.
This reflects the principle that rational agents should keep higher-level beliefs in
preference to lower-level beliefs whenever possible. The beliefs in the hierarchy
of a rational agent should also be *coherent*; that is, they should, in some sense,
be jointly consistent. Roughly, an agent's belief hierarchy is coherent if every
belief in the hierarchy is consistent with every belief which is at least as reliable
as it; a precise definition is given in the sequel. If a rational agent realises that its
beliefs are incoherent, the agent should revise them in order to restore coherence.
In doing so the agent should retain more preferred beliefs in favour of less preferred ones wherever coherence permits. Moreover, the agent should only make
those changes which are necessary in order to restore coherence. For example,
Zhisheng's belief that the departures board was correct was inconsistent with
his belief that the published timetable was correct, so he restored consistency
by dropping the latter, less preferred, belief.

Belief hierarchies can perhaps be seen as providing a formalization of Quine's
"Web of Belief" metaphor [11,12,13], especially as explicated by Dummett [5].
There are also interesting similarities and differences between our theory and
the theory of belief revision developed by Alchourrón, Gärdenfors and Makinson

[6,7], the "AGM theory", and a comparison is given in the sequel. Our theory is intended as part of a larger theory of practical reasoning and rationality [2]; in particular, it has been used in the development of a common sense theory of the adoption of perception-based beliefs [4].

Our theory is expressed in the language $\mathcal{CA}$ [1] which has been extended to include the preference operator of ALX [8,9]. In the following section we discuss the representation of time ad preferences. In Section 3 we give the formal definition of beliefs and belief hierarchies, and study their static properties. In the final section we show how preferential entailment can be used to formalize the rational revision of belief hierarchies, show how the opening example can be formalized, and discuss the relationship between our theory and the AGM theory.

2   Time, Preference, and Indifference

$\mathcal{CA}$ is a many-sorted, modal temporal language. The atomic sentences of $\mathcal{CA}$ all have a temporal index. For example, the sentence $OnTable(B)(3)$ states that block B is on the table at time point 3. Thus time is taken to be composed of points and, for simplicity, we will assume that it is discrete and linear.[1]

The models of $\mathcal{CA}$ are fairly complex possible-worlds structures. Each model comes equipped with an interpretation function $\mathcal{V}$ which assigns an n-ary relation to each n-ary relation symbol at each time point at each possible world. Thus, for model M, world w in M and variable assignment g:[2]

$$M, w, g \models r(u_1, \ldots u_n)(t) \ i \quad (u_1, \ldots, u_n) \in \mathcal{V}(r, t, w)$$

A sentence of the form $Pref\,(a, \phi, \psi)(t)$ states that agent a prefers ϕ to ψ at time t. The semantics of the preference operator begin with von Wright's conjunction expansion principle [16]. According to this principle, to say that you prefer an apple to an orange is to say that you prefer situations in which you have an apple and no orange to those in which you have an orange and no apple. In possible-worlds terms this principle might be stated as follows: agent a prefers ϕ to ψ if a prefers $\phi \wedge \neg\psi$-worlds to $\psi \wedge \neg\phi$-worlds. However, this semantics is too simple, as it leads to paradoxes involving conjunction and disjunction. If ϕ is preferred to ψ then $\phi \vee \chi$ is preferred to ψ, and ϕ is preferred to $\psi \wedge \chi$. For example, if a prefers coffee to tea, then a prefers coffee or poison to tea, and a prefers coffee to tea and a million dollars. Clearly we need to capture the ceteris paribus nature of preferences: we should compare $\phi \wedge \neg\psi$-worlds and $\psi \wedge \neg\phi$-worlds which otherwise differ as little as possible from the actual world. In order to do so we introduce the selection function from the Stalnaker-Lewis analysis of conditionals [10,15]. Thus the function cw is of type $W \times \mathcal{P}(W) \to \mathcal{P}(W)$, and, intuitively, $cw(w, [\![\phi]\!]_g^M)$ is the set of closest worlds

---

[1] The extension to intervals is straightforward; see e.g. [3].

[2] For the sake of simplicity of presentation we will let the distinction between terms and their denotations in M given g take care of itself.

to w in which ϕ is true.[3] Formally, cw is required to satisfy the conditions imposed by Lewis in [10]. The agent's preferences over time are represented by the function $\succ: A \times T \to \mathcal{P}(\mathcal{P}(W) \times \mathcal{P}(W))$, which assigns a comparison relation over sets of worlds to each agent at each time point. Intuitively, for sets of worlds X and Y, $X \succ_{(a,t)} Y$ means that agent a prefers the worlds in X to the worlds in Y at time t. Preferences are required to be irreflexive and transitive, and should satisfy left and right disjunction. Accordingly, let $X \sqsupset_{(a,t,w)} Y$ abbreviate $cw(w, X \cap \overline{Y}) \succ_{(a,t)} cw(w, Y \cap \overline{X})$. Then each $\sqsupset_{(a,t,w)}$ is required satisfy the following properties:

(irp) $X \not\sqsupset_{(a,t,w)} X$.
(trp) If $X \sqsupset_{(a,t,w)} Y$ and $Y \sqsupset_{(a,t,w)} Z$ then $X \sqsupset_{(a,t,w)} Z$.
(orl) If $X \sqsupset_{(a,t,w)} Z$ and $Y \sqsupset_{(a,t,w)} Z$ then $X \cup Y \sqsupset_{(a,t,w)} Z$.
(orr) If $X \sqsupset_{(a,t,w)} Y$ and $X \sqsupset_{(a,t,w)} Z$ then $X \sqsupset_{(a,t,w)} Y \cup Z$.

The truth condition for preferences is then as follows:

$$M, w, g \models \mathit{Pref}\,(a, \phi, \psi)(t) \quad i \quad [\![\phi]\!]_g^M \sqsupset_{(a,t,w)} [\![\psi]\!]_g^M.$$

Given these semantics, we have the following axioms:

(IRP) $\neg \mathit{Pref}\,(a, \phi, \phi)(t)$
(TRP) $\mathit{Pref}\,(a, \phi, \psi)(t) \wedge \mathit{Pref}\,(a, \psi, \chi)(t) \to \mathit{Pref}\,(a, \phi, \chi)(t)$
(ORL) $\mathit{Pref}\,(a, \phi, \chi)(t) \wedge \mathit{Pref}\,(a, \psi, \chi)(t) \to \mathit{Pref}\,(a, \phi \vee \psi, \chi)(t)$
(ORR) $\mathit{Pref}\,(a, \phi, \psi)(t) \wedge \mathit{Pref}\,(a, \phi, \chi)(t) \to \mathit{Pref}\,(a, \phi, \psi \vee \chi)(t)$
(CEP) $\mathit{Pref}\,(a, \phi, \psi)(t) \leftrightarrow \mathit{Pref}\,(a, (\phi \wedge \neg\psi), (\neg\phi \wedge \psi))(t)$

(IRP) and (TRP) state the irreflexivity and transitivity of preferences respectively, while (ORL) and (ORR) respectively state left and right disjunction of preferences.[4] Finally, (CEP) states the conjunction expansion principle. The following are theorems:

(AS) $\mathit{Pref}\,(\phi, \psi)(t) \to \neg \mathit{Pref}\,(\psi, \phi)(t)$
(CP) $\mathit{Pref}\,(a, \phi, \psi)(t) \to \mathit{Pref}\,(a, \neg\psi, \neg\phi)(t)$

Thus preferences are asymmetric (AS) and contraposable (CP). Note that $\mathit{Pref}\,(a, \phi, \psi)(t)$ implies neither $\mathit{Pref}\,(a, \phi \vee \chi, \psi)(t)$ nor $\mathit{Pref}\,(a, \phi, \psi \wedge \chi)(t)$, so the paradoxes of conjunction and disjunction of preferences are avoided.

We also require *indierence* and *weak preference* operators. Informally, $Ind(a, \phi, \psi)(t)$ states that agent a is indifferent between ϕ and ψ at time t, while *PrefInd* $(a, \phi, \psi)(t)$ states that a weakly prefers ϕ to ψ at time t; that is, either a strongly prefers ϕ to ψ at t, or a is indifferent between ϕ and ψ at t. In order to do so, we require a stronger notion of (strong) preference. Each $\sqsupset_{(a,t,w)}$ should now also be almost connected:

---

[3] As usual, $[\![\phi]\!]_g^M$ denotes the set of worlds in M in which ϕ is satisfied by g; i.e., $[\![\phi]\!]_g^M = \{w \in W : M, w, g \models \phi\}$.

[4] The disjunctive properties of preferences were suggested by Pierre-Yves Schobbens.

(acp) If $X \sqsupset_{(a,t,w)} Y$ then for any $Z \in \mathcal{P}(W)$ either $X \sqsupset_{(a,t,w)} Z$ or $Z \sqsupset_{(a,t,w)} Y$.

Then the indifference relation, $\sim_{(a,t,w)}$, can be defined as follows:

$$X \sim_{(a,t)} Y \text{ i } X \not\sqsupset_{(a,t,w)} Y \text{ and } Y \not\sqsupset_{(a,t,w)} X.$$

We thus have the following additional axioms for preference and indifference:

(ACP) $Pref\,(a,\phi,\psi)(t) \wedge \neg Pref\,(a,\phi,\chi)(t) \rightarrow Pref\,(a,\chi,\psi)(t)$
(IND) $Ind(a,\phi,\psi)(t) \leftrightarrow \neg Pref\,(a,\phi,\psi)(t) \wedge \neg Pref\,(a,\psi,\phi)(t)$
(TRI) $Ind(a,\phi,\psi)(t) \wedge Ind(a,\psi,\chi)(t) \rightarrow Ind(a,\phi,\chi)(t)$

(ACP) states that preferences are almost connected and (TRI) states that indifference is transitive. Obviously it follows from (IND) that indifference is also reflexive (REI), and symmetric (SYI):

(REI) $Ind(a,\phi,\phi)(t)$
(SYI) $Ind(a,\phi,\psi)(t) \rightarrow Ind(a,\psi,\phi)(t)$

Finally, the weak preference operator is introduced by definition:

(WP) $PrefInd\,(a,\phi,\psi)(t) \leftrightarrow Pref\,(a,\phi,\psi)(t) \vee Ind(a,\phi,\psi)(t)$

Proposition 1. *Properties of (strong) preference, weak preference and indierence.*

1. Consistency of preference and indierence:

$$Pref\,(a,\phi,\psi)(t) \wedge Ind(a,\phi,\chi)(t) \rightarrow Pref\,(a,\chi,\psi)(t)$$
$$Pref\,(a,\phi,\psi)(t) \wedge Ind(a,\psi,\chi)(t) \rightarrow Pref\,(a,\phi,\chi)(t)$$

2. Weak preference is reflexive, transitive, and comparable:

$$PrefInd\,(a,\phi,\phi)(t)$$
$$PrefInd\,(a,\phi,\psi)(t) \wedge PrefInd\,(a,\psi,\chi)(t) \rightarrow PrefInd\,(a,\phi,\chi)(t)$$
$$PrefInd\,(a,\phi,\psi)(t) \vee PrefInd\,(a,\psi,\phi)(t)$$

3. Consistency of indierence and weak preference:

$$Ind(a,\phi,\psi)(t) \leftrightarrow PrefInd\,(a,\phi,\psi)(t) \wedge PrefInd\,(a,\psi,\phi)(t)$$

4. Consistency of (strong) preference and weak preference:

$$Pref\,(a,\phi,\psi)(t) \leftrightarrow \neg PrefInd\,(a,\psi,\phi)(t)$$

5. Exactly one of the following holds:

$$Pref\,(a,\phi,\psi)(t), Ind(a,\phi,\psi)(t), Pref\,(a,\psi,\phi)(t)$$

Proof. (1) For the first part, suppose that *Pref* $(a, \phi, \psi)(t)$ and $Ind(a, \phi, \chi)(t)$ but that $\neg Pref$ $(a, \chi, \psi)(t)$. If *Pref* $(a, \psi, \chi)(t)$ then, by transitivity of preference, we have *Pref* $(a, \phi, \chi)(t)$, contradicting the supposition that $Ind(a, \phi, \chi)(t)$. So it must be the case that $\neg Pref$ $(a, \psi, \chi)(t)$. Hence, by definition, $Ind(a, \chi, \psi)(t)$. But then, as indifference is transitive, we have $Ind(a, \phi, \psi)(t)$, contradicting the supposition that *Pref* $(a, \phi, \psi)(t)$. So it must be the case that *Pref* $(a, \chi, \psi)(t)$.

For the second part, suppose that *Pref* $(a, \phi, \psi)(t)$ and $Ind(a, \psi, \chi)(t)$ but that $\neg Pref$ $(a, \phi, \chi)(t)$. If *Pref* $(a, \chi, \phi)(t)$ then, by transitivity of preference, *Pref* $(a, \chi, \psi)(t)$, contradicting the supposition that $Ind(a, \psi, \chi)(t)$. So it must be the case that $\neg Pref$ $(a, \chi, \phi)(t)$. Hence, by definition, $Ind(a, \phi, \chi)(t)$. But then, as indifference is transitive, we have $Ind(a, \phi, \psi)(t)$, contradicting the supposition that *Pref* $(a, \phi, \psi)(t)$. So it must be the case that *Pref* $(a, \phi, \chi)(t)$.

(2) Reflexivity. Since *Pref* is irreflexive, we have $\neg Pref$ $(a, \phi, \phi)(t)$. By the definition of indifference, this means that $Ind(a, \phi, \phi)(t)$. Thus *PrefInd* $(a, \phi, \phi)(t)$.

Transitivity. Suppose that *PrefInd* $(a, \phi, \psi)(t) \wedge PrefInd$ $(a, \psi, \chi)(t)$, then there are four cases to consider.

Case 1. *Pref* $(a, \phi, \psi)(t) \wedge Pref$ $(a, \psi, \chi)(t)$. Since preference is transitive, we have *Pref* $(a, \phi, \chi)(t)$. So, by definition, *PrefInd* $(a, \phi, \chi)(t)$.

Case 2. *Pref* $(a, \phi, \psi)(t) \wedge Ind(a, \psi, \chi)(t)$. By part (1), *Pref* $(a, \phi, \chi)(t)$ holds. So, by definition, *PrefInd* $(a, \phi, \chi)(t)$.

Case 3. $Ind(a, \phi, \psi)(t) \wedge Pref$ $(a, \psi, \chi)(t)$. Similarly, by part (1), we have *PrefInd* $(a, \phi, \chi)(t)$.

Case 4. $Ind(a, \phi, \psi)(t) \wedge Ind(a, \psi, \chi)(t)$. By the transitivity of indifference we have $Ind(a, \phi, \chi)(t)$, so, by definition, *PrefInd* $(a, \phi, \chi)(t)$.

Comparability. Suppose that $\neg PrefInd$ $(a, \phi, \psi)(t)$. Then, by definition, $\neg Pref(a, \phi, \psi)(t)$ and $\neg Ind(a, \phi, \psi)$. So it follows from the definition of indifference that *Pref* $(a, \psi, \phi)(t)$. So it follows from the definition of weak preference that *PrefInd* $(a, \psi, \phi)(t)$.

For (3), suppose that $Ind(a, \phi, \psi)(t)$. By the definition of weak preference we have *PrefInd* $(a, \phi, \psi)(t)$. And, by the symmetry of indifference and the definition of weak preference, we have *PrefInd* $(a, \psi, \phi)(t)$. Conversely, suppose that *PrefInd* $(a, \phi, \psi)(t) \wedge PrefInd$ $(a, \psi, \phi)(t)$. If $\neg Ind(a, \phi, \psi)(t)$ holds, then by the symmetry of indifference, we also have $\neg Ind(a, \psi, \phi)(t)$. Furthermore, from the definition of weak preference, we have *Pref* $(a, \phi, \psi)(t) \wedge Pref$ $(a, \psi, \phi)(t)$. So, by the transitivity of (strong) preference, we have *Pref* $(a, \phi, \phi)(t)$. But this contradicts the irreflexivity of preference. Thus, we conclude that $Ind(a, \phi, \psi)(t)$.

For (4), suppose that *Pref* $(a, \phi, \psi)(t)$. If *PrefInd* $(a, \psi, \phi)(t)$, it follows by definition that either *Pref* $(a, \psi, \phi)(t)$ or $Ind(a, \psi, \phi)(t)$. But, the former contradicts the asymmetry of preference, and the latter contradicts the irreflexivity of preference by part (1). Conversely, suppose that $\neg PrefInd$ $(a, \psi, \phi)(t)$. Then, by definition of weak preference, $\neg Pref$ $(a, \psi, \phi)(t)$ and $\neg Ind(a, \psi, \phi)(t)$. As $\neg Ind(a, \psi, \phi)(t)$, it follows that either *Pref* $(a, \psi, \phi)(t)$ or *Pref* $(a, \phi, \psi)(t)$. The former contradicts $\neg Pref$ $(a, \psi, \phi)(t)$. So we conclude the latter.

(5) is straightforward from (4).   □

3   Belief Hierarchies

We now proceed to the definition of beliefs and belief hierarchies, beginning with *candidate beliefs* . Intuitively a sentence ϕ is a candidate belief of agent a at time t, written $CBel(a, \phi)(t)$, if a has reason to believe that ϕ is true at t. The formal semantics for the new operator are, for simplicity, the standard possible-worlds semantics, but indexed by agent and time point. Thus, for each agent a, time point t and world w, $\mathcal{R}_{(Bel,a,t,w)}$ is a binary accessibility relation on worlds which represents a's candidate beliefs in w at t. As usual, $\mathcal{R}_{(Bel,a,t,w)}$ is required to be transitive and Euclidean, corresponding to positive and negative introspection. However $\mathcal{R}_{(Bel,a,t,w)}$ is not required to be serial, so a's candidate beliefs at t need not be jointly consistent. The truth condition for the candidate belief operator is thus as follows:

$$M, w, g \models CBel(a, \phi)(t) \; i \quad M, w', g \models \phi \; for \; all \; (w, w') \in \mathcal{R}_{(Bel,a,t,w)}.$$

We will use the preference and indifference operators to represent the comparative importance of the agent's candidate beliefs and, in due course of the agent's beliefs. Thus *Pref* $(a, CBel(a, \phi)(t), CBel(a, \psi)(t))(t)$ states that, at t, a considers candidate belief ϕ to be more reliable than candidate belief ψ. In order to abbreviate complex sentences such as this we will adopt the convention that a missing agent term is the same as the closest agent term to its left and that a missing temporal term is the same as the closest temporal term to its right; thus the last sentence is abbreviated to *Pref* $(a, CBel(\phi), CBel(\psi))(t)$. Preferences between (candidate) beliefs are required to satisfy the following conditions:

$(RPCB)$ *Pref* $(a, CBel(\phi), CBel(\psi))(t) \rightarrow CBel(a, \phi)(t) \wedge CBel(a, \psi)(t)$
(RPB) *Pref* $(a, Bel(\phi), Bel(\psi))(t) \rightarrow Bel(a, \phi)(t) \wedge Bel(a, \psi)(t)$

$(RPCB)$ is a realism condition on preferences between candidate beliefs. To say that at t, a prefers candidate belief ϕ to candidate belief ψ should imply that ϕ and ψ are candidate beliefs for a at t. Similarly (RPB) is a realism condition on preferences between beliefs.

By introducing preferences on an agent's candidate beliefs at time t we obtain the agent's candidate belief hierarchy at t, and this will be used to define the agent's belief hierarchy at t. As our ultimate concern is with finite, resource-bounded, agents we will assume that at any time point the agent has a finite number of logically distinct candidate beliefs.

The agent's belief hierarchy at t should be a subhierarchy of the agent's candidate belief hierarchy at t. In order to ensure that this is the case, we require the additional conditions:

$(PBCB)$ *Pref* $(a, Bel(\phi), Bel(\psi))(t) \rightarrow$ *Pref* $(a, CBel(\phi), CBel(\psi))(t)$
$(PCBB)$ *Pref* $(a, CBel(\phi), CBel(\psi))(t) \wedge Bel(a, \phi)(t) \wedge Bel(a, \psi)(t) \rightarrow$
$\quad\quad\quad\quad\quad\quad\quad\quad\quad\quad$ *Pref* $(a, Bel(\phi), Bel(\psi))(t)$

$(PBCB)$ and $(PCBB)$ together ensure the agent's preferences on candidate beliefs are consistent with its preferences on beliefs. The last three conditions are, of course, equivalent to the following one:

$$Pref\,(a, Bel(\phi), Bel(\psi))(t) \leftrightarrow$$
$$Pref\,(a, CBel(\phi), CBel(\psi))(t) \wedge Bel(a, \phi)(t) \wedge Bel(a, \psi)(t)$$

The axioms for the irreflexivity and transitivity of preferences, (IR) and (TR), ensure that the preference orderings on beliefs and candidate beliefs are strict partial orderings. The corresponding weak preference orderings on (candidate) beliefs are, of course, pre-orderings. Finally, preference between a belief and a candidate belief can be defined as follows:

$$Pref\,(a, Bel(\phi), CBel(\psi))(t) \leftrightarrow Pref\,(a, CBel(\phi), CBel(\psi))(t) \wedge$$
$$Bel(a, \phi)(t).$$

We are now in a position to give the formal definition of coherence and thus of beliefs.

Definition 2. *A candidate belief is* P-coherent *if the agent believes that it is jointly consistent with every belief that the agent prefers to it:* [5]

$$PCoherent(a, \phi)(t) \leftrightarrow$$
$$\neg CBel(a, \phi \wedge \bigwedge\{[\psi] : Pref(a, Bel(\psi), CBel(\phi))(t)\} \rightarrow \bot)(t)).$$

Definition 3. *A candidate belief is* PI-coherent *if it is P-coherent, and it coheres with all peer candidate beliefs which are P-coherent:*

$$PICoherent(a, \phi)(t) \leftrightarrow$$
$$PCoherent(a, \phi)(t) \wedge$$
$$PCoherent(a, \phi \wedge \bigwedge\{[\psi] : Ind(a, CBel(\phi), CBel(\psi)) \wedge PCoherent(\psi)\})(t).$$

Definition 4. *A* belief *is a PI-coherent candidate belief:*

$$Bel(a, \phi)(t) \leftrightarrow CBel(a, \phi)(t) \wedge PICoherent(a, \phi)(t).$$

Proposition 5. *Static properties of candidate beliefs and beliefs.*

1. Any maximal candidate belief is a belief:

$$CBel(a, \phi)(t) \wedge \neg \exists \psi \neq \phi(PrefInd\,(a, CBel(\psi), CBel(\phi))(t)) \rightarrow Bel(a, \phi)(t).$$

2. All beliefs are candidate beliefs:

$$Bel(a, \phi)(t) \rightarrow CBel(a, \phi)(t).$$

---

[5] Recall that we are assuming that at any time point an agent has a finite number of logically distinct candidate beliefs. In this and the following definition $[\psi]$ is the representative member of the class of all formulas which are logically equivalent to ψ. As usual, for finite formula set S, $\bigwedge S$ is the conjunction of the formulas in S and $\bigwedge \emptyset \leftrightarrow \top$.

3. *Beliefs are consistent.*

$$Bel(a, \phi)(t) \rightarrow \neg Bel(a, \neg\phi)(t).$$

4. *Beliefs are decomposable under conjunction.*

$$Bel(a, \phi \wedge \psi)(t) \rightarrow Bel(a, \phi)(t) \wedge Bel(a, \psi)(t).$$

5. *Beliefs are closed under conjunction.*

$$Bel(a, \phi)(t) \wedge Bel(a, \psi)(t) \rightarrow Bel(a, \phi \wedge \psi)(t).$$

6. *Beliefs are closed under implication.*

$$Bel(a, \phi)(t) \wedge Bel(a, \phi \rightarrow \psi)(t) \rightarrow Bel(a, \psi)(t)$$

7. *Consistency principle for peer beliefs:*

$$PrefInd\ (a, CBel(\phi), CBel(\psi))(t) \wedge \neg PICoherent(a, \phi \wedge \psi)(t) \rightarrow$$
$$\neg(Bel(\phi)(t) \wedge Bel(\chi)(t))$$

8. *Maximality principle for peer beliefs:*

$$Ind(a, CB(\phi), CB(\psi))(t) \wedge PCoherent(a, \phi)(t) \wedge PCoherent(a, \psi)(t) \rightarrow$$
$$Bel(a, \phi \vee \psi)(t).$$

Proof. For (1), if ϕ is a candidate belief, for an agent a at time t,[6] and there is no more reliable candidate belief than ϕ, then ϕ is a maximal CBel. As ϕ is a maximal CBel, it is coherent, and hence it is also a Belief.

(2) and (3) follow from the definition of beliefs.

For (4), suppose that $\phi \wedge \psi$ is a belief for a at t. If $\neg Bel(a, \phi)(t)$ holds, then by the definition of belief, either $\neg PCoherent(a, \phi)(t)$ holds, or $PCoherent(a, \phi)(t)$ $\wedge \exists \chi (ICBel(a, \phi, \chi)(t) \wedge PCoherent(a, \chi)(t) \wedge \neg PCoherent(a, \phi \wedge \chi)(t)$ holds.[7] The former contradicts $Bel(a, \phi \wedge \psi)(t)$. While from the latter it follows, by $PCoherent(a, \chi)(t)$ and $Bel(a, \phi \wedge \psi)(t)$, that $PCoherent(a, \chi \wedge \phi \wedge \psi)(t)$. We thus have $PCoherent(a, \chi \wedge \phi)(t)$, contradicting $\neg PCoherent(a, \phi \wedge \chi)(t)$. Thus, we conclude that $Bel(a, \phi)(t)$ holds. The proof for $Bel(a, \psi)(t)$ is similar.

For (5), suppose that $Bel(a, \phi)(t) \wedge Bel(a, \psi)(t)$ holds. We know that either *Pref* $(a, CBel(\phi), CBel(\psi))(t)$ or *Pref* $(a, CBel(\psi), CBel(\phi))(t)$ or $Ind(a, CBel$ $(\phi), CBel(\psi))(t)$ holds. Suppose that *Pref* $(a, CBel(\phi), CBel(\psi))(t)$ holds. Then, from $Bel(a, \psi)(t)$, we know that $PCoherent(a, \phi \wedge \psi)(t)$ holds. If $\neg Bel(a, \phi \wedge \psi)(t)$ holds, then this means that there exists a χ such that $ICBel(a, \phi \wedge \psi, \chi)(t) \wedge$ $PCoherent(a, \chi)(t) \wedge \neg PCoherent(a, \phi \wedge \psi \wedge \chi)(t)$ holds. However, from $PCoher$ $ent(a, \chi)(t)$ and *Pref* $(a, CBel(\phi), CBel(\psi))(t)$ and *Pref* $(a, CBel(\psi), CBel(\chi))$,

---

[6] In the sequel, we will often omit the agent name a and the time point t in proofs when it does not cause any ambiguity.

[7] Where $ICBel(a, \phi, \chi)(t)$ denotes that χ is a conjunction of candidate beliefs which are peers of ψ. Thus $Ind(a, CBel(\phi), CBel(\psi))(t) \rightarrow ICBel(a, \phi, \psi)(t)$, and $Ind(a, CBel(\phi), CBel(\psi_1))(t) \wedge ICBel(a, \phi, \psi_2)(t) \rightarrow ICBel(a, \phi, \psi_1 \wedge \psi_2)(t)$.

we have $PCoherent(a, \phi \wedge \psi \wedge \chi)(t)$, contradicting $\neg PCoherent(a, \phi \wedge \psi \wedge \chi)(t)$. The proof for the case where $Pref\ (a, CBel(\psi), CBel(\phi))(t)$ holds is similar.

For the case where $Ind(a, CBel(\phi), CBel(\psi))(t)$ holds we know by the definition of beliefs that $PCoherent(a, \phi \wedge \psi)(t)$ and there exists no other peer χ such that $\neg PCoherent(a, \phi \wedge \psi \wedge \chi)(t)$. Therefore, we conclude that $Bel(a, \phi \wedge \psi)(t)$. (6) follows from (4) and (5). (7) is straightforward from the definition of belief and the consistency of belief hierarchies.

For (8), suppose that $PrefInd\ (a, CBel(\phi), CBel(\psi))(t) \wedge PCoherent(a, \phi)(t) \wedge PCoherent(a, \psi)(t)$. If $\neg Bel(a, \phi \vee \psi)(t)$ holds, then by the definition of belief, we have either $\neg PCoherent(a, \phi \vee \psi)(t)$ or there exists a χ such that $ICBel(a, \chi, \phi \vee \psi)(t) \wedge PCoherent(a, \chi)(t) \wedge \neg PCoherent(a, \chi \wedge (\phi \vee \psi))(t)$. In the former case it follows that either $\neg PCoherent(a, \phi)(t)$ or $\neg PCoherent(a, \psi)(t)$, giving a contradiction in each case. While from the latter it follows that χ is inconsistent with $\phi \vee \psi$, which contradicts the supposition that χ is P-Coherent. $\square$

4   Belief Revision

Thus far our analysis has been concerned with the static properties of beliefs and belief hierarchies, with the properties of agents' beliefs and belief hierarchies at particular points in time. In this section we consider the dynamic properties of beliefs and belief hierarchies; that is, how they should be revised over time. Clearly a rational agent should only revise its beliefs if they become incoherent. Moreover when revising the agent should keep higher-level beliefs in preference to lower-level beliefs wherever coherence permits, and should only make those changes which are necessary in order to restore coherence.

In order to represent the persistence of beliefs and preferences, we use the affected operator, A , of $\mathcal{CA}$. This modal operator is analogous to the Ab predicate of the Situation Calculus. Let Φ be a meta-variable which ranges over the non-temporal component of atomic modal formulas.[8] Then a formula $\Phi(t)$ is affected at t if its truth value at t differs from its truth value at $t + 1$:

$$M, w, g \models A\ (\Phi)(t) \ i \ M, w, g \models \neg(\Phi(t) \leftrightarrow \Phi(t + 1)).$$

We thus have the following *persistence rule* :

$$\Phi(t) \wedge \neg A\ (\Phi)(t) \rightarrow \Phi(t + 1).$$

Intuitively we are interested in models in which this schema is used from left-to-right only in order to reason "forwards in time" from instances of its antecedent to instances of its consequent. Typically also we want to be able to infer the second conjunct of each instance nonmonotonically whenever it is consistent to do so. For example, if we have $Bel(a, \phi)(t)$ then we want to be able

---

[8] Atomic modal formulas are formulas of the form $op(a, \phi_1, \ldots, \phi_n)(t)$, where $n \geq 1$ and op is a modal operator other than A .

to use the rule to infer $Bel(a, \phi)(t+1)$ if $A \ (Bel(a, \phi))(t)$ cannot be inferred. In order to enforce this interpretation, we define a prioritized form of preferential entailment [14].

Definition 6. *Let $A_1, \ldots, A_n$ be a partition of the atomic modal sentences of n dierent types according to their type.* [9] *For each A_i, model M and time point t, let $M_{A_i}/t = \{\alpha_i(t') \in A_i \mid t' \leq t, M \models \alpha_i(t')\}$. Then a model M is chronologically less defined than a model M' on the basis of the priorities $\langle A_1, \ldots, A_n \rangle$, written $M \prec_{\langle A_1, \ldots, A_n \rangle} M'$ i M and M' dier at most on the interpretation of $A_1, \ldots, A_n$ and there is a time point t such that:*

- *for some i such that $1 \leq i \leq n, M_{A_i}/t \subset M'_{A_i}/t$, and*
- *for all j such that $1 \leq j \leq i, M_{A_j}/t \subseteq M'_{A_j}/t$.*

Definition 7. *A model M is an $\langle A_1, \ldots, A_n \rangle$-preferred model of a sentence ϕ if $M \models \phi$ and there is no model M' such that $M' \models \phi$ and $M' \prec_{\langle A_1, \ldots, A_n \rangle} M$. Similarly, M is an $\langle A_1, \ldots, A_n \rangle$-preferred model of a set of sentences Θ if $M \models \Theta$ and there is no model M' such that $M' \models \Theta$ and $M' \prec_{\langle A_1, \ldots, A_n \rangle} M$.*

Definition 8. *A set of sentences Θ preferentially entails a sentence ϕ given the priorities $\langle A_1, \ldots, A_n \rangle$ (written $\Theta \mathrel{\rawtilde}_{\langle A_1, \ldots, A_n \rangle} \phi$) if, for any $\langle A_1, \ldots, A_n \rangle$-preferred model M of Θ, $M \models \phi$.*

In the sequel we will say that a set of sentences Θ is a *belief theory* if it contains the axioms of our theory of belief. We are therefore interested in the $\langle CBel, Pref, A \rangle$-preferred models models of belief theories. In models of belief theories candidate beliefs, preferences and affected atoms should be minimized chronologically while, at any time point, candidate beliefs should be minimized before preferences, and preferences should be minimized before affected atoms. In the sequel we will abbreviate $\Theta \mathrel{\rawtilde}_{\langle CBel, Pref, Aff \rangle} \phi$ to $\Theta \mathrel{\rawtilde} \phi$.

As a result of the definitions we have:

Proposition 9. *Dynamic properties of beliefs and belief hierarchies.*

1. *Beliefs persist by default.*
2. *Preferences on beliefs persist by default.*
3. *Belief hierarchies persist by default.*
4. *Belief hierarchies are upwardly stable.*

Proof. For (1), let Θ be a belief theory such that $\Theta \mathrel{\rawtilde} Bel(a, \phi)(t)$ and $\Theta \mathrel{\rawtilde} \neg A \ (Bel(a, \phi))(t)$. Then it follows from the persistence rule that $\Theta \mathrel{\rawtilde} Bel(a, \phi)$ $(t + 1)$. The proof for (2) is similar. Part (3) follows from (1) and (2). Part (4) follows from the maximality and default persistence of belief hierarchies. □

---

[9] For example, A_1 might be the set *Bel* of all belief atoms $Bel(a, \phi)(t)$, A_2 might be the set Pref of all preference atoms Pref $(a, \phi, \psi)(t)$, etc.

By way of illustration, we show how the opening example can be formalized.

Example 1. Let $1, 2, ..$, denote time points, and *one* and *two* denote the two platforms, and let Θ be a belief theory which contains the following sentences representing agent a's beliefs, preferences and candidate beliefs:

(A) Pref $(a, CBel(Timetable(one)), CBel(\forall x(Timetable(x) \rightarrow Platform(x))))(1)$,
(B) Pref $(a, CBel(Board(two)), CBel(\forall x(Board(x) \rightarrow Platform(x))))(2)$,
(C) Pref $(a, CBel(\forall x(Board(x) \rightarrow Platform(x))),$
$\qquad\qquad CBel(\forall x(Timetable(x) \rightarrow Platform(x))))(2)$,
(D) Pref $(a, CBel(Infoman(two)), CBel(\forall x(Infoman(x) \rightarrow Platform(x))))(3)$,
(E) Pref $(a, CBel(\forall x(Infoman(x) \rightarrow Platform(x))),$
$\qquad\qquad CBel(\forall x(Board(x) \rightarrow Platform(x))))(3)$,
(F) Pref $(a, CBel(Train(one)), CBel(\forall x(Train(x) \rightarrow Platform(x))))(4)$,
(G) Pref $(a, CBel(\forall x(Board(x) \rightarrow Platform(x))),$
$\qquad\qquad CBel(\forall x(Train(x) \rightarrow Platform(x))))(4)$,
(H) Pref $(a, CBel(Signman(one)), CBel(\forall x(Signman(x) \rightarrow Platform(x))))(5)$,
(I) Pref $(a, CBel(\forall x(Signman(x) \rightarrow Platform(x))),$
$\qquad\qquad CBel(\forall x(Infoman(x) \rightarrow Platform(x))))(5)$,
(J) $\forall \psi$Pref $(a, CBel((Platform(one) \vee Platform(two)) \wedge$
$\qquad\qquad \neg(Platform(one) \wedge Platform(two)), CBel(a, \psi))(1)$.

For natural numbers n_1 and n_2 such that $1 \leq n_1 \leq n_2 \leq 7$, we will use $\Phi([n_1 \ldots n_2])$ to denote the conjunction $\Phi(n_1) \wedge \Phi(n_1 + 1) \wedge ... \wedge \Phi(n_2)$. Then the following sentences are true in all $\langle CBel, Pref, A \rangle$-preferred models of Θ:

(a) Pref $(a, CBel(Timetable(one)), CBel(\forall x(Timetable(x)$
$\qquad\qquad \rightarrow Platform(x))))([1 \ldots 5])$,
(b) Pref $(a, CBel(Board(two)), CBel(\forall x(Board(x) \rightarrow Platform(x))))([2 \ldots 5])$,
(c) Pref $(a, CBel(\forall x(Board(x) \rightarrow Platform(x))),$
$\qquad\qquad CBel(\forall x(Timetable(x) \rightarrow Platform(x))))([2 \ldots 5])$,
(d) Pref $(a, CBel(Infoman(two)), CBel(\forall x(Infoman(x)$
$\qquad\qquad \rightarrow Platform(x))))([3 \ldots 5])$,
(e) Pref $(a, CBel(\forall x(Infoman(x) \rightarrow Platform(x))),$
$\qquad\qquad CBel(\forall x(Board(x) \rightarrow Platform(x))))([3 \ldots 5])$,
(f) Pref $(a, CBel(Train(one)), CBel(\forall x(Train(x) \rightarrow Platform(x))))([4 \ldots 5])$,
(g) Pref $(a, CBel(\forall x(Board(x) \rightarrow Platform(x))),$
$\qquad\qquad CBel(\forall x(Train(x) \rightarrow Platform(x))))([4 \ldots 5])$,
(h) Pref $(a, CBel(Signman(one)), CBel(\forall x(Signman(x) \rightarrow Platform(x))))(5)$,
(i) Pref $(a, CBel(\forall x(Signman(x) \rightarrow Platform(x))),$
$\qquad\qquad CBel(\forall x(Infoman(x) \rightarrow Platform(x))))(5)$,
(j) $\forall \psi$Pref $(a, CBel((Platform(one) \vee Platform(two)) \wedge$
$\qquad\qquad \neg(Platform(one) \wedge Platform(two)), CBel(a, \psi))([1 \ldots 5])$.

So in all $\langle CBel, Pref, A \rangle$-preferred models of Θ a's beliefs change as follows during the period:

(0) $Bel(a, (Platform(one) \lor Platform(two)) \land$
$\quad \neg(Platform(one) \land Platform(two)))([1 \ldots 5])$ (j),
(1) $Bel(a, Timetable(one))(1)$ (a)
(2) $Bel(a, \forall x(Timetable(x) \to Platform(x))(1)$ $(1), (a)$
(3) $Bel(a, Platform(one))(1)$ $(1), (2)$
(4) $\neg Bel(a, Platform(two))(1)$ $(0), (3)$
(5) $Bel(a, Board(two))(2)$ (b)
(6) $Bel(a, \forall x(Board(x) \to Platform(x))(2)$ $(b), (c)$
(7) $\neg Bel(a, \forall x(Timetable(x) \to Platform(x))(2)$ (c)
(8) $Bel(a, Platform(two))(2)$ $(5), (6))$
(9) $\neg Bel(a, Platform(one))(2)$ $(0), (8)$
(10) $Bel(a, Infoman(two))(3)$ (d)
(11) $Bel(a, \forall x(Infoman(x) \to Platform(x)))(3)$ (10)
(12) $Bel(a, Platform(two)(3)$ $(10), (11)$
(13) $\neg Bel(a, Platfrom(one))(3)$ $(0), (12)$
(14) $Bel(a, Train(one))(4)$ (f)
(15) $\neg Bel(a, \forall x(Train(x) \to Platform(x))(4)$ (g)
(16) $Bel(a, Platform(two))(4)$ $(Persistence)$
(17) $\neg Bel(a, Platform(one))(4)$ $(0), (16)$
(18) $Bel(a, Signman(one))(5)$ (h)
(19) $Bel(a, \forall x(Signman(x) \to Platform(x))(5)$ (h)
(20) $\neg Bel(a, \forall x(Infoman(x) \to Platform(x))(5)$ (i)
(21) $Bel(a, Platform(one))(5)$ $(18), (19)$
(22) $\neg Bel(a, Platform(two))(5)$ $(0), (21)$

$\square$

It is interesting to compare our work with the AGM theory of belief revision developed by Alchourrón, Gärdenfors and Makinson, e.g. [6,7]. In the AGM theory an agent's beliefs are represented by a knowledge set; a deductively closed set of sentences which, at any stage, can be modified in one of three ways:

Expansion: A proposition ϕ, which is consistent with a knowledge set K, is added to K. The result is denoted $K + \phi$.

Revision: A proposition ϕ, which may be inconsistent with a knowledge set K, is added to it. In order to maintain consistency some of the propositions which were in K may have to be removed. A revision of K by ϕ is denoted by $K * \phi$.

Contraction: A proposition ϕ is removed from a knowledge set K. A contraction of K by ϕ is denoted by $K \dot{-} \phi$.

Alchourrón, Gärdenfors and Makinson propose a number of plausible postulates which any definition of these operations should satisfy. The postulates for expansion are straightforward. Those for revision are as follows:[10]

(a) [Closure] $K * \phi$ is a closed theory.

---

[10] Where, $Cn(S)$ is the deductive closure of S.

(b) [Inclusion] $K * \phi \subseteq K + \phi$.

(c) [Vacuity] If $\neg\phi \notin K$, then $K + \phi \subseteq K * \phi$.

(d) [Success] $\phi \in K * \phi$.

(e) [Consistency] If $\bot \in K * \phi$, then $\neg\phi \in Cn(\emptyset)$.

(f) [Extensionality] If $Cn(K) = Cn(K')$, then $K * \phi = K' * \phi$.

The postulates for contraction need not concern us as the *Harper identity* shows that the contraction operation can be defined in terms of the revision operation:

$$K \dot{-} \phi = (K * \neg\phi) \cap K.$$

Our theory differs from the AGM theory in at least three important respects. In our theory beliefs are represented as hierarchies of propositions, rather than sets of sentences, and the preferences among beliefs must be considered when revision takes place. Moreover, revision of a hierarchy from one time point to the next may correspond to several AGM operations; several beliefs may have to be removed in order to incorporate new ones, while several others may simply be added or deleted. Finally, the revision of a hierarchy will always be unique; unlike the result of an AGM revision.

In order to make a comparison we consider the special case in which each revision of a belief hierarchy corresponds to a single AGM operation. For belief theory Θ and resulting belief hierarchy at time t, we can define an agent a's *belief set* at t as follows:

$$Bel(a, t) = \{\psi : \Theta \approx Bel(a, \psi)(t)\}.$$

Given an operation on a's belief set at t and the proposition ϕ, we are thus interested in a's belief set at $t + 1$.

An AGM-type expansion operator can be partially defined as follows:

$$Bel(a, t) + \phi = \{\psi : \Theta \approx Bel(a, \psi)(t)\} \cup \{\psi : \Theta \approx Bel(a, \phi \rightarrow \psi)(t + 1)\}$$
$$\text{when } \Theta \approx Bel(a, \phi)(t + 1).$$

The assumption that the expansion $Bel(a, t) + \phi$ is the only operation which occurs at t is captured by the following condition:

(Uni+) If $Bel(a, t) + \phi$ is defined, then $Bel(a, t) + \phi = Bel(a, t + 1)$.

An AGM-type revision operator can be partially defined in a similar way:

$$Bel(a, t) * \phi = \{\psi : \Theta \approx Bel(a, \psi)(t) \wedge \neg A \quad (Bel(a, \psi)(t))\} \cup$$
$$\{\psi : \Theta \approx Bel(a, \phi \rightarrow \psi)(t + 1)\}$$
$$\text{when } \Theta \approx Bel(a, \phi)(t + 1).$$

The assumption that the revision $Bel(a,t) * \phi$ is the only operation which occurs at t is captured by the following condition:

(Uni*) If $Bel(a,t) * \phi$ is defined, then $Bel(a,t) * \phi = Bel(a, t+1)$.

Proposition 10. *The belief revision operator defined above satisfies AGM Postulates (a)-(f).*

Proof. (a) follows from part (6) of Proposition 5. (b) is straightforward from the definitions. For (c), if $\neg\phi \notin Bel(a,t)$, by definition, $Bel(a, \neg\phi)(t)$ does not hold. Thus, the expansion and revision operations are defined, and (c) follows from (Uni+). For (d), we know that if $Bel(a,t)*\phi$ is defined, then $\Theta \approx Bel(a, \phi)(t+1)$. Thus, $\phi \in Bel(a,t)*\phi$. For (e), it follows from Proposition 5 that $\perp \in Bel(a,t)*\phi$ is undefined when ϕ is inconsistent, hence (e) holds vacuously. For (f), if $Cn(Bel(a,t)) = Cn(Bel(a',t'))$, then $Bel(a,t) = Bel(a',t')$. Thus, for any ψ, $Bel(a, \psi)(t) \leftrightarrow Bel(a', \psi)(t')$. By the definition of the revision operator, we thus have $Bel(a,t) * \phi = Bel(a',t') * \phi$.   □

When the appropriate uniqueness assumptions hold our theory can be viewed as a realisation of the AGM theory, and when they do not hold our theory can be viewed as an extension of it.

Our theory is also of interest as part of a larger theory of practical reasoning and rationality [2]; in particular, it has been used in the development of a common sense theory of the adoption of perception-based beliefs [4].

Acknowledgements

This research forms part of the Ratio Project and is supported by the United Kingdom Engineering and Physical Sciences Research Council under grant number GR/L34914.

References

1. J. Bell. Changing Attitudes. In: M.J. Wooldridge and N.R. Jennings (Eds.). Intelligent Agents . Post-Proceedings of the ECAI'94 Workshop on Agent Theories, Architectures, and Languages. Springer Lecture Notes in Artificial Intelligence, No. 890. Springer, Berlin, 1995. pp. 40-55.   22
2. J. Bell. A Planning Theory of Practical Rationality. Proceedings of the AAAI-95 Fall Symposium on Rational Agency: Concepts, Theories, Models and Applications   , M.I.T, November 1995, pp. 1-4.   22, 34
3. J. Bell and Z. Huang. Dynamic Obligation Hierarchies. In P. McNamara and H. Prakken (Eds.) Norms, Logics and Information Systems: New Studies in Deontic Logic and Computer Science   , Ios Press, Amsterdam, 1999, pp. 231-246.   22
4. J. Bell and Z. Huang. Seeing is believing: A common sense theory of the adoption of perception-based beliefs. Artificial Intelligence for Engineering Design, Analysis and Manufacturing   13, 1999, pp. 133-140.   22, 34

5. M. Dummett. The Significance of Quine's Indeterminacy Thesis. Synthese 27 1974, pp. 351-97. 21
6. P. Gärdenfors. Knowledge in Flux; Modeling the Dynamics of Epistemic States . MIT Press, Cambridge, Massachusetts, 1988. 22, 32
7. P. Gärdenfors and D. Makinson. Revisions of knowledge systems using epistemic entrenchment, in: M. Vardi (ed.), Proceedings of TARK'88 , Morgan Kaufmann, San Francisco, 1988. pp. 83-95. 22, 32
8. Z. Huang. Logics for Agents with Bounded Rationality , ILLC Dissertation series 1994-10, University of Amsterdam, 1994. 22
9. Z. Huang, M. Masuch and L. Pólos. ALX: an action logic for agents with bounded rationality, Artificial Intelligence 82 (1996), pp. 101-153. 22
10. D. Lewis. Counterfactuals , Basil Blackwell, Oxford, 1973. 22, 23
11. W.V.O. Quine. Two Dogmas of Empiricism. In: From a Logical Point of View . Harvard University Press, Cambridge, Massachusetts, 1953. 21
12. W.V.O. Quine. Word and Object . MIT Press, Cambridge, Massachusetts, 1960. 21
13. W.V.O. Quine and J.S. Ullian. The Web of belief , Random house, New York, 1970. 21
14. Y. Shoham. Reasoning About Change . MIT Press, Cambridge, Massachusetts, 1988. 30
15. R.A. Stalnaker. A theory of conditionals, Studies in Logical Theory, American Philosophical Quarterly 2 (1968), pp. 9 8-122. 22
16. G. von Wright. The Logic of Preference , Edinburgh University Press, Edinburgh, 1963. 22

Modelling Internal Dynamic Behaviour of BDI Agents

Frances Brazier[1], Barbara Dunin-Keplicz[2], Jan Treur[1], and Rineke Verbrugge[1]

[1] Vrije Universiteit Amsterdam
Department of Mathematics and Computer Science, Artificial Intelligence Group
De Boelelaan 1081a, 1081 HV Amsterdam, The Netherlands
{frances,treur,rineke}@cs.vu.nl
http://www.cs.vu.nl

[2] Warsaw University
Institute of Informatics, ul. Banacha 2, 02-097 Warsaw, Poland
keplicz@mimuw.edu.pl

Abstract. A generic model for the internal dynamic behaviour of BDI agents is proposed. This model, a refinement of a generic agent model, explicitly specifies beliefs and motivational attitudes such as desires, goals, intentions, commitments, and plans, and their relations. A formal meta-language is used to represent beliefs, motivational attitudes and strategies. Dynamic aspects of reasoning about and revision of beliefs and motivational attitudes are modelled in a compositional manner within the modelling framework DESIRE.

1 Introduction

In the last five years multi-agent systems have been a major focus of research in AI. The concept of agents, in particular the role of agents as participants in multi-agent systems, has been subject to discussion. In (Wooldridge and Jennings, 1995) different notions of strong and weak agency are presented. In other contexts big and small agents have been distinguished (Velde and Perram, 1996). In this paper, a model for a rational agent is proposed: a rational agent described using cognitive notions such as beliefs, desires and intentions.

Beliefs, intentions, and commitments play a crucial role in determining how rational agents will act. Shoham defines an agent to be "an entity whose state is viewed as consisting of mental components such as beliefs, capabilities, choices, and commitments. (...) What makes any hardware or software component an agent is precisely the fact that one has chosen to analyze and control it in these mental terms" (Shoham, 1993). This definition provides a basis to study, model and specify mental attitudes; see (Rao and Georgeff, 1991; Cohen and Levesque, 1990; Shoham, 1991; Dunin-Keplicz and Verbrugge, 1996).

The goal of this paper is to define a generic BDI agent model in the compositional multi-agent modelling framework DESIRE. To this purpose, a generic agent model is presented and refined to incorporate beliefs, desires and intentions (in which intentions with respect to goals are distinguished from intentions with respect to plans). The result is a more specific BDI agent in which dependencies between beliefs, desires and intentions are made explicit. The BDI model includes knowledge of different intention/commitment strategies in which these dependencies are used to

J.-J. Ch. Meyer, P.-Y. Schobbens (Eds.): Formal Methods of Agents, LNAI 1760, pp. 36-56, 1999.
© Springer-Verlag Berlin Heidelberg 1999

reason about beliefs, desires, and intentions, but also to explicitly revise specific beliefs, desires and intentions.

The main emphasis in this paper is on static and dynamic relations between mental attitudes. DESIRE (framework for DEsign and Specification of Interacting REasoning components) is a framework for modelling, specifying and implementing multi-agent systems, see (Brazier, Dunin-Keplicz, Jennings, and Treur, 1995, 1996; Dunin-Keplicz and Treur, 1995). Within the framework, complex processes are designed as compositional models consisting of interacting task-based hierarchically structured components. Agents are modelled as composed components. The interaction between components, and between components and the external world, is explicitly specified. Components may be primitive reasoning components using a knowledge base, but may also be subsystems capable of performing tasks using methods as diverse as decision theory, neural networks, and genetic algorithms.

In this paper a small, simplified part of an application, namely meeting scheduling, is used to illustrate the way in which dependencies and strategies are used to model revision.

The paper is structured in the following manner. In Section 2, a generic classification of mental attitudes is presented and a more precise characterization of a few selected motivational attitudes is given. Next, in Section 3, the specification framework DESIRE for multi-agent systems is characterized. In Section 4 a general agent model is described. The framework of modelling motivational attitudes in DESIRE is discussed in Section 5. In Section 6 the use of the explicit knowledge of dependencies and strategies for belief, intention and commitment revision is explained. Finally, Section 7 presents some conclusions and possible directions for further research.

2 Intention and Commitment Strategies

A number of motivational attitudes, and the static and dynamic relations between motivational attitudes and agents' activities, are modelled in this paper. Individual agents are assumed to have intentions and commitments both with respect to goals and with respect to plans. Joint motivational attitudes and joint actions are not discussed in this paper. The following classification of an agent's attitudes is used:

1. Informational attitudes
   1.1 Knowledge
   1.2 Beliefs

2. Motivational attitudes
   2.1 Desires
   2.2 Intentions
      2.2.a Intended goals
      2.2.b Intended plans
   2.3 Commitments
      2.3.a Committed goals
      2.3.b Committed plans

In this classification the weakest motivational attitude is desire. Desires may be ordered according to preferences and they are the only motivational attitudes subject to inconsistency. A limited number of intended goals are chosen by an agent, on the basis of its (beliefs and) desires. In this paper only achievement goals (and not, for example, maintenance goals) are considered. Moreover, agents are assumed to assure consistency of intentions. With respect to intentions, the conditions elaborated in (Bratman, 1987; Cohen and Levesque, 1990) are adopted.

On the basis of intentions, an agent commits to itself to achieve both goals and to execute plans. In addition an agent may also make commitments to other agents. Such social commitments (Castelfranchi, 1995; Dunin-Keplicz and Verbrugge, 1996) are also explicitly modelled. As proposed in (Castelfranchi, 1995), contrary to some other approaches, social commitments are stronger than intentions, because the aspects of obligation and of interest in the commitment by the other agent are involved.

After committing to a goal and an associated plan, an agent starts plan realization. Knowledge of strategies and dependencies is required to determine in which situations an agent drops an intention or commitment, and how. The kind of behavior that agents manifest depends on immanent behavioral characteristics and environment, including their intention and commitment strategies. As a result individual agents may behave differently in analogical situations. In (Rao and Georgeff 1991) intention strategies were introduced, which inspired the definition of social commitment strategies in (Dunin-Keplicz and Verbrugge, 1996). These commitment strategies include the additional aspects of communication and coordination.

In this paper, three commitment strategies are distinguished. The strongest commitment strategy is followed by the *blindly committed* agent, that maintains its commitments until it believes they have been achieved, irrespective of changes in its own goals and desires, and irrespective of other beliefs with respect to the feasibility of the commitment. A *single-minded* agent may drop commitments when it believes they can no longer be attained, irrespective of changes in its goals and desires. However, as soon as a single-minded agent abandons a commitment, communication and coordination are necessary with agents to whom the single-minded agent is committed. An *open-minded* agent may drop commitments when it believes they can no longer be attained or when the relevant goals are no longer desired. Communication and coordination with agents to whom the single-minded agent is committed, are also performed when commitments are abandoned.

For simplicity, in this paper each agent is assumed to follow a single commitment strategy during the whole process of plan realization. Moreover, it should be stressed that commitment strategies are used for both committed goals and committed plans.

3 A Modelling Framework for Multi-agent Systems

The compositional BDI model introduced in this paper is based on an analysis of the tasks performed by a BDI agent. Such a task analysis results, among others, in a (hierarchical) task composition, which is the basis for a compositional model: components in a compositional model are directly related to tasks in a task composition. Interaction between tasks is modelled and specified at each level within a task composition, making it possible to explicitly model tasks which entail interaction between agents. The hierarchical structures of tasks, interaction and knowledge are fully preserved within compositional models. Task coordination is of importance both within and between agents. Below the formal compositional framework for modelling multi-agent tasks DESIRE is briefly introduced, in which the following aspects are modelled and specified (for more details, see (Brazier, Dunin-Keplicz, Jennings, Treur, 1997)):

(1) a task composition,
(2) information exchange,
(3) sequencing of tasks,
(4) task delegation,
(5) knowledge structures.

3.1 Task Composition

To model and specify composition of tasks, knowledge of the following types is required:

- a *task hierarchy*,
- information a task requires as *input*,
- information a task produces as a *result* of task performance
- *meta-object* relations between tasks

Within a task hierarchy *composed* and *primitive* tasks are distinguished: in contrast to primitive tasks, composed tasks consist of a number of other tasks, which, in turn, may be either composed or primitive. Tasks are directly related to components: composed tasks are specified as composed components and primitive tasks as primitive components.

Information required/produced by a task is defined by *input* and *output signatures* of a component. The signatures used to name the information are defined in a predicate logic with a hierarchically ordered sort structure (order-sorted predicate logic). Units of information are represented by the ground *atoms* defined in the signature.

The role information plays within reasoning is indicated by the level of an atom within a signature: different (meta)levels may be distinguished. In a two-level situation the lowest level is termed *object-level information*, and the second level *meta-level information*. Meta-level information contains information about object-level information and reasoning processes; for example, for which atoms the values are still unknown (*epistemic information*). Similarly, tasks which include reasoning about other tasks are modelled as meta-level tasks with respect to object-level tasks. Often more than two levels of information and reasoning occur, resulting in meta-meta-... information and reasoning.

3.2 Information Exchange between Tasks

Information links between components are used to specify information exchange between tasks. Two types of information links are distinguished: *private* information links and *mediating* information links. For a given parent component, a private information link relates output of one of its components to input of another, by specifying which truth value of a specific output atom is linked with which truth value of a specific input atom. Atoms can be renamed: each component can be specified in its own language, independent of other components. In a similar manner mediating links transfer information from the input interface of the parent component to the input interface of one of its components, or from the output interface of one of its components to the output interface of the parent component iteself. Mediating links specify the relation between the information at two adjacent levels in the component hierarchy. The conditions for activation of information links are explicitly specified as task control knowledge.

3.3 Sequencing of Tasks

Task sequencing is explicitly modelled within components as *task control knowledge*. Task control knowledge includes not only knowledge of which tasks should be activated, when and how, but also knowledge of the goals associated with task activation and the extent to which goals should be derived. These aspects are specified as component and link activation together with task control foci and extent to define the component's goals. Components are, in principle, black boxes to the task control of an encompassing component: task control is based purely on information about the success and/or failure of component reasoning. Reasoning of a component is considered to have been successful with respect to an evaluation criterion if it has reached the goals specified by this evaluation criterion to the extent specified (e.g., any or every).

3.4 Delegation of Tasks

During knowledge acquisition a task as a whole is modelled. In the course of the modelling process decisions are made as to which tasks are (to be) performed by which agent. This process, which may also be performed at run-time, results in the delegation of tasks to the parties involved in task execution. In addition to these specific tasks, often generic agent tasks, such as interaction with the world (observation) and other agents (communication and cooperation) are assigned.

3.5 Knowledge Structures

During knowledge acquisition an appropriate structure for domain knowledge must be devised. The meaning of the concepts used to describe a domain and the relations between concepts and groups of concepts, are determined. Concepts are required to identify objects distinguished in a domain (domain-oriented ontology) , but also to express the methods and strategies employed to perform a task (task-oriented ontology). Concepts and relations between concepts are defined in hierarchies and rules based on order-sorted predicate logic. In a specification document references to appropriate knowledge structures (specified elsewhere) suffice; compositional knowledge structures are composed by reference to other knowledge structures.

4 Global Structure of a Generic Agent

To model an agent capable of reasoning about its own tasks, processes and plans, its knowledge of other agents, its communication with other agents, its knowledge of the world and its interaction with the world, a generic agent architecture has been devised in which such types of reasoning are transparently allocated to specific components of an agent (see (Brazier, Jonker and Treur, 1997)).

This generic architecture can be applied to different types of agents. In this paper this architecture is refined to model a rational agent with motivational attitudes: other architectures are more applicable for other types of agents. The generic architecture is described in this section, while the refined BDI architecture is the subject of Section 5.

Four of the five types of knowledge distinguished above in Section 3 are used to describe this generic architecture: task composition, information exchange, sequencing of tasks and knowledge structures. Within an individual agent, task delegation is trivial.

4.1 Task Composition

As stated above an agent needs to be capable of reasoning about its own processes, its own tasks, other agents and the world. In other words, an agent needs to be capable of six tasks:

(1) controlling its own processes,
(2) performing its own specific tasks,
(3) managing its interaction with the world (observation, execution of actions),
(4) managing its communication with other agents,
(5) maintaining information on the world, and
(6) maintaining information on other agents.

4.2 Information Exchange

Information links are defined for the purpose of information exchange between components. The component *agent_interaction_management*   receives information from, and sends information to, other agents. The component *world_interaction_management* on the other hand exchanges information with the external world. Both components also exchange information with the component *own_process_control* . Which information is required by an agent specific task depends on the task itself and therefore cannot be predefined. To fully specify the exchange of information, a more specific analysis of the types of information exchange is required. In Figure 1, a number of information links defined for information exchange at the top level of the agent, are shown together with the names of the components they connect.

Link name	From component	To component
import_world_info	agent (input interface)	world_interaction_management
export_world_info	world_interaction_management	agent (output interface)
transfer_comm_world_info	agent_interaction_management	maintenance_of_world_information
provide_world_state_info	world_interaction_management	own_process_control
import_agent_info	agent (input interface)	agent_interaction_management
export_planned_comm	agent_interaction_management	agent (output interface)
provide_agent_info	agent_interaction_management	own_process_control
transfer_committed_acts&obs	own_process_control	world_interaction_management
transfer_agent_commitments	own_process_control	agent_interaction_management
transfer_planned_comm	own_process_control	agent_interaction_management

Fig. 1. Links for information exchange at the top level of an agent

In Figure 2 a graphical representation of the generic architecture for an agent is shown; in this figure a number of the information links and the components they connect, are depicted.

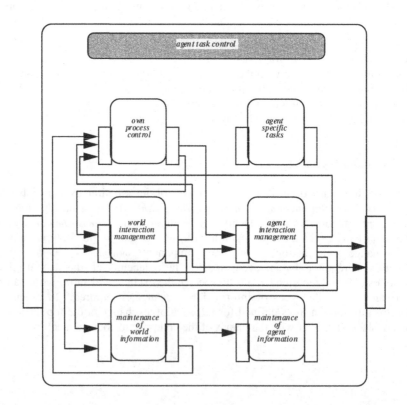

Fig. 2. Top level composition and information links of a generic agent

4.3 Task Sequencing

Minimal task control has been modelled and specified for the top level of the generic agent. Task control knowledge specifies that all generic components and links are initially awakened. The awake status specifies that as soon as new information arrives, it is processed. This allows for parallel processing of information by different components. The links which connect an agent to other agents are activated by the agents from which they originate. Global task control includes specifications such as the following rule:

> *if start*
> *then next_component_state(own_process_control, awake)*
> *and next_component_state(world_interaction_management, awake)*
> *and next_component_state(agent_interaction_management, awake)*
> *and next_link_state(import_agent_info, awake)*
> *and next_link_state(export_agent_info, awake)*
> *and next_link_state(import_world_info, awake)*
> *and next_link_state(export_world_info, awake)*
> *and next_link_state(transfer_comm_world_info, awake)*
> *.......*

4.4 Knowledge Structures

Generic knowledge structures are used within the specification of a generic agent, a number of which have been shown above. In the following section more detailed examples of specifications of knowledge structures will be shown for a rational agent with motivational attitudes.

4.5 Building a Real Agent

Each of the six components of the generic agent model presented above can be refined in many ways, resulting in models of agents with different characteristics. (Brazier, Jonker and Treur, 1996) describe a model of a generic cooperative agent, based on the generic agent model and Jenning's model of cooperation, see (Jennings, 1995). In (Brazier and Treur, 1996) another refinement of the generic agent model is proposed for reflective agents capable of reasoning about their own reasoning processes and other agents' reasoning processes.   In the following section a refinement of the component *own_process_control* is presented in which motivational attitudes (including beliefs, desires and intentions) play an important role.

5 A Model for Rational Agents with Motivational Attitudes

The generic model and specifications of an agent described above, can be refined to a generic model of a rational BDI agent capable of explicit reasoning about its beliefs, desires, intentions and commitments. First, some of the assumptions behind the model are discussed (Section 5.1). Next the specification of the model is presented for the highest level of abstraction (in Section 5.2 and 5.3), and for the more specific levels of abstraction (Section 5.4).

5.1 Rational Agents with Motivational Attitudes

Before presenting the model, some of the assumptions upon which this model is based, are described. Agents are assumed to be rational: they must be able to generate goals and act rationally to achieve them, namely planning, replanning, and plan execution. Moreover, to fully adhere to the strong notion of agency, an agent's activities are described using mentalistic notions usually applied to humans. This does not imply that computer systems are believed to actually "have" beliefs and intentions, but that these notions are believed to be useful in modelling and specifying the behaviour required to build effective multi-agent systems (see, for example, (Dennett, 1987) for a description of the "intentional stance").

A first assumption is that motivational attitudes, such as beliefs, desires, intentions and commitments are defined as *reflective statements* about the agent itself and about the agent in relation to other agents and the external world. These reflective statements are modelled in DESIRE in a meta-language, which is order sorted predicate logic. Functional or logical relations between motivational attitudes and between motivational attitudes and informational attitudes are expressed as meta-knowledge, which may be used to perform meta-reasoning resulting in further conclusions about motivational attitudes. For example, in a simple instantiation of the model, beliefs can be inferred from meta-knowledge that any observed fact is a believed fact and that any fact communicated by a trustworthy agent is a believed fact.

A second assumption is that information is classified according to its *source*: internal information, observation, communication, deduction, assumption making. Information is explicitly labeled with these sources. Both informational attitudes (such as beliefs) and motivational attitudes (such as desires) depend on these sources of information. Explicit representations of the dependencies between attitudes and their sources are used when update or revision is required.

A third assumption is that the *dynamics* of the processes involved are explicitly modelled. For example, a component may be made awake from the start, which means that it always processes incoming information immediately. If more components are awake, their processes will run in parallel. But, if tasks depend on each other, sequential activation may be preferred. Both parallel and sequential activation may be specified explicitly. If required, update or revision takes place and is propagated through different components by active information links.

A fourth assumption is that the model presented below is *generic*, in the sense that the explicit meta-knowledge required to reason about motivational and informational attitudes has been left unspecified. To tune the model to a given application this knowledge has to be added. In this paper, examples of the types of knowledge are given for the purpose of illustration.

A fifth assumption is that intentions and commitments are defined with respect to both *goals and plans*. An agent accepts commitments towards itself as well as towards others (social commitments). In this paper, an agent determines which goals it intends to fulfill, and commits to a selected subset of these goals. Similarly, an agent determines which plans it intends to perform, and commits to a selected subset of these plans.

Most reasoning about beliefs, desires, and intentions can be modelled as an essential part of the reasoning an agent needs to perform to control its own processes. A refinement of the generic component *own_process_control* described in Section 4 is presented below.

5.2 A Refined Model of Own Process Control

Finally, to design a BDI agent, the component *own_process_control* is refined. The component *own_process_control* is composed of three components, which reason about:

(1) the agent's beliefs
(2) its desires
(3) its intentions and commitments with respect to both goals and plans.

The extended task hierarchy for a BDI agent is shown in Figure 3. The component *belief_determination* performs reasoning about relevant beliefs in a given situation. In the component *desire_determination* an agent determines which desires it has, related to its beliefs. Intended and committed goals and plans are derived by the component *intention_and_commitment_determination* . This component first determines the goals and/or plans it intends to pursue before committing to the specific selected goals and/or plans. All three components are further refined in Section 5.4.

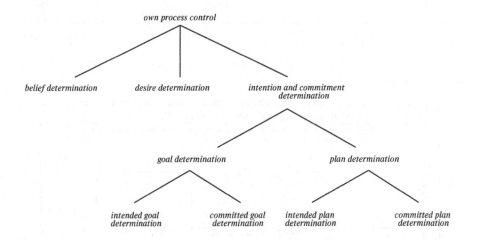

Fig. 3. Task hierarchy of own process control within a BDI agent

In the model, beliefs and desires influence each other reciprocally. Furthermore, beliefs and desires both influence intentions and commitments. This is explicitly modelled by information links between the components and meta-knowledge within each of the components.

In Figures 4.1 and 4.2, the composition of *own_process_control* is shown, together with the exchange of information. This is specified in DESIRE graphically as in Figure 4.1.

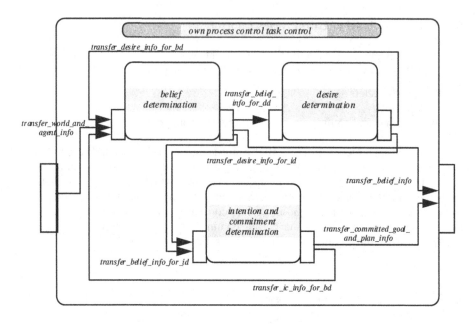

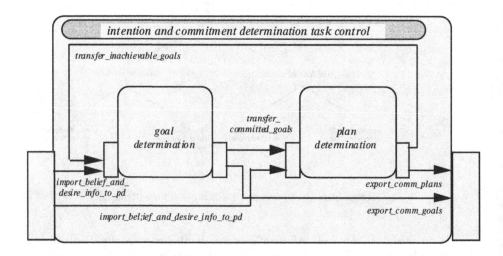

Fig. 4.1. Refinement of own process control within the BDI agent

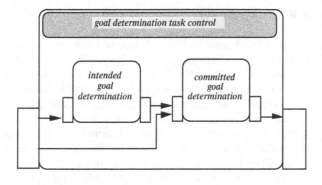

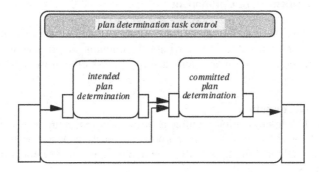

Fig. 4.2. Further refinement of goal determination and plan determination

Task control knowledge of the component *own_process_control*   determines that:

(1) initially all links within the component *own_process_control*   are awakened, and the component *belief_determination* is activated,

(2) once the component *belief_determination* has succeeded in reaching all possible conclusions (specified in the evaluation criterion *goals*) *desire_determination* is activated and *belief_determination* is made continually active (awake),

(3) once the component *desire_determination*   has succeeded in reaching all possible conclusions (specified in the evaluation criterion *desires*), the component *intention_and commitment_determination*   is activated and *desire_determination*   is made continually active (awake). In addition, the desires in which the agent may want to believe (wishful thinking) are transferred to the component *belief_determination* .

Task control of the component *intention_and_commitment_determination* , in turn, is described in Section 5.4.3.

5.3 The Global Reasoning Strategy

The global reasoning strategy specified by task control knowledge in the model is that some chosen desires (depending on knowledge in the component *intended_goal_determination,* existing beliefs and specific agent characteristics) become intentions, and some selected intentions (depending on knowledge in the component *committed_goal_determination* and specific agent characteristics) are translated into *committed_goals* to the agent itself and to other agents. The agent then reasons about ways to achieve the *committed_goals* on the basis of knowledge about planning in the component *committed_plan_determination* , resulting in the construction of a *committed_plan* . This plan is transferred to one or more of the other high-level components of the agent (depending on the plan in question), namely *world_management* , *agent_management* , and *agent_specific_tasks* , to be executed.

5.4 Further Refinement of Components

In the previous two sections the model for reasoning about motivational attitudes was described in terms of the three tasks within the component *own_process_control* and their mutual interaction. In this section each of the tasks themselves is described in more detail.

5.4.1 Belief Determination
The task of belief determination requires explicit meta-reasoning to generate beliefs. The specific knowledge used for this purpose obviously depends on the domain of application. The adopted model specifies meta-knowledge about beliefs based on six different sources:

(1) *internal beliefs of an agent*
Internal beliefs are beliefs which an agent inherently has, with no further indication of their source. They can be expressed as meta-facts of the form *internal_belief(X:Statement)* , meaning that *X:Statement* is an internal belief. These meta-facts can be specified as initial facts or be inferred from other internal meta-information. By meta-knowledge of the form

$$if\ internal\_belief(X{:}Statement)\ then\ belief(X{:}Statement)$$

beliefs can be derived from the internal beliefs.

(2) *beliefs based on observations*
Beliefs based on observations are acquired on the basis of observations of the world, either at a particular moment or over time. Simple generic meta-knowledge can be used to derive such beliefs:

$$if\ observed\_world\_fact(X{:}Statement)\ then\ belief(X{:}Statement)\ .$$

(3) *beliefs based on communication with other agents*
Communication with other agents may, if agents are considered trustworthy, result in beliefs about the world or about other agents. Generic meta-knowledge that can be used to derive such beliefs is:

if communicated_fact_by(X:Statement, A:Agent)   and trustworthy(A:Agent)
then belief(X:Statement)

(4) *beliefs deduced from other beliefs*
Deduction from other beliefs can be performed by means of an agent's own (domain-dependent) knowledge of the world, of other agents and of itself.

(5) *beliefs based on assumptions*
Beliefs based on assumptions may be derived from other beliefs (and/or from epistemic information on the lack of information) on the basis of default knowledge, knowledge about likelihood, et cetera. For example, a default rule *(a : b) / c*   can be specified as meta-knowledge (e.g. according to the approach described by (Tan and Treur, 1992)).

(6) *beliefs based on desires*
In the case of wishful thinking beliefs may be implied by generated desires. For example, as an extreme case, a strongly wishful-thinking agent may have the following knowledge in *belief_determination* :

if not belief(not(X:Statement)) and desired(X:Statement)   then belief(X:Statement)

A more sophisticated model to generate beliefs can also keep track of the source of a belief. This can be specified in the meta-language by adding labels to beliefs reflecting their source, for example by *belief(X:Statement, L:Label)* . Here the label *L:Label* can denote a single source, such as *observed* , or *communicated_by(A:Agent)* , but if beliefs have been combined to generate other beliefs, also combined labels can be generated as more complex term structures, expressing that a belief depends on a number of sources.

Another aspect of importance is the omniscience problem (Fagin et al., 1995), which requires the control of the belief generation process. In practical reasoning processes, only those beliefs are generated that are of specific interest. Specific solutions to the omniscience problem may be modelled explicitly within this component.

5.4.2 Desire Determination
Desires can refer to a (desired) state of affairs in the world (and the other agents), but also to (desired) actions to be performed. Often, desires are influenced by beliefs. Because beliefs can be based on their source, as discussed in Section 5.4.1, desires can inherit these sources. In addition, desires can have their own internal source, for example desires can be inherent to an agent. Knowledge on how desires are generated is left unspecified in the generic model.

5.4.3 Intention and Commitment Determination
Intended and committed goals and plans are determined by the component *intention_and_commitment_determination* ; this component is composed of the component *goal_determination* and *plan_determination*. Each of these two components first determines the intended goals and/or plans it wishes to pursue before committing to a specific goal and/or plan.

In the component *goal_determination* commitments to goals are generated in two stages. In the component *intended_goal_determination* , based on beliefs and desires, but also on preferences between goals, specific goals become intended goals. Different agents have different strategies to choose which desires will become intentions. For example:

• some (eager) agents may choose a desire as an intention as soon as it is consistent with their previously established intended goals;
• others (socially complying agents) may select an intention when it is one of their desires which is an intention of other agents with which they automatically comply;
• and still others (apathetic agents) may select no intentions at all.

These differences in agent characteristics can be expressed in the (meta-)knowledge specified for *intended_goal_determination* . For each intended goal a condition (in the form of *not inadequate_intended_goal(X:Statement)*) is specified that expresses the adequacy of the goal, i.e., that the goal is not subject to revision. As soon as it has been established that the intention has to be dropped, the intended goal becomes inadequate, so this condition no longer holds, which in turn leads to the retraction of the intended goal on the basis of the revision facilities built-in in the semantics and execution environment of DESIRE.

In the component *committed_goal_determination* a number of intended goals are selected to become goals to which the agent commits; again, different agents have different strategies to select committed goals, and these different strategies can be expressed in the (meta-)knowledge specified for the component *committed_goal_determination* . The committed goals are transferred to the component *plan_determination* . In a manner similar to intended goal determination, the knowledge specified for the component *committed_goals* includes a condition *inadequate_committed_goal(X:Statement)* that plays a role in revision.

In the component *plan_determination* commitments to goals are analysed and commitments to plans are generated in two stages. In the component *intended_plan_determination* plans are generated dynamically, combining primitive actions and predefined plans known to the agent (stored in an implementation, for example, in a library). On the basis of knowledge of the quality of plans, committed goals, beliefs and desires, a number of plans become intended plans. The component *committed_plan_determination* determines which of these plans should actually be executed. In other words, to which plans an agent commits. If no plan can be devised to reach one or more goals to which an agent has committed, this is made known to the component *goal_determination* . If a plan has been devised, execution of a plan includes determining, at each point in time, which actions are to be executed. During plan execution, monitoring information can be acquired by the agent through observation and/or communication. Plans can be adapted on the basis of observations and communication, but also on the basis of new information on goals to which an agent has committed. If, for example, the goals for which a certain plan has been devised, are no longer relevant, and thus withdrawn from an agent's list of committed goals, it may no longer make sense to execute this plan.

6 Modelling Commitment Strategies

Specifications in DESIRE define in a declarative manner the behaviour of a multi-agent system with respect to their integrated reasoning processes and acting processes (observing, communicating, executing actions in the world). Characteristic to this approach to modelling multi-agent systems is that strategies, revision, and the integration of communication, observation and action in the reasoning process, are explicitly modelled and specified.

6.1 Specification of Commitment Strategies

After plan construction, the phase of plan realization starts. During this phase, all components of *own_process_control* are continually awake, so that any revision of an agent's informational and motivational attitudes is propagated immediately by transfer of the new information through links to other components. The fact that both information links and components are always awake ensures that this happens without further explicit specification of activation. Thus, new information is not necessarily expected at specific points in the process.

In our model, the crucial difference between the three kinds of agents, defined according to their commitment strategies as discussed in Section 2, manifests itself in their reaction to different kinds of information received through different links. For all types of agents final revision of commitments takes place in the component *intention_and_commitment_determination* , namely in the components *committed_goal_determination* and *committed_plan_determination* . These are the components in which the knowledge about different commitment strategies resides.

To be more specific, the *blindly committed agent* only drops a *committed_goal* as a reaction to the receipt of information that the relevant goal has been realized. This information is transferred from the component *belief_determination* through the link *transfer_belief_info_for_id* , which in turn receives it through the link *import_ws_info_for_bd* , from the higher level components *world_management* and possibly from the component *agent_specific_tasks* . Some of the relevant generic knowledge present in the component *committed_goal_determination* is the following:

> *if own_commitment_strategy(blind)   and goal_reached(X:Statement)*
> *then to_be_dropped_committed_goal(X:Statement)*

If this rule succeeds, an information link from *committed_goal_determination* to itself transfers the conclusion *to_be_dropped_committed_goal(X:Statement)* to update the atom *inadequate_committed_goal(X:Statement)* to *true*, which, in turn leads to the retraction of the committed goal, as described in Section 5.4.3. For simplicity these update links have not been depicted in Figure 4.

The *single-minded agent*, in addition, drops a *committed_goal* as a reaction to the information that the relevant goal can no longer be realized. This information is transferred from the component *belief_determination* . The knowledge present in the component *committed_goal_determination* includes the following:

> *if own_commitment_strategy(single_minded)   and goal_reached(X:Statement)*
> *then to_be_dropped_committed_goal(X:Statement)*

> *if own_commitment_strategy(single_minded)   and goal_not_achievable(X:Statement)*
> *then to_be_dropped_committed_goal(X:Statement)*

The information *goal_not_achievable(X:Statement),*   in turn, may depend on beliefs. In the first case the information may be transferred through the link *import_ws_info_for_bd* , from the higher level component *world_management* . In the second case plan revision is involved. In either case the relevant *committed_plan* is dropped using knowledge in the component *committed_plan_determination* :

> *if own_commitment_strategy(single_minded)   and plan_not_achievable(X: plan)*
> *then to_be_dropped_committed_plan(X: plan)*

Next, in the second case, in order to check whether the relevant goal is achievable, the component *plan_determination* tries to design a plan. If this component succeeds in designing a new plan, this plan is adopted, and the original goal is maintained. If not, the component comes to the conclusion (based on exhaustive search) that no new plan can be designed. The component *committed_goal_determination* derives that the original goal must be retracted. Information specifying the success or failure of the design of a new plan is transferred from the component *plan_determination* to the component *committed_goal_determination* .

The *open-minded agent,* finally, in addition to the reasons adopted by the blindly committed agent and the single-minded agent, also drops a *committed_goal* in reaction to information that the goal is no longer desired, received from the component *desire_determination* through the link *transfer_desire_info_for_id* . The knowledge included in the component *committed_goal_determination* includes the following:

> *if own_commitment_strategy(open_minded)   and goal_reached(X:Statement)*
> *then to_be_dropped_committed_goal(X:Statement)*

> *if own_commitment_strategy(open_minded)   and goal_not_achievable(X:Statement)*
> *then to_be_dropped_committed_goal(X:Statement)*

> *if own_commitment_strategy(open_minded)   and goal_not_desired(X:Statement)*
> *then to_be_dropped_committed_goal(X:Statement)*

In the last case the desire may have been dropped for many different reasons, not to be elaborated in this paper.

For all three agents, the stage of dropping a committed goal and/or a committed plan is followed by communication to the relevant agents. After this, a new committed   goal   should   be   established   in   the   component *intention_and_commitment_determination* .

6.2 An Example: Meeting Scheduling

To illustrate the use of explicit knowledge of dependencies and strategies for belief, intention and commitment revision, within the BDI model (specified within the DESIRE framework), a small, simplified example of an application, namely meeting scheduling, is described.

Three agents A1, A2 and A3 all believe that a meeting is required, and that their presence at this meeting is desired. They also believe that all three agents' presence is required. As agreement has been reached on a specific time slot, they all have an additional desire, namely to be at a meeting at the specific time slot.

The goal to be at a meeting in general, and at the specific meeting in particular, has been adopted by all three agents as an intended and committed goal.   To accomplish this goal they all intend, and have committed to a plan to be at the specific meeting. In this example all three agents are single-minded. Below, the revision of attitudes is described from the point of view of A3. Agent A1 discovers that agent A2 is no longer available at the given time slot for the meeting.

Communication is required:
Agent A1 informs agent A3 of this fact.
As agent A3 believes that information A1 conveys is true, agent A3 also believes that agent A2 is no longer available.

Belief revision:
Given this new belief, agent A3 realizes that a prerequisite for the meeting (namely that all three participants' presence is required) no longer holds, and that the meeting can not be held as planned.

Dropping of committed goal:
As A3 is a single-minded agent, it is now allowed to drop its committed goal and the associated committed plan of meeting at the specific meeting.

Desire revision:
The desire to hold a meeting remains.   The desire to hold the specific meeting is retracted.

Intention and commitment revision:
Agent A3's intention and commitment to the general goal of holding a meeting with the three other agents, still holds. Its intention and commitment to the goal of holding the specific meeting are retracted.
The intention and commitment to the plan for the specific meeting are also retracted.

The stage *Dropping of committed goal* follows the specification for single-minded agents elaborated in Section 6.1; the other stages can be described similarly (see (Brazier, Dunin-Keplicz, Treur and Verbrugge, 1997) for an extended specification).
In the example above, both committed and intended goals are dropped during intention and commitment revision. However, there are examples in which a committed goal is retracted while the corresponding intended goal remains; for example, a single-minded agent may become ill and retract its commitment to be present at the meeting, while still keeping its intention to be there (hoping to have recovered before the meeting).

7 Discussion and Conclusions

In this paper a generic model for a rational BDI agent with explicit knowledge of dependencies between motivational attitudes has been modelled in DESIRE. The BDI model also includes knowledge of different commitment strategies in which these dependencies are used to reason about beliefs, desires and intentions, but also to explicitly revise specific beliefs, desires and/or intentions. Communication, action and observation may influence an agent's beliefs, desires, goals and plans dynamically.

The formal specification in DESIRE provides a bridge between logical theory, e.g. (Rao and Georgeff, 1991) and practice of BDI agents. Another bridge is described in (Rao, 1996), in which the operational semantics of a language corresponding to the implemented system dMARS, are formalized. Our model, in contrast, emphasizes the analysis and design methods of BDI systems, as do the architectures of (Jennings, 1995; Kinny, Georgeff and Rao, 1996). However, there are differences as well: our specification is more formal than Jennings' specification in (Jennings, 1995). DESIRE has a logical basis for which a temporal semantics has been defined (Brazier, Treur, Wijngaards and Willems, 1995). In contrast to the BDI architecture described in (Kinny, Georgeff and Rao, 1996), in our approach dynamic reasoning about beliefs, desires and goals, during plan execution, may lead to the construction of a (partially) new plan. This is partly caused by the parallel nature of specific reasoning processes in this model, but is also a consequence of the nature of explicit strategic knowledge of commitment strategies in the model. Strategic knowledge is used to revise, for example, beliefs, but also to revise intentions and commitments to goals and plans, during a dynamic process. Revisions are propagated by transfer of updated information on beliefs, desires and intentions to the components that need the information: components that reason about beliefs, desires, intentions, goals and plans.

The nature of continual activation of components and links makes it possible to transfer updated or new beliefs "automatically" to the relevant components. (The compositional revision approach incorporated in DESIRE is discussed in more depth in (Pannekeet, Philipsen and Treur, 1992)). In the paper the example of new information received from another agent, which may influence beliefs on which a goal has been chosen, is used to illustrate the effect this may have on the execution of a plan. Retraction of beliefs may lead to retraction of a number of goals that were based on these beliefs, which in turn may lead to retraction of a commitment to these goals. If the belief is the basis for a commitment to a plan, retraction of the belief may result in the retraction of the commitment to the plan and thus to its execution.

The DESIRE framework provides support in distinguishing the types of knowledge required to model rational agents based on mental attitudes. An existing agent architecture provided the basis for the model and the specification language provided a means to express the knowledge involved. By declaratively specifying task control knowledge and information exchange for each task, the dynamic process of revision has been explicitly specified.

The model as such provides a basis for further research: within this model more specific patterns of reasoning and interaction can be modelled and specified. Maintenance goals can be considered, joint commitments and joint actions can be modelled, more extensive communication patterns between agents can be analysed and represented, relative importance of intentions can be expressed, et cetera.

In contrast to general purpose formal specification languages such as Z and VDM, DESIRE is committed to well-structured compositional models. Such models can be specified in DESIRE at a higher level of conceptualisation than in Z or VDM and can be implemented automatically through use of automated implementation generators.

Acknowledgments

This work was partially supported by the Polish KBN Grants 3 P406 019 06 and 8T11C 03110.

References

Bratman, M.A. (1987). Intentions, Plans, and Practical Reason, Harvard University Press, Cambridge, MA.

Brazier, F.M.T. , Dunin-Keplicz, B., Jennings, N.R. and Treur, J. (1995). Formal specification of Multi-Agent Systems: a real-world case. In: V. Lesser (Ed.), Proc. of the First International Conference on Multi-Agent Systems, ICMAS-95, MIT Press, Cambridge, MA, pp. 25-32.

Brazier, F.M.T. , Dunin-Keplicz, B., Jennings, N.R. and Treur, J. (1997). DESIRE: modelling multi-agent systems in a compositional formal framework, International Journal of Cooperative Information Systems, M. Huhns, M. Singh, (Eds.), special issue on Formal Methods in Cooperative Information Systems: Multi-Agent Systems, vol. 6, to appear.

Brazier, F.M.T., Dunin-Keplicz, B., Treur, J., Verbrugge, R. (1997) A generic BDI architecture. Technical Report, Department of Mathematics and Computer Science Vrije Universiteit Amsterdam.

Brazier, F.M.T., Treur, J. (1996). Compositional modelling of reflective agents. In: B.R. Gaines, M.A. Musen (Eds.), Proc. of the 10th Banff Knowledge Acquisition for Knowledge-based Systems workshop, KAW'96, Calgary: SRDG Publications, Department of Computer Science, University of Calgary, pp. 23/1-13/12.

Brazier, F.M.T., Jonker, C.M., Treur, J., (1997). Formalisation of a cooperation model based on joint intentions. In: Proc. of the ECAI'96 Workshop on Agent Theories, Architures and Languages, ATAL'96. In: J.P. Muller, M.J. Wooldridge, N.R. Jennings, Intelligent Agents III, Lecture Notes in AI, vol. 1193, Springer Verlag, 1997, pp. 141-156.

Brazier, F.M.T., Treur, J., Wijngaards, N.J.E. and Willems, M. (1996). Temporal semantics of complex reasoning tasks. In: B.R. Gaines, M.A. Musen (Eds.), Proc. of the 10th Banff Knowledge Acquisition for Knowledge-based Systems workshop, KAW'95, Calgary: SRDG Publications, Department of Computer Science, University of Calgary, pp. 15/1-15/17

Castelfranchi, C. (1995). Commitments: From individual intentions to groups and organizations. In: V. Lesser (Ed.), Proc. of the First International Conference on Multi-Agent Systems, ICMAS-95, MIT Press, Cambridge, MA, pp. 41-48.

Cohen, P.R. and Levesque, H.J. (1990). Intention is choice with commitment, Artificial Intelligence 42, pp. 213-261.

Dennett, D. (1987). The Intentional Stance, MIT Press, Cambridge, MA.

Dunin-Keplicz, B. and Treur, J. (1995). Compositional formal specification of multi-agent systems. In: M. Wooldridge and N.R. Jennings, Intelligent Agents, Lecture Notes in Artificial Intelligence, Vol. 890, Springer Verlag, Berlin, pp. 102-117.

Dunin-Keplicz, B. and Verbrugge, R. (1996). Collective commitments. To appear in: Proceedings of the Second International Conference on Multiagent Systems, ICMAS-96.

Fagin, R., Halpern, J., Moses, Y. and Vardi, M. (1995). Reasoning about Knowledge. Cambridge, MA, MIT Press.

Jennings, N.R. (1995). Controlling cooperative problem solving in industrial multi-agent systems using joint intentions, Artificial Intelligence 74 (2).

Kinny, D., Georgeff, M.P., Rao, A.S. (1996). A Methodology and Technique for Systems of BDI Agents. In: W. van der Velde, J.W. Perram (Eds.), Agents Breaking Away, Proc. 7th European Workshop on Modelling Autonomous Agents in a Multi-Agent World, MAAMAW'96, Lecture Notes in AI, vol. 1038, Springer Verlag, pp. 56-71

Pannekeet, J.H.M., Philipsen, A.W. and Treur, J. (1992). Designing compositional assumption revision, Report IR-279, Department of Mathematics and Computer Science, Vrije Universiteit Amsterdam, 1991. Shorter version in: H. de Swaan Arons et al., Proc. Dutch AI-Conference, NAIC-92, 1992, pp. 285-296.

Rao, A.S. (1996). AgentSpeak(L): BDI Agents Speak Out in a Logical Computable Language. In: W. van der Velde, J.W. Perram (eds.), Agents Breaking Away, Proc. 7th European Workshop on Modelling Autonomous Agents in a Multi-Agent World, MAAMAW'96, Lecture Notes in AI, vol. 1038, Springer Verlag, pp. 42-55.

Rao, A.S. and Georgeff, M.P. (1991). Modeling rational agents within a BDI architecture. In: R. Fikes and E. Sandewall (eds.), Proceedings of the Second Conference on Knowledge Representation and Reasoning, Morgan Kaufman, pp. 473-484.

Shoham, Y. (1993). Agent-oriented programming, Artificial Intelligence 60 (1993) 51- 92.

Shoham, Y. (1991). Implementing the intentional stance. In: R. Cummins and J. Pollock (eds.), Philosophy and AI, MIT Press, Cambridge, MA, 1991, pp. 261-277.

Shoham, Y. and Cousins, S.B. (1994). Logics of mental attitudes in AI: a very preliminary survey. In: G. Lakemeyer and B. Nebel (eds.) Foundations of Knowledge Representation and Reasoning, Springer Verlag, pp. 296-309.

Tan, Y.H. and Treur, J. (1992). Constructive default logic and the control of defeasible reasoning, Report IR-280, Vrije Universiteit Amsterdam, Department of Mathematics and Computer Science, 1991. Shorter version in: B. Neumann (ed.), Proc. 10th European Conference on Artificial Intelligence, ECAI'92, Wiley and Sons, 1992, pp. 299-303.

Velde, W. van der and J.W. Perram J.W. (Eds.) (1996). Agents Breaking Away, Proc. 7th European Workshop on Modelling Autonomous Agents in a Multi-Agent World, MAAMAW'96, Lecture Notes in AI, vol. 1038, Springer Verlag.

Wooldridge, M. and Jennings, N.R. (1995). Agent theories, architectures, and languages: a survey. In: M. Wooldridge and N.R. Jennings, Intelligent Agents, Lecture Notes in Artificial Intelligence, Vol. 890, Springer Verlag, Berlin, pp. 1-39.

Towards an Agent-Oriented Framework for Specification of Information Systems

Stefan Conrad, Gunter Saake, and Can Türker

Otto-von-Guericke-Universität Magdeburg
Institut für Technische und Betriebliche Informationssysteme
Postfach 4120, D-39016 Magdeburg, Germany
{conrad|saake|tuerker}@iti.cs.uni-magdeburg.de

Abstract. Objects in information systems usually have a very long life-span. Therefore, it often happens that during the life of an object external requirements are changing, e.g. changes of laws. Such changes often require the object to adopt another behavior. In consequence, it is necessary to get a grasp of dynamically changing object behavior. Unfortunately, not all possible changes can in general be taken into account in advance at specification time. Hence, current object specification approaches cannot deal with this problem. Flexible extensions of object specification are needed to capture such situations.

The approach we present and discuss in this paper is an important step towards a specification framework based on the concept of agents by introducing a certain form of knowledge as part of the internal state of objects. Especially, we concentrate on the specification of evolving temporal behavior. For that, we propose an extension (called Evolving Temporal Logic) of classical temporal logic approaches to object specification.

Keywords: modeling information systems, agent-oriented specification, dynamically changing behavior, evolving temporal logic.

1 Introduction

Currently, nearly every enterprise or organization has to face the situation that in order be competitive the use of modern information systems is indispensable. Considering the frequent and dramatic changes in the international economy and politics, there is clear demand for advanced information systems which are able to deal with highly dynamic environments, e.g. rapidly changing markets, increasing (world-wide) competition, and new trade agreements as well as (inter)national laws. In the recent years, there are obvious efforts in several computer science communities to build cooperative intelligent information systems which can deal with such aspects (see for example [HPS93]).

Today, object-oriented techniques are in general used for modeling such advanced information systems [Buc91,Bro92]. Most of the existing object-oriented

This research was partially supported by the CEC ESPRIT Basic Research Working Groups No. 8319 ModelAge and No. 22704 ASPIRE as well as by the Deutsche Forschungsgemeinschaft under Sa 465/19 (SAW).

approaches are successful in capturing the properties and behavior of the real-world entities. However, it seems that the concept of "object" (at least in its current understanding) cannot cover all aspects of modern information systems. Whereas structural aspects of such systems can easily be dealt with by current object-oriented approaches, these approaches succeed to cope with *dynamic* behavior only up to a certain degree.

Typically, information system objects have a longer life-span than application programs, environmental restrictions, etc. Therefore, we need a semantic model where the behavior specification of an object or object system may be modified during its existence, which is not expressible in current formalisms underlying traditional (object-oriented) specification languages until now.

The concept of *agent* [WJ95,GK94] which can be seen as a further development of the concept of object seems to provide a more adequate basis for modeling such information system dynamics. In comparison to traditional objects, agents are flexible in that sense they may change their behavior dynamically during system run-time, i.e. the behavior of an agent is not (or can not be) completely determined at compile or specification time. In order to get a grasp of such properties, we need an agent-oriented specification framework which goes beyond the existing object-oriented ones.

Therefore, we propose and discuss several extensions for object specification languages. These extensions are intended to be first steps towards an own agent-oriented specification framework. For that, we present a first formalization based on an extended temporal logic.

The remainder of this paper is organized as follows. Section 2 starts with a brief presentation of current object specification technology for modeling information systems. Further, we introduce the concept of agent as a further evolution of the concept of object. In Section 3, we propose first extensions of existing object specification languages for capturing dynamically changing behavior. An extended temporal logic, called Evolving Temporal Logic, as formal basis is sketched in Section 4. Finally, we conclude by summarizing and pointing out future work.

2   From Object Specification to Agent Design

In the recent years, object-oriented conceptual modeling of information systems has become a widely accepted approach. Meanwhile, there exists a lot of object-oriented models and specification languages (e.g. Oblog [SSE87,SSG+91], LCM [FW93] or TROLL [HSJ+94,JSHS96,SJH93]) proposed for those purposes. In this section, we briefly recall the basic ideas of the concept of object, whereby we base our presentation on the object model as introduced in [SSE87].

Basically, objects are characterized as *coherent units of structure and behavior*. An object has an *internal state* of which certain properties can be observed. The internal state can be manipulated explicitly through a properly defined *event interface*. Objects can be considered as *observable processes*. *Attributes*

are the observable properties of objects which may only be changed by event
occurrences.

The *behavior* of objects are described by *life cycles (or traces)*, which are built
from sequences of (sets of simultaneously occurring) events. Thus, each object
state is completely characterized by a *life cycle prefix (or event snapshot)*, which
determines the current attribute values. The possible evolution of objects can be
restricted by a set of *state constraints* which can be used to define the admissible
state transitions for an object.

For textual presentation of object specifications, we use a notation close to
the syntactical conventions of the object-oriented specification language TROLL.
In Figure 1 we introduce an example of a TROLL specification. For the purposes
of this paper, we have chosen a small universe of discourse (UoD) consisting of
one or more account objects. Here, we assume an account to have an (unique)
account number, a bank by which it is managed, a holder, a balance, and a limit
for overdrawing. Moreover, we specify some basic events like opening an account,
withdrawing money from or depositing money to an account.

```
object class Account
   identification   ByAccountID: (Bank, No);
   attributes       No:            nat constant;
                    Bank:          |Bank|;
                    Holder:        |Customer|;
                    Balance:       money initialized 0.00;
                    Limit:         money initialized 0.00 restricted >= -5000.00;
                    Counter:       nat initialized 0;
   events Open(BID:|Bank|, AccNo:nat, AccHolder:|Customer|) birth
                         changing   Bank    := BID,
                                    No      := AccNo,
                                    Holder  := AccHolder;
          Withdraw(W:money) enabled   Balance - Limit >= W;
                         changing   Balance := Balance - W;
                         calling    IncreaseCounter;
          Deposit(D:money)  changing   Balance := Balance + D;
                         calling    IncreaseCounter;
          IncreaseCounter   changing   Counter := Counter + 1;
          Close death;
end object class Account;
```

Fig. 1. TROLL specification of an Account class.

In TROLL-like languages, an object template specification mainly consists out of
two parts: a *signature* section which lists object events and attributes together
with parameter and co-domain types, and a *behavior* section containing the
axioms. As axioms we do not have general temporal logic formulas but special
syntactic notations for typical specification patterns.

In the declaration section for events, we mark some events as *birth* events or as *death* events corresponding to creation and destruction of objects, e.g. Open and Close. The occurrence of events can be restricted by *enabling conditions*, which are formulae built over attributes and event parameters. In connection with temporal quantifiers these conditions may refer to object histories. Changes of attribute values are caused by event occurrences, i.e. the event Withdraw decreases the balance of an account.

The allowed values for object attributes may also be restricted, e.g. we may constrain the credit limit to maximal 5000.00. Interactions inside (composite) objects are expressed by the *event calling mechanism*, e.g. a withdrawal event enforces the event IncreaseCounter to occur simultaneously. Similar to attribute valuations, conditional event calling is supported, too.

The object specification concepts presented so far have a major drawback: *they succeed in capturing dynamic behavior (of information systems) only up to a certain degree.* Indeed, languages like TROLL or Oblog are expressive enough to model even changing object behavior depending on state changes, *but these modifications have to be fixed during specification time, e.g. before object creation.* But, this is too restrictive for handling object evolution in information systems. Typically, information system objects are characterized by long life-spans.

Usually, during that long time-span an object and the environment of object may change in a way that cannot be foreseen in advance. Consequently, dynamic specification changes are needed to overcome the problem that generally not all possible future behaviors of an object can be anticipated in the original system specification. In order to support the aspect of object and object system evolution, respectively, in an adequate way, we need an extended, logic-based framework where object class descriptions may be modified during system runtime.

Recently, the *concept of agent*, which can be seen as a further evolution of the concept of object (cf. [Sho93,GK94,WJ95]), is proposed as an adequate means for modeling information systems. Basically, an agent may be seen as an *intelligent* and *evolutionary* object which is equipped with knowledge and reasoning capabilities and is able to deal with dynamic aspects, e.g. to change its state as well as its behavior dynamically.

Like objects, agents have an *internal state* which is based on their history and influence their behavior. Whereas the internal state of objects is determined by the values of their attributes, agents have a more general notion of internal state: beside (conventional) attribute values it may contain disjunctive information, partial knowledge, default assumptions, etc.

Essentially, the internal state of an agent reflects the knowledge (belief, intention, obligations, goals, etc.) of that agent at a given time. In contrast to traditional object concepts, this *knowledge is not fixed at specification time, but it is changeable during the lifetime of an agent.* In conclusion, we can state that the internal state of an agent contains strict knowledge (which is fixed at creation time and may not be revised) as well as some changeable knowledge (which may be revised or replaced under given constraints during the agent evolution).

Agents have *goals* which they try to achieve (by cooperation) under given constraints. Each agent is obliged to satisfy its goals. Since goals are part of the internal state of agents, they may be changed during an agent's lifetime, too. They can be extended, revised or replaced through other (more important) goals. In contrast, goals to be satisfied by traditional objects are fixed at specification time, and may serve as formal requirements for implementing behavior. Therefore they have to be logically consistent.

On the other hand, the agent's goals may also be conflicting. Hence, agents must be able to resolve conflict situations in which not all goals may be achieved. In such cases, agents must be able either to revise some of their goals or to decide to satisfy only a few of their goals which are not conflicting.

Agents are able to (re)act and communicate by executing sequences of *actions*. Thus, agents show an external *behavior* that obeys the given *constraints*. In contrast to traditional objects, agents exhibit reactive behavior as well as goal-driven (or pro-active) behavior. Because agents are assumed to be autonomous, they are able to act without direct (user) intervention.

In most cases agents have to cooperate to achieve their goals. Because of the fact that agents may change their behavior and/or may even change their signature, there must exist varying communication structures. For cooperation reasons agents require knowledge about other agents, i.e. their capabilities and goals, respectively. However, agents have in general not the same and complete knowledge about other agents. In such cases, agents have to deal with partial or incomplete knowledge.

Considering all these properties agents can have, it becomes clear that the current object specification technology as sketched in the beginning of this section cannot fulfill all these requirements. This is due to the fact that several concepts are not given in current object-oriented approaches. Nevertheless, the existing object specification approaches can be used as a stable basis for extensions which try to get a grasp of those agent-specific properties.

By carefully extending the underlying semantic models and logics it should be possible to come closer and closer to the idea of "agents" as sketched before. A detailed discussion on the differences between traditional object concepts and the presented concept of agent can be found in [SCT95,TCS96].

In the following section, we propose a first agent specification language in which some of the agent-specific concepts are respected. This language is an extension of an existing object-oriented specification language. Instead of inventing a completely new specification language the extension of an existing and well-understood specification language offers us the possibility to experiment on a stable and well-understood basis.

3   Towards an Agent-Oriented Specification Language

In this section, we sketch the basic frame of an agent-oriented specification language by giving example specifications. We point out that in this first approach only a few, but very important agent-specific concepts like dynamic behavior are respected.

Our starting point is the idea of "*considering states as theories*" (a similar approach was taken in [Rei84]). In comparison to usual object-oriented approaches where the state of an object is described by a simple value map assigning each attribute a corresponding value, the "states as theories" approach is much more powerful by assuming that a state is described by a set of formulas. Depending on the underlying logic that we apply for formulating such formulas, we can then express different kinds of knowledge, for example knowledge about the future behavior of an agent as part of its own state as well as knowledge about the states of other agents.

In this way, simple state changes can become changes of theories by which we can even express the change of knowledge or goals of an agent. Thereby, knowledge revision as well as dynamic knowledge acquisition can be specified. Furthermore, partial knowledge is possible and default knowledge could be integrated.

We propose a two-level specification framework for modeling of information systems in terms of agents. The first level contains usual attributes and events, which describe the fixed behavior of an agent. In the second level, the possible evolution of the agent specification is specified.

In Figure 2 the structure of a possible specification of an agent class **Account** is sketched. The specification language used here can be considered as an extension of the object-oriented language TROLL sketched in Section 2. Similar to objects, agents have attributes (e.g. **Balance**) and events (e.g. **Withdraw**). The part of the behavior specification which must not be changed is specified in the **rigid axioms** section. In our example the effect of the events **Withdraw** and **Deposit** on the attribute **Balance** is fixed.

In addition to the concepts used for objects, an agent have **axiom attributes** which contain sets of axioms which are valid under certain circumstances. In our example we have the axiom attribute **Axioms** which is initialized by the empty set of axioms. In case we specify several axiom attributes we have to explicitly mark one of them as the current axiom set. Each formula which is included in the value of this special axiom attribute at a certain state must be fulfilled in that state.

Similar to basic attributes, axiom attributes are changed by **mutators** which can be seen as special events. The effect of mutators is described in the **dynamic specification** section. Here, we allow the manipulation of the axiom attribute **Axioms**. We may add further axioms to **Axioms**, remove existing axioms from **Axioms** and reset **Axioms** to the initial state.

Specification of Dynamic Behavior

As already mentioned, one main difference between agents and traditional objects is that agents may change their behavior dynamically during their lifetime. There are several different ways how dynamic behavior can be specified:

```
agent class Account
    identification      ByAccountID: (Bank, No);
    attributes          No:           nat constant;
                        Bank:         |Bank|;
                        Holder:       |Customer|;
                        Balance:      money initialized 0.00;
                        Limit:        money initialized 0.00;
                        Counter:      nat initialized 0;
    events              Open(BID:|Bank|, AccNo:nat, AccHolder:|Customer|) birth;
                        Withdrawal(W:money);
                        Deposit(D:money);
                        IncreaseCounter;
                        Close death;
                        Warning(S:string);
    rigid axioms        Open(BID:|Bank|, AccNo:nat, AccHolder:|Customer|)
                                    changing    Bank   := BID,
                                                No     := AccNo,
                                                Holder := AccHolder;
                                    calling     ResetAxioms;
                        Withdraw(W)  enabled     Balance - Limit >= W;
                                    changing    Balance := Balance - W;
                                    calling     IncreaseCounter;
                        Deposit(D)   changing    Balance := Balance + D;
                                    calling     IncreaseCounter;
                        IncreaseCounter changing Counter := Counter + 1;
    axiom attributes    Axioms initialized {};
    mutators            ResetAxioms;
                        AddAxioms(P:Formula);
                        RemoveAxioms(P:Formula);
    dynamic specification ResetAxioms     changing Axioms := {};
                        AddAxioms(P)     changing Axioms := Axioms ∪ P;
                        RemoveAxioms(P) changing Axioms := Axioms - P;
end agent class Account;
```

Fig. 2. Specification of an agent class Account

1. Using only one dynamically changeable axiom attribute:

This case is presented in the example in Figure 2. Here, the axiom attribute must be modifiable during the lifetime of an agent in order to be able to represent changing dynamic behavior of that agent. In our example the axiom attribute Axioms can be manipulated by the mutators AddAxioms, RemoveAxioms and ResetAxioms. Whereas AddAxioms and RemoveAxioms adds further axioms to and removes existing axioms from Axioms, respectively, ResetAxioms resets Axioms to the initial state. Possible values for the parameter P of the mutator AddAxioms could be the following ones:

```
{ Withdraw(W)
    calling    { W > 400.00 } Warning("Withdrawal limit exceeded!"); }
```

```
{ Withdraw(W)
    enabled   (W >= 0.00) and (Balance - W >= Limit); }

{ Withdraw(W)
    calling   { not(occurs(Clock.NextDay))
                since last occurs(Withdraw(W)) }
              Warning("Two withdrawals within one day!"); }

{ Close
    enabled  Balance = 0.00; }
```

The values above are sets of axioms written in the syntax of our specification language. The first value contains an axiom which requires to trigger a warning if the amount of a withdrawal is larger than 400. In the next value there is an additional restriction saying that a `Withdraw` event may only occur with an amount smaller than the current value of the attribute `Balance` minus the current value of the attribute `Limit`. Thereby, overdrawing of an account is ruled out.

The third value ensures that a warning is triggered if two withdrawals occur within one day (in this formula we refer to a `Clock` assuming that it is specified elsewhere as a part of the same system). The last listed value contains a formula which specifies that an account may only be closed if there is no money on this account.

2. Using a set of predefined, unchangeable axiom attributes:

Here, a set of axiom attributes, which contain predefined sets of axioms and which cannot be modified during the lifetime of an agent, can be defined to model dynamically changing behavior of an agent. One of these axiom attributes must be declared as the current valid set of axioms which determines the current behavior of the agent. By switching between the axiom attributes the behavior of the agent can be changed dynamically.

```
axiom attributes
  Axioms(N:nat) initialized
    N=0: {} default,
    N=1: { Withdraw(W)
            calling   { W > Balance }
                      Warning("Account has been overdrawn")) },
    N=2: { Withdraw(W)
            calling   { not(occurs(Clock.NextDay))
                        since last occurs(Withdraw(W)) }
                      Warning("Two withdrawals within one day!"); }
    ...
mutators
  ResetAxioms;
  SwitchAxioms(N:nat);
dynamic specification
  ResetAxioms      changing Axioms(0) := {};
  SwitchAxioms(N) changing Axioms(0) := Axioms(N);
```

In the example above we define a parameterized attribute **Axioms** (for details see [HSJ⁺94]) which contains different sets of axioms. Here, we declare implicitly the attribute term **Axioms(0)** to be the set with the current valid axioms. By using the mutator **SwitchAxioms** we are able to change the agent's behavior dynamically.

Please notice that this approach restricts the behavior evolution of an agent to various predefined behavior pattern. This is due to the fact that the axioms sets can not be modified during the lifetime of an agent. Furthermore, note that in the rigid axioms part the common behavior of all possible behaviors are specified.

3. Using several dynamically changeable axiom attributes:

Here, the ideas of the other cases are combined. We allow to specify several axiom attributes which may be modified during the lifetime of an agent. As in the second case, these attributes may be predefined and one of these attributes is marked as the currently valid one. In the following example we have specified two mutators **AddAxioms** and **RemoveAxioms** (in addition to the mutator of the example above) for adding a set of axioms to and for removing a set of axioms from a given axiom attribute, respectively.

```
mutators
  ⋮
  AddAxioms(N:nat, P:setOfAxioms);
  RemoveAxioms(N:nat, P:setOfAxioms);
dynamic specification
  ⋮
  AddAxioms(N, P)    changing Axioms(N) := Axioms(N) ∪ P;
  RemoveAxioms(N, P) changing Axioms(N) := Axioms(N) - P;
```

We emphasize that it might be useful to combine changing as well as predefined, unchangeable axiom attributes. In such cases we have to specify for each changeable axiom attribute own mutators. Further, please note that mutator events may be equipped with enabling conditions as usual events in order to prevent arbitrary manipulations. Moreover, mutator events may also cause the occurrence of other basic as well as mutator events. This fact can be expressed by using the well-known event calling mechanism.

However, for the agent specification approach presented so far we need a logical framework, a *logic of agents*, in which several non-standard logics (e.g. logic of knowledge, default logic, deontic logic [Mey92,Rya93,Rya94,JS93]), can be integrated. First results already show that the composition of different logics can really work [FM91]. In [SSS95,CRSS98] first steps towards the specification of dynamically changeable behavior in an object-oriented setting are presented and discussed. The following section gives a first formalization of dynamically changing behavior based on an extended temporal logic [CS97].

4 Evolving Temporal Logic

In this section we present the basic ideas for formalizing an extension of temporal logic we need for capturing the properties sketched in the previous section. We will call this extension *Evolving Temporal Logic* (ETL). Afterwards, we show how the example given in the previous section is formulated in ETL.

4.1 Basic Ideas for Formalization

Temporal Logic. The starting point is a first-order, discrete, future-directed linear temporal logic for objects which can be considered as a slightly modified version of the *Object Specification Logic (OSL)* which is presented in full detail in [SSC95]. In [Jun93] a comprehensive translation of TROLL object specifications into OSL is given. The following basic types of elementary propositions are used in the logic:

1. $o.\text{Attr} = v$ expresses that the attribute Attr of an object o has the value v (we have adopted this form from the specification language used for our example; instead we could also take a predicate expression like $\text{Attr}(o, v)$).
2. $o.\nabla e$ stands for the occurrence of event e in object o.

With these elementary propositions we may build formulas in the usual way: for this we may use for instance the boolean operators $\neg$ (negation) and $\wedge$ (conjunction) as well as all operators which can be defined by these ones. Furthermore, we have the future-directed temporal operators $\bigcirc$ (next), $\square$ (always in the future), and $\diamond$ (sometime in the future; defined as $\diamond f \equiv \neg\square\neg f$). By introducing variables and quantifiers we obtain a first-order variant of linear temporal logic: provided x is a variable and f a formula, then $\forall x : f$ and $\exists x : f$ are formulas.

The semantics of temporal logic formulas is defined w.r.t. life cycles which are infinite sequences of states: $\lambda = \langle s_0, s_1, s_2, \ldots \rangle$. We define λ^i as the life cycle which is obtained by removing the first i states from λ, i.e. $\lambda^i = \langle s_i, s_{i+1}, s_{i+2}, \ldots \rangle$. Each state in a life cycle is assumed to be equipped with a mapping assigning a truth value to each elementary proposition. Based on that we can define the semantics of composed formulas in the usual way. For instance, the semantics of temporal operators is defined as follows ($\lambda \models \phi$ means that ϕ is satisfied in λ):

$$\lambda \models \square f \quad \text{if} \quad \text{for all } i \geq 0: \lambda^i \models f.$$
$$\lambda \models \bigcirc f \quad \text{if} \quad \lambda^1 \models f.$$

For brevity we omit the treatment of variables. This can be done in the usual straightforward way. All variables which are not explicitly bound by a quantifier are assumed to be universally quantified. Fully-fledged definitions of syntax and semantics of first-order order-sorted temporal logics for object specification can be found for instance in [SSC95] or [Con96].

Example. Here, we only present some temporal logic formulas representing properties of the objects described in Fig. 1. We start with the effect an event occurrence has on attributes. For instance the effect of **Open** events for account objects is represented by the following temporal logic formula:

$$\Box(\ a.\nabla\text{Open}(B,N,H) \to \bigcirc(a.\text{Bank} = B \wedge a.\text{No} = N \wedge a.\text{Holder} = H)\ )$$

Due to the fact that **Open** is a birth event it may only occur once in the life of an object. This property being inherent to the object model of the specification language TROLL can be expressed by:

$$\Box(\ a.\nabla\text{Open}(B,N,H) \to \bigcirc\Box\neg(\exists B',N',H': a.\nabla\text{Open}(B',N',H'))\ )$$

Event calling as it may be specified for **Transfer** events in bank objects could be expressed by temporal logic formulas as follows (where b refers to a bank object):

$$\Box(\ b.\nabla\text{Transfer}(A_1,A_2,M) \to (\ \text{Account}(A_1).\nabla\text{Withdrawal}(M)\wedge$$
$$\text{Account}(A_2).\nabla\text{Deposit}(M)\qquad)\ )$$

Evolving temporal Logic (ETL). Based on the linear temporal logic described before we have to find an extension for the treatment of the special attribute having sets of first-order formulas as values. In order to represent this special property we introduce a corresponding predicate $\mathcal{V}$ into our logic. This predicate is used to express the current validity of the dynamic behavior axioms. For simplicity, we restrict our consideration to one special predicate over first-order temporal formulas.[1]

This predicate is used to express the state-dependent validity of first-order formulas: $\mathcal{V}(\tilde\varphi)$ holds in a state (at an instant of time) means that the specification φ is valid w.r.t. that state.

In a more formal way we can express this as follows: if $\mathcal{V}(\tilde\varphi)$ holds for a (linear) life cycle λ (i.e., $\lambda \models \mathcal{V}(\tilde\varphi)$) then φ holds for λ as well:

$$\lambda \models \mathcal{V}(\tilde\varphi) \quad \textbf{implies} \quad \lambda \models \varphi$$

In order to avoid severe problems especially caused by substitution we assume $\mathcal{V}$ to work only on syntactic representations of first-order temporal formulas instead of the formulas themselves. Here, we use the notation $\tilde\varphi$ to distinguish such a syntactic representation from the formula φ. For a correct formal treatment we have to define an abstract data type **Formula** for first-order temporal formulas as possible parameter values for $\mathcal{V}$. In addition a function translating values of this abstract data type into corresponding formulas is needed.

W.r.t. the reflection of $\mathcal{V}(\tilde\varphi)$ on the first-order level, we may establish the following axiom for ETL:

$$\mathcal{V}(\tilde\varphi) \to \varphi$$

---

[1] For dealing with several objects having different sets of currently valid behavior axioms, we could extend this view to several predicates or to introduce an additional parameter to the predicate for referring to different objects. In the same way, we can deal with the case that one object has several of these attributes.

By means of the predicate $\mathcal{V}$ we simulate the finite set of behavior axioms which are currently valid. Thus $\mathcal{V}(\widetilde{\varphi})$ can be read as "$\widetilde{\varphi}$ is in the set of currently valid behavior axioms". Due to $\mathcal{V}(\widetilde{\varphi}) \rightarrow \varphi$, it is sufficient that $\mathcal{V}$ holds only for a finite set of specification axioms because the theory induced by these axioms is generated on the first-order level in the usual way.

Please note that $\mathcal{V}(\widetilde{\varphi})$ can be considered as an elementary proposition in ETL. Therefore, we may assume that for each state s_i in a life cycle λ there is a truth assigning function denoting the validity of $\mathcal{V}(\widetilde{\varphi})$ for each first-order formula φ.

From the definition given before and from the usual properties of the temporal operators we can now immediately conclude:

$$\lambda \models \mathcal{V}(\widetilde{\Box\varphi}) \quad \textbf{implies} \quad \forall i \geq 0 : \lambda^i \models \varphi$$
$$\lambda \models \mathcal{V}(\widetilde{\Diamond\varphi}) \quad \textbf{implies} \quad \exists i \geq 0 : \lambda^i \models \varphi$$

This is due to $\lambda \models \mathcal{V}(\widetilde{\Box\varphi})$ implies $\lambda \models \Box\varphi$ and $\lambda \models \Box\varphi$ is defined by $\forall i \geq 0 : \lambda^i \models \varphi$ (and analogously for $\Diamond\varphi$). This special property is depicted in Fig. 3: Assume $\mathcal{V}(\widetilde{\Box\varphi})$ holds in state s_i in a life cycle λ. Then φ holds in all the states $s_i, s_{i+1}, s_{i+2}, \ldots$ — independent of whether $\mathcal{V}(\widetilde{\Box\varphi})$ is true in $s_{i+1}, s_{i+2}, \ldots$ Therefore, it should be clearly noted that there is a big difference between $\mathcal{V}(\widetilde{\Box\varphi})$ and $\mathcal{V}(\widetilde{\varphi})$. Once $\mathcal{V}(\widetilde{\Box\varphi})$ has become true, φ remains true forever. In contrast, if $\mathcal{V}(\widetilde{\varphi})$ becomes true, φ needs only to remain true as long as $\mathcal{V}(\varphi)$ does.

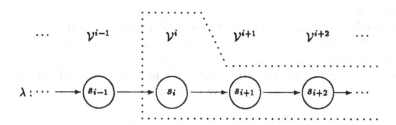

Fig. 3. Interpreting Evolving Temporal Logic.

For the events manipulating the special attribute **Axioms** (in the specification called mutators) we need counterparts in the logic. For a general manipulation of the predicate $\mathcal{V}$ we introduce two special events $axiom^+(\widetilde{\varphi})$ and $axiom^-(\widetilde{\varphi})$ for adding an axiom to $\mathcal{V}$ and for removing an axiom from $\mathcal{V}$, respectively. From the logical point of view these two events are sufficient for representing all possible ways of manipulating the attribute **Axioms**. As introduced before we use the notation $\nabla axiom^+(\widetilde{\varphi})$ for denoting the occurrence event $axiom^+$ (analogously for $axiom^-$). For occurrences of these events the following axioms are given:

$$\nabla axiom^+(\widetilde{\varphi}) \rightarrow \bigcirc\mathcal{V}(\widetilde{\varphi})$$
$$\nabla axiom^-(\widetilde{\varphi}) \rightarrow \bigcirc\neg\mathcal{V}(\widetilde{\varphi})$$

$\nabla axiom^+(\widetilde{\varphi})$ (or $\nabla axiom^-(\widetilde{\varphi})$) leads to $\mathcal{V}(\widetilde{\varphi})$ ($\neg\mathcal{V}(\widetilde{\varphi})$, resp.) in the subsequent state. Frame rules are assumed restricting the evolution of $\mathcal{V}$ to changes which are caused by occurrences of the events $axiom^+$ and $axiom^-$:

$$\neg\mathcal{V}(\widetilde{\varphi}) \wedge \bigcirc\mathcal{V}(\widetilde{\varphi}) \rightarrow \nabla axiom^+(\widetilde{\varphi})$$

$$\mathcal{V}(\widetilde{\varphi}) \wedge \bigcirc\neg\mathcal{V}(\widetilde{\varphi}) \rightarrow \nabla axiom^-(\widetilde{\varphi})$$

Before we show how to formulate some properties specified in Fig. 2 we want to briefly discuss the understanding of negation w.r.t. the predicate $\mathcal{V}$. The question to answer is whether $\mathcal{V}(\widetilde{\neg\varphi})$ is different from $\neg\mathcal{V}(\widetilde{\varphi})$. The answer is quite simple: From $\lambda \models \mathcal{V}(\widetilde{\neg\varphi})$ it follows that $\lambda \models \neg\varphi$. In contrast we cannot derive the same from $\neg\mathcal{V}(\widetilde{\varphi})$. Therefore, $\mathcal{V}(\widetilde{\neg\varphi})$ and $\neg\mathcal{V}(\widetilde{\varphi})$ have to be distinguished. This is of course not surprising because it corresponds to our intuition about the predicate $\mathcal{V}$.

Another important issue we do not discuss in full detail is a proof system for ETL. In fact, we think of taking a proof system for first-order linear temporal logic (like OSL [SSC95]) and extending it a little bit in order to get a grasp of the predicate $\mathcal{V}$.

4.2 Expressing the Example Using ETL

In the example given in Fig. 2 several properties are specified for the special attribute **Axioms**. Here, we formulate some of them as ETL formulas where the attribute **Axioms** is represented by the special predicate $\mathcal{V}$. Due to the fact that we have to distinguish between different agents we prefix each occurrence of $\mathcal{V}$ in a formula by a variable (or an agent name) referring to the agent concerned. This corresponds to the way we have prefixed predicates denoting an event occurrence for an agent before.

In all formulas given below there is an implicit universal quantification over all variables (including $\widetilde{\varphi}$). Please recall that we assume $\widetilde{\varphi}$ to be a variable over an abstract data type **Formula**.

The way we express the initial value property for **Axioms**, i.e., that directly after the occurrence of the birth event **Open** there is no formula $\widetilde{\varphi}$ for which $\mathcal{V}(\widetilde{\varphi})$ holds is a little bit tricky:

$$\Box(\ \bigcirc a.\mathcal{V}(\widetilde{\varphi}) \rightarrow \neg a.\nabla\mathrm{Open}(B,N,H)\ )$$

The effect the so-called mutator event **AddAxioms** has on the value of **Axioms** can be described by simply reducing the occurrence of **AddAxioms** to occurrences of the special pre-defined event $axiom^+$:

$$\Box(\ a.\nabla\mathrm{addAxioms}(\widetilde{\Phi}) \wedge \widetilde{\varphi} \in \widetilde{\Phi} \rightarrow a.\nabla axiom^+(\widetilde{\varphi})\ )$$

For the mutator event **ResetAxioms** we choose a similar way of expressing its effect:

$$\Box(\ a.\nabla\mathrm{ResetAxioms} \wedge a.\mathcal{V}(\widetilde{\varphi}) \rightarrow a.\nabla axiom^-(\widetilde{\varphi})\ )$$

Considering the property of $axiom^+$ described before we can immediately conclude:

$$\Box(\ a.\nabla\text{ResetAxioms} \wedge a.\mathcal{V}(\widetilde{\varphi}) \rightarrow \bigcirc\neg a.\mathcal{V}(\widetilde{\varphi})\ )$$

Finally, the effect of the mutator event **RemoveAxioms** can be described by:

$$\Box(\ a.\nabla\text{RemoveAxioms}(\widetilde{\Phi}) \wedge \widetilde{\varphi} \in \widetilde{\Phi} \rightarrow a.\nabla axiom^-(\widetilde{\varphi})\ )$$

Obviously, it is possible to express a nearly arbitrary manipulation of the behavior specification. From a pragmatic point of view this is not a desirable property. Therefore, we think of restricting the possibilities by means of the specification language. The specification language should only allow those ways of manipulating the dynamic behavior specification which can be captured by the logic in a reasonable way. Furthermore, we have to make sure that only certain users (represented by special objects or agents) are allowed to change the dynamic part of the specification. For that, additional mechanisms are needed in the specification framework.

5   Conclusions

In this paper we have motivated the necessity of evolving specifications in the area of information systems. As a rather straightforward step to modeling information systems dynamics, we presented a first approach of an agent-oriented specification framework. For that, we sketched the concept of an agent as a further evolution of the traditional concept of object. Here, we showed that the concept of agent overcomes the limitations of current object models to describe object behavior evolution. This is due to the fact that the agent paradigm allows agents to have changing goals, behavior, constraints, etc.

Our presented approach bases on the idea of "states as theories" as described, for instance, in [SSS95]. We proposed a two-level specification framework. The first level contains basic axioms describing usual events and their fixed effects on the specified attributes. In the second level we allow to specify (meta) axioms which describe the possible evolution of the agent specification. Thereby, we are able to consider dynamically changing behavior of agents and agent systems. Furthermore, we sketched an extension of linear temporal logic (called ETL, Evolving Temporal Logic) which allows us to express dynamically changing behavior within the logic. Thereby, it becomes possible to reason about changes of behavior. In [CRSS98] the same idea of separating two levels of specification is applied as extension to OSL [SSC95].

We do not want to conceal that there are several properties of agents of which we do not exactly know at the moment how to integrate them into the framework we proposed, for example planning and conflict resolving facilities of agents, and autonomy issues (e.g. which request must be fulfilled by an agent).

A nice application area for agent-oriented specification is the area of federated database or information systems. In a federation the component systems are allowed to operate in an autonomous way (at least, up to a certain degree). Most of the concepts which distinguish agent-oriented specification from traditional object-oriented specification can be applied in a natural way in such a scenario. In [TSC97b,TSC97a] we present first examples and discuss basic principles for applying an agent-oriented approach to specifying federated systems.

Besides, we have to investigate how far we can allow dynamic *signature modification*. In order to model evolutionary behavior adequately, it seems to be necessary to allow the dynamic specification of additional events. If we allow arbitrary formulas as parameters for the mutators, it is easy to add new events into the specification during the lifetime of an agent. When defining such events we also may need the specification of additional mutators which describe the evolution of these events.

On the other hand, if we do not allow arbitrary formulas as parameters, only the behavior of existing events may be changed and thus we have a restricted evolution of agents. Furthermore, we have to check if we need additionally attributes which may be integrated into the specification during the lifetime of an agent.

In conclusion, we can state that although there are many open questions, it is obvious that the concept of *agent* can be useful especially for modeling information systems consisting of components which are partially autonomous.

References

[Bro92]   M. L. Brodie. The Promise of Distributed Computing and the Challenges of Legacy Systems. In P. M. Gray and R. J. Lucas, editors, *Advanced Database Systems, Proc. of the 10th British National Conf. on Databases, BNCOD 10, Aberdeen, Scotland, July 1992*, Lecture Notes in Computer Science, Vol. 618, pages 1–28. Springer-Verlag, Berlin, 1992.

[Buc91]   A. P. Buchmann. Modeling Heterogeneous Systems as an Active Object Space. In *Implementing Persistent Object Bases, Principles and Practice, Proc. of the 4th Int. Workshop on Persistent Object Systems, Martha's Vineyard, MA, USA, September 23–27, 1990*, pages 279–290. Morgan Kaufmann Publishers, San Mateo, CA, 1991.

[Con96]   S. Conrad. A Basic Calculus for Verifying Properties of Interacting Objects. *Data & Knowledge Engineering*, 18(2):119–146, March 1996.

[CRSS98] S. Conrad, J. Ramos, G. Saake, and C. Sernadas. Evolving Logical Specification in Information Systems. In J. Chomicki and G. Saake, editors, *Logics for Databases and Information Systems*, chapter 7, pages 199–228, Kluwer Academic Publishers, Boston, 1998.

[CS97]   S. Conrad and G. Saake. Extending Temporal Logic for Capturing Evolving Behaviour. In Z.W. Raś and A. Skowron, editors, *Foundations of Intelligent Systems (Proceedings, 10th International Symposium, ISMIS'97, Charlotte, North Carolina, USA, October 1997)*, Lecture Notes in Artificial Intelligence, Vol. 1325, pages 60–71. Springer-Verlag, Berlin, 1997.

[FM91]   J. Fiadeiro and T. Maibaum. Towards Object Calculi. In G. Saake and A. Sernadas, editors, *Information Systems – Correctness and Reusability*, Informatik-Bericht No. 91–3, pages 129–178, Technische Universität Braunschweig, 1991.

[FW93]   R. B. Feenstra and R. J. Wieringa. LCM 3.0: A Language for Describing Conceptual Models. Technical Report, Faculty of Mathematics and Computer Science, Vrije Universiteit Amsterdam, 1993.

[GK94]   M. R. Genesereth and S. P. Ketchpel. Software Agents. *Communications of the ACM*, 37(7):48–53, July 1994.

[HPS93]   M. Huhns, M. P. Papazoglou, and G. Schlageter, editors. *Proc. of the Int. Conf. Intelligent and Cooperating Information Systems, Rotterdam, The Netherlands.* IEEE Computer Society Press, May 1993.

[HSJ+94]   T. Hartmann, G. Saake, R. Jungclaus, P. Hartel, and J. Kusch. Revised Version of the Modelling Language TROLL (Version 2.0). Informatik-Bericht 94–03, Technische Universität Braunschweig, 1994.

[JS93]   A. Jones and M. Sergot. On the Characterisation of Law and Computer Systems: The Normative System Perspective. In J.-J. Ch. Meyer and R. J. Wieringa, editors, *Deontic Logic in Computer Science: Normative System Specification*, chapter 12, John Wiley & Sons, Inc., 1993.

[JSHS96]   R. Jungclaus, G. Saake, T. Hartmann, and C. Sernadas. TROLL – A Language for Object-Oriented Specification of Information Systems. *ACM Transactions on Information Systems*, 14(2):175–211, April 1996.

[Jun93]   R. Jungclaus. *Modeling of Dynamic Object Systems — A Logic-Based Approach.* Advanced Studies in Computer Science. Vieweg-Verlag, Wiesbaden, 1993.

[Mey92]   J.-J. Ch. Meyer. Modal Logics for Knowledge Representation. In R. P. van de Riet and R. A. Meersman, editors, *Linguistic Instruments in Knowledge Engineering*, pages 251–275. North-Holland, Amsterdam, 1992.

[Rei84]   R. Reiter. Towards a Logical Reconstruction of Relational Database Theory. In M. L. Brodie, J. Mylopoulos, and J. W. Schmidt, editors, *On Conceptual Modeling*, pages 191–239, Springer-Verlag, New York, NJ, 1984.

[Rya93]   M. Ryan. Defaults in Specifications. In A. Finkelstein, editor, *Proc. of the IEEE Int. Symposium on Requirements Engineering (RE'93), San Diego, CA*, pages 142–149, IEEE Computer Society Press, 1993.

[Rya94]   M. Ryan. Belief Revision and Ordered Theory Presentation. In A. Fuhrmann and H. Rott, editors, *Logic, Action and Information*, De Gruyter Publishers, 1994.

[SCT95]   G. Saake, S. Conrad, and C. Türker. From Object Specification towards Agent Design. In M. Papazoglou, editor, *OOER'95: Object-Oriented and Entity-Relationship Modeling, Proc. of the 14th Int. Conf., Gold Coast, Australia, December 1995*, Lecture Notes in Computer Science, Vol. 1021, pages 329–340. Springer-Verlag, Berlin, 1995.

[Sho93]   Y. Shoham. Agent-Oriented Programming. *Artificial Intelligence*, 60(1):51–92, March 1993.

[SJH93]   G. Saake, R. Jungclaus, and T. Hartmann. Application Modelling in Heterogeneous Environments Using an Object Specification Language. *Int. Journal of Intelligent and Cooperative Information Systems*, 2(4):425–449, 1993.

[SSC95]   A. Sernadas, C. Sernadas, and J. Costa. Object Specification Logic. *Journal of Logic and Computation*, 5(5):603–630, 1995.

[SSE87]   A. Sernadas, C. Sernadas, and H.-D. Ehrich. Object-Oriented Specification of Databases: An Algebraic Approach. In P. M. Stocker and W. Kent, editors, *Proc. of the 13th Int. Conf. on Very Large Data Bases (VLDB'87), Brighton, England*, pages 107–116. Morgan Kaufmann Publishers, Los Altos, CA, September 1987.

[SSG⁺91]   A. Sernadas, C. Sernadas, P. Gouveia, P. Resende, and J. Gouveia. OBLOG
— Object-Oriented Logic: An Informal Introduction. Technical Report, IN-
ESC, Lisbon, 1991.

[SSS95]   G. Saake, A. Sernadas, and C. Sernadas. Evolving Object Specifications. In
R. Wieringa and R. Feenstra, editors, *Information Systems — Correctness
and Reusability. Selected Papers from the IS-CORE Workshop*, pages 84–99,
World Scientific Publishing, Singapore, 1995.

[TCS96]   C. Türker, S. Conrad, and G. Saake. Dynamically Changing Behavior: An
Agent-Oriented View to Modeling Intelligent Information Systems. In Z. W.
Raś and M. Michalewicz, editors, *Foundations of Intelligent Systems, Proc. of
the 9th Int. Symposium on Methodologies for Intelligent Systems, ISMIS'96,
Zakopane, Poland*, Lecture Notes in Artificial Intelligence, Vol. 1079, pages
572–581. Springer-Verlag, Berlin, June 1996.

[TSC97a]   C. Türker, G. Saake, and S. Conrad. Modeling Database Federations in
Terms of Evolving Agents. In F. Pin, Z. W. Ras, and A. Skowron, editors,
*ISMIS 1997 — Poster Proceedings of the 10th Int. Symposium on Method-
ologies for Intelligent Systems, Charlotte, North Carolina, October 15–18,
1997*, pages 197–208, Oak Ridge National Laboratory, 1997.

[TSC97b]   C. Türker, G. Saake, and S. Conrad. Requirements for Agent-based Modeling of Federated Database Systems (Extended Abstract). In A. Cesta and
P.-Y. Schobbens, editors, *ModelAge 97, Proc. of the 4th ModelAge Workshop on Formal Models of Agents, Certosa di Pontignano, Italy, January
15–17, 1997*, pages 335–343, National Research Council of Italy, Institute of
Psychology, 1997.

[WJ95]   M. J. Wooldridge and N. R. Jennings. Agents Theories, Architectures, and
Languages: A Survey. In M. J. Wooldridge and N. R. Jennings, editors, *Intelligent Agents, Proc. of the ECAI'94 Workshop on Agent Theories, Architectures, and Languages, Amsterdam, The Netherlands, August 1994*, Lecture
Notes in Artificial Intelligence, Vol. 890, pages 1–39. Springer-Verlag, Berlin,
1995.

The Impossibility of Modelling Cooperation in PD-Game

Rosaria Conte, Cristiano Castelfranchi, and Roberto Pedone

IP-CNR - Division of AI, Cognitive and Interaction Modelling
Social Behaviour Simulation Project
{rosaria,cris}@pscs2.irmkant.rm.cnr.it

Abstract. The possibility of Cooperation is still a matter of debate in the field of GT. Generally speaking, the emergence of cooperation is seen in the prospect of re-encounter as a forward-looking, calculated, and self-interested decision to cooperate. In this paper, it is argued that neither one-shot nor repeated versions of PD-game can account for a theory of cooperation as distinct from other forms of social action, and particularly bargaining it. It is also argued that in order to provide a theory of cooperation it is necessary to ground social interdependence on a general theory of action and planning. More precisely, two theses are presented and discussed: (i) When the PD-game structure is applied to ideal-type situations, one or other of its formal property does not hold. (ii) A plan-based model of social dependence is necessary for disentangling cooperation from other types of social action, especially bargaining: while PD-game applies to the latter, it does not apply to the former! Even in its repeated version, PD-game cannot account for cooperation as distinct from honest bargaining.

1 Introduction

The impossibility of cooperation in the one-shot Prisoners' Dilemma (PD) game is largely acknowledged. Indeed, some authors (Howard, 1971; Gauthier, 1986; 1993) have attempted to enable PD-game to account for one-shot cooperation; but others (Binmore, 1994) claim such an attempt to be irrational.

In short, the possibility of cooperation is still a matter of debate in the field of GT. Generally speaking, the emergence of cooperation is seen in the prospect of re-encounter. To use the words of Axelrod (1997: 12), game-theoretical models explain cooperation in the *shadow of the future*, as a forward-looking, calculated, and self-interested (although an "enlightened" self-interest, as is precised by Binmore, 1994) decision to cooperate (see also Macy, 1998). If one-shot PD-game leaves no room for cooperation, repeated versions of the same game do (see Axelrod 1984).

In this paper we will endeavour to show that *neither one-shot nor repeated* versions of the PD-game can account for a theory of cooperation as *distinct* from other forms of social action, and particularly bargaining. We will argue that in order to provide a theory of cooperation it is necessary to ground social interdependence on a general theory of action and planning as provided within the cognitive science and AI framework (for the most classical version of a theory of planned action, see Miller

J.-J. Ch. Meyer, P.-Y. Schobbens (Eds.): Formal Methods of Agents, LNAI 1760, pp. 74-89, 1999.

et al., 1960). More precisely, this paper will present a discussion of the following theses:

(a) although PD-game has been said to be applicable to several social phenomena and in different domains (Axelrod, 1990), *the limits of application are yet unclear*: to which ideal-type social conditions does the PD-game applies? In this paper we will show that a *plan*-based model of social dependence (Castelfranchi et al., 1992) allows to *deduce* applicability of the PD-game; in other words, instead of testing game-theoretical models against empirical evidence, we suggest a lower-level theoretical approach for checking the applicability of the Prisoner's Dilemma, and predicting the emergence of either defection or cooperation;

(b) a plan-based model of dependence is also necessary   for *disentangling cooperation from other types of social action*, especially bargaining: while PD-game applies to the latter, it does *never* apply to the former! Even in its repeated version, PD-game cannot account for cooperation as distinct from honest bargaining.

The paper is organised as follows:
- in the following section, after a brief summary of the PD-game properties, a plan-based model of interdependence, defined in terms of goals and actions, will be shortly presented. Some ideal-type social situations will be thereby distinguished, in particular *cooperation* and *bargaining*. One-shot cooperation will be shown to be feasible, although unaccountable in terms of a PD-game. A repeated version of the game is therefore proved to be *unnecessary* to account for cooperation.
- In the third section, the repeated version of the PD-game will shown to be also *insufficient*. In order to model cooperation, it is no use to extend the temporal perspective of the PD-game. This solution is inadequate because again it fails to distinguish cooperation from reciprocity.
- Finally, in the fourth section, we will summarise the advantages of a notion of cooperation as distinct from bargaining.

2   A Plan-Based View of Social Dependence and the Applicability of PD-Game

In AI, cognitive science, and even in the common intuition, actions are (tentative) solutions to existing problems, or, *means* for achieving *goals*, applicable under given *conditions*. The structure of action cannot be essentially incorporated into the PD-game structure, because such a structure does not allow for goals, conditions, and problems, but only for payoffs (which are explicitly considered as primitive in game-theoretical models, see Binmore 1994), to be represented. While building its theoretical foundations on a game-theoretic grounds, social scientists actually dispense with at least one the major contributions that AI and cognitive science have given to the scientific community: a theory of action and planning. We will resort to such a contribution to give grounds and reasons to the interdependent payoffs displayed in a game-theoretical matrix.

2.1   PD-Game Properties

The PD-game is a fundamental game applied in several fields for several purposes (Axelrod 1990). One of its major applications is the study of human cooperation (see, for example, G. Hardin, 1968; R. Hardin, 1982; Margolis, 1982; Olson, 1965; Taylor, 1987; Axelrod, 1984). The idea underneath was that if we are not able to get people to cooperate in a simple situation like that depicted by the PD game, we can forget about *deriving* rational cooperation at all.

Here, we will clarify what is usally meant by a game, and in particular by a PD-game.

A game is a situation of interdependence between the payoffs of two or more agents' (usually called, players) moves. Given a set of moves and a set of players (e.g., m_j and m_j, and two players), and their possible combinations (in our case, (m_j, m_j), (m_j,m_j), (m_j, m_j), (m_j, m_j)), a game is a situation in which, (a) the players' actual moves instantiate one combination, (b) the payoffs that each player obtains are interdependent: the player performing m_j will obtain a different payoff according to whether the opposer plays m_j or m_j. A PD-game is a game in which agents choose among two possible moves (C and D, which stand for cooperate and defect; however, it should be noted that the "cooperative" or "non-cooperative" character of the moves is illusory[1], and lies only in the specific structural properties of the game, which will be expressedbelow.

The PD-game moves give rise to four possible combinations (DC, CC, DD, CD), with the relative payoffs. Let us present the payoff matrix of the PD using, for purpose of clarity, the Maynard-Smith's (1982) moves of dove and hawk, where *dove* stands for the cooperative move (keep silent) and *hawk* stands for the non-cooperative move (confess):

	dove	hawk
	y	x
dove	y	0
	0	z
hawk	x	z

	dove	hawk
	2	3
2		0
	0	1
3		1

	dove	hawk
	3	6
3		0
	0	1
6		1

Fig. 1: Prisoners' Dilemmas (drawn from Binmore, 1994: 103)

where $x > y > z > 0$. For brevity, we use Axelrod's symbols:

(a) 1, 2 = players
(b) dove, hawk = possible actions

---

[1] The structure of PD-game more is usually applied to a fictitious and rather cumbersome example, of which many variants circulate. The originary draft (as reported by Binmore, 1994, is as follows: the questor of Chicago is on the tracks of two well-known delinquents, but he has no sufficient elements to arrest them. Consequently, he constructs a plan: he tells them that if they both will deliver information on each other (non-cooperative move), they will obtain a discount on the sentence (D,D). If, alternatively, they both keep silent, they will be sentenced to a mild penalty (in absence of elements for a serious virdict). But if one delivers information on the other while the latter keeps silent (D,C), ther latter will be emprisoned, while the former will be set free.

(c) R (reward) = (dove,dove) payoff
(d) T (temptation) = (hawk,dove) payoff
(d) S (sucker) = (dove,hawk) payoff

to which we add

(e) B (boomerang) = (hawk, hawk) payoff

A number of properties apply to this structure. These explicit properties of the structure of the Prisoner's Dilemma, which allow to set the payoffs to given values, are as follows:

(a) *Preference order*: payoffs are such that T > R > B > S; this in substance means that a PD-game structure is such that temptation to cheat is always possible and that hawk is a dominant strategy (Eichberger, 1993), since it is one's best move whatever the opponent decides to do (in fact, T > R, and B > S); it is actually a strongly dominating strategy (Binmore, 1994), because hawk is always the best choice, not only one that which provides the highest payoff in a subset of the extended form of the game (this latter would be a weakly dominating strategy). In short, a PD-game is one in which cheat is always convenient.

(b) *Pareto-inefficiency assumption*: payoffs are such that $R > \dfrac{T+S}{2}$. The outcome of the PD-game is Pareto-inefficient, since the average outcome of cooperation (R) is higher than the average result of non cooperating $\dfrac{T+S}{2}$.

(c) The actions remain the same, but their payoffs vary interdependently. Actions must produce benefits with different payoffs, but variability depends exclusively on the players' interdependence.

But there are also some implicit assumptions, namely:

(d) actions are executed to achieve goals, to obtain benefits, which have payoffs
(e) actions imply costs,
(f) payoffs should be greater than costs.

2.2   Main Theses

As game-theorists are well-aware of (see, for example Binmore 1994: 102), the assignment of payoffs is arbitrary: payoffs are not derived from a theory of action. They are inputs to decision, rather than results of a model of action. As a consequence, the matrix does not *derive* from a model of cooperative action. Indeed, it itself *is*, or claims to be, one such model, that is to say, a mathematical representation of social interdependence.

We claim that just because of this, PD game is inapplicable to cooperation. If one tries to apply it to real-life situations, one of the following consequences occurs,

- the preference order is modified in such a way that hawk is no more a dominating strategy (it is not always preferable), and/or
- $R = \dfrac{T+S}{2}$, meaning that the Pareto-inefficiency assumption does not hold. This in substance means that there is no incentive to cooperate, and/or
- agents do not achieve a common goal, but individually different goals.

To see this, we will try to apply the PD-game to a number of paradigmatic social situations. But beforehand, we will present a plan-based model of social dependence (Castelfranchi et al., 1992) which will help us identify ideal-type cases cooperation situations.

2.3   Interdependence in *Action*

Let us distinguish two types of dependence.

Mutual dependence. This occurs when two or more agents $<x_1, x_2, ..., x_n>$ have a shared goal and depend on each other to achieve it. Two or more agents are said (Conte et al., 1991) to have a *shared* goal when they have the same world state p as a goal $<(GOAL\ x_1\ p)\ \&\ (GOAL\ x_2\ p)\ \&\ ...\ \&\ (GOAL\ x_n\ p)>$, and p does *not* mention the goal holder as a beneficiary of one's own goal (e.g., "Have the left coalition party win the elections", or "Have the cake cooked", etc.). More formally (for a complete formal definition of this notion in terms of a first-order language, see Castelfranchi et al., 1992), two agents x and y depend upon each other tow achieve a shared goal g_i, when for any plan p_i $<a_1, a_2,..., a_n>$ belonging to the set of plans P_i which is believed to achieve g_i, there are at least,

- one action a_i *not* belonging to the set of actions A_x that x is competent upon;
- and one action a_j -with a_i always $\neq a_j$- *not* belonging to the set of actions A_y that y is competent upon.

Reciprocal dependence. This occurs when two agents x and y depend upon each other to achieve two (or more) different goals. More formally (see again Castelfranchi et al., 1992), x and y are in reciprocal dependence iff, for any two goals g_x and g_y - with g_x always $\neq g_y$ - such that g_x is an instance of x's goal set G_x and g_y is an instance of y's goal set G_y, it is the case that

- for any plan p_i belonging to the set of plans P_x which is believed to achieve g_x there is at least one action a_i *not* belonging the set of actions A_x that x is competent upon;
- and for any plan p_j belonging to P_y which is believed to achieve p_y , there is at least one action a_j -with a_i always $\neq a_j$- *not* belonging to the set of actions A_y that y is competent upon.

Two rather different types of social action follows from the above definition:

- *cooperation* occurring when mutually dependent agents execute the plan p_i to achieve their common goal g_i;
- *exchange*[2], occurring when reciprocally dependent agents execute each a share of the other's plan to achieve their different goals.

In what follows, it will be argued that PD-game applies to reciprocal dependence, and therefore depicts exchange; but it does not apply to mutual dependence and therefore does not represent cooperation.

2.4   PD-Game and Mutual Dependence

The agents goals vary along the following dimensions.

(a) *Cost-dependent Vs independent*: either the benefit[3] is a continuous variable depending on the cost of contribution (e.g., the control of pollution), or it is a none-or-all phenomenon (for example, a surgery); if the benefit is cost-dependent, the amount of benefit achieved if all contributors cooperate to it will be higher than would be the case if some contributors cheat. Viceversa, if the benefit is cost-independent, the amount of benefit produced is the same, whether someone is cheating or not.

(b) *Global Vs distributed*: the common benefit may be enjoyed either jointly (to dethrone a tyrant) or distributedly (to split a booty) by contributors.

To the goal dimensions, we will add an action dimension of variability:

(c) *iterated Vs complementary actions:* the cooperative plan is either iterated (including several instances of one action, as in the case of jointly lifting a sofa) by, or distributed among, contributors (including several distinct types of action, like in a football team). Complementary actions imply that the benefit cannot be achieved if complementary actions are not carried out.

These dimensions are not exhaustive but they allowed us to distinguish several prototypical situations. They seem particularly relevant in the context of the present argument because they specify the conditions for cheating: cheat can take place at at least two levels:

---

[2]We speak here about exchange, rather than bargaining, since in the present context we are not distinguishing the exchange of actions from the exchange of resources. However, the notion of reciprocal dependence defined above includes dependence from each others' resources. In the latter case, we speak of bargaining. Throughout the rest of the paper, bargaining will be preferred over exchange because the notion of bargaining seems to fit better the PD-game context.

[3]From now on, we will speak about benefit, rather than goals, in order to emphasize the quantitative aspect of goal-achievement, which is essential within a game-theoretical model. Quantity, by the way, is neither a primary nor a necessary specification of goals, which are symbolic representations.

(a) at the level of the goal: in which case the hawk move is "don"t share"; this obvioulsy implies that, when the benefit is global, cheat cannot occur at the level of the benefit;

(b) at the level of the action: in which case, the hawk move is "don't contribute"; this implies that cheat cannot occur with complementary actions.

In particular, the strongest mutual dependence holds with global benefit and complementary action, and the weakest in the opposite situations. While mutual dependence never leaves room to PD-game, it may allow for defection (although not as a dominant strategy). In particular,

- mutual dependence does never allow for PD-game, and
- strong dependence does not even allow for defection; but
- weak mutual dependence allows for defection as a non-dominant strategy.

Let us examine the situations which are drawn from the interplay between these dimensions.

Cost-dependent global benefit with iterated actions. The benefit achievement is a continuous variable, but cannot be split and therefore enjoyed separately by contributors; furthermore the plan to achieve it is iterated by them.

Let us consider as an example the control of pollution, (this is a typical example of a public good in the Olson's sense). This can be formulated in terms of a PD-game structure by instantiating action *dove* to 'reduce production of poison gas', and in turn action *hawk* to 'not reduce' such production. Obviously, the degree of pollution can vary on a continuous scale depending on the entity of reduction. Therefore, the joint benefit (b) is a continuous variable based upon cost of reduction (c).

Thesis 1.

Either the preference order $(R > T > B > S)$ does not hold (and as a consequence, hawk is not always preferable), or the assumption of rational action does not hold.

Proof 1.

Premises

(p1) On the grounds of the implicit assumption (iii) mentioned above, the joint benefit is supposed to be greater than the cost sustained to achieve it: $b > c$.

(p2) *A fortiori*, the cooperative global reward is higher than costs, which are distributable; since for simplicity we are assuming that the game is played by two agents only: $R = (b - c/2) > 0$

(p3) The benefit of temptation must be lower than the benefit of global cooperation ($b_{DC}^4 < b_{CC}$) since the benefit is proportioned to costs.

(p4) B= 0 since no-one is contributing to the benefit.

(p5) D = "don't contribute", since benefit is global.

Consequences

---

[4] This stands for the total benefit of the (D,C) combination.

(c1) By (p3), $b_{CC} > b_{DC}$.

(c2) For (p5), $T = (b_{DC} - 0)$.

(c3) Two alternatives,

If $b_{DC} \leq (b_{CC} - c/2)$,

then $R \geq T$; preference order: $(R > T > B > B) \neq (T > R > B > S)$

If $b_{DC} > (b_{CC} - c/2)$,

if $(b_{DC} - c/2) > 0$

then $S > B$; preference order: $(T > R > S \geq B) \neq (T > R > B > S)$

if $(b_{DC} - c/2) < 0$

then $c > b$; thereby infringing the assumption of rational action.

Therefore, either the preference order is different from that which is assumed by the PD-game structure or the assumption of rational action does not hold.

Cost-independent global benefit with iterated actions. The benefit is none-or-all, independent on the entity of the costs sustained from contributors, and cannot be split among them, and is achieved by several instances of the same action.

Typical examples are the parliamentary obstructionism, where deputies belonging to the same party or coalition take successively the word to prevent that a given law is voted. (Political) elections also belong to this category: people vote for a given candidate, who will be elected only if the votes received will exceed a certain threshold. If their candidate will be elected, supporters will enjoy a joint benefit.

Suppose the common benefit is to have the labour party winning the elections. The cooperative action C is therefore 'vote' while the non-cooperative action D, by those expected supporters who went instead to the beach, is 'not vote'.

We have two alternatives here: the agents will obtain their global benefit (the candidate will be elected) or they will not. For the purpose of our reasoning, the former alternative is all we need to consider.

Thesis 2.

The outcome of S is no-lower than the outcome of B, thereby infringing the preference order $(R > T > B > S)$. As a consequence, hawk is not a dominating strategy (is not always preferable).

Proof 2.

Premises

(p1) Since benefit is not distributable, the payoff of the (dove, dove) combination is equal to the benefit minus the cost of each contributor: $R = b - c/2$.

(p2) $b > c/2$ for the assumption of rational action.

(p3) Since benefit is independent of cost, there is no difference between the (dove,dove) benefit and the (hawk, dove) benefit $b_{CC} = b_{DC}$.

(p4) D = don't contribute (don't vote).

(p5) Since no benefit will be obtained if no-one votes, B is always ≤ 0.

Consequences

We have two possible consequences, depending on whether (') or not (") the quorum is reached and the candidate is elected:

(c1') T > R, for the premises (p1) and (p3),	(c1") T > R, for the premise (p1);
(c2') R > 0, for premise (p2);	(c2") R < 0, by definition (the candidate has not been elected but the cost of contribution has been sustained);
(c3') S = R, for the premises (p1) and (p3), and therefore > 0;	(c3") S = R, by premise (p3), and therefore < 0;
(c4') therefore S > B, for the premise (p4);	(c4") B ≤ O, by premise (p4), and therefore ≤ S. But since, S = R, B ≤ R.
If candidate is elected, the preference order will be (T>R=S>B) ≠ (T >R > B > S).	If candidate is not elected, the preference order will be (T>R=S=B) ≠ (T >R > B > S).

In any case, the preference order infringes that which is assumed by the PD-game assumption.

Cost-independent distributed benefit with complementary actions. The quantity of benefit does not depend on the contribution: it is a yes/no effect of (cooperative) action. However, it must be enjoyed distributedly, as opposed to jointly, by its contributors. A typical example is to split a booty[5]: suppose two thieves decide to rob a jewellery. One executes the actual robbery while the other does the car driving. We have a multi-agent plan (MAP) -rob the jewellery and drive the car- and an alternative between C and D: C is 'share' the booty; D equals to 'not share' the booty.

Suppose the value of the booty is b and the cost of the whole MAP equals to c, where (b - c) > 0according to the assumption of rational action -e.(iii)-, the outcomes payoffs are as follows:

---

[5]This may be considered by the reader to be equivalent to the Stag Hunt Game (inspired by Rousseau (1755/1913)), where the cooperative enterprise is to hunt a deer (cf. Binmore 1994:121; several examples of this game are applied to the international relations literature (see, for example, Jervis, 1978). Unless the players play their part in the eneterprise, this is bound to fail. However, once the players have separated to execute each one's share of the plan, one or the other may be tempted to trap a hare, since this is an activity which requires no help by anyone. However, if both end up by trapping hares, they will hinder each other. The similarity between this situation and the one we are describing is only apparent because, unlike our example, in the Stag Hunt game, R > T, and it is not clear why a player should be induced to defeat:

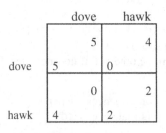

Fig. 2: Stag Hunt Game

Thesis 3

The outcome of S is no-lower than the outcome of B, thereby infringing the preference order *(R > T > B > S)*. As a consequence, hawk is not a dominating strategy (is not always preferable).

Proof 3

Premises
(p1) Benefit is distributed and cost-independent: $R = b/2 - c/2$
(p2) $(b/2 - c/2) > 0$ (rational action)
(p3) b is not obtained if anyone agent does not contribute (heterogenous actions): D = "don't share".

Consequences
(c1) by premise (p1 and p3), $T = b - c/2$; cheat consists of not sharing the booty;
   (c2) by p3 and the definition of the game: if the hawk move is "don't share", the (hawk, hawk) combination equals to contribute (do action needed) and then snatch the booty from each other's hands: $B = 0 - c/2$;
   (c3) by p1 and p3, $S = 0 - c/2$, and therefore $S = B$. The preference order is $(T>R>S = B) \neq (T>R>B>S)$.

Cost-independent distributed benefit with iterated actions. The benefit is a yes-or-no effect to be enjoyed separately, but the MAP includes several (in our example, two) instances of the same action, as when two predators run at each side of the prey. If any stops, the prey will run away, and no-one will achieve any share of the booty. This is equal to the previous case[6].

Cost-independent global benefit with complementary actions. The benefit of cooperation is a yes-or-no effect, to be enjoyed jointly but it is achieved by complementary actions. A typical example is teamwork, for example a car convoy: one does the driving of a car that both want to get to destination, while the other does the leading (the example is drawn from Cohen and Levesque 1991). Here, interestingly, the PD-game properties do not apply. In fact to cheat at the level of actions, which are both necessary to obtain the benefit, is impossible. But to cheat at the level of the goal is useless, since the benefit is not distributable!

Thesis 4

Preference order is different from that which defines the PD-game structure (the hawk move is not a dominating strategy).

Proof 4

Premises
(p1) By definition, b is not distributable: $R = (b - c/2)$.

---

[6] As in the previous case, the actions are both necessary to catch the prey. The argument follows therefore the same line as before.

(p2) By definition, actions are complementary.
(p3) $b > c$.

Consequences
(c1) by p1, the hawk move (D) must be different from "don't share"; therefore, the hawk move is "don't contribute";
(c2) by p1, $R = b - c/2$
(c3) by p2, $B = 0$ and $T = 0$
(c4) the previous consequences and (p3), $R > T = B$;
(c4) by p1, $S = 0 - c/2$; $B > S$
The preference order is $(R > T = B > S) \neq T > R > B > S$.

Cost-dependent global benefit with complementary actions. Here, the benefit cannot be enjoyed separately, but it depends on the costs sustained by contributors. Actions are complementary. The example is an orchestra giving a concert: the elements of the orchestra are complementary, and the final result depends on the costs sustained by each of them. The more each contributes, the better the final result they will jointly enjoy.

Thesis 5

Either the preference order is different from that which defines the PD-game structure (hawk is not a dominating strategy), or the assumption of rational action does not hold.

Proof 5

Premises
(p1) By definition, b is not distributable: $R = b - c/2$
(p2) By definition, benefit is cost-dependent: the (hawk, dove) combination (DC) produces a global benefit lower than the (dove, dove) dombination (CC): $b_{CC} > b_{DC}$
(p3) By definition, actions are complementary: $D =$ "don't contribute" and $B = 0$
(p4) $b > c$.

Consequences
(c1) By (p3): $T = b_{DC} - O$, and $B = 0$
(c2) by (p2), $b_{DC} < b_{CC}$;
(c3) Either $b_{DC} \leq (b_{CC} - c/2)$, in which case, by previous consequence, the preference order is $R > T > B > S$, or, if it is higher, it must also be the case that $(b_{DC} - c/2) > 0$, otherwise $b < c$, which is ruled out py (p4; see *Proof 1*). But if $(b_{DC} - c/2) > 0$, $S = b_{DC} - c/2 > 0$, and, $S > B$.

Either the preference order is different from $(T > R > B > S)$, or the assumption of rational action does not hold ($b < c$).

Cost-dependent distributed benefit with iterated actions. Here, the benefit can be shared and its amount depends on contributors: agents can both cheat at the level of goal and at the level of contribution. The ideal-type example are the (seasonal) restrictions in resource exploitation: people refrain from harvesting or fishing for each to obtain a better fish or harvest after some time. The more they respect the constraints, the more likely each will find resurces in the future.

Thesis 6

Either the Pareto-inefficiency assumption does not hold, or the preference order is different from the one assumed by the PD-game structure.

Proof 6

Premises
(p1) By definition, b is distributable: $R = b/2 - c/2$.
(p2) By definition, benefit is cost-dependent: $b_{DC} < b_{CC}$
(p3) D = either "don't share", in which case $T = b_{DC} - c/2$, while $B = (0 - c/2)$
or
(p4) D = "don't contribute", in which case $T = b_{DC}/2 - 0$, and $B = 0$
(p5) $b/2 > c/2$.

Consequences
Two alternatives may occur:
(c'1) D = don't share: $T = (b_{DC} - c/2)$, and $S = (0 - c/2) = B$;
(c"1) D = don't contribute: $T = (b_{DC}/2 - 0)$, and $B = 0$,
If $b_{DC}/2 \le (b_{CC}/2 - c/2)$,
then (by p2) $R > T$; preference order is (T>R>S=B)
if $b_{DC}/2 > (b_{CC}/2 - c/2)$,
if $(b_{DC}/2 - c/2) > 0$,
then $S > 0$; preference order is (R>T>S>B)
if $(b_{DC}/2 - c/2) \le 0$
then $b/2 < C/2$, which is ruled out by (p5).
Either the preference order is diferent from that which defines the PD-game structure, or the assumption of rational action does not hold.

Cost-dependent distributed benefit with complementary actions. This is close to split a booty except that the amount of benefit is a function of whether complementary actions are performed. Cheat can occur at the level of action, ("don't contribute"), and at the level of the benefit, ("don't share"). The typical example is farming, in which agents perform complementary actions, and the amount (harvest) is determined by how much each contributes. However, since actions are complementary, all agents must contribute. Participants will equally share the benefit, although some (cheaters) will have contributed less than others.

Thesis 7

Preference order is different from that which defines the PD-game structure (hawk is not a dominating strategy).

Proof 7

Premises

(p1) By definition, benefit is distributable: $R = b/2 - c/2$

(p2) By definition, benefit is cost-dependent: $b_{CC}/2 > b_{DC}/2$

(p3) By definition, actions are complementary: $D =$ "don't share"

(p4) $b > c$.

Consequences

(c1) By (p3) $T = (b_{DC} - c/2)$ and $B = (0 - c/2)$

(c2) By previous consequence, $S = (0 - C/2) = B$

Preference order $(T>R>S=B) \neq (T>R>B>S)$.

To sum up, in all the situations examined agents are coooperating to achieve a common goal. There is mutual dependence, but the degree of dependence varies with the benefit and action dimension considered. PD-game applies to none of those situations since one or other of its properties are infringed. In weaker dependence situations (distributable benefit and iterated actions) defection is possible although not dominant (see Figure 3).

		Cooperation	
		benefit *global*	benefit *distributable*
benefit *cost-dependent*	*iterated*	Mild dep. Cheat the level of action. Mild incentive to cheat.	Mild dep.Cheat possible at act.& benefit levels. Mild incentive to cheat
	compl.	**Strongest dep. Cheat impossible**	Strong dep. Cheat at benefit level. Low incent. to cheat.
benefit *cost-independent*	*iterated*	Weak dep. Cheat possible at action level. Hi. incentive to cheat	**Weakest dep. Cheat at act. & benefit. Highest inc.to cheat**
	compl.	Strong dep. Cheat at action level. Low incent. to cheat.	Weak dep. Cheat at benefit level. Low incent. to cheat.

Fig. 3: Strong and weak dependence. Room for defection

2.5 Reciprocal Dependence and Bargaining

Two agents enter a relation of exchange when each contributes to the partial achievement of the other's goal. In particular, a special case of exchange, namely barter, fits comfortably the framework of a PD-game. In bargaining, x gives y r_x to obtain r_y, and y gives x r_y to obtain r_x; the value of r_x for its recipient = value of r_y for its recipient, but value of r_x for the giver is higher than the value of r_x for the recipient (and the same is true for r_y).

dove = give one's resource to obtain the other's;
hawk = give nothing.
Recipient value = b;
giver's cost = c;
b > c
R = (b - c) >0;
T = b;
S = (Ø- c) <0;
B=0.

In such a situation, all the properties of PD-game and the assumptions hold. Indeed, in one-shot bargaining, defection *is* a strongly dominating strategy [...].

3 Cooperation Is More than Honest Bargaining

Obviously, things change if we add a temporal perspective: in repeated games, the more convenient solution at the individual level will also be closer to a Pareto-efficient solution: as mathematical analysis, and many experimental findings, and simulation results converge to show, the dove strategy becomes rational in repeated versions of the game.

However, the dove strategy in the repeated version of the PD-game does not emerge from mutual dependence and cooperation: in the prospect of re-encounter, agents realise that they depend *reciprocally* on each other. In other words, they realise that each needs the other to reciprocate herself. But still there is no actual cooperation; there is no joint achievement of a common goal. There is not even a weak form of mutual dependence. Social intelligence leads agents to understand that they must come to an agreement, committing one before the other to reciprocate. Indeed, commitment is needed precisely when dependence does not provide a sufficient instrumental bind, which is another way to say that dependence is not mutual! A self-interested agent does not care about the achievement of a goal he does not share. Reciprocally depending agents do not share goals. Therefore, each will care about the other's goal only as long as she is able to ensure the achievement of her own goal. This is true also in the repeated version of the PD-game. To sees this suffice to recall that in finite repeated games, rational agents will reciprocate *only up to what they believe to be the last but one move*. If they were cooperating in the full sense of the word, they would do so until *completion of the plan* (unless they drop their goal earlier).

PD is inapt to model cooperation as distinct from bargaining. Indeed, it actually obscures an important social matter of fact, namely, that *one-shot* cooperation *is* feasible. Actually in order to model cooperation, it is no use to extend the temporal perspective of the PD-game! This solution is still inadequate because it fails to distinguish cooperation from honest bargaining. GT indeed, deals with the problem of social contract, reciprocity, etc.. We believe such a problem exists and is important. But it does not cover all important pro-social phenomena. Cooperation is more than simply avoiding the Hobbesian state of nature. It includes executing multi-agent plans, that is, plans which must be executed by more than one agent in order to achieve a common goal. In order to grasp this notion of cooperation, it seems necessary to ground social interdependence on a lower-level theoretical ground, namely on a theory of action and planning.

4   Concluding Remarks: Why Bother with Feasible Cooperation?

In this paper, we endeavoured to show the role of a plan-based model of dependence as a baseline for checking the applicability of PD-game to ideal-type social situations. Thanks to such a model, we have distinguished cooperation, as occurring among mutually depending agents achieving a shared goal, from bargaining, which holds between reciprocally depending agents which achieve different goals. Furthermore, we have distinguished levels of mutual dependence, and shown that while PD-game never applies to a situation of mutual dependence, weaker forms of mutual dependence allow for defection as a non-dominant strategy, while stronger forms of mutual dependence do not allow for defection at all.

However, a game-theorist would probably ask now, where is the problem with feasible emergent cooperation? If cooperation is feasible, and does not pose any social dilemma, paradox, etc., why bother with it? The problem for a social scientists becomes interesting when a dilemma is at stake.

There are several answers to this question. First, we need a theory which provides grounds for payoffs interdependence. Why? Because we must be able to explain and predict temptation to cheat. The reasons for cheating reside in the structure of cooperative and non-cooperative actions and plans. Only on such grounds, we are able to predict when one-shot cooperation is possible and when, instead, cheating is likely to occur: in the case of Olson's public good, a theory of cooperation in terms of goals enables us to predict that agents will not cheat when they think: (a) they are necessary to obtain the benefit and (b) this is global! Only a theory of action which give grounds for payoffs enables us to make such a prediction.

To disentangle cooperation from bargaining seems useful not only to develop a more exhaustive view of the variety and complexity of social life, or to predict the likelihood of free-riding, cheat, etc.; but also to relinquish the legend of a steadily ominous state of nature, calling for a "mutually agreed upon mutual coercion".

References

Axelrod, R. *The evolution of cooperation*. Basic Books, New York, 1984

Axelrod, R. The emergence of cooperation among egoists. In P.K. Moser, editor, *Rationality in action. Contemporary approaches*. Cambridge University Press, Cambridge, 1990.

Axelrod, R. *The complexity of cooperation*. Princeton University Press, Princeton, 1997.

Binmore, K. *Game Theory and the social contract. Playing fair*. The MIT Press, Cambridge, MA., 1994.

Castelfranchi,C.,Miceli, M.,Cesta,A. *Dependence Relations among Autonomous Agents*. In Y. Demazeau, E. Werner (eds),*Decentralized AI - 3*, 215-31. Elsevier, Amsterdam, 1992.

Cohen,P. R. , Levesque,H. J. *Teamwork.*. Tech. Rep. 504, :SRI-International, Menlo Park, CA., 1991.

Conte, R., Miceli, M., Castelfranchi, C., *Limits and Levels of Cooperation. Disentangling Various Types of Prosocial Interaction*. In Demazeau,J.P. Mueller (eds), *Decentralized AI-2*, Y. , 147-157, Elsevier, Armsterdam, 1991.

Eichberger, J. *Game Theory for economists*, Academic Press, San Diego, 1993.

Gauthier, D. *Morals by agreement*, Clarendon press, Oxford, 1986.

Gauthier, D. Unite separate persons. In D. Gauthier and R. Sugden, editors, *Rationality, justice, and social contract*, Harvester heatsheaf, Hemel Hempstead, UK., 1993.

Hardin, G., *The Tragedy of the Commons, Science*,162,   1243-1248, 1968.

Hardin, R. *Collective action*, Johns Hopkins Press, Baltimore, 1982.

Howard, N. *Paradoxes of rationality: Theory of metagames and political behavior*. The MIT Press, Cambridge, MA., 1971.

Jervis, R. Cooperation under the security dilemma. World Politics, 30, 167-214, 1978.

Macy, M. Social order in artificial worlds, Journal of Artificial Societies and Social Simulation, 1, 1998.

Margolis, H. *Selfishness, altruism and rationality*, Cmbridge University Press, Cambridge, 1982.

Olson, M. *The logic of collective action*. Harvard University Press, Cambridge, MA., 1965.

Miller, G., Galanter, E., Pribram, K.H.Plans and the structure of behavior, Holt, Rinehart & Winston, New York, 1960. .

Rousseau, J.J. The inequality of man. In G. Cole, editor, Rousseau's social contract and discourses,J. M. Dent, London, 1913 (1755).

Taylor, M. The possibility of cooperation. Cambridge University Press, Cambridge, 1987.

Ullman-Margalit, E. The emergence of norms. Oxford University Press, New York, 1977.

Designing Multi-agent Systems around an Extensible Communication Abstraction

Enrico Denti and Andrea Omicini

LIA - DEIS - Università di Bologna
Viale Risorgimento, 2 – 40136, Bologna (Italy)
Ph.: +39 51 6443087 - Fax: +39 51 6443073
{edenti,aomicini}@deis.unibo.it
http://www-lia.deis.unibo.it/Staff/

Abstract. What is relevant for the effectiveness of a multi-agent system is the interaction between agents, rather than their peculiar internal model. The design of a single agent architecture should then concentrate on agent observable behaviour and on its interface towards the outside. Moreover, a multi-agent architecture should be designed around the choice of a suitable coordination model, accounting for all the aspects of agent interaction. Accordingly, the effective design of a multi-agent architecture should focus on the role and properties of the coordination media (the communication abstractions) within the coordination model, instead of the coordination entities (the agents).

The main aim of this paper is to show how a multi-agent system may benefit by a coordination model whose flexibility and expressive power lies in the extensibility of the coordination medium. Extensibility can result from the embodiment of computational properties typically in charge of the agents into the communication abstraction.

As an example, we show how a shared communication device à la Linda works as the core of a flexible coordination architecture in the Linda-based $\mathcal{ACLT}$ coordination model. $\mathcal{ACLT}$ tuple spaces are enhanced so as to be reactive to communication events, rather than to communication state changes only. So, $\mathcal{ACLT}$ tuple spaces are programmable . Reactions to communication events can be defined through a logic-based specification language, and have the semantics of asynchronous, mutually-independent atomic transactions. By defining different observable behaviours for $\mathcal{ACLT}$ tuple spaces through reaction programming, a multi-agent architecture can exploit a number of different agent coordination policies without affecting the single agent behaviour.

Keywords: Multi-Agent Systems, Coordination Model, Transactions, Extensible Communication Abstraction

1 Introduction

According to [14], *interaction* adds a fundamental dimension to computing, in that complexity of interactive systems makes them unsuitable for a complete characterisation in terms of a formal system such as, for instance, an operational

J.-J. Ch. Meyer, P.-Y. Schobbens (Eds.): Formal Methods of Agents, LNAI 1760, pp. 90–102, 1999.
© Springer-Verlag Berlin Heidelberg 1999

semantics based on state transitions. Being intrinsically interactive, multi-agent systems are naturally better characterised by the model of component interaction, as well as by the observational behaviour of their components, rather than by the rules of agent inner computation. As a result, agent architectures can be designed independently of agent internal models, by focussing on agent observational behaviour, thus intrinsically providing for agent heterogeneity. As a further consequence, the design of a multi-agent system crucially depends on the choice of an adequate *coordination model* , suitably accounting for communication, synchronisation, cooperation, and competition among agents.

Due to this shifting focus from agents to agent interaction, the communication abstraction is asked to play a major role within the coordination model. In particular, this paper aims to show the benefits of a flexible coordination model based on an extensible coordination medium for a multi-agent system. Extensibility can be achieved by suitably embodying computational properties into the communication abstraction, so that its behaviour can be properly modified according to the system needs. One important expected consequence of this approach is that, once the coordination model for the multi-agent system is given, the choice of a particular interaction policy should not affect agent design. Agents could be designed according to a quite abstract model of observational behaviour that the communication abstraction should be able to interpret and handle according to the required interaction model. Indeed, this seems to be quite a desirable property, from both a conceptual and a practical viewpoint. In fact, this makes interaction policy be in charge of the *coordination media* [5], where interaction actually takes place, instead of the single *coordination entities* , which should not be conceived as having a view of the system as a whole. In practice, agents of a multi-agent system may often be difficult or even impossible to modify, so their observable behaviour could not be (easily) accommodated to accomplish a range of different interaction strategies.

To show the effectiveness of this approach, we discuss the Linda-based $\mathcal{ACLT}$ coordination model [12]. By introducing the notion of *generative communication* and promoting the separation between the computation model and the coordination model [11], based on a shared memory communication abstraction (called *tuple space*), Linda [9] provides an effective approach to the design of multi-agent architectures. $\mathcal{ACLT}$ adopts and extends the basic Linda communication kernel. What is relevant to the main topic of this paper is the $\mathcal{ACLT}$ notion of *reactive tuple space*, based on the idea of providing the communication abstraction with the capability to react to *communication events* rather than just to the global *communication state* as in standard Linda, thus lifting the system observability from tuples to operations on tuples. Communication operations can then be associated to *reactions* by means of a simple *specification language* (which is also based on logic tuples and basic operations over tuple spaces, thus reusing the same communication pattern) making it possible to program the behaviour of the communication abstractions in terms of event reactions. Different agent interaction policies can be accomplished given the same agent behaviour, since agents can delegate part of the synchronisation, cooperation, and competition load to the (extensible) communication abstraction.

This work is structured as follows. section 2 describes briefly $\mathcal{ACLT}$ reactions, and discusses the enhanced role of the coordination medium in the $\mathcal{ACLT}$ coordination model. section 3 shows two examples of how a simple multi-agent system can be designed around the communication abstraction behaviour, by properly programming tuple space reactions to communication events. A third example shows how the interaction policy of a multi-agent system can be changed by suitably programming the behaviour of the coordination medium, without affecting the agent interaction protocol. Conclusions and final remarks are reported in section 4.

2   Enhancing the Communication Abstraction

The $\mathcal{ACLT}$ coordination model (first presented in [12], and originating from research activities in the robotics field [15]) extends the basic Linda coordination model with the notions of *logic tuple space* (see also [3,4]), of *multiple tuple spaces* [10], and of *reactive tuple space* [6]. In the $\mathcal{ACLT}$ model, communication takes place through a multiplicity of named logic tuple spaces, which are collections of first-order unitary clauses, uniquely identified by a ground term. In particular, a logic tuple space may be given a twofold interpretation, either as a simple communication device, or or as a knowledge repository. According to the latter reading, a logic tuple space can be used as a logic theory, where deductive activities over the communication state can be performed. For this purpose, $\mathcal{ACLT}$ provides for a family of *demo* primitives, along with a coherent notion of logic consequence in a time-dependent environment [12].

The $\mathcal{ACLT}$ model is based on the notion of *reactive tuple space*, making tuple spaces reactive to *communication events* rather than to *communication state changes* only [6]. In addition, the response of the tuple space to communication events is not fixed once and for all by the communication protocol. Instead, it can be specified by programming the tuple space behaviour, by defining *reactions* to relevant communication events. A specification language, founded on the same model adopted for agent interaction, based on logic tuples and tuple spaces, is then defined for reaction programming.

2.1   The Reaction Model

The $\mathcal{ACLT}$ reaction model is based on the idea of defining a set of *logical events*, each denoted by a unique name, which are associated with *physical* (communication) *events*. Multiple physical events may correspond to the same logical event, and, conversely, multiple logical events may be connected to the same physical event. The association between communication events and logical events is represented by a special tuple of the form map(*Operation, Event*), which captures the idea that each time *Operation* is performed on the tuple space, a logical *Event* occurs.

Logical events can be associated with *reactions* triggered in response to the event occurrence. The behaviour of each reaction is specified through a tuple of the form react(*Event*,*Goal*), where the *reaction body* *Goal* is the collection of the primitive operations to be executed in response to the occurrence of the logical *Event*. Syntactically, a reaction body is defined as a conjunction of *reaction goals*. A reaction goal is an atomic formula of one of the following kinds:

- non-blocking communication primitives (out, in_noblock, rd_noblock, ...)
- state primitives (current_agent/1, current_tuple/1, current_op/1, ...)
- term predicates (term equality/inequality, term unifiability/non-unifiability, ...)

Since reaction goals are actually executed sequentially at the system level, their relative order may influence the result of the reaction. For instance, supposing the tuple space initially empty, the reaction

⟨in_noblock(x_value(X)), out(x_value(X+1)), out(x_value(1))⟩

fails, while the reaction

⟨out(x_value(1)), in_noblock(x_value(X)), out(x_value(X+1))⟩

succeeds, emitting a tuple of the form x_value(1+1).

Since a multiplicity of react/2 tuples can be specified for the same logical event, multiple reactions may correspond to one logical event. Such reactions are executed as mutually-independent actions in a non-deterministic order.

2.2   Reactions as Transactions

ACLT reactions are executed with an *all-or-nothing* transaction semantics: a reaction is brought to an end if and only if all its reaction goals succeed, in which case all side-effect operations possibly associated with the reaction itself are realised simultaneously. Instead, if even one subgoal fails, the reaction is virtually cancelled, yielding no effect at all.[1] Consider, for instance, the following reaction, which is supposed to have been associated with the *out* operation:[2]

⟨current_tuple(p(_)), in_noblock(p(a)), in_noblock(p(X)), out(pp(a,X))⟩

Each time a new tuple is inserted in the tuple space, this reaction checks for the presence of two p/1 tuples (whose one should be p(a)) and then replaces them with one single pp/2 tuple. If some part of the reaction fails (possibly because there is only one p/1 tuple instead of the two required), the reaction has no effect

---

[1] As a further consequence, reactions executed in response to communication events triggered by another reaction are handled only after such reaction has been successfully completed (or, of course, are cancelled if the same reaction fails). Accordingly, the *ACLT* reaction scheme does not allow reaction nesting.

[2] Although *ACLT* exploits multiple tuple spaces, we will henceforth leave this feature aside, since it is not relevant in the context of this work. Thus, we will always refer any communication primitive to a sort of "default tuple space", without specifying any tuple space name.

at all, and appears as never having happened at the agent perception level. So, no tuples are actually removed from the tuple space, nor are any other side-effects ever performed.[3] As a result, the communication abstraction behaves so that the simultaneous presence of the two p/1 tuples is perceived by the multi-agent system as the single pp/2 tuple.

As shown in subsection 2.1, multiple reactions to the same logical event, as well as multiple logical events mapping the same communication event, trigger the execution of a multiplicity of reactions. In addition, a reaction may trigger other reactions as a consequence of its successful completion, since it may contain communication primitives. So, it is possible for many reactions to be executed in response to one communication event. The key point is that all such reactions (both those directly triggered by the event, and those triggered by other reactions produced by the event) are actually executed before serving any other agent-triggered communication event. As a result, agents can only perceive but the final result of the execution of both the communication event and the set of all the reactions triggered by it both directly and indirectly.

Generally speaking, reactions enhance the expressive power of the coordination model. Thanks to the execution model of $\mathcal{ACLT}$ reactions, agents still perceive the response of a tuple space to a communication event as a single computational step, a single transition of the tuple space state. However, such a transition is no longer bounded to be simple (adding/deleting one tuple) and fixed by the model, but can instead be defined to be as complex as desired by programming reactions. For instance, in the example above, when viewed from an agent perspective, the simultaneous presence of the two p/1 tuples is never perceived, and one single out operation results both in the removal of a tuple and in the insertion of another. Moreover, the inserted tuple is not exactly the one specified by the out operation, but is related both to that one, and to the state of the tuple space.

As a result, the observational behaviour of the communication abstraction in response to a communication event can be modelled through reaction programming. This can be used to carry out different agent interaction policies without affecting agent models. By freeing agents from the charge of explicitly handling a (possibly complex) interaction protocol, $\mathcal{ACLT}$ allows coordination entities to be designed according to a straightforward communication protocol, while charging the coordination media of most of the coordination tasks.

The following section shows some meaningful examples of small multi-agent systems.

3   Examples

3.1   Transmission of an Encrypted Message

Suppose that a long message has to be transmitted in an encrypted form by agent A to agent B. Due to the message length, the computational load required

---

[3] In particular, no implicit knowledge classification is performed in response to the in_noblock operation: see [12,7] for further details.

to encode and decode it with a safe (yet computationally heavy) two-key (private and public) algorithm would likely be unacceptable. A typical approach consists then of encrypting the message using a (much simpler) single-key algorithm, which calls for a safe way to let the receiver know the encoding key. Since this key is always relatively short, it can be safely transmitted using the two-key algorithm without a high computational cost.

More precisely, to safely send message M to B, the sender A should:

- choose the key KM to encrypt M, producing the encrypted message CM ;
- read from the key directory the public key of B, $KpubB$, and use it to encrypt the key KM , thus producing CKM ;
- emit both CM and CKM in the proper tuple space, by means of two *out* operations.

On its side, the receiver B should:

- wait for the tuple representing the encrypted key, CKM ;
- using its private key, $KprivB$, decrypt CKM so as to restore the message encryption key, KM ;
- wait for the encrypted message CM ;
- use the key KM to decode the message, thus rebuilding the original message M.

While the sender's activity is just a sequential process, requiring no synchronisation, the receiver's activity requires that two distinct message components are available in order to rebuild the message. So, B should either remain waiting for such components or poll regularly the tuple space checking for their availability. In either case, it would be in explicit charge of handling an irrelevant activity, yet without knowing which of the two message components will appear first. This may result in a deadlock situation in the case that one of them, for whatever reason, is not produced properly.

Suppose, for instance, that B's activity is expressed in a code like

```
in_noblock(msg_key(To,MsgID,CKM)),
in(encoded_msg(MsgID,CM)), ...
```

If, after getting a tuple like msg_key(To,MsgID,CKM), the subsequent message tuple encoded_msg(MsgID,CM) is never received (for instance, because it gets lost), B would remain suspended forever. If, in order to avoid this behaviour, in(encoded_msg(MsgID,M)) is transformed into a non-blocking *in* operation in_noblock(encoded_msg(MsgID,M)), B should then handle the message queue on its own, while it would be preferable to not be concerned with such synchronisation activities at all.

In $\mathcal{ACLT}$, instead, the deadlock risk could be avoided by programming the tuple space behaviour so as to make the simultaneous presence of the two required information chunks perceivable at the agent level as a single event. This could be done by simply associating the following reaction to all *out* events, succeeding only if both message components are available:

⟨in_noblock(msg_key(To,MsgID,CKM)), in_noblock(encoded_msg(MsgID,CM)),
out(decode(To,CKM,CM))⟩

The result of such a (successful) reaction would then be the production of a tuple of the form decode(To,CKM,CM), which can be decoded by the receiver by means of its private key, thus obtaining the encryption key K, to be used to decode the message from A. Thus, B has simply to either regularly poll the tuple space with a in_noblock(decode(BID,CKM,CM)), or to suspend itself on an in(decode(BID,CKM,CM)), waiting for such a tuple to become available.

3.2   The Dining Philosophers

As an example of the flexibility provided by the extensibility of the communication abstraction to the $\mathcal{ACLT}$ model, we discuss an implementation of the classical *dining philosopher* problem [8], based on reactions. The main characteristic of this problem is that, in order to avoid deadlock situations, a philosopher should either get the two forks he needs to eat, or get none. This means that the two forks should be obtained through a transaction. Moreover, in order to ensure fairness, both fork acquisition and fork release should be performed atomically.

When trying to express the solution to this problem in Linda, the main problem is that the natural choice of modelling the fork acquisition as a sequence of two *in* operations is not transactional, thus yielding a potential risk of deadlock. In that framework, a safe solution requires that the user explicitly handles a locking mechanism, thus affecting the agent behaviour. Instead, using $\mathcal{ACLT}$ reactions, transactionality is guaranteed by suitably programming the tuple space behaviour, with no need for a more complex agent protocol.

Philosopher agents are designed according to a very straightforward interaction protocol, which can be described as follows. When a philosopher wants to eat, he tries to acquire the two forks through an in(forks(F1,F2)) operation. When he is satiated, and wants to start thinking, he gives the forks back by means of an out(release(F1,F2)) operation. Given such a simple protocol, it should be obvious that all the charge of the interaction policy is up to the communication abstraction.

The request for forks is recorded in the tuple space with a tuple of the form required(F1,F2)), signalling the philosopher is waiting to eat, and is retracted when the philosopher has been served and can start eating. This is achieved by the following reaction, which transforms a communication event (a performed in) into an explicit tuple, recording such an event into the tuple space state. In fact, the required(F1,F2) tuple indicates that a hungry philosopher has performed a fork request through an in operation, and that it is currently suspended waiting for fork availability.

```
map(in,  hungry).
react(hungry, (current_tuple(forks(F1,F2)), pre,
                    out(required(F1,F2))
            )).
```

```
react(hungry, (current_tuple(forks(F1,F2)), post,
                    in_noblock(required(F1,F2))
               )).
```

Each available fork is represented by a tuple of the form fork(*Fork*). Fork release by a philosopher is handled by the following reaction.

```
map(out, thoughtful).
react(thoughtful, (current_tuple(release(F1,F2)),
                    out(fork(F1)),
                    out(fork(F2)),
                    in_noblock(release(F1,F2))
               )).
```

Reaction atomicity ensures that the two forks are released at the same time, thus avoiding the unfairness which could be produced by any sequentialisation of the two out operations.

Finally, the tuple space is programmed so as to try to serve a request, if possible, whenever a fork is released, or a new fork request is performed.

```
map(out, reserve).
react(reserve, (current_tuple(required(F1,F2)),
                    in_noblock(fork(F1)),
                    in_noblock(fork(F2)),
                    out(forks(F1,F2))
               )).
react(reserve, (current_tuple(fork(F)),
                    rd_noblock(required(F1,F)),
                    in_noblock(fork(F1)),
                    in_noblock(fork(F)),
                    out(forks(F1,F))
               )).
react(reserve, (current_tuple(fork(F)),
                    rd_noblock(required(F,F2)),
                    in_noblock(fork(F)),
                    in_noblock(fork(F2)),
                    out(forks(F,F2))
               )).
```

The transaction semantics ensures that the forks are reserved only when they are both available and needed by someone, and reserved for the proper philosopher. Should one of these conditions not hold, reaction would fail and would not have any effect on the tuple space at all.

The agent model does not need to be specialised in order to accomplish the competition protocol: a philosopher simply asks for forks when hungry, and sets them free when satiated. Agent design can then concentrate on modelling its internal architecture, while its interaction model results in being quite simple and intuitive. A good deal of the intelligence of the system is then in charge of the interaction protocol, which is only of little concern for the single agent. Thus, the communication abstraction is extended through suitable reaction programming until it makes the system behave correctly, independently from the agent internal model: the only thing needed is that philosopher agent emerging behaviour (its interaction model) accomplishes the very straightforward *acquire/release* protocol.

3.3   Philosophers Dining with Labelled Forks

In order to show how an interaction policy can be modified and made more complex by changing the behaviour of the coordination medium, without affecting the interaction protocol of the coordination entities, we discuss a slight variation of the Dining Philosopher example, discussed in subsection 3.2. The basic problem is changed in that now there are three forks for each position on the table, each one labelled differently according to the kind of meal for which it has to be used: breakfast, lunch, or dinner. At any moment in the multi-agent system, it is either breakfast, lunch, or dinner time. When it is lunch time, for instance, only lunch forks can be given for eating. However, a slowly-eating philosopher is allowed to keep on having his meal as long as he needs. So, if he starts eating at dinner time, he will be given dinner forks, and will be allowed to keep them for eating even when breakfast time comes around.

With respect to subsection 3.2, the tuple space representation of the forks is changed from fork(*Fork*) to labelledfork(*Meal,Fork*), representing the fork *Fork* which can be used at *Meal* time. Moreover, a timefor(*Meal*) tuple is assumed to be always in the tuple space, so that at any time it is possible to determine which forks to allocate to hungry philosophers. This task obviously may be charged to a simple agent, signalling the system when it is time to switch (from breakfast to lunch, from lunch to dinner, and from dinner back to breakfast). Such an agent could simply perform an out(switch) operation on the tuple space, which could be simply programmed to properly react consistently, for instance as follows:

```
map(out, next).
react(next, (current_tuple(switch), in_noblock(switch),
             in_noblock(timefor(breakfast)),
             out(timefor(lunch)))).
react(next, (current_tuple(switch), in_noblock(switch),
             in_noblock(timefor(lunch)),
             out(timefor(dinner)))).
react(next, (current_tuple(switch), in_noblock(switch),
             in_noblock(timefor(dinner)),
             out(timefor(breakfast)))).
```

The main thing here is that philosophers are supposed to be totally unaware of this (as of most of the things of life). In fact, whenever a philosopher gets hungry, he simply asks for forks, unconcerned with time, whose handling is instead in charge of the tuple space reactions. As a result, the philosopher protocol is exactly the same of the Dining Philosopher example in subsection 3.2. Unlike that example, however, it may happen that two contiguous philosopher sharing a fork position can eat at the same time, thus exploiting the availability of more resources - three forks instead of one. Take for instance the case of a two-philosopher system, in which both get hungry at breakfast time. Only one of them (the *lucky philosopher*) will be assigned of the breakfast forks, while the other (the *unlucky philosopher*) will be forced to wait. When lunch time comes, and the lucky philosopher insists on eating, the unlucky one may still be allowed to eat on his own, since the lucky philosopher is using breakfast forks, and lunch forks are free. Thus, the two philosophers can eat together, one having lunch, the other continuing his breakfast.

In order to achieve this behaviour, we have simply to modify slightly the reactions of subsection 3.2:

```
map(out, reserve).
react(reserve, (current_tuple(required(F1,F2)),
                    rd_noblock(timefor(M)),
                    in_noblock(labelledfork(M,F1)),
                    in_noblock(labelledfork(M,F2)),
                    out(used(M,F1,F2)),
                    out(forks(F1,F2))
               )).
react(reserve, (current_tuple(labelledfork(M,F)),
                    rd_noblock(required(F1,F)),
                    rd_noblock(timefor(M)),
                    in_noblock(labelledfork(M,F1)),
                    in_noblock(labelledfork(M,F)),
                    out(used(M,F1,F)),
                    out(forks(F1,F))
               )).
react(reserve, (current_tuple(labelledfork(M,F)),
                    rd_noblock(required(F,F2)),
                    rd_noblock(timefor(M)),
                    in_noblock(labelledfork(M,F)),
                    in_noblock(labelledfork(M,F2)),
                    out(used(M,F,F2)),
                    out(forks(F,F2))
               )).
react(reserve, (current_tuple(timefor(M)),
                    rd_noblock(required(F1,F2)),
                    in_noblock(labelledfork(M,F1)),
                    in_noblock(labelledfork(M,F2)),
                    out(used(M,F1,F2)),
                    out(forks(F1,F2))
               )).
```

```
map(out, thoughtful).
react(thoughtful, (current_tuple(release(F1,F2)),
                   in_noblock(used(M,F1,F2)),
                   out(labelledfork(M,F1)),
                   out(labelledfork(M,F2)),
                   in_noblock(release(F1,F2))
                   )).
```

The interaction policy discussed in this example can be adapted to any case of renewable cyclic shared resources with limited lifespan, like in the case of clerks in a postoffice: some of them working (i.e., being available) from 6am to 12pm, some others from 12pm to 6pm, (supposedly) every day. However, what this example really aims to show is how reaction programming can be exploited to modify the behaviour of a multi-agent system with no change to the behaviour of the agents. New notions (like meal time, and labelled forks) are introduced in the system, new resources are made available (more forks), a new policy for resource assignment is adopted, but the philosopher agents are allowed to keep on using the same straightforward *acquire/release forks* protocol of the example in subsection 3.2.

4   Conclusions

This work is inspired by the observation that multi-agent systems are intrinsically interactive systems [14] whose effectiveness crucially depends on the model adopted for agent coordination. Thus, as far as a single agent architecture is concerned, only agent observational behaviour needs be accounted for in the multi-agent system design. Instead, a major role has to be played by the communication abstraction, which has to be expressive and flexible enough to support the definition of a wide range of communication and synchronisation policies.

As an example, we discussed the $\mathcal{ACLT}$ coordination model. We showed how the behaviour of $\mathcal{ACLT}$ logic tuple spaces can be programmed by specifying reactions to communication events. Reactions are defined through a conveniently expressive specification language, and have the semantics of asynchronous, mutually-independent atomic transactions. By exploiting reactions, multi-agent systems can delegate synchronisation, cooperation, and competition charges to the communication abstraction.

Other different coordination models deeply rely on a notion of reaction. The chemical metaphor of Gamma [1] allows very general coordination laws to be specified in terms of reaction conditions and of consequent actions. However, no communication abstraction is provided, nor is any agent interaction protocol. As it can be argued from the Dining Philosopher example shown in [2], reactions are the only means for the evolution of a multi-agent system based on Gamma, since the model does not account for agent deliberative activity. Moreover, Gamma reactions are to be seen as high-level specifications ruling the evolution of a multi-agent system, independent of any computation model, while the specification of an $\mathcal{ACLT}$ reaction actually corresponds to a precise operational behaviour of the system.

Like $\mathcal{ACLT}$, the ESP coordination language [4] is based on the notion of multiple logic tuple space, and exploits reactiveness of the tuple space. However, the computational shift from the agents to the communication abstraction is even stronger than the $\mathcal{ACLT}$ one. ESP tuple spaces are at the core of all the computational activity, and the ESP notion of agent is reduced to a purely reactive execution thread.

Even though the examples discussed in this paper are quite simple, we are confident that the benefits of such an approach emerge more clearly when more complex applications are considered. Thus, further work will be devoted to test the effectiveness of the model in more complex domains, by exploiting the $\mathcal{ACLT}$ implementation based on SICStus Prolog 3 [13], which is currently working on a network of workstations.

References

1. J.-P. Banâtre and D. le Métayer. The Gamma model and its discipline of programming. Science of Computer Programming , 15(1):55–77, November 1990. 100
2. J.-P. Banâtre and D. le Métayer. Programming by multiset transformation. Communications of the ACM , 36(1):98–111, January 1993. 100
3. A. Brogi and P. Ciancarini. The concurrent language, Shared Prolog. ACM Transactions on Programming Languages and Systems , 13(1), January 1991. 92
4. P. Ciancarini. Distributed programming with logic tuple spaces. New Generation Computing , 12, 1994. 92, 101
5. P. Ciancarini. Coordination models and languages as software integrators. ACM Computing Surveys , 28(2), June 1996. 91
6. E. Denti, A. Natali, A. Omicini, and M. Venuti. An extensible framework for the development of coordinated applications, 1996. First International Conference, COORDINATION'96, Cesena, Italy, April 15–17, 1996. 92, 92
7. E. Denti, A. Natali, A. Omicini, and M. Venuti. Logic tuple spaces for the coordination of heterogeneous agents. In F. Baader and K.U. Schulz, editors, Frontiers of Combining Systems , pages 147–160. Kluwer Academic Publishers, 1996. First International Workshop "Frontiers of Combining Systems", FroCoS'96, Munich, Germany, March 26-29, 1996. 94
8. E.W. Dijkstra. Co-operating sequential processes . Academic Press, London, 1965. 96
9. D. Gelernter. Generative communication in Linda. ACM Transactions on Programming Languages and Systems , 7(1), January 1985. 91
10. D. Gelernter. Multiple tuple spaces in Linda. In Proceedings of PARLE , volume 365 of LNCS , 1989. 92
11. D. Gelernter and N. Carriero. Coordination languages and their significance. Communications of the ACM , 35(2):97–107, February 1992. 91
12. A. Omicini, E. Denti, and A. Natali. Agent coordination and control through logic theories. In Topics in Artificial Intelligence - 4th Congress of the Italian Association for Artificial Intelligence, AI*IA'95 , volume 992 of LNAI , pages 439–450, Firenze, Italy, October 11–13 1995. Springer-Verlag. 91, 92, 92, 94

13. Swedish Institute of Computer Science, Kista, Sweden. SICStus Prolog User's Manual , 1994. 101
14. P. Wegner. Interactive foundations of computing. Technical report, Brown University, Providence (RI), August 1996. 90, 100
15. F. Zanichelli, S. Caselli, A. Natali, and A. Omicini. A multi-agent framework and programming environment for autonomous robotics. In Proceedings of the International Conference on Robotics and Automation (ICRA'94)   , pages 3501–3506, S. Diego, CA, USA, May 1994. 92

Social Interactions of Autonomous Agents: Private and Global Views on Communication

F. Dignum

Fac. of Maths. & Comp. Sc., Eindhoven University of Technology
P.O. Box 513, 5600 MB Eindhoven, The Netherlands
e-mail: `dignum@win.tue.nl`
phone: +31-402473705, fax: +31-402463992

Abstract. In describing the interactions between agents we can take either a global view, where the set of all agents is seen as one big system, or a private view, where the system is identified with a single agent and the other agents form a part of the environment. Often a global view is taken to fix some protocols (like contract net) for all the possible social interactions between agents within the system. Privately the agents then have fixed reaction rules to respond to changes in the environment. In a sense the agents are no longer autonomous in that they always respond in a fixed way and their behaviour can be completely determined by other agents. In this paper we investigate the case where there might not be a (or one) fixed protocol for the social interaction and where the agents do not necessarily react in the same way to each message from other agents. We distinguish between the agents perception of the world and the "real" state of the world and show how these views can be related.

Keywords: Multi-Agent Systems, Multi-Modal logic, Communication, Speech acts.

1 Introduction

In the area of Multi-Agent Systems much research is devoted to the coordination of the agents. Many papers have been written about protocols (like contract net) that allow agents to negotiate and cooperate (e.g. [19,4]). Most of the cooperation between agents is based on the assumption that they have some joint goal or intention. Such a joint goal enforces some type of cooperative behaviour on all agents (see e.g. [3,13,23]). The conventions according to which the agents coordinate their behaviour is hard-wired into the protocols that the agents use to react to the behaviour (cq. messages) of other agents.

This raises several issues. The first issue is that, although agents are said to be autonomous, they always react in a predictable way to each message. Namely their response will follow the protocol that was built-in. The question then arises how autonomous these agents actually are. It seems that they react always in standard ways to some stimulus from other agents, that can therefore determine their behaviour.

J.-J. Ch. Meyer, P.-Y. Schobbens (Eds.): Formal Methods of Agents, LNAI 1760, pp. 103–122, 1999.
© Springer-Verlag Berlin Heidelberg 1999

Besides autonomy, an important characteristic of agents is that they can react to a changing environment. However, if the protocols that they use to react to (at least some part of) the environment are fixed, they have no ways to respond to changes. For instance, if an agent notices that another agent is cheating it cannot switch to another protocol to protect itself. (At least this is not very common). In general it is difficult (if not impossible) for agents to react to violations of the conventions by other agents.

As was also argued in [21], autonomous agents need a richer communication protocol than contract net (or similar protocols) to be able to retain their autonomy. A greater autonomy of the agent places a higher burden on the communication. An autonomous agent might negotiate over every request it gets. In this paper we will describe a mechanism to avoid excessive communication. It is similar to the one employed in [21], but defined more formally and still more generally applicable.

Negotiation between autonomous agents is only necessary if the agents do not have complete knowledge of the state of the world. If they did have complete knowledge (including knowledge about the state of minds of the other agents) they could calculate the optimum deal for both agents and agree in one step. This fact makes it important to distinguish between private and global views of the state of the world. And even more important the private and global view of actions and communication. We argue that agents do not only have limited knowledge of the world, but that they also can only *acquire* limited knowledge about the world. This holds especially for knowledge about the state of mind of other agents. In general it is not efficient for each agent to be able to "test" the truth of any statement about the world. This would require that all agents use the same language and have access to all facts about the world. However, one reason to introduce agents is to split up the work in manageable packets that can be handled by different agents. Each agents only reasons about its own part of the data. I.e. one agent for managing the weather reports and another agent to handle stock prices.

The same principle holds for the reasoning about actions. An agent cannot take into account all possible actions of other agents and possible events occurring in the environment. If an agent could do this, no unforeseen circumstances could arise and the goals would always be reached. Therefore, we assume that agents can only reason about a limited set of influences on their actions.

However, in order to describe the "actual" effect of actions (and especially communication) we need to use a global (agent independent) view. In this case the set of all agents is seen as one system. Using a global view on communication we can describe properties of communication protocols and proof their termination, fairness, etc.

In this paper we show how to describe the formal effects of communication both in the private view as well as in the global view. This gives rise to an integrated formal framework for communicating agents. An important aspect in the description of the effects of the communication is the use of deontic concepts.

This enables us to describe commitments resulting from communication without destroying the autonomy of the agents.

The second important point in this paper is the distinction between the private and the global view of the world in a formal framework and more specifically what are the consequences for the communication between agents. We describe a formal framework for communication that can be used to model all types of protocols. Instead of fixing some protocol the framework indicates possible meaningful sequences of messages for certain situations and goals of the agents. For instance, after a proposal is received a counterproposal can be given. However, it does not make sense to follow up a proposal with an identical counterproposal. The ultimate goal is to formally describe communication rules for autonomous agents. With these rules the effects of communication protocols (like contract net) can be calculated and more flexible ways of dealing with communication protocols can be devised.

In the next section we describe the four components that we use to describe autonomous communicating agents. In section 3 we show how communication can be formally described using our formalism, using the communication primitives for negotiating agents in the ADEPT system ([21]) as example. In section 4 we describe the differences between the local and global view on communication. In section 5 we give a sketch of a formalisation of the framework given in the previous sections. We give some conclusions in section 6.

2   Communicating Agents

The definition of the agents is based on the framework developed in [8,9]. However, we added a private view on the actions. The concepts that we formalise can roughly be divided over four different components: the informational component, the action component, the motivational component and the social component. For readability we will mention all the concepts (including the ones described in previous publications) of each of these components in the following subsections. However, we will only go into the details of those concepts that are new for this paper.

2.1   The Informational Component

At the informational level we consider both knowledge and belief. Many formalisations have been given of these concepts and we will follow the more common approach in epistemic and doxastic logic: the formula $K_i\phi$ denotes the fact that agent i knows ϕ and $B_i\phi$ that agent i believes ϕ. We demand knowledge to obey an S5 axiomatisation, belief to validate a KD45 axiomatisation, and agents to believe all the things that they know.

2.2   The Action Component

In the action component we consider both dynamic and temporal notions. The main dynamic notion that we consider is that of actions, which we interpret as functions that map some some state of affairs into another one. Following [12,26] we use parameterised actions to describe the event consisting of a particular agent's execution of an action. We let $\alpha(i)$ indicate that agent i performs the action α.

We can reason about the results of actions on both a private level and a global level. The global level reasoning is the "standard" one using dynamic logic as described by Harel in [11]. We use $[\alpha(i)]\phi$ to indicate that *if* agent i performs the action indicated by α the result will be ϕ. I.e. no matter what happens, if agent i performs α the system will change to a state where ϕ holds. Note that this is a very strong statement! No unforeseen action can disturb the execution of α by i.

We also introduce a private level of reasoning about actions in this paper. We use $[\alpha(i)]_j\phi$ to indicate that agent j concludes that ϕ will hold *if* agent i performs the action indicated by α. Each agent j will only consider a subset of all possible actions that might intervene with α. For instance, it might be that $[\mathbf{read} - \mathbf{record}]_j\mathbf{K_j}(\mathbf{correct\ number\ of\ computers\ sold\ this\ year})$. But if j did not consider that agent i could just update the sales database at the same time we also have (globally) $\neg[\mathbf{read} - \mathbf{record}]\mathbf{K_j}(\mathbf{correct\ number\ of\ computers\ sold\ this\ year})$.

Besides these formulas that indicate the results of actions we also would like to express that an agent has the reliable opportunity to perform an action. This is done through the predicate OPP: $OPP(\alpha(i))$ indicates that agent i has the opportunity to do α, i.e. the event $\alpha(i)$ will possibly take place.

Besides the OPP operator, which already has a temporal flavour to it, we introduce two genuinely temporal operators: $PREV$, denoting the events that actually just took place, and the "standard" temporal operator $NEXT$, which indicates, in our case, which event will actually take place next. We also define a more traditional $NEXT$ operator on formulas in terms of the $NEXT$ operator on events.

$$NEXT(\phi) \text{ iff } NEXT(\alpha(i)) \wedge [\alpha(i)]\phi$$

This means that the formula ϕ is true in all next states iff an action $\alpha(i)$ is performed next and the formula ϕ is true after the performance of $\alpha(i)$.

In this paper we introduce two special action types. These are the *test* action and the *Reveal* action. Both actions have an epistemic character. Although the test action is already introduced in standard dynamic logic, we give it an epistemic flavour conform [17]. I.e. after i tests the truth of a formula i knows whether the formula is true or not. The test action on formula ϕ is written as $\phi?$. So, more formally we have:

$$\phi \rightarrow [\phi?(i)]K_i(\phi)$$
$$\neg\phi \rightarrow [\phi?(i)]K_i(\neg\phi)$$

As we argued before, an agent cannot test every possible formula. Every agent has a restricted domain on which it can perform tests. However, an agent i can reveal certain information to an agent j by using the reveal action. The result of this action is that agent j can test the truth of that formula himself. Formally:

$$[Reveal(i, j, \phi)]OPP(\phi?(j))$$

The reveal action is especially useful to function as grounding mechanism for discussions about the validity of some formula. It is equivalent to the physical action of showing some evidence as support to your claim.

2.3   The Motivational Component

In the motivational component we consider a variety of concepts, ranging from preferences, goals and decisions to intentions and commitments. The most fundamental of these notions is that of conditional preferences.(See also [1,16]). Formally, (conditional) preferences are defined as the combination of implicit and explicit preferences. A formula ϕ is preferred by an agent i in situation ψ, denoted by $Pref_i(\phi|\psi)$, iff ϕ is true in all the states that the agent considers desirable when ψ is true, and ϕ is an element of a predefined set of (explicitly preferred) formulas. We assume a (total) ordering between the explicit preferences of each agent in each world. (The ordering may vary between worlds because the preferences are conditional upon some statement to hold true.) The use of conditional preferences, instead of the traditional "desires", makes it possible to use the qualitative decision theory developed in [1,16] and also to make a connection with game theoretic work used for negotiations between agents (see e.g. [22]).

Goals are not primitive in our framework, but instead defined in terms of preferences. Informally, a preference of agent i constitutes one of i's goals iff i knows that the preference does not hold yet, but is *achievable*. Formally:

$$Achiev_i\phi \equiv \exists\beta : [\beta(i)]_i\phi \wedge OPP(\beta(i))$$

Note that we use $[\beta(i)]_i\phi$ to indicate that agent i privately concludes that ϕ holds after performing β. In most cases it will hold that (globally) $\neg[\beta(i)]\phi$ or even $[\beta(i)]\neg\phi$.

A goal is now formally defined as a preference that does not hold but is achievable:

$$Goal_i(\phi|\psi) \equiv Pref_i(\phi|\psi) \wedge \neg\phi \wedge Achiev_i\phi$$

Note that our definition implies that there are three ways for an agent to drop one of its goals: since it no longer considers achieving the goal to be desirable, since the preference now holds, or since it is no longer certain that it can achieve the goal. This shows that our framework complies to the standard notions of goals given in e.g. [2].

Goals can either be known or unconscious goals of an agent. Most goals will be known, but we will later on see that goals can also arise from commitments and these goals might not be known explicitly.

Intentions are divided in two categories, viz. the intention to perform an action and the intention to bring about a proposition. The latter category of intentions is seen as goals in our framework. We define the intention of an agent i to perform a certain action α as primitive, denoted by $INT_i\alpha$. An intention to perform an action is based on the decision to try to reach a goal. The agent can only make a decision to try to achieve the goal that has the highest preference (the utility principle). Because the order of the preferences may differ in each world, this does not mean that once a goal has been fixed the agent will always keep on trying to reach that goal (at least not straight away). The above is described formally by

$$\gamma \to OPP(DEC(i,\alpha)) \text{ iff } \exists\phi : Goal_i(\phi|\gamma)\wedge$$
$$\gamma \to [\alpha; \beta(i)]\phi \wedge \neg\exists\psi(Pref_i(\psi|\gamma) \wedge \phi <_i \psi)$$

$$OPP(DEC(i,\alpha)) \to [DEC(i,\alpha)]INT_i\alpha$$

There is no direct relation between the intention to perform an action and the action that is actually performed next. We do, however, establish an indirect relation between the two through a binary *implementation* predicate, ranging over pairs of actions. The idea is that the formula $IMP_i(\alpha_1,\alpha_2)$ expresses that for agent i executing α_2 is a reasonable attempt at executing α_1.

Having defined the binary IMP predicate, we may now relate intended actions to the actions that are actually performed. We demand the action that is actually performed by an agent to be an attempt to perform one of its intentions. Formally, this amounts to the formula

$$(INT_i(\alpha_1(i)) \wedge NEXT(\alpha_2(i))) \to IMP_i(\alpha_1,\alpha_2)$$

The last concept that we consider at the motivational level is that of commitment. Many interpretations have been given to the concept of commitment (see e.g. [2,13,15]). We chose a deontic interpretation of commitment. That is, a commitment of an agent to reach a goal is expressed as an obligation of the agent towards itself to reach the goal. Although the obligation does not ensure the actual performance of the action by the agent, it does have two practical consequences. If an agent commits itself to an action and afterwards does not perform the action a *violation* condition is registered, i.e. the state is not ideal (anymore).

The second consequence of registering a commitment as an obligation is, as we argued in [6], that obligations lead to (conditional) preferences which are ordered. From this it follows that an agent will be very committed to a goal if the preference following from a commitment has a very high ranking. In the other hand the commitment of an agent towards a goal is low if the generated preferences get a low ranking.

The relation between obligations and preferences is formally described as follows:

$$\forall i, j, \phi Pref_i(\phi|O_{ij}(\phi))$$

and for actions:

$$\forall i, j, \alpha Pref_i(PREV(\alpha(i))|O_{ij}(\alpha(i)))$$

Note that the latter is sufficient to create a goal if i has the opportunity to perform α, because $PREV(\alpha(i))$ does not hold presently (the action is not performed yet when the obligation arises) and it is achievable (by performing the action $\alpha(i)$.

The above connection between commitments and preferences (and thus goals) makes our agents sincere. Whenever an agent commits itself there automatically arises a preference to fulfil the commitment. Whether the commitment is kept depends on the priority of the resulting preference and the achievability of it. This is especially important if the commitment is made towards other agents. In that case the commitment forms a part of the social component. We will say more about the social component in the next section.

2.4   The Social Component

The $COMMIT$ described in the previous section is one of the four types of *speech acts* [24] that play a role in the social component. Speech acts are used to communicate between agents. The result of a speech act is a change in the doxastic or deontic state of an agent, or in some cases a change in the state of the world. The speech acts are the main actions for which synchronization between agents is essential. A speech act always involves at least two agents; a speaker and a hearer. If an agent sends a message to another agent but that agent does not "listen" (does not receive the message) the speech act is not successful. We will describe the speech acts first on the global level to indicate the interaction between the agents. Then we will show the private views of the agents on the speech acts.

The most important feature in which our framework for speech acts differs from other frameworks for speech acts (based on the work of Searle) is that a speech act in our framework is not just the sending of message by an agent but is the composition of sending and receiving of a message by two (or more) agents!

We distinguish the following speech act types: *commitments, directions, declarations* and *assertions* . The idea underlying a direction is that of giving orders, i.e. an utterance like 'Pay the bill before next week'. A typical example of a declaration is the utterance 'Herewith you are granted permission to access the database', and a typical assertion is 'I tell you that the earth is flat'. Each type of speech act should be interpreted within the background of the relationship between the speaker and the hearer of the speech act. In particular for directions and declarations the agent uttering the statement should have some kind of basis of authority for the speech act to have any effect.

We distinguish three types of relations between agents: *peer* relation, *power* relation and *authorization* relation. The first two relations are similar to the ones used in the ADEPT system [21,14]. The power relation is used to model hierarchical relations between agents. We assume that these relations are fixed during the lifecycle of the agents. Within such a relation less negotiation is possible about requests and demands. This reduces the amount of communication and therefore increases the efficiency of the agents.

The peer relation exists between all agents that have no prior contract or obligations towards each other (with respect to the present communication). This relation permits extensive negotiations to allow a maximum of autonomy for the agents.

The last relation between agents is the authorization relation which is a type of temporary power relation that can be build up by the agents themselves.

The power relation is formalized as a partial ordering between the agents, which is expressed as follows: $i \ll j$ means that j has a higher rank than i.

The authority relation is formalized through a binary predicate $auth$; $auth(i, \alpha)$ means that agent i is authorised to perform α. It seems that this specifies a property of one agent, however, the other agent is usually part of the specification of α. Therefore the authorization to perform an action implicitly determines an authorization relation between the agents involved in that action as well.

One way to create the authorisation relations is by agent j giving an implicit authorisation to i to give him some directives. For example, when agent i orders a product from agent j it implicitly gives the authorisation to agent j for demanding payment from i for the product (after delivery). We will see later that most communicative actions have also implicit components and effects that are usually determined by the context and conventions within which the communication takes place.

Besides the implicit way to create authorizations, they can also be created explicitly by a separate speech act which is formally a declaration that the authorization is true.

The speech acts themselves are formalised as meta-actions (based on earlier work [5]):

- $DIR(x, i, j, \alpha)$ formalises that agent i directs agent j to perform α on the basis of x, where x can be either *peer*, *power* or *authority*.
- $DECL(i, f)$ models the declaration of i that f holds.
- $ASS(x, i, j, f)$ formalises the assertion of i to agent j that f holds.
- $COMMIT(i, j, \alpha)$ describes that i commits itself towards j to perform α.

Note that the commit and the declarative do not take a relation parameter. This is basically because the effect of a commit is the same irrespective of the relation between the agents, while the declarative does only involve one agent.

A directive from agent i to agent j to perform α results in an obligation of j towards i to perform that action *if* agent i was either in a power relation towards j or was authorized to give the order. In a similar way the assertion of proposition f by i to j results in the fact that j will believe f *if* I had authority over j. Creating the authorizations is an important part of the negotiation between agents when they are establishing some type of contract. On the basis of the authorizations that are created during the negotiation some protocol for the transactions between the agents can be followed quick and efficiently. (See [25] for more details on contracts between agents).

Formally, the following formulas hold for the effects of commitments, orders and declaratives:

- $[COMMIT(i,j,\alpha)][DECL(j,P_{ij}(\alpha(i)))]O_{ij}\alpha$
- $auth(i,DIR(authority,i,j,\alpha)) \rightarrow [DIR(authority,i,j,\alpha)]O_{ji}\alpha$
- $j \ll i \rightarrow [DIR(authority,i,j,\alpha)]O_{ji}\alpha$
- $[DIR(peer,i,j,\alpha)]K_jINT_i\alpha(j)$
- $auth(i,DECL(i,f)) \rightarrow [DECL(i,f)]f$
- $[DECL(i,f)]Pref_i(f|true)$
- $[ASS(peer,i,j,f)]K_jB_if$
- $auth(i,ASS(authority,i,j,f)) \rightarrow [ASS(authority,i,j,f)]B_jf$
- $j \ll i \rightarrow [ASS(power,i,j,f)]B_jf$

A commitment always results in a kind of conditional obligation. The obligation is conditional on the permission of the agent towards which the commitment is made. (This is very close to the ACCEPT action in other frameworks). The giving of permission is formally described by $[DECL(j,P_{ij}(\alpha(i)))]$, where $P_{ij}(\alpha(i)) \equiv \neg O_{ij}(\overline{\alpha(i)})$. I.e. the permission to perform α is equivalent to the fact that there is no obligation to perform the negation of α.

The permission of j is necessary because j might play a (passive) role in the action α initiated by i. Of course j must be willing to play its part. It signifies this by giving the permission to i. In contrast to the other speech acts no precondition has to hold for a commitment to obtain its desired result.

A directive from agent i results in an obligation of agent j (towards i) if agent i was authorised to give the order or i has a power relation towards j.

If i has no authority or power over j then the directive is actually a request. It results in the fact j knows that i wants him to perform α. If j does not mind to perform it can commit himself to perform α and create an obligation.

Assertions can be used to transfer beliefs from one agent to another. Note that agent j does not automatically believe what agent i tells him. We do assume that agents are sincere and thus we have the following axiom:

$$OPP(ASS(x,i,j,f)) \rightarrow B_if$$

That is, an agent can only assert facts that it believes itself.

The only way to directly transfer a belief is when agent i is authorised to make a statement. Usually this situation arises when agent j first requested some information from i. Such a request for information (modelled by a directive without authorisation) gives an implicit authorisation on the assertions that form the answer to the request.

A declaration can change the state of the world if the agent making the declaration is authorised to do so. (This is the only speech act that has a direct effect on the states other than a change of the mental attitudes of the agents!). If agent i has no authority to declare the fact, then the only result of the speech act is that i establishes a preference for itself. It prefers the fact to be true.

Although we do not attempt to give a (complete) axiomatization, we want to mention the following axioms for the declaratives, because they are very fundamental for creating relationships between agents.

$$[DECL(i,auth(j,DIR(authority,j,i,\alpha(i))))]auth(j,DIR(authority,j,i,\alpha(i)))$$

which states that an agent i can create authorisations for an agent j concerning actions that i has to perform.

The following axiom is important for the acceptance of offers:

$$[DECL(i, P_{ji}(\alpha(i)))]P_{ji}(\alpha(i))$$

which states that an agent can always give permission to another agent to perform some action.

Note that it may very well be that another agent forbids j to perform α! The permission is only with respect to i!

3   Formal Communication

In the previous section we gave a brief overview of the basic messages that agents can use in our framework. To show the power of our framework and to show the relation with other work on communication between agents we show how the basic illocutions that are used for the negotiating agents in the ADEPT system (and that also form the heart of many other negotiation systems) can be modelled within our framework. We only show this for the negotiation because it forms an important part of the communication between agents. In a later paper we will show how the communication in the stages after the negotiation (the performance and satisfaction stages) can also be formally modelled in our framework.

The negotiating agents in the ADEPT system use the four illocutions: PROPOSE, COUNTERPROPOSE, ACCEPT and REJECT. These four illocutions also form the basic elements of many other negotiation systems.

The PROPOSE is directly translated into a COMMIT. The obligation that follows from a proposal depends on the acceptance of the receiving party. However, the ACCEPT that is used as primitive in ADEPT and most other systems involves more than the giving of permission that we already indicated above.

The ACCEPT message has three components. That is, we consider the ACCEPT to be the simultaneous expression of three illocutions.

1. Giving permission to perform the action
2. Commitment to perform those actions that are necessary to make the proposal succeed
3. Giving (implicit) authority for subsequent actions (linked to the proposal by convention)

For example if agent i sends the following message to j:

PROPOSE,i,j,
I will deliver 20 computers (pentium, 32M, etc.) to you for $1000,- per computer

then the ACCEPT message of j to i:

ACCEPT,j,i,
You will deliver 20 computers (pentium, 32M, etc.) to me for $1000,- per computer

means:

1. You are permitted to deliver the computers: $DECL(j, P_{ij}(deliver))$
2. I will receive the computers (sign a receipt): $COMMIT(j, i, receive)$
3. I give you authority to ask for payment after delivery:
   $DECL(j, [deliver]auth(i, DIR(authority, i, j, pay)))$

It is important to notice that only the first component of the meaning of the ACCEPT message is fixed. The other two components depend on the action involved and the conventions (contracts) under which the transaction is negotiated.

The REJECT message is the denegation of the ACCEPT message. It means that the agent is either not giving permission for the action, not committing itself to its part of the action or not willing to give authority to subsequent actions. Formally this is expressed as the disjunction of the negation of these three parts. Due to space limitations we will not work this out any further.

The COUNTERPROPOSE is a composition of a REJECT and PROPOSE message. Formally it can thus be expressed as the parallel execution of these two primitives.

Besides the formal representation of the illocution of the message we can also give some preconditions on the basic message types. Only the PROPOSE message type does not have preconditions. This is as expected because the PROPOSE is used to start the negotiation. The other types of messages are all used as answer to a PROPOSE (or COUNTERPROPOSE) message. We can formally describe the precondition that these message types can only be used after a PROPOSE or COUNTERPROPOSE as follows:

- $OPP(ACCEPT(j, i, \alpha)) \leftrightarrow$
  $(PREV(PROPOSE(i, j, \alpha)) \vee PREV(COUNTERPROPOSE(i, j, \alpha)))$
- $OPP(REJECT(j, i, \alpha)) \leftrightarrow$
  $(PREV(PROPOSE(i, j, \alpha)) \vee PREV(COUNTERPROPOSE(i, j, \alpha)))$
- $OPP(COUNTERPROPOSE(j, i, \beta)) \leftrightarrow$
  $$\beta \neq \alpha \wedge (PREV(PROPOSE(i, j, \alpha)) \vee$$
  $PREV(COUNTERPROPOSE(i, j, \alpha)))$

In the precondition of the COUNTERPROPOSE we included the fact that a counterproposal should differ from the proposal that it counters. (Although not mentioned in this paper, the semantics of actions does give an equivalence relation between actions). More elaborate conversation rules are needed to describe long term dependencies within protocols. E.g. one cannot repeat the same proposal later on if it already has been rejected. These rules should be incorporated within the protocols that the agents are using.

We do not want to give the formalisation of complete protocols at this place due to space limitations. However, we can indicate quite easily the results of the most common pairs of messages where agent i first proposes something to agent j after which agent j can accept it, reject it or counterpropose it. These moves are formally described as follows:

- $[PROPOSE(i,j,\alpha)(i)][ACCEPT(j,i,\alpha)(j)]O_{ij}(\alpha(i)) \wedge P_{ji}(\alpha(i))$ (accept)
  Furthermore, if the success of $\alpha(i)$ depends on the performance of $\beta(j)$ by j:
  $[PROPOSE(i,j,\alpha)(i)][ACCEPT(j,i,\alpha)(j)]O_{ji}(\beta(j))$
  And if conventions determine that i can perform $\beta(i)$ after acceptance of the proposal then:
  $[PROPOSE(i,j,\alpha)(i)][ACCEPT(j,i,\alpha)(j)][\alpha(i)]auth(i,\beta(i))$
- $[PROPOSE(i,j,\alpha)(i)][REJECT(j,i,\alpha)(j)]\neg O_{ij}(\alpha(i))$ (reject)
- $[PROPOSE(i,j,\alpha)(i)][COUNTERPROPOSE(j,i,\beta)(j)]\neg O_{ij}(\alpha(i))$
  (counter)

Note that the counterproposal has no effect of itself yet. Only the reject component of the counterproposal has immediate effect. The proposal component of the counterproposal only takes effect after an appropriate answer of i.

For the reject we only indicated that the obligation does not arise. The rest of the effect depends on the context and is usually not of prime interest.

The formalisation of the basic messages in the ADEPT system shows two things.

First, that our framework is powerful enough to formally describe the negotiation in the ADEPT system including the effects of the communication.

Secondly, that seemingly simple message types, like ACCEPT, have complicated meanings that partly depend on the context in which they are used.

4   Private and Global Views on Communication

In the previous sections we gave a formal description of communication between agents. This description was given from a global viewpoint. That is, the communication was seen as actions that change the complete system of agents from one state to another state. This is quite natural when considering material actions like database updates. If an agent changes a database, the system will be in a different state where some values in the database are changed. No other agents are necessarily (directly) involved in this action. However, communicative actions (except for the declaratives) always require the participation of two agents: the speaker and the hearer.

In this section we will give a private view on communication based on the global view defined in the previous sections. In a private view of the system we try to ascribe each action, that takes place in the system, to an agent that has control over that action. Also we try to make clear which part of the system can be "seen" by each of the agents. I.e. which formulas can be checked by the agents.

To explain the private description of the communication between agents we will use only one type of message. All remarks hold mutatis mutandis for the other types of messages.

In a global view we have the following axiom for directives:

$$auth(i, DIR(authority, i, j, \alpha)) \rightarrow [DIR(authority, i, j, \alpha)]O_{ji}\alpha$$

I.e. after an authorized directive an obligation arises.

In the private view the following features of communication can be better described:

1. Communication consists of speaking and listening.
2. Speaker and hearer might not share the same language.
3. Not all pre-conditions and effects of communications can be (directly) checked by both speaker and hearer.

Ad.1. The first and most important step that should be taken to privatize the view on this communication is to split up this action into a speaker and hearer part. Agent i can never perform the complete directive by itself. It can only send the message and hope that agent j receives the message. So, although agent i initiates the action it does not have complete control over it. It cannot assure that the action completes successfully. Because there is not a single entity that has control over the communicative actions we will split up the communicative actions into a send and receive action to get a private view on them. $DIR(authority, i, j, \alpha) \equiv$

$$send(DIR(authority, i, j, \alpha))(i)\&receive(DIR(authority, i, j, \alpha))(j)$$

The parallel decomposition of the directive should be read as a synchronization between the agents. In an actual implementation the actions might be serialized.

Although in the global view we cannot assume that an obligation holds after the sending of (an authorized) directive by agent i, agent i can privately conclude this if we assume the following axiom:

$$auth(i, DIR(authority, i, j, \alpha)) \rightarrow [send(DIR(authority, i, j, \alpha))]_i O_{ji}\alpha$$

This means that agent i assumes that agent j will always receive the messages that agent i sends.

In the same way we have of course (and with more right probably):

$$auth(i, DIR(authority, i, j, \alpha)) \rightarrow [receive(DIR(authority, i, j, \alpha))]_j O_{ji}\alpha$$

That is, if agent j receives an authorized directive it will conclude that it now has an obligation towards i.

Ad.2. Because the communication is now split up into a send and receive part it is also possible to indicate whether the receiver can "understand" the message that was send. I.e. whether the receiving agent talks the same language in terms of formulas that it incorporates in its private language. It is possible to incorporate some general *translation rules* in the system that indicate how terms can be translated from one agent's language to another's. In this paper we will assume that all agents use the same language in order not to complicate the formalisation to much. See [20] for an example how an agent system can be described in which agents can use different languages.

Ad.3. The last part that plays a role in the privatization of communication is the checking of the pre-conditions and effects of communication. If agent j does not know that agent i is authorized to give him an order it might not accept the consequent obligation. Often agent j can also not check the authority directly. Therefore, we think that in each protocol it should be possible for j to question the authority of i if j cannot check this authority himself. This is conform the theory from Habermas about communication protocols [10] where this is classified as an attack on the validity claims. Agent j can attack the validity of the authority of i by directing agent i to make the authority available for inspection of agent j. We get the following possibilities:

1. $(auth(i, DIR(authority, i, j, \alpha)) \wedge$
   $OPP(auth(i, DIR(authority, i, j, \alpha))?(j))) \rightarrow$
   $$[DIR(authority, i, j, \alpha)]O_{ji}\alpha$$
   I.e. if agent j has the opportunity to check the authority of agent i then the authoritative direction of i to j to perform α results in an obligation.

2. $(auth(i, DIR(authority, i, j, \alpha)) \wedge$
   $\neg OPP(auth(i, DIR(authority, i, j, \alpha))?(j))) \rightarrow$
   $[DIR(authority, i, j, \alpha)]$
   $auth(j, DIR(auth., j, i, Reveal(i, j, (auth(i, DIR(auth., i, j, \alpha))))))$
   If agent j does not have the opportunity to check the authority of i then the direction of i only results in the authority of j to direct i to reveal the status of his authority to j. We admit that this formula is not very readable, but it is of course very easy to find some suitable abbreviations for these standard formulas.

The establishment of the truth of the authority of i does not have to be the end of the discussion, because, according to Habermas, agent j might now question the reason for this authority. For instance, it is based on law, on a previous agreement, on a contract, etc. We will not go further into this at this place.

The above points indicate that the private view on communication between agents reveals new aspects of the communication that are not visible in the global view. Especially the difference in awareness about actions and facts by different agents leads to new communicative acts that did not seem necessary in the global view.

5   A Sketch of a Formalisation

In this section we precisely define the language that we use to formally represent the concepts described in the previous sections, and the models that are used to interpret this language. We will not go into too much detail with regard to the actual semantics, but try to provide the reader with an intuitive grasp for the formal details without actually mentioning them.

The language that we use is a multi-modal, propositional language, based on three denumerable, pairwise disjoint sets: Π, representing the propositional symbols, Ag representing agents, and At containing atomic action expressions. The language $FORM$ is defined in four stages. Starting with a set of propositional formulas ($PFORM$), we define the action- and meta-action expressions, after which $FORM$ can be defined.

The set Act of regular action expressions is built up from the set At of atomic (parameterised) action expressions (denoted by $\underline{a}$...) using the operators ; (sequential composition), + (nondeterministic composition), & (parallel composition), and ⁻ (action negation). The constant actions **any** and **fail** denote 'don't care what happens' and 'failure' respectively.

Definition 1. *Let* $\underline{a} \in At$ *then the set* Act *of action expressions is given by the following BNF:*

$$\alpha :: -\underline{a}|\textbf{any}|\textbf{fail}|\alpha_1 + \alpha_2|\alpha_1\&\alpha_2|\overline{\alpha}$$

The set $MAct$ of general action expressions contains the regular actions and all of the special meta-actions informally described in section 2. For simplicity, we restrict ourselves in this paper to closing the set $MAct$ under sequential composition.

Definition 2. *Let* $\alpha \in Act$, $i, j \in Ag$ *and* $x \in \{peer, authority, power\}$ *then the set* $MAct$ *of general action expressions is given by the following BNF:*

$$\gamma\alpha :: -\alpha|DEC(i, \alpha)|COMMIT(i, j, \alpha)|DIR(x, i, j, \alpha)|\gamma\alpha_1; \gamma\alpha_2$$

Not all actions can be defined at this level, because some actions like $DECL$ contain formulas from $FORM$ as parameters. These actions will be defined in the next stage.

The complete language $FORM$ is now defined to contain all the constructs informally described in the previous section. That is, there are operators representing informational attitudes, motivational attitudes, aspects of actions, and the social traffic between agents.

Definition 3. *Let* $\psi \in PFORM$, $\gamma\alpha \in Mact$, $\alpha, \alpha_1, \alpha_2 \in Act$, $i, j, k \in Ag$ *and* $x \in \{peer, authority, power\}$ *then the language* $FORM$ *of formulas is given by the following BNF:*

$$\phi :: - \psi|\neg\phi|\phi_1 \wedge \phi_2|K_i\phi|B_i\phi|[\gamma\alpha]\phi|[\gamma\alpha]_i$$
$$[DECL(i, \psi)]\phi|[ASS(x, i, j, \psi)]\phi|[Reveal(i, j, \psi)]\phi|[\psi?(i)]\phi$$
$$[DECL(i, \psi)]_k\phi|[ASS(x, i, j, \psi)]_k\phi|[Reveal(i, j, \psi)]_k\phi|[\psi?(i)]_k\phi$$
$$[\gamma\alpha; \gamma\beta]\theta|[\gamma\alpha; \gamma\beta]_i\theta|PREV(\alpha)|OPP(\alpha)|NEXT(\phi)$$
$$Pref_i(\phi|\psi)|\psi <_i \phi|i \ll j|INT_i\alpha|IMP_i(\alpha_1|\alpha_2)|O_{ij}(\alpha)|auth(i, \alpha)$$

Note that the ASS, $DECL$, $Reveal$ and $test$ action are introduced in $FORM$ at this stage. The postcondition ϕ does not have any meaning except as a placeholder in these formulas.

The models used to interpret $FORM$ are based on Kripke-style possible worlds models. That is, the backbone of these models is given by a set Σ of states, and a valuation π on propositional symbols relative to a state. Various relations and functions on these states are used to interpret the various (modal) operators. These relations and functions can roughly be classified in four parts, dealing with the informational component, the action component, the motivational component and the social component, respectively. We assume tt and ff to denote the truth values 'true' and 'false', respectively.

Definition 4. *A model* Mo *for* $FORM$ *from the set* CMo *is a structure* $(\Sigma, \pi, I, A, M, S)$ *where*

1. Σ *is a non-empty set of states and* $\pi : \Sigma \times \Pi \rightarrow \{tt, ff\}$.
2. $I = (Rk, Rb)$ *with* $Rk : Ag \rightarrow \wp(\Sigma \times \Sigma)$ *denoting the epistemic alternatives of agents and* $Rb : Ag \times \Sigma \rightarrow \wp(\Sigma)$ *denoting the doxastic alternatives.*
3. $A = (Sf, Mf, Sfa, Mfa, Ropp, Rprev, Rnext)$ *with* $Sf : Ag \times Act \times \Sigma \rightarrow \wp(\Sigma)$ *yielding the global interpretation of regular actions,* $Mf : Ag \times MAct \times (CMo \times \Sigma) \rightarrow (CMo \times \Sigma)$ *yielding the global interpretation of meta-actions,* $Sfa : Ag \times Ag \times Act \times \Sigma \rightarrow wp(\Sigma)$ *yielding the private interpretation of of regular actions,* $Mfa : Ag \times Ag \times MAct \times (CMo \times \Sigma) \rightarrow (CMo \times \Sigma)$ *yielding the private interpretation of meta-actions,* $Ropp : Ag \times \Sigma \rightarrow \wp(Act)$ *denoting opportunities,* $Rprev : Ag \times \Sigma \rightarrow Act$ *yielding the action that has been performed last and* $Rnext : Ag \times \Sigma \rightarrow Act$ *yielding the action that will be performed next.*
4. $M = (Rp, Rep, <, Ri, Ria, Ro)$ *with* $Rp : Ag \times \Sigma \rightarrow \wp(\Sigma)$ *denoting implicit preferences,* $Rep : Ag \times \Sigma \rightarrow \wp(FORM)$ *yielding explicit preferences,* $< \subseteq Ag \times \Sigma \rightarrow FORM \times FORM$ *which is a preference relation on preferences,* $Ri : Ag \times \Sigma \rightarrow \wp(Act)$ *denoting intended actions,* $Ria : Ag \times \Sigma \rightarrow \wp(Act) \times \wp(Act)$ *denoting implementation relations between actions and* $Ro : Ag \times Ag \rightarrow \wp(\Sigma \times \Sigma)$ *denoting obligations.*
5. $S = (Auth, \prec)$ *with* $Auth : Ag \times \wp(MAct) \rightarrow \{tt, ff\}$ *yielding authorisations and* $\prec : Ag \times Ag \rightarrow \{tt, ff\}$ *yielding hierarchical relations between agents.*

such that the following constraints are validated:

1. $Rk(i)$ *is an equivalence relation for all* i, *and* $Rb(i, s) \neq \emptyset$, $Rb(i, s) \subseteq \{s' \mid (s, s') \in Rk(i)\}$ *and* $(s, s') \in Rk(i) \implies Rb(i, s) = Rb(i, s')$, *which ensures that knowledge validates an S5 axiomatisation and belief obeys a KD45 axiomatisation, while agents indeed believe all things they know.*
2. Sf *yields the global state-transition interpretation for regular actions. This function satisfies the usual constraints ensuring an adequate interpretation of composite actions in terms of their constituents.* Sfa *satisfies the same constraints as* Sf *but also should satisfy that* $Sfa(i, j, \alpha, s) \subseteq Sf(j, \alpha, s)$. *I.e. the private interpretation of an action is more limited than the global one. The function* Mf *models the global model-transforming interpretation of meta-action. Because we do not allow the composition of meta-actions with other actions yet, we require for the moment that* $Mf \equiv Mfa$. *Below we elaborate on the definition of* Mf *for the meta-actions introduced in the previous section.*

3. $Rnext(i, s) \in Ropp(i, s) \subseteq \{\alpha \mid Sf(i, \alpha, s) \neq \emptyset\}$, *which ensures that oppor-
    tunities are a subset of the actions that are possible by virtue of the circum-
    stances and that the next action performed is an opportunity. Furthermore,
    $Rprev(i, s) = \alpha$ i $\alpha \in Ropp(i, s')$ for some s' with $s \in Sf(i, \alpha, s')$, which
    relates previously executed actions to past opportunities.*
4. $Ri(i, s) \subseteq \{\alpha \mid Sf(i, \alpha, s) \neq \emptyset\}$ *and for all* $s \in \Sigma$ *some* $s' \in \Sigma$ *exists with*
    $(s, s') \in Ro$.

The complete semantics contains an algebraic semantics of action expresses,
based on the action semantics of Meyer [18]. In this paper we will abstract from
the algebraic interpretation of actions and instead interpret actions as functions
on states of affairs. For the meta-actions the state-transition interpretation is not
adequate, because meta-actions do not change states but they change relations
between states. For instance, in the case of an assertion, the effect is to change
the doxastic state of the receiving agent, and nothing else. To formalise this
behaviour, we interpret meta-actions as model-transforming functions. In the
case of an assertion, the resulting model will differ from the starting model in
the doxastic accessibility relation of the receiving agent.

Definition 5. *The binary relation* $\models$ *between an element of* $FORM$ *and a pair
consisting of a model* Mo *in* CMo *and a state* s *in* Mo *is for propositional
symbols, conjunctions and negations defined as usual. Epistemic formulas* $K_i\phi$
and doxastic formulas $B_i\phi$ *are interpreted as necessity operators over* Rk *and
Rb respectively. For the other formulas* $\models$ *is defined as follows:*

$$Mo, s \models [\alpha(i)]\phi \iff Mo, s' \models \phi \text{ for all } s' \in Sf(i, \alpha, s)$$
$$Mo, s \models [\alpha(i)]_j\phi \iff Mo, s' \models \phi \text{ for all } s' \in Sfa(j, i, \alpha, s)$$
$$Mo, s \models [\gamma\alpha(i)]\phi \iff Mo', s' \models \phi \text{ for all } Mo', s' \in Mf(i, \alpha, Mo, s)$$
$$Mo, s \models [\gamma\alpha(i)]_j\phi \iff Mo', s' \models \phi \text{ for all } Mo', s' \in Mfa(j, i, \alpha, Mo, s)$$
$$Mo, s \models PREV(\alpha(i)) \iff \alpha \in Rprev(i, s)$$
$$Mo, s \models OPP(\alpha(i)) \iff \alpha \in Ropp(i, s)$$
$$Mo, s \models NEXT(\alpha(i)) \iff \alpha(i) \in Rnext(i, s)$$
$$Mo, s \models Pref_i(\phi|\psi) \iff \text{If } Mo, s \models \psi \text{ then}$$
$$Mo, s' \models \phi \text{ for all } s' \in Rp(i, s) \text{ and } \phi \in Rep(i, s)$$
$$Mo, s \models \psi <_i \phi \iff (\psi, \phi) \in< (i, s)$$
$$Mo, s \models i \ll j \iff i \prec j$$
$$Mo, s \models INT_i\alpha \iff \alpha \in Ri(i, s)$$
$$Mo, s \models IMP_i(\alpha_1, \alpha_2) \iff (\alpha_1, \alpha_2) \in Ria(i, s)$$
$$Mo, s \models O_{ij}(\phi) \iff Mo, s' \models \phi \text{ for all } s' \text{ with } (s, s') \in Ro(i, j)$$
$$Mo, s \models O_{ij}(\alpha) \iff Mo, s \models [\mathbf{any}(i)]O_{ij}(PREV(\alpha(i)))$$
$$Mos, \models auth(i, \alpha) \iff Auth(i, \alpha, s) = tt$$

The functions interpreting the special meta-actions (**?**, *Reveal*, *DEC*, *COM-
MIT*, *DIR*, *DECL* and *ASS*) can be described in terms of the preconditions and
the postconditions for execution of the actions. Due to space limitations we leave
them out here. See [9] for more details.

6 Conclusions

In this paper we have shown that it is possible to formally describe communicating agents. The emphasis in this paper was on the formal description of the communication between agents. A very important aspect of this formalism is that it is possible to (formally) describe the effects of the communication. Therefore it is possible to check what is the resulting situation after a communication protocol has been followed. We can analyze a protocol and find out what are reasonable moves at any point in the protocol. We have shown how the message types of the ADEPT system can be described in our primitives. This revealed that a seemingly simple primitive like ACCEPT contains a lot of hidden meanings.

We have also shown in this paper that there exists an important difference between a private and global view on actions and in particular communications. The private view opens up new communication moves in the negotiation because the agents involved have different information!

The difference becomes of prime importance when we want to implement agents that have to follow the rules of our logical formalism. By using a private view of actions it becomes clear which agent has control over each action. This is important because in the implemented system each action has to be initiated by some agent.

The private view on actions also makes it possible to introduce unforeseen actions, which seems more realistic in a multi-agent system which usually has an open character. I.e. not all the actions of all agents can be checked all the time.

Two remarks should be made about the logical formalism. First, it is not our aim to build an automated theorem prover that can prove theorems in this very rich logic. The use of a logical formalism gives the opportunity to automatically generate the logical effects of a sequence of steps in a protocol. These could be subsequently implemented in a more efficient formalism. The logical description, however, can be used as a very general and precise specification of that implementation.

Secondly, the use of logic forces a very precise formal description of the communication. The use of logic led to the discovery that the primitive ACCEPT message has actually several components, some of which depend on the context within which the ACCEPT is used. It is very important that this is realized when the communication protocols are automatized. (As is the aim in communication between agents.)

We admit that the logical formulas get very complicated and are not very readable. However, it is easy to define suitable abbreviations for standard formulas. At least, working this way, it is clear what these abbreviations mean exactly!

References

1. C. Boutilier. Toward a Logic for Qualitative Decision Theory. In Jon Doyle, Erik Sandewall and Pietro Torasso (eds.), Principles of Knowledge Representation and

Reasoning, proceedings of the fourth international conference   , pages 75-86, 1994, Morgan Kaufmann Publishers, San Francisco, California. 107, 107

2. P. Cohen and H. Levesque. Intention is choice with commitment. Artificial Intelligence, vol.42, pages 213-261, 1990. 107, 108

3. P. Cohen and H. Levesque. Teamwork Nous, vol.35, pages 487-512, 1991. 103

4. R. Davis and R. Smith. Negotiation as a metaphor for distributed problem solving. Artificial Intelligence , vol.20, pages 63-109, 1983. 103

5. F. Dignum and H. Weigand. Communication and deontic logic. In R. Wieringa and R. Feenstra, editors, Information Systems, Correctness and Reusability   , pages 242–260. World Scientific, Singapore, 1995. 110

6. F. Dignum. Autonomous Agents and Social Norms. Submitted to ICMAS workshop on Norms, Obligations and Conventions. 108

7. F. Dignum, J.-J.Ch. Meyer, R. Wieringa and R. Kuiper. A modal approach to intentions, commitments and obligations: intention plus commitment yields obligation. In M.A. Brown and J. Carmo (eds.) DEON'96 Workshop on deontic logic in computer science , pages 174-193, Lisbon, Jan. 1996.

8. F. Dignum and B. van Linder. Modelling Rational Agents in a Dynamic Environment: Putting Humpty Dumpty Together Again. In J.L. Fiadeiro and P.-Y. Schobbens (eds.) ModelAge-96, pages 81-92,Sesimbra, Portugal, 1996. 105

9. F. Dignum and B. van Linder. Modeling Social Agents: Communication as Action In J. Mueller, M. Wooldridge and N. Jennings (eds.) Intelligent Agents III - Proceedings of the Third International Workshop on Agent Theories, Architectures, and Languages (ATAL-96) , pages 83-93, Budapest, Hungary, 1996. 105, 119

10. J. Habermas. The Theory of Communicative Action: Reason and Rationalization of Society. Polity Press, Cambridge, 1984. 116

11. D. Harel. First Order Dynamic Logic. LNCS 68 Springer, 1979. 106

12. W. van der Hoek, B. van Linder and J.-J.Ch. Meyer. A logic of capabilities. In Nerode and Matiyasevich, eds, Proceedings of LFCS'94 , LNCS 813, pages 366-378, 1994. 106

13. N. Jennings. Commitments and Conventions: The foundation of coordination in Multi-Agent systems. Knowledge Engineering Review , vol. 8(3), pages 223-250, 1993. 103, 108

14. N. Jennings, P. Faratin, M. Johnson, P. O'Brien and M. Wiegand. Using Intelligent Agents to Manage Business Processes. In Proceedings The Practical Application of Intelligent Agents and Multi-Agent Technology   , pages 345-360, London, 1996. 109

15. D. Kinny and M. Georgeff. Commitment and Effectiveness of Situated Agents. In Proceedings Int. Joint Conf. on Artificial Intelligence   , pages 82-88, Sydney, Australia, 1991. 108

16. J. Lang. Conditional Desires and Utilities - an alternative logical approach to qualitative decision theory. In W. Wahlster, editor, Proceedings of ECAI-96 , pages 318-327, Budapest, Hungary, 1996, John Wiley & Sons Ltd. 107, 107

17. B. van Linder, W. van der Hoek and J.-J.Ch. Meyer. Tests as Epistemic Updates. Pursuit of Knowledge. Technical Report, UU-CS-1994-08, Utrecht University, 1994. 106

18. J.-J.Ch. Meyer. A different approach to deontic logic. In Notre Dame Journal of Formal Logic , vol.29, pages 109–136, 1988. 119

19. J. Muller. A cooperation model for autonomous agents. In J. Muller, M. Wooldridge and N. Jennings, eds, Intelligent Agents III - Proceedings of the Third International Workshop on Agent Theories, Architectures, and Languages (ATAL-96), pages 135-147, Budapest, Hungary, 1996. 103

20. P. Noriega and C. Sierra. Towards layered Dialogical Agents In J. Muller, M. Wooldridge and N. Jennings, eds, Intelligent Agents III - Proceedings of the Third International Workshop on Agent Theories, Architectures, and Languages (ATAL-96), pages 69-82, Budapest, Hungary, 1996. 115

21. T. Norman, N. Jennings, P. Faratin and E. Mamdani Designing and Implementing a Multi-Agent Architecture for business process management. In J. Mueller, M. Wooldridge and N. Jennings (eds.) Intelligent Agents III - Proceedings of the Third International Workshop on Agent Theories, Architectures, and Languages (ATAL-96), pages 149-162, Budapest, Hungary, 1996. 104, 104, 105, 109

22. J. Rosenschein and G. Zlotkin Rules of Encounter MIT Press, Cambridge Massachusetts, 1994. 107

23. G. Sandu. Reasoning about collective goals. In J. Muller, M. Wooldridge and N. Jennings, eds, Intelligent Agents III - Proceedings of the Third International Workshop on Agent Theories, Architectures, and Languages (ATAL-96)   , pages 35-47, Budapest, Hungary, 1996. 103

24. J.R. Searle. Speech Acts. Cambridge University Press. 1969. 109

25. H. Weigand, E. Verharen and F. Dignum. Interoperable Transactions in Business Models: A Structured Approach. In P. Constantopoulos, J. Mylopoulos and Y. Vassiliou, eds, Advanced Information Systems Engineering (LNCS 1080)   , pages 193-209, Springer, 1996. 110

26. R. Wieringa, J.-J.Ch. Meyer and H. Weigand. Specifying dynamic and deontic integrity constraints. Data & knowledge engineering , vol.4, pages 157-189, 1989. 106

Towards a Proof-Theoretic Foundation for Actor Specification and Verification

Carlos H. C. Duarte

Department of Computing, Imperial College
180 Queen's Gate, London, SW7 2BZ, United Kingdom
e-mail: cd7@doc.ic.ac.uk, tel: +44 171 594 8341, fax: +44 171 581 8024

Abstract. Actors has been regarded as a promising model for open distributed systems. Although the operational semantics of actor programs has already been studied in some recent work, means of reasoning about the behaviour of communities of interconnected actors at a high abstraction level are still lacking. In this paper we argue that a proof-theoretic semantics would be better suited to this purpose. We present an abstract data type like axiomatisation of the kernel primitives of Actors, showing how to reason from specifications of actor communities and how to compose them within the framework of temporal logics of objects.

Keywords: Actors, Specification, Verification, Proof-Theory, Distributed Systems.

1 Introduction

Actors has been regarded as a promising model for open distributed systems. An actor is a computational agent with mutable encapsulated state that changes by processing messages in a side-effect free manner. Message passing between actors is buffered, point-to-point, asynchronous and relies on a local naming scheme. As a result of processing messages, new concurrent actors can be created and actor names can be communicated. With all these characteristics, actors support desirable run-time capabilities such as configurability and extensibility. In addition, the Actors model integrates the functional and object-oriented approaches to software development, enforcing design principles as modularity and incrementability.

Due to these peculiarities, it seems natural to search for a semantic foundation that could permit the rigorous step-by-step development of actor systems. Since the work described in [1], we know how to execute actor programs correctly. In [2] and [19], the operational semantics of individual actors and of communities of interacting actors is further studied formally. Yet the authors recognise that it would be necessary to characterise properties of interest to specifiers and users of systems organised as actor communities and also that it would be nice to have logical means of reasoning about such objects. This is the motivating factor for the present paper.

We believe that a sufficiently abstract semantic foundation for the specification, composition and verification of actors should encode in the axioms and inference rules of a deductive system the meaning of the Actor primitives. Ultimately, designers and programmers need to deal in a rigorous and systematic

J.-J. Ch. Meyer, P.-Y. Schobbens (Eds.): Formal Methods of Agents, LNAI 1760, pp. 123-142, 1999.
© Springer-Verlag Berlin Heidelberg 1999

manner with the syntactic representation of such primitives as parts of specifications and programs. Our view can be captured in a development process where such software artifacts are represented as theory presentations of some logic and are interconnected by means of translations between their languages [15]. Techniques for constructing similar formalisms have been popularised by Institutions [11] in studying the theory of abstract data types (ADTs) using some sort of equational logic. However, we have to point out that, when concurrency comes to place, and particularly because in the Actors model there are some fairness assumptions, the use of a temporal logic for specification and verification is almost unavoidable.

This leaves us very close to the view put forward in [10]. Hence, we organise actor specifications using signatures and presentations of temporal theories. We axiomatise the primitives for sending and receiving asynchronous messages and for creating new objects, deriving inference rules to support modular reasoning about concurrent behaviour in terms of safety and liveness properties. Having developed such a formalism, we see our main contribution as a logic that establishes a firm proof-theoretic basis for actor specification, composition and verification, which follows to some extent previous work of the ADT school.

We proceed by discussing some of the issues in designing a proof-theory for Actors. Subsequently, we introduce our approach to the specification and verification of actor systems, illustrating the involved technicalities by means of an example. Our conclusions, a comparison with related work and a description of our future research are presented in the final section.

2   Issues in the Design of a Proof-Theory for Actors

One question naturally arises in working out a proof-theory for Actors: Can we apply directly some *existing logic* to provide the desired semantics? To the best of our knowledge, the answer is negative, because no such a logic captures all the required ingredients and provides the proper level of abstraction. Other logics for concurrent object-based systems development are described in [3, 13, 17, 20]. In the concluding section, we shall compare them with our work.

Because the constituent entities of the Actors model are formal and our approach to specification is logical, we need to determine the characteristics of a logic to make possible the rigorous representation of all these entities. To begin with, an *actor* deals with distinct sets of *values* in message exchange and computation. Values may be considered actors with unserialised behaviour [1], which are not history sensitive and have a fixed meaning in every computation. Here, however, in order to keep a clear distinction between values and actors, we represent the first family as objects of a sort in a many-sorted language, instead of using an unsorted language. In a way, sorts define types for values, which is indeed the usual representation of properties of fixed meaning objects in programming languages. Actors, in turn, have observable behaviour, state-independent identity and can be considered modules. Hence, they are specified using theory presentations as suggested in [10].

Actors interact via buffered message passing. Since [18], temporal logic has been the preferred framework for studying *buffered communication*. Even among such logics, there are many possibilities to choose. Due to the infinite character of some *data domains* of messages, propositional logic cannot be used [8]. Because the Actors model requires message delivery to be guaranteed and message consumption to be eventually performed, *fairness* requirements which demand specifying when these actions may occur as it is impossible to determine *a priori* how the environment will evolve, branching time logic has to be used [14].

To complete the picture, we need to address the *naming* and *creation* schemes adopted by the Actors model. In producing a specification, we are in fact defining a template for the behaviour of a population of similar actors so that each receives a mail address at creation time to serve as its name in communications. The usual way of representing this is to regard the specification as implicitly parameterised by a sort of names, extending the original specification [6]. In addition, to avoid conflicts between the creation of new actors and the satisfiability of Barcan formulae, which state that the quantification domain of variables do not vary, every actor needs to carry an existential attribute [9]. According to this approach, objects that have not been created do not play any role, paraphrasing [3].

Considering this rationale, actor specifications should look like Figure 1. There is represented a buffer cell, which dynamically allocates other cells for the integers stored. Attribute symbols represent the actor state, while messages and local computations are represented by action symbols. The symbols **E**, **X**, $\leftarrow$ and $\leftrightarrows$ are temporal connectives to state that a property holds in some behaviour, in the next local instant, only if preceded by the occurence of another property and that occurrences of two properties are causally connected. Axiom 1.2, e.g., states that in any behaviour, if *item* happens, in the next instant the cell will hold a value equal to the v provided. Then, the cell will not be empty (*empty* = F) and will be the last element in the queue of integers (*lst* = T). We shall continue to explain this example in Section 3.

3   Axiomatising the Actors Model

3.1   Representing Actors

A theory signature provides the language to be used in a specification. Signatures bring both the notion of scope and interface to the logic, by forcing every used symbol to be declared locally and by enabling the definition of translations between symbols in order to connect distinct specifications. Theory signatures for actor specification are defined as follows:

Definition 1 (Actor Signature). An actor signature Δ is a triple of disjoint and finite families $(\Sigma, \mathcal{A}, \Gamma)$ where:

- $\Sigma = (S, \Omega)$ is an universe signature in the usual algebraic sense [7], i.e., S is a set of sort symbols and Ω is an $S^* \times S$-indexed family of operation symbols. We also require that addr $\in S$;

Actor BUFFERCELL
  data types addr, bool, int
  attributes $cont$: int, nxt : addr, $empty$, lst : bool
  actions nil, $item$(int) : **local** + **extrn birth**;
           $void$, $link$(addr) : **local comput**;
           put(int), get(addr) : **local** + **extrn message**;
           $reply$(int) : **extrn message**
  axioms n, m : addr, u, v : int, b : bool

$$nil \rightarrow empty = \text{T} \wedge lst = \text{T} \tag{1.1}$$
$$item(v) \rightarrow cont = v \wedge empty = \text{F} \wedge lst = \text{T} \tag{1.2}$$
$$void \wedge nxt = n \wedge lst = b \rightarrow \mathbf{X}(nxt = n \wedge empty = \text{T} \wedge lst = b) \tag{1.3}$$
$$link(n) \wedge cont = v \wedge empty = b \rightarrow \mathbf{X}(cont = v \wedge nxt = n \wedge empty = b \wedge lst = \text{F}) \tag{1.4}$$
$$put(v) \wedge lst = \text{T} \rightarrow \mathbf{X}(\exists n \cdot \mathbf{new}(item, n, v) \wedge link(n)) \tag{1.5}$$
$$\exists n \cdot \mathbf{new}(item, n, v) \vee link(n) \leftarrow put(v) \wedge lst = \text{T} \tag{1.6}$$
$$put(v) \wedge lst = \text{F} \wedge nxt = m \leftrightarrows \mathbf{send}(put, m, v) \tag{1.7}$$
$$get(n) \wedge empty = \text{F} \wedge cont = u \leftrightarrows \mathbf{send}(reply, n, u) \tag{1.8}$$
$$get(n) \wedge empty = \text{F} \leftrightarrows void \tag{1.9}$$
$$get(n) \wedge empty = \text{T} \wedge lst = \text{F} \wedge nxt = m \leftrightarrows \mathbf{send}(get, m, n) \tag{1.10}$$
$$nil \vee item(u) \rightarrow \mathbf{G}(\mathbf{E}(\mathbf{deliv}(put, v)) \wedge \mathbf{E}(\mathbf{deliv}(get, n))) \tag{1.11}$$
$$nil \vee item(u) \rightarrow \mathbf{XG}(\neg(void \vee link(n)) \rightarrow \mathbf{E}(put(v)) \wedge \mathbf{E}(get(m))) \tag{1.12}$$
End

Fig. 1. Specification of buffer cells

- $\mathcal{A}$ is an $S^* \times S$-indexed family of attribute symbols;
- $\Gamma = (\Gamma_e, \Gamma_l, \Gamma_c)$ is a triple of S^*-indexed families of action symbols such that $(\Gamma_e \cup \Gamma_l) \cap \Gamma_c$ is empty. Γ_c is a set of local computation symbols. The elements of Γ_e and Γ_l represent respectively events to be requested from the environment and provided locally[1]. Each of these two sets contains distinguished sub-sets of message and birth computation symbols, e.g. $\Gamma_l - \Gamma_{l_b}$ and Γ_{l_b}.

For ϵ denoting the empty sequence, we write an $\epsilon \times s$-indexed family of symbols as if s were its index. Also, given a set or a sequence X, we denote the sub-set of X symbols of sort $\langle s_1, \ldots, s_n \rangle \times s$ as $X_{\langle s_1, \ldots, s_n \rangle, s}$. In making reference to specific sets of signature symbols, we shall operate with subscripts ($\Gamma_{e_b \cap l_b}$) to denote operations on sub-sets of Γ ($\Gamma_{e_b} \cap \Gamma_{l_b}$).

In our previous example, addr, bool and int are the sorts that constitute, together with their implicitly defined constants and operations, the universe signature Σ. Clearly, the sort of mail addresses addr must be part of every signature. Otherwise, some specified actors would be useless without the ability of exchanging messages or creating new actors. Still in the example, we can see that $cont$, nxt,

---

[1] Since the mail addresses of actors requesting and providing the occurrence of an event can be determined at run time only and may denote the same object, Γ_e and Γ_l should not be disjoint in general.

empty and *lst* are the attributes in $\mathcal{A}$. In the Actors model peculiar terminology, such attributes are called acquaintances, which may be instantiated at creation time or in processing subsequently received messages.

The structure of the set of action symbols differs from other similar logics [10, 17]. Each actor may provide some externally visible functionality and may request provision of functionality from other actors. An actor may also perform purely local computations. Because of these distinctions, the set of action symbols is divided into three sub-sets, Γ_e, Γ_l and Γ_c. The first two are dismembered in sub-sets of actions to represent synchronous and asynchronous interactions, Γ_{e_b} and Γ_{e-e_b} for instance. In general, actors interact using asynchronous messages, members of Γ_{e-e_b} like *put* in $\mathbf{send}(put, nxt, v)$. In some particular cases, however, synchrony is also required. This is the mode of interaction when a newly created actor receives its name because the occurrence of birth action of Γ_{e_b} has just been requested[2]. For our example, all these families can be inferred from the statements in Figure 1.

As it is usual in a proof-theoretic approach to specification (cf. [6, 9, 20]), we need to extend signatures with some logical symbols. The situation here resembles the use of hidden symbols in algebraic specifications [7]. There, the specifier wants to use the language of previously defined data types to specify a more complex one. Here, we want a simpler language to specify complex patterns of behaviour presented by every actor, defined in terms of a more complex language. This extended language will be used in providing a semantics for the actor primitives and that is why it should not be required from the specifier of each signature.

Definition 2 (Extended Actor Signature). Given an actor signature $\Delta = (\Sigma, \mathcal{A}, \Gamma)$, the triple $\lambda\Delta = (\lambda\Sigma, \lambda\mathcal{A}, \lambda\Gamma)$ is said to be the extended signature of Δ, where:

- $\lambda\Sigma = (S \oplus \{\mathsf{bool}\}, \Omega \oplus \{\mathsf{T_{bool}}, \mathsf{F_{bool}}, \mathsf{NOT_{bool \to bool}}\})$;
- $\lambda\mathcal{A} = (\mathcal{A}_l, \mathcal{A}_i, \mathcal{A}_s, \mathcal{A}_d)$, such that $\mathcal{A}_l = \mathcal{A}$; for each $c \in \Gamma_{l_b}$ of sort $\langle s_1, \ldots, s_n \rangle$ there is an $init_c \in \mathcal{A}_{i_{\langle s_1, \ldots, s_n \rangle, \mathsf{bool}}}$; for each $c \in \Gamma_{(e-e_b) \cup (l-l_b)}$ of sort $\langle s_1, \ldots, s_n \rangle$ there is a $sent_c \in \mathcal{A}_{s_{\langle s_1, \ldots, s_n \rangle, \mathsf{bool}}}$ and for each $c \in \Gamma_{l-l_b}$ of sort $\langle s_1, \ldots, s_n \rangle$ there is a $delivd_c \in \mathcal{A}_{d_{\langle s_1, \ldots, s_n \rangle, \mathsf{bool}}}$;
- $\lambda\Gamma = (\Gamma_e, \Gamma_{out}, \Gamma_l, \Gamma_{in}, \Gamma_c, \Gamma_{rcv})$, where for each $c \in \Gamma_e$ of sort $\langle s_1, \ldots, s_n \rangle$ there is an $out_c \in \Gamma_{out_{\langle addr, addr, s_1, \ldots, s_n \rangle}}$; for each $c \in \Gamma_l$ of sort $\langle s_1, \ldots, s_n \rangle$ there is an $in_c \in \Gamma_{in_{\langle addr, addr, s_1, \ldots, s_n \rangle}}$ and for each $c \in \Gamma_{l-l_b}$ of sort $\langle s_1, \ldots, s_n \rangle$ there is a $rcv_c \in \Gamma_{rcv_{\langle s_1, \ldots, s_n \rangle}}$ such that $\Gamma_{(in \cup out) \cap rcv} = \{\}$ and that $in_c = out_c$ whenever $c \in \Gamma_{e \cap l}$.

That is to say, the original universal signature is extended with the sort of booleans, new attributes are provided to deal with the existence of actors and buffering of messages, and new actions are introduced to handle creation and interaction. Hereafter, we will not make any distinction between extended signatures and actor signatures.

---

[2] For simplicity, we assume that there are only two modes of interaction between objects, synchronous and asynchronous, and that creation follows the first one.

A central feature of actors is interaction. Here, it is simulated using the synchronous case by the actions out_c and in_d happening simultaneously for $c \in \Gamma_e$ and $d \in \Gamma_l'$, which belong to the actor communities (populations of actors with same specification) requesting and providing the event respectively. The occurrence of these logical actions plays the role of the interaction steps in [19]. For an interaction between actors of the same community represented by action c, hence required and provided internally and member of $\Gamma_{e \cap l}$, the occurrence of the new actions above has already been synchronised since their symbols are equalised by the constraint $in_c = out_c$ in Definition 2. Otherwise, this synchronisation must be supported by the existence of a morphism identifying shared actions in the distinct signatures, as discussed in Section 3.4. Asynchrony is guaranteed by obliging rcv_d to happen after $out_c | in_d$ and before d itself. Finally, (double) buffering is captured by the attribute $delivd_d$ ($sent_c$) becoming true for some values when they are delivered (sent) in a message. Of course, all these new symbols do not explicitly appear in specifications but their behavioural constraints will have to be captured by our axiomatisation. Also according to the proposed extended signatures, ill formed messages are not allowed (as actions, messages always have a locally correct representation at the sender) and messages sent to actors which cannot provide the required functionality are never delivered.

According to [3], in a given state of the system, it should only be possible to mention the objects which exist in that state. In our case, objects will have some $init_c$ attribute set to $\top$ for some sequence of values $\vec{v_c}$ if the occurrence of an action $in_c(\vec{v_c})$, $c \in \Gamma_{l_b}$, created it. The structure of communities of similar actors is defined below and provides a syntactic (although static) representation for the configurations of [2] and the fragments of [19]:

Definition 3 (Actor Community Signature). Given a signature $\Delta = (\Sigma, \mathcal{A}, \Gamma)$, a community signature Δ^P is obtained by parameterising Δ with sort P. That is, $\Sigma^P = (S \oplus \{P\}, \Omega)$; $\mathcal{A}^P$ is obtained from $\mathcal{A}$ by adding the parameter sort P to each of its attribute symbols; and Γ^P is obtained from Γ by adding the parameter sort P to each action symbol of Γ_e, Γ_l, Γ_c and Γ_{rcv}. The other symbols of Δ remain the same in Δ^P.

It seems obvious that the parameter sort P of every community should be addr. Indeed, according to [19], actor semantics should be parameterised by sets of actor addresses. Due to our definition, a new parameter is added to each relevant signature symbol and its instances will represent an actor name. In this way, the basic operations on object references, equality test and dereferencing [3], are supported. However, signatures alone do not support a modular design discipline, obliging the entire structure of complex systems to be represented by single entities. The required means of composition shall be provided in Section 3.4.

3.2   Specifying and Interpreting Actor Behaviours

Actor specifications stand for the behaviour definitions of [1]. To define them, we assume that an infinite family of variables and its classification Ξ according to a set of sorts are given.

Terms stand for meaningful values. In their definition, a signature Δ and a classification Ξ indexed by the set of sorts are used. These are assumed to be given in the sequel.

Definition 4 (Terms). The S-indexed set of terms $T_\Delta(\Xi)$ is defined as follows, assuming $q \in \Xi_s \cup \Omega_s \cup \mathcal{A}_s$, $p \in \Omega_{\langle s_1,\ldots,s_n\rangle,s}$, $f \in \mathcal{A}_{\langle s_1,\ldots,s_n\rangle,s}$ and $t_i \in T_\Delta(\Xi)_{s_i}$:

$$t := q \mid p(t_1,\ldots,t_n) \mid f(t_1,\ldots,t_n)$$

That is, terms consist in variables, nulary function and attribute symbols, or function and attribute symbols applied to terms. We usually write a sequence of similar terms $t_1,\ldots,t_n$ as $\vec{t}$.

As explained previously, to give an account of actor behaviour in terms of formulae, first-order branching time temporal logic is required. In what follows, we take formulae as defined in CTL* [8] and introduce the necessary extensions:

Definition 5 (Formulae). The set $F_\Delta(\Xi)$ of formulae is defined by the mutual recursion below, assuming $c \in \Gamma_{\langle s_1,\ldots,s_n\rangle}$, $t_i \in T_\Delta(\Xi)_{s_i}$, $y \in \Xi_s$ and $g_i \in F_\Delta(\Xi)$:

$$g := \mathbf{beg} \mid c(t_1,\ldots t_n) \mid t_1 =_s t_2 \mid \mathbf{E}g' \mid g_1 \rightarrow g_2 \mid \neg g_1 \mid \exists y \cdot g_1$$
$$g' := g \mid \mathbf{X}g'_1 \mid g'_1\mathbf{U}g'_2 \mid g'_1 \rightarrow g'_2 \mid \neg g'_1 \mid \exists y \cdot g'_1$$

Formulae stand for the initial instant; action occurrences; term equality; a formula holding in some possible behaviour, in the next instant or until another formula holds; or formulae aggregation using first-order logic connectives.

A formal definition of actor specifications, exemplified here by BUFFERCELL, is as follows:

Definition 6 (Actor Specification). An actor specification is a pair $\Phi = (\Delta, \Psi)$ where Δ is an actor signature and Ψ is a finite set of formulae over Δ (the specification axioms).

Formulae containing other first-order logic connectives and inequalities stand for their usual translations. Free variables in axioms are considered to be universally quantified. Moreover, we write a parameterised formula $g(n, \vec{v}_g)$ as $n.g(\vec{v}_g)$. The connectives defined below are also admissible in specifications:

FOR	IN	FORMULA	READS	REPRESENTS
—	—	$\mathbf{init}$	initialisation	$\bigvee_{c \in \Gamma_{l_b}} \exists \vec{v}_c \cdot c(\vec{v}_c)$
$n_i, \vec{v}_c$	$T_\Delta(\Xi)$	$n_1.\mathbf{new}(c, n_2, \vec{v}_c)$	actor creation	$out_c(n_1, n_2, \vec{v}_c), c \in \Gamma_{e_b}$ $in_c(n_1, n_2, \vec{v}_c), c \in \Gamma_{l_b}$
$n_i, \vec{v}_c$	$T_\Delta(\Xi)$	$n_1.\mathbf{send}(c, n_2, \vec{v}_c)$	message dispatch	$out_c(n_1, n_2, \vec{v}_c), c \in \Gamma_{e-e_b}$ $in_c(n_1, n_2, \vec{v}_c), c \in \Gamma_{l-l_b}$
$n, \vec{v}_c$	$T_\Delta(\Xi)$	$n.\mathbf{deliv}(c, \vec{v}_c)$	message delivery	$n.rcv_c(\vec{v}_c), c \in \Gamma_{l-l_b}$
g	$F_\Delta(\Xi)$	$\mathbf{A}g$	in any behaviour	$\neg\mathbf{E}\neg g$
g	$F_\Delta(\Xi)$	$\mathbf{F}g$	eventually	$(g \rightarrow g)\mathbf{U}g$
g	$F_\Delta(\Xi)$	$\mathbf{G}g$	henceforth	$\neg\mathbf{F}\neg g$
g_1, g_2	$F_\Delta(\Xi)$	$g_1\mathbf{W}g_2$	unless	$\mathbf{G}(g_1 \wedge \neg g_2) \vee g_1\mathbf{U}g_2$
g_1, g_2, p	$F_\Delta(\Xi)$	$g_1 \overset{i}{\leftarrow}_p g_2$	initially precedes	$p \rightarrow (\neg g_1)\mathbf{W}(g_2 \wedge \neg g_1)$
g_1, g_2, p	$F_\Delta(\Xi)$	$g_1 \leftarrow_p g_2$	precedes	$g_1 \overset{i}{\leftarrow}_p g_2 \wedge g_1 \rightarrow \mathbf{X}(g_1 \overset{i}{\leftarrow}_{(p\rightarrow p)} g_2)$
g_1, g_2, p	$F_\Delta(\Xi)$	$g_1 \overset{\leftarrow}{\rightarrow}_p g_2$	cause/consequence	$g_1 \rightarrow \mathbf{X}g_2 \wedge g_2 \leftarrow_p g_1$

The unary temporal connectives above are defined to be non-strict (they include the present). Conversely, the precedence connectives are strict and forbid the simultaneous occurrence of some properties. In specifications, where usually $p =$ **init**, their subscripts are omitted. In particular, $\leftrightarrows$ is used to establish causality relations; for instance that an occurrence of a *get* causes the subsequent dispatch of a *reply* which cannot happen otherwise. The primitives are the usual in the Actors model [1][3].

There is just another Actor primitive not treated by our syntax: **become**, which defines that an actor will behave according to a distinct specification in its subsequent computation. In fact, local computations in Γ_c like *void* of our example together with a selective use of attributes simulate this in an awkward manner. It would be easy to present **become** as another definition, by introducing death actions in signatures (cf. [9]) and by considering the primitive as the death of an actor and its subsequent resurrection with a distinct behaviour, keeping the same mail address in this process. However, we have reasons to avoid treating this here: in the first place, in order to simplify our presentation, and secondly because it would bring methodological complications for reasoning. These complications shall be addressed in the last section.

Concerning the formal meaning of signature symbols, we assume that sorts are interpreted as constant sets, while variables and operations on sorts denote constant functions. Attributes differ from operations in that they may have a distinct meaning at each instant (i.e. they are non-rigid). Actions, in turn, may happen concurrently if this is allowed by specification axioms. Indeed, action symbols are a syntactic representation of the events of [12], which may proceed concurrently if unrelated. Specifications are only satisfied by branching infinite sequences of states representing an actor community behaviour. As a result of all these assumptions, it is easy to see that we are adopting a model of parallelism where actions have a fixed granularity. Since our approach here is proof-theoretic, the reader is referred to [8, 10] for some semantic considerations.

3.3   Axiomatising Actor Behaviours

In this section, we develop a deductive system ACT for Actors consisting of a set of axiom schemes and inference rules. We assume the existence of a deductive system $BTLO$ for the many-sorted, first-order, branching time temporal logic of objects used here (see [9, 17] for axiomatisations of particular linear time versions) and concentrate on the peculiarities of our work.

We shall develop axiom schemes for a consequence relation $\vdash_\Phi$ wherein a specification is used as an index to remind us that it depends of the structure of a signature to support localised reasoning. We will assume that a specification $\Phi = ((\Sigma, \mathcal{A}, \Gamma), \Psi)$ is given. Also, we will drop from the schemes sorts in quantifications to simplify our presentation, using the variable n for actor names decorated with indexes when necessary. The following notation shall be used to express the invariance of an attribute or a modification in its value, the fact that

---

[3] Notice that, since $|\Gamma_{l_b}| \in [0, \infty[$, we allow actors to have "multiple constructors".

an actor name has become known and that a property continuously holds unless that happens, and the fairness requirement over the occurrence of an action:

FOR s AS	FORMULA	REPRESENTS
t	$Inv(s)$	$\forall k \cdot (\mathbf{X}(t = k) \leftrightarrow t = k)$
$\bigwedge f_i(\vec{v_{f_i}}) = v_i$	$Mod(s)$	$\bigwedge \mathbf{X}(f_i(\vec{v_{f_i}}) = v_i))$
n	$Acq(s)$	$\bigvee_{d \in \Gamma_{l-l_b}} \exists \vec{v_d} \cdot (\mathbf{deliv}(d, \vec{v_d}) \wedge n \in \vec{v_d}) \vee$ $\bigvee_{d \in \Gamma_{l_b}} \exists \vec{v_d} \cdot (d(\vec{v_d}) \wedge n \in \vec{v_d}) \vee \bigvee_{d \in \Gamma_{e_b} \cup l_b} \exists \vec{v_d} \cdot \mathbf{new}(d, n, \vec{v_d})$
(n, g)	$Wait(s)$	$(g)\mathbf{W}(\mathbf{init}) \wedge (g)\mathbf{W}(Acq(n))$
$c(\vec{v_c})$	$Fair(s)$	$\mathbf{F}\left(c(\vec{v_c}) \vee \mathbf{G}\left(\bigwedge_{d \in \Gamma^c} \forall \vec{v_d} \cdot \neg\mathbf{E}(d(\vec{v_d}))\right)\right)$

In logics of objects, the so-called locality property is regarded as a crucial assumption to support modular reasoning [10, 17]. It is also a key feature of the Actors model [12]. Generally speaking, locality requires that either an action of the object occurs or its attribute values remain invariant. This means that each actor has encapsulated state — changes must be witnessed by the occurrence of its own actions. Locality is captured by the following schemes:

$\overline{\mathbf{L}}_\phi^1.$ $\bigvee_{c \in \Gamma_c} \exists \vec{v_c} \cdot n.c(\vec{v_c}) \vee \bigwedge_{f \in \mathcal{A}_l} \forall \vec{v_f} \cdot n.Inv(f(\vec{v_f}))$

$\mathbf{L}_\phi^2.$ $\bigwedge_{c \in \Gamma_{l_b}} \forall \vec{v_c} \cdot \exists n_1 \cdot n_1.\mathbf{new}(c, n_2, \vec{v_c}) \vee n_2.Inv(init_c(\vec{v_c}))$

$\mathbf{L}_\phi^3.$ $\bigwedge_{c \in \Gamma_{l-l_b}} \forall \vec{v_c} \cdot \bigvee_{d \in \Gamma_{l_b}} \exists n_2, \vec{v_d} \cdot n_2.\mathbf{new}(d, n_1, \vec{v_d}) \vee n_2.\mathbf{send}(c, n_1, \vec{v_c}) \vee n_1.\mathbf{deliv}(c, \vec{v_c}) \vee$
 $n_1.Inv(sent_c(\vec{v_c}))$

$\mathbf{L}_\phi^4.$ $\bigwedge_{c \in \Gamma_{l-l_b}} \forall \vec{v_c} \cdot \bigvee_{d \in \Gamma_{l_b}} \exists n_2, \vec{v_d} \cdot n_2.\mathbf{new}(d, n_1, \vec{v_d}) \vee n_1.\mathbf{deliv}(c, \vec{v_c}) \vee n_1.c(\vec{v_c}) \vee n_1.Inv(delivd_c(\vec{v_c}))$

The first scheme says that, either a local computation happens, or all the non-logical attributes remain invariant. In the BUFFERCELL example, this captures the fact that either *void* or *link* occurs or else *cont*, *nxt*, *empty* and *lst* do not change. According to the second scheme, or an actor is created with some name, or the possible existence of an object with such name is not disturbed. The other two schemes are to guarantee that buffering attributes vary only when the actor is created or message passing takes place.

Permission schemes constrain the occurrence of actions:

$\overline{\mathbf{P}}_\phi^1.$ $\bigwedge_{c \in \Gamma_{(e-e_b) \cup (l-l_b)}} \forall \vec{v_c} \cdot \mathbf{beg} \rightarrow \mathbf{G}(\neg n_1.\mathbf{init}) \vee \bigwedge_{n \in \vec{v_{c_{addr}}} \cup \{n_2\}} n_1.Wait(n, \neg\mathbf{send}(c, n_2, \vec{v_c}))$

$\overline{\mathbf{P}}_\phi^2.$ $\bigwedge_{c \in \Gamma_{l-l_b}} \forall \vec{v_c} \cdot \mathbf{beg} \rightarrow (\neg n.\mathbf{deliv}(c, \vec{v_c}))\mathbf{W}(n.\mathbf{init})$

$\overline{\mathbf{P}}_\phi^3.$ $\bigwedge_{c \in \Gamma_{(l-l_b) \cup c}} \forall \vec{v_c} \cdot \mathbf{beg} \rightarrow (\neg n.c(\vec{v_c}))\mathbf{W}(n.\mathbf{init})$

$\overline{\mathbf{P}}_\phi^4.$ $\bigwedge_{c \in \Gamma_{e_b} \cup l_b} \forall \vec{v_c} \cdot \mathbf{beg} \rightarrow \mathbf{G}(\neg n_1.\mathbf{init}) \vee \bigwedge_{n \in \vec{v_{c_{addr}}} \cup \{n_2\}} n_1.Wait(n, \neg\mathbf{new}(c, n_2, \vec{v_c}))$

$\mathbf{P}_\phi^5.$ $\bigwedge_{c, d \in \Gamma_{l_b}} \exists n_1, \vec{v_c} \cdot n_1.\mathbf{new}(c, n_2, \vec{v_c}) \rightarrow \forall \vec{v_d} \cdot n_2.init_d(\vec{v_d}) = \mathrm{F}$

$\overline{\mathbf{P}}_\phi^6.$ $\bigwedge_{c \in \Gamma_{l_b}} \mathbf{beg} \rightarrow \mathbf{G}(\exists n_1, n_2, \vec{v_c} \cdot \mathbf{E}(n_1.\mathbf{new}(c, n_2, \vec{v_c})))$

$\overline{\mathbf{P}}_\phi^7.$ $\bigwedge_{c \in \Gamma_{l_b}} \forall \vec{v_c} \cdot \exists n_1 \cdot n_1.\mathbf{new}(c, n_2, \vec{v_c}) \leftrightharpoons_{\mathbf{beg}} n_2.c(\vec{v_c})$

$\overline{\mathbf{P}}_{\phi}^{\mathbf{8}}$. $\bigwedge_{\substack{c,d\in\Gamma_{l_b} \\ d\neq c}} \forall \vec{v_c} \cdot n_1.\mathbf{new}(c,n_2,\vec{v_c}) \rightarrow \nexists n_3, \vec{v_c}', \vec{v_d} \cdot ((n_3 \neq n_1 \vee \vec{v_c}' \neq \vec{v_c}) \wedge n_3.\mathbf{new}(c,n_2,\vec{v_c}')) \vee$

$\qquad n_3.\mathbf{new}(d,n_2,\vec{v_d})$

$\mathbf{P}_{\phi}^{\mathbf{9}}$. $\bigwedge_{c\in\Gamma_{l-l_b}} \forall \vec{v_c} \cdot n.\mathbf{deliv}(c,\vec{v_c}) \rightarrow n.sent_c(\vec{v_c}) = \mathrm{T}$

$\overline{\mathbf{P}}_{\phi}^{\mathbf{10}}$. $\bigwedge_{\substack{c,d\in\Gamma_{l-l_b} \\ d\neq c}} \forall \vec{v_c} \cdot n.\mathbf{deliv}(c,\vec{v_c}) \rightarrow \nexists \vec{v_c}', \vec{v_d} \cdot (\vec{v_c}' \neq \vec{v_c} \wedge n.\mathbf{deliv}(c,\vec{v_c}')) \vee n.\mathbf{deliv}(d,\vec{v_d})$

$\mathbf{P}_{\phi}^{\mathbf{11}}$. $\bigwedge_{c\in\Gamma_{l-l_b}} \forall \vec{v_c} \cdot n.c(\vec{v_c}) \rightarrow n.delivd_c(\vec{v_c}) = \mathrm{T}$

$\overline{\mathbf{P}}_{\phi}^{\mathbf{12}}$. $\bigwedge_{\substack{c,d\in\Gamma_{(l-l_b)\cup c} \\ c\neq d}} \forall \vec{v_c} \cdot n.c(\vec{v_c}) \rightarrow \nexists \vec{v_c}', \vec{v_d} \cdot (\vec{v_c}' \neq \vec{v_c} \wedge n.c(\vec{v_c}')) \vee n.d(\vec{v_d})$

The first four schemes say that dispatch, delivery and consumption of messages plus local computations and requests for creation do not happen before the birth of each actor. Notice that the first and forth schemes are more liberal if the actor is never created within a certain community but are more restrictive otherwise by requiring actor names to become known due to the delivery of a message, the birth of the source or the creation of the target before they could be used in the task. This is to prevent using arbitrary names and modes of interaction distinct from point-to-point message passing such as broadcasting [12, 19]. The other schemes say: a new actor can only be created if this has not happened before (5); it is always possible to create some new actors (6); the occurrence of birth actions is causally connected to requests for creation (7); two actors with the same name cannot be concurrently created (8); messages can be delivered only if they were previously sent (9); only one message can be delivered to each actor at any instant (10); messages can be consumed only if they were previously delivered (11); consumption of messages and local computations are totally ordered (12), meaning that two such actions cannot occur in parallel.

Many logical attributes are introduced in the extension of actor signatures. The variation of their values as the actor community evolves is defined as follows:

$\mathbf{V}_{\phi}^{\mathbf{1}}$. $\bigwedge_{c\in\Gamma_{l_b}} \forall \vec{v_c} \cdot \exists n_1 \cdot n_1.\mathbf{new}(c,n_2,\vec{v_c}) \rightarrow n_2.Mod(init_c(\vec{v_c}) = \mathrm{T})$

$\mathbf{V}_{\phi}^{\mathbf{2}}$. $\bigwedge_{\substack{c\in\Gamma_{l_b} \\ d\in\Gamma_{l-l_b}}} \forall \vec{v_c}, \vec{v_d} \cdot \exists n_1 \cdot n_1.\mathbf{new}(c,n_2,\vec{v_c}) \rightarrow n_2.Mod(sent_d(\vec{v_d}) = \mathrm{F} \wedge delivd_d(\vec{v_d}) = \mathrm{F})$

$\mathbf{V}_{\phi}^{\mathbf{3}}$. $\bigwedge_{c\in\Gamma_{l-l_b}} \forall \vec{v_c} \cdot \exists n_1 \cdot n_1.\mathbf{send}(c,n_2,\vec{v_c}) \rightarrow n_2.Mod(sent_c(\vec{v_c}) = \mathrm{T})$

$\mathbf{V}_{\phi}^{\mathbf{4}}$. $\bigwedge_{c\in\Gamma_{l-l_b}} \forall \vec{v_c} \cdot n.\mathbf{deliv}(c,\vec{v_c}) \rightarrow n.Mod(sent_c(\vec{v_c}) = \mathrm{F} \wedge delivd_c(\vec{v_c}) = \mathrm{T})$

$\mathbf{V}_{\phi}^{\mathbf{5}}$. $\bigwedge_{c\in\Gamma_{l-l_b}} \forall \vec{v_c} \cdot n.c(\vec{v_c}) \rightarrow n.Mod(delivd_c(\vec{v_c}) = \mathrm{F})$

That is, if the creation of an actor has been requested, there will exist a new actor in the next instant with empty message buffers (1,2); if a message is sent, it will be buffered for output (3); if a delivery happens, the message will be removed from the output buffer and transfered to the input buffer (4); and if a message is processed, it will be removed from the input buffer (5). Notice that the delay in buffering messages, in the next instant only, rules out the existence of Zeno actors, which could reply infinitely fast.

It is important to mention that, even though the two sets of axiom schemes above severely constrain the behaviour of actor communities, such constraints are almost always necessary. For instance, we require the continuous ability to create new actors using $\overline{\mathbf{P}}_{\Phi}^{6}$ in order to prevent that the address space used by some community could become completely used. However, we do not constrain the initial value of $n.init_c(\vec{v_c})$ for every n and this permits the existence of actors in the initial instant. What would happen otherwise is that no actor could exist according to $\overline{\mathbf{P}}_{\Phi}^{7}$ since any birth could not be requested first. On the other hand, the permission scheme $\overline{\mathbf{P}}_{\Phi}^{12}$ above is not necessary and is provided here just to facilitate specification and reasoning. We can allow actors to have full internal concurrency instead, as soon as we guarantee that attribute consistency (in the sense of [16]) is preserved using additional axioms [5]. Notice that actors can always present some internal concurrency anyway: they can create many other actors and send several messages at the same time.

Finally, fairness schemes are required to guarantee a correct collective actor behaviour. Without fairness, it could be the case that messages fail to be delivered, because the receiver always postpones the delivery or due to transmission failures, and that received messages are never consumed.

$\mathbf{F}_{\Phi}^{1}$. $\bigwedge\limits_{c \in \Gamma_{l-l_b}} \forall \vec{v_c} \cdot n.delivd_c(\vec{v_c}) = \mathrm{T} \wedge \mathbf{E}(n.c(\vec{v_c})) \rightarrow n.Fair(c(\vec{v_c}))$

$\mathbf{F}_{\Phi}^{2}$. $\bigwedge\limits_{c \in \Gamma_{l-l_b}} \forall \vec{v_c} \cdot n.sent_c(\vec{v_c}) = \mathrm{T} \wedge \mathbf{E}(n.\mathbf{deliv}(c, \vec{v_c})) \rightarrow n.Fair(\mathbf{deliv}(c, \vec{v_c}))$

The first scheme says that, if the processing of a message is obliged, because the message was delivered and has been locally buffered, and it is also permitted (enabled), the message will be processed or the actor will become always disabled for processing — unable to consume any pending message. *Mutatis mutandis*, this is what the second scheme says for message delivery. These schemes capture the assumptions of bounded buffering and reliable message passing respectively.

A crucial simplification was made in our axiomatisation concerning message passing. We should have treated the fact that messages may be exchanged both concurrently or in sequence and thus some of them could be missed or duplicated [8]. In Actors, the usual treatment of this problem is to attach tags to messages so that they become distinct from each other [1]. To avoid obliging the specifier to deal with such details, logical means could have been provided, much in the way that buffering is treated through auxiliary attributes. Although omitted here, this additional treatment is indeed necessary, say, to determine the effects of messages simultaneously sent to the same actor, which would have been equalised otherwise since this situation is not covered by axiom $\mathbf{V}_{\Phi}^{3}$.

All the properties above have already been stated in the literature — many appear in [12], for instance — although they remained without an axiomatisation. Hereafter, we call the set of logical axioms of Φ containing $\{\mathbf{L}_{\Phi}^{1..4}, \mathbf{P}_{\Phi}^{1..12}, \mathbf{V}_{\Phi}^{1..5}, \mathbf{F}_{\Phi}^{1,2}\}$ as Ax_{Φ}, while the set $\overline{Ax}_{\Phi}$ contains only the axioms with barred labels, wherein logical attributes do not appear.

The axiom schemes above allow us to derive more or less standard rules for reasoning about concurrent actor communities. In what follows, we use Hoare triples $\{p\}\,a\,\{q\}$ to represent $a \wedge p \to \mathbf{X}q$. Moreover, sequents like $P \vdash_\Phi q$ stand for the fact that formula q is derivable from the set of formulae P together with the (logical and non-logical) axioms of Φ using the inference rules of the proof system. We drop the index from the sequent when it is clear from the context.

Proposition 7 (Derived Rules of Inference). Given an actor specification $\Phi = ((\Sigma,\, \mathcal{A},\, \Gamma),\, \Psi)$, the following are inference rules for deriving properties of existing Φ-actors, where each p, p' and q is an arbitrary formula over a single actor and n, n' and m are terms of sort addr:

$$
[EXIST] \quad
\begin{array}{l}
1.\ p' \to n'.\mathbf{new}(d, m, \vec{v_d}) \\
2.\ p \to q \vee \bigvee_{c \in \Gamma_{l_b}} \exists \vec{v_c} \cdot n.\mathbf{new}(c, m, \vec{v_c})
\end{array}
\qquad d \in \Gamma_{l_b}
$$
$$
\overline{\quad p' \to \mathbf{XG}(p \to q) \quad}
$$

$$
[SAFE] \quad
\begin{array}{l}
1.\ \bigwedge_{c \in \Gamma_{l_b}} \forall \vec{v_c} \cdot n.c(\vec{v_c}) \to q \\
2.\ \bigwedge_{c \in \Gamma_c} \forall \vec{v_c} \cdot \{q\}\, n.c(\vec{v_c})\, \{q\}
\end{array}
$$
$$
\overline{\qquad \mathbf{G}q \qquad}
$$

$$
[INV] \quad
1.\ \bigwedge_{c \in \Gamma_c} \forall \vec{v_c} \cdot \{q\}\, n.c(\vec{v_c})\, \{q\}
$$
$$
\overline{\qquad q \to \mathbf{G}q \qquad}
$$

$$
[RESP] \quad
\begin{array}{l}
1.\ \bigwedge_{c \in \Gamma_c} \forall \vec{v_c} \cdot \{p\}\, n.c(\vec{v_c})\, \{p \vee n.d(\vec{v_d})\} \\
2.\ n.d(\vec{v_d}) \to \mathbf{F}q \\
3.\ p \to \mathbf{FE}(n.d(\vec{v_d}))
\end{array}
\qquad d \in \Gamma_{l-l_b}
$$
$$
\overline{\quad n.\mathbf{deliv}(d, \vec{v_d}) \to \mathbf{X}(\mathbf{F}p \to \mathbf{F}q) \quad}
$$

$$
[COM] \quad
\begin{array}{l}
1.\ \bigwedge_{c \in \Gamma_c} \forall \vec{v_c} \cdot \{p\}\, n.c(\vec{v_c})\, \{p \vee n.\mathbf{deliv}(d, \vec{v_d})\} \\
2.\ n.\mathbf{deliv}(d, \vec{v_d}) \to \mathbf{F}q \\
3.\ p \to \mathbf{FE}(n.\mathbf{deliv}(d, \vec{v_d}))
\end{array}
\qquad d \in \Gamma_{l-l_b}
$$
$$
\overline{\quad n'.\mathbf{send}(d, n, \vec{v_d}) \to \mathbf{X}(\mathbf{F}p \to \mathbf{F}q) \quad}
$$

Using our axiom schemes Ax_Φ and the axiomatisation of the temporal logic $BTLO$, it is not difficult to derive the inference rules above, which are more convenient to use together with the axioms of $\overline{Ax_\Phi}$ because the logical attributes have been eliminated. Rule $EXIST$ is a direct consequence of $\{\mathbf{L}^2_\Phi, \mathbf{P}^5_\Phi, \mathbf{V}^1_\Phi\}$. The $SAFE$ and INV rules, which enable the deduction of properties that actors will always have and correspond to forms of actor induction as described in [12], are consequences of axioms $\mathbf{L}^1_\Phi$ and $\mathbf{P}^{3,12}_\Phi$. The other rules are a consequence of $\{\mathbf{L}^4_\Phi, \mathbf{P}^{11,12}_\Phi, \mathbf{V}^{4,5}_\Phi, \mathbf{F}^1_\Phi\}$ and $\{\mathbf{L}^3_\Phi, \mathbf{P}^{9,10}_\Phi, \mathbf{V}^{3,4}_\Phi, \mathbf{F}^2_\Phi\}$ respectively. Although these last two rules are both for the derivation of properties in the general liveness family, which an actor will eventually present, they are distinguished to keep apart properties arising as a result of local and cooperative behaviour.

The COM rule is to be used in proving properties that arise from the interaction between two (potentially distinct) actors. The situation here differs from that described in [4], where interaction is captured through action sharing in a more explicit and unconstrained manner. Therein, a very strong form of fairness is proposed, since in general a shared action may loose its permission to happen in some of the components while it has been obliged to take place. For designing actor systems, however, such a fairness strengthening is not required: a shared action must be locally provided by one actor only and cannot have its permission to occur externally constrained in this way.

Let us illustrate the use of our proof system. From the BUFFERCELL specification, we can see that each cell is created and may be subsequently consumed or linked to another cell of the buffer. If a cell is empty and it is not the last element of the list, the cell will never perform any local computation again. Hence, the cell will forward every incoming message to the next buffer element (if any). Assuming familiarity with temporal logic, this is stated and verified as:

$$\vdash_{\text{BUFFERCELL}} \mathbf{G}(empty = \text{T} \wedge lst = \text{F} \rightarrow \mathbf{G}(\neg void \wedge \neg link(n))) \tag{1}$$

1. $void \wedge empty = \text{T} \rightarrow \mathbf{X}(empty = \text{T})$ — from 1.3
2. $link(n) \wedge empty = \text{T} \rightarrow \mathbf{X}(empty = \text{T})$ — from 1.4
3. $empty = \text{T} \rightarrow \mathbf{G}(empty = \text{T})$ — 1, 2 INV
4. $void \rightarrow \mathbf{X}((\neg void)\mathbf{W}(get(n) \wedge empty = \text{F} \wedge \neg void))$ — from 1.9, $DEF \leftarrow$
5. $(\neg void)\mathbf{W}(empty = \text{F}) \rightarrow (\mathbf{G}(empty = \text{T}) \rightarrow \mathbf{G}(\neg void))$ — DEF $\mathbf{W}$, bool Ax
6. $void \rightarrow \mathbf{X}\mathbf{G}(empty = \text{T})$ — 1, 3, K $\mathbf{X}$
7. $void \rightarrow \mathbf{X}\mathbf{G}(empty = \text{T} \rightarrow \neg void)$ — 4, 5, 6, $WEAK$ $\mathbf{G}$
8. $beg \rightarrow (\neg void)\mathbf{W}(\mathbf{init})$ — from $\mathbf{P}^3$
9. $init \rightarrow (\neg void)\mathbf{W}(get(n) \wedge empty = \text{F} \wedge \neg void)$ — from 1.9, $DEF \leftarrow$
10. $beg \rightarrow (\neg void)\mathbf{W}(get(n) \wedge empty = \text{F} \wedge \neg void)$ — 8, 9 $TRANS$ $\mathbf{W}$
11. $get(n) \wedge empty = \text{F} \rightarrow \neg void \wedge \mathbf{X}(empty = \text{F} \wedge void)$ — from 1.9, $\mathbf{L}^1, \mathbf{P}^{12}$
12. $get(n) \wedge empty = \text{F} \wedge \neg void \rightarrow \mathbf{G}(empty = \text{T} \rightarrow \neg void)$ — 7, 11, $WEAK$ $\mathbf{X}$, FIX $\mathbf{G}$
13. $beg \rightarrow \mathbf{G}(empty = \text{T} \rightarrow \neg void)$ — 10, 12, DEF $\mathbf{G}$, $TRANS$ $\mathbf{W}$
14. $empty = \text{T} \rightarrow \neg void$ — 13 beg $\mathcal{E}$
15. $\mathbf{G}(empty = \text{T}) \rightarrow \mathbf{G}(\neg void)$ — 14 $\mathbf{G}$ $\mathcal{I}, K$ $\mathbf{G}$
16. $empty = \text{T} \wedge lst = \text{F} \rightarrow \mathbf{G}(\neg void)$ — 3, 15, $WEAK$ $\rightarrow$

using *Modus Ponens* and generalisation as the inference rules of the underlying logic. In a similar way, it is easy to prove $\vdash empty = \text{T} \wedge lst = \text{F} \rightarrow \mathbf{G}(\neg link(n))$. Therefore, conjoining these partial results and using the fact that $\mathbf{G}p \wedge \mathbf{G}q \rightarrow \mathbf{G}(p \wedge q)$ and a $\mathbf{G}$ introduction, we conclude that the property above holds.

3.4   Composing Actor Communities

In Section 3.1 we discovered that, to give an account of what is usually considered to be a component in Actors, we need at least to be able to put distinct signatures together to represent the structure of yet another component or an entire system. The view that complex components should be defined in terms of smaller components connected together has been developed within the theory of Institutions [11], which requires the definition of basic entities to be regarded as connectable units. In our case, these will be actor community specifications.

Next, it is necessary to provide means of connecting these entities to each other. Traditionally, in a logical approach to design, this is achieved by providing translations between the languages of the related theories [15]. If a symbol-to-symbol mapping (morphism) between two actor signatures is given, the existence of a translation between the respective languages can be guaranteed along with an interpretation between their theories.

Definition 8 (Signature Morphisms). Given two actor signatures $\Delta_1 = (\Sigma_1, \mathcal{A}_1, \Gamma_1)$ and $\Delta_2 = (\Sigma_2, \mathcal{A}_2, \Gamma_2)$, a signature morphism $\tau : \Delta_1 \rightarrow \Delta_2$ consists of:

- a limit preserving morphism of algebraic structures $\tau_\upsilon : \Sigma_1 \rightarrow \Sigma_2$ such that $\tau_\upsilon(\mathsf{addr}_1) = \mathsf{addr}_2$ and $\tau_\upsilon(\mathsf{bool}_1) = \mathsf{bool}_2$, and also that $\tau_\upsilon(\mathrm{T}_1) = \mathrm{T}_2$, $\tau_\upsilon(\mathrm{F}_1) = \mathrm{F}_2$ and $\tau_\upsilon(\mathrm{NOT}_1) = \mathrm{NOT}_2$;
- for each $f \in \mathcal{A}_{1_{(s_1,\ldots,s_n),s}}$, an attribute symbol $\tau_\alpha(f) : \tau_\upsilon(s_1) \times \ldots \times \tau_\upsilon(s_n) \rightarrow \tau_\upsilon(s)$ in $\mathcal{A}_2$ such that $\tau_\alpha(\mathcal{A}_{l_1}) \subseteq \mathcal{A}_{l_2}$, $\tau_\alpha(\mathcal{A}_{i_1}) \subseteq \mathcal{A}_{i_2}$, $\tau_\alpha(\mathcal{A}_{s_1}) \subseteq \mathcal{A}_{s_2}$ and $\tau_\alpha(\mathcal{A}_{d_1}) \subseteq \mathcal{A}_{d_2}$, where for each $f_c \in \mathcal{A}_{(i \cup s \cup d)_1}$, $\tau_\alpha(f_c) = f_{\tau_\gamma(c)}$;
- for each $c \in \Gamma_{1_{(s_1,\ldots,s_n)}}$, an action symbol $\tau_\gamma(c) : \tau_\upsilon(s_1) \times \ldots \times \tau_\upsilon(s_n)$ in Γ_2 such that $\tau_\gamma(\Gamma_{e_1}) \subseteq \Gamma_{e_2}$, $\tau_\gamma(\Gamma_{l_1}) \subseteq \Gamma_{l_2}$, $\tau_\gamma(\Gamma_{c_1}) \subseteq \Gamma_{c_2}$, $\tau_\gamma(\Gamma_{rcv_1}) \subseteq \Gamma_{rcv_2}$, $\tau_\gamma(\Gamma_{out_1}) \subseteq \Gamma_{out_2}$ and $\tau_\gamma(\Gamma_{in_1}) \subseteq \Gamma_{in_2}$, where $\tau_\gamma(\Gamma_{e_{b_1}}) \subseteq \Gamma_{e_{b_2} \cup l_{b_2}}$ and $\tau_\gamma(\Gamma_{e_1 - e_{b_1}}) \subseteq \Gamma_{(e_2 - e_{b_2}) \cup (l_2 - l_{b_2})}$, $\tau_\gamma(\Gamma_{l_{b_1}}) \subseteq \Gamma_{l_{b_2}}$ and $\tau_\gamma(\Gamma_{l_1 - l_{b_1}}) \subseteq \Gamma_{l_2 - l_{b_2}}$ so that $\tau_\gamma(\Gamma_{e_1 \cap l_1}) \subseteq \Gamma_{e_2 \cap l_2}$ and also $\tau_\gamma(\Gamma_{out_1 \cap in_1}) \subseteq \Gamma_{out_2 \cap in_2}$. In addition, for each $d_c \in \Gamma_{(in \cup out \cup rcv)_1}$, $\tau_\gamma(d_c) = d_{\tau_\gamma(c)}$.

It is straightforward to define inductively the translation of symbols, classifications, terms, formulae and sets thereof under τ.

Since renaming is one of the features of translations, morphisms capture the re-labelling operation described in [1], used to equalise identifiers in distinct components. In addition, the translation of symbols belonging to extended signatures only is determined by the translation of the original symbols provided. This means that the specifier, in defining a morphism to connect distinct signatures, does not need to be concerned with the new symbols introduced in their extension. Furthermore, signature morphisms allow some external symbols (members of Γ_e) to become local as well. This stems from the fact that, in a complex configuration, there may be events required from the environment of a sub-component which are not required by the whole component, because they are provided by another sub-component of the same configuration.

Of course, we want to be always able to combine distinct signatures in such a way that the structure to support actor interaction is provided. This can be accomplished if we can show that, for every three generic signatures connected through morphisms so that one contains symbols to be shared by the others, there is a unique way of collapsing such objects into a new larger signature wherein the shared-to-be symbols are equalised. As a consequence, any such aggregations through morphisms will be possible. Using Category Theory, this is equivalent to show that the category of signatures has an initial object (the empty signature shared by disjoint components) and pushouts. A category with these characteristics is called co-complete:

Theorem 9 (Category of Actor Signatures). Actor signatures and morphisms constitute a finitely co-complete category where $\Delta_\perp = ((\{\text{addr}, \text{bool}\},$ $\{\text{T}, \text{F}, \text{NOT}\}), (\{\}, \{\}, \{\}, \{\}), (\{\}, \{\}, \{\}, \{\}, \{\}, \{\}))$ is the initial object.

Interpretations between theories induced by the signature morphisms above do not capture the expected combination of behavior as usual in Institutions [11]. This happens because such morphisms do not translate the logical axioms of source theories, which are needed to guarantee a correct collective behaviour. To support this, non-standard specification morphisms are used:

Definition 10 (Specification Morphisms). Given two actor specifications $\Phi_1 = (\Delta_1, \Psi_1)$ and $\Phi_2 = (\Delta_2, \Psi_2)$, a specification morphism $\tau : \Phi_1 \to \Phi_2$ is a signature morphism such that $\vdash_{\Phi_2} \tau(g)$ for every $g \in \Psi_1 \cup Ax_{\Phi_1}$.

The inclusion of the translated logical axioms $\tau(Ax_{\Phi_1})$ into Φ_2 is necessary as they represent properties which are not always a consequence of Ax_{Φ_2}, since they rely on the existence of only the original signature symbols. Once the signature is augmented with new symbols using a morphism, these properties may fail to hold. The locality of non-logical symbols, say, is not preserved by the translation [10]. It is not difficult to see that some other schemes also fail to hold.

Another category is determined by specification morphisms:

Theorem 11 (Category of Actor Specifications). Actor specifications and morphisms constitute a finitely co-complete category.

A comparison between our notion of composability and that of [2, 19] is in order here. Given a set of specifications with their pairwise shared sub-components fixed, pushouts of specification morphisms are commutative and have $\Delta_\perp$ as their identity. In addition, all their possible compositions in any order are isomorphic among themselves, which yields associativity up to isomorphism (in the Category Theory sense). Apart from that, the composability notion therein is dynamic and fails to compose configurations having in common identical names of existing actors. This is syntactically immaterial, though, since there is a canonical way of relating actor syntax and semantics, as hinted in [1] and followed here, by obliging the composed specifications to entail configurations with disjoint sets of existing actor addresses. Consequently, we have presented an alternative syntactic formalisation of the composability notion for Actors.

3.5   Example Revisited and Extended

Using the technique described in the previous section, we can now study communities of heterogeneous actors. A good example is obtained by composing a buffer as described in Section 2 with a processor and a set of terminals, to represent a uniprocessor time-sharing architecture. The intended behaviour of this complex component, whose specification shall be called UTSA, is to allow commands typed by terminal users to be always eventually executed. The specification of terminal and processor actors for this purpose appears in Figure 2.

Actor TERMINAL
  data types addr, int
  attributes buf : addr
  actions
      rst(addr) : **local + extrn birth**;
      rd(int) : **local comput**;
      trx(addr) : **extrn message**
  axioms n : addr, v : int
$$rst(n) \rightarrow buf = n \tag{2.1}$$
$$rd(v) \wedge buf = n \leftrightarrows send(trx, n, v) \tag{2.2}$$
End

Actor PROCESSOR
  data types addr, int
  attributes inp, me : addr, $done$: int
  actions
      ini(addr, addr) : **local + extrn birth**;
      exc(int), nop : **local comput**;
      rcv(int) : **local + extrn message**;
      req(addr) : **extrn message**
  axioms n, p : addr, u, v : int
$$ini(n, p) \rightarrow me = n \wedge inp = p \tag{3.1}$$
$$(nop \vee exc(v)) \wedge me = n \rightarrow \mathbf{X}(me = n) \tag{3.2}$$
$$(nop \vee exc(v)) \wedge inp = p \rightarrow \mathbf{X}(inp = p) \tag{3.3}$$
$$nop \wedge done = v \rightarrow \mathbf{X}(done = v) \tag{3.4}$$
$$nop \leftrightarrow send(req, inp, me) \tag{3.5}$$
$$exc(v) \rightarrow \mathbf{X}(done = v) \tag{3.6}$$
$$ini(n, p) \rightarrow \mathbf{G}(rcv(v) \vee exc(v) \leftrightarrow \neg nop) \tag{3.7}$$
$$rcv(v) \leftrightarrows exc(v) \tag{3.8}$$
$$ini(n, p) \rightarrow \mathbf{GE}(\mathbf{deliv}(rcv, v)) \tag{3.9}$$
$$ini(n, p) \rightarrow \mathbf{XG}(\neg exc(v) \rightarrow \mathbf{E}(rcv(u))) \tag{3.10}$$
End

Fig. 2. Simplified specification of terminals and processors

Terminals become aware of the mail address of a cell to serve as their buffer at creation time (2.1). Afterwards, they always transmit typed commands to the buffer to wait for processing (2.2). Processors, in turn, have a more complex behaviour, since they have to request the next command from the buffer at each free processing cycle (3.5). Commands may always be delivered to the processor (3.9). Once received, they are subsequently executed (3.8). The computation cycle of the processor alternates among the occurrence of nop, rcv and exc (3.7), which starts only when its behaviour is initialised using ini (3.1).

Clearly, these actors cannot work as a single component unless the proper connections between them are provided. Morphisms must establish "physical" shared channels to enable message exchange, like in Figure (3.i). As expected, COMPONENT1, COMPONENT2 and UTSA, which result from the composition of the three specified components, are defined up to isomorphism, by the pushout of the respective sub-components. This means that any name for each of their symbols suffices as long as the symbols to be shared and only them are equalised. They are defined according to the two connectors and the morphisms in Figure (3.ii). The signature of CONNECTOR1 contains one external message symbol only, called x, which is mapped to the trx action of terminals and to the put action of buffers. CONNECTOR2 has two actions, which are mapped to get and $reply$ at the buffer side and to req and rcv at the processor side respectively. These morphisms clearly satisfy the requirements of Definition 8.

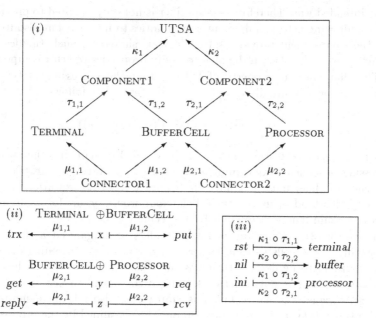

Fig. 3. Static configuration of the system

So far, we have described components consisting of individual actors. To describe communities of similar actors, though, morphisms can also be used. Each diamond in Figure (3.i) should actually have a cube structure, to allow several similar actors to exist concurrently. Considering that the sort symbols of each specification define a category whose morphisms are determined by their use as symbol parameters, as proposed in [9], each diamond vertex becomes source of a signature morphism which adds a new sort morphism to each parameter sort[4]. For instance, the sort p, which is the parameter of *item* with projection $\pi_a : p \to$ int, should be mapped accordingly to p' and to π'_a, such that p' has another projection $\pi'_b : p' \to$ addr to cater for the new parameter sort. Using this kind of structure, it is possible to state properties like

$$\exists n \cdot (k.\mathbf{new}(buffer, n) \wedge (\exists m \cdot k.\mathbf{new}(processor, m, m, n)) \wedge \qquad (2)$$
$$\exists t_1 \cdot k.\mathbf{new}(terminal, t_1, n) \wedge \ldots \wedge \exists t_l \cdot k.\mathbf{new}(terminal, t_l, n))$$

provided that the translations for the birth actions in Figure (3.iii) are given. This kind of property should be guaranteed the environment (some other component connected to UTSA) to ensure the creation of a set of actors configured

---

[4] That is why we consider that morphisms of algebraic structures are limit preserving in Definition 8. Otherwise, the translation of signature symbols would not yield theory interpretations.

in the intended way. Therefore, the specifier is not only required to provide morphisms, allowing actors in different communities to interact, but also to assume that the environment provides some "logical" shared channels (names to bind the actors to each other) to be able to verify properties of actor components.

The characteristic property of UTSA, that the processing of typed commands is always eventually completed, can be stated as follows:

$$\vdash_{\text{UTSA}} \mathbf{G}(t_i.rd(v) \rightarrow \mathbf{F}(m.done = v)) \tag{3}$$

This is an instance of the so-called Fair Merge Problem. In other words, the processing of sequences of commands from each user must be fair, which means that each of them must not have the completion of its execution indefinitely delayed. This kind of inacceptable behaviour would occur, for example, if the processor could ignore commands from specific users.

To verify (3), we use the fact that buffers are organised as finite queues of logically linked cells so that each cell either processes incoming messages or forwards them to be dealt with by its successors, because the cell has already been consumed or is not the last element of the queue, or else it ignores each message, because the entire buffer is empty. We also rely on assumption (2) which insures that user commands can only be consumed by the processor with mail address m. Some auxiliary definitions are required to state these properties:

$$R_n(x,y) \equiv y.nxt = x \wedge y.lst = \text{F}$$
$$P(v) \equiv \exists y \cdot y.cont = v \wedge y.empty = \text{F}$$
$$Q(m,v) \equiv \exists y \cdot y.cont = v \wedge y.\mathbf{send}(reply, m, v)$$

Notice that R_n determines a well-founded relation, whose bottom element is n and which can be formalised as follows, considering always that x and y range over all the address of buffer cells existing in the configuration:

$$\begin{aligned} &\wedge \neg R_n(x,x) \\ &\wedge \mathbf{G}((y.Mod(nxt = x) \wedge \mathbf{X}(R_n(x,y))) \vee y.Inv(nxt)) \rightarrow \mathbf{FG}(y.Inv(nxt)) \end{aligned} \tag{4}$$

The anti-reflexivity of R_n can be verified by first using rule $EXIST$ together with (2) and axioms 1.5/6 to prove as an invariant that a cell cannot be linked to itself ($n.lst = \text{T} \vee n.nxt \neq n$). This implies that the anti-reflexivity of R_n is preserved by the occurrence of $link$. The same can be easily proved for the other actions of BUFFERCELL. By using rule $SAFE$, the anti-reflexivity proof is completed. The second half of (4) is a consequence of the proof in Section 3.3.

The verification of (3) is then decomposed by κ, μ and τ as follows: (i) prove $\vdash_{\text{COMP1}} t_i.rd(v) \rightarrow \mathbf{F}P(v)$ using R_n in the proof rule $WELL$ [8, p. 1057], followed by COM and $RESP$ letting p as in Definition 7 be the invariant above; (ii) prove $\vdash_{\text{PROC}} m.\mathbf{send}(req, n, m) \vee \neg m.nop$ as a consequence of 3.5; (iii) prove $\vdash_{\text{COMP2}} P(v) \rightarrow (m.\mathbf{send}(req, n, m) \vee \neg nop \rightarrow \mathbf{F}Q(m,v))$ as in (i), and (iv) prove $\vdash_{\text{COMP2}} Q(m,v) \rightarrow \mathbf{F}(m.done = v)$ likewise. The formal proof appears elsewhere.

4   Concluding Remarks

In this paper, we have presented an axiomatisation of the kernel primitives of Actors [1] using the framework of temporal logics of objects [9]. We showed not only how actor systems can be specified and verified but also how to compose specifications and decompose proofs using Category Theory. Our main contribution is therefore a logic (in the Institutions sense [11]) for the Actors model. This logic provides a syntactic and more elegant formalisation of interfacing and modularisation structures previously proposed in [1, 2, 19]. In addition, as it is easy to capture in Actors control structures usually found in computing applications such as recursion, they become tractable using our logic.

What makes our logic interesting is the integrated treatment of object creation, asynchronous message passing, fairness and dynamic reconfigurability as they appear in Actors. Other logics for concurrent object-based systems development also exist. We could have extended as a basis for our work the linear time logic proposed in [17] for specifying objects based on action sharing interaction. A proof system for object creation in POOL is described in [3] based on the CSP synchronous primitives. A logic resembling UNITY is proposed in [13] considering asynchrony and fairness. None of these logics provide built-in support to all the characteristics of the Actors model mentioned above.

Having treated all these characteristics, we still have to address the axiomatisation of **become**, which allows an actor to behave according to a distinct specification in its subsequent computation. As we have already pointed out, we could have treated this primitive herein. However, any simplistic treatment would make reasoning a lot more difficult in general. To verify a safety property, for example, we would have to show that it does not depend on the mutations suffered by the actor. Since to maintain the balance between ease to specify and ease to verify is not straightforward, a methodological study of this primitive within our logic — perhaps following [20] — is required.

Acknowledgements: This work has been supported by CNPq, the Brazilian National Research Council. Partial financial support from the ESPRIT WG 8319 *Modelage* is also acknowledged. The diagrams herein were produced using the LATEX style by Paul Taylor. Thanks are due to the anonymous referees for their helpful comments and to the workshop participants for the lively discussions.

References

1. Gul Agha. *Actors: A Model of Concurrent Computation in Distributed Systems.* MIT Press, 1986.
2. Gul Agha, Ian A. Mason, Scott Smith, and Carolyn Talcott. A foundation for actor computation. *Journal of Functional Programming*, 7(1), 1997.
3. Pierre America and Frank de Boer. A proof system for process creation. In Manfred Broy and Cliff B. Jones, editors, *Programming Concepts and Methods*, pages 303–332. North Holland, 1990.
4. Nuno Barreiro, José Fiadeiro, and Tom Maibaum. Politeness in object societies. In Roel Wieringa and Remco Feenstra, editors, *Proc. Information Systems: Correctness and Reusability*, pages 119–134. World Scientific, 1995.

5. Carlos H. C. Duarte. Acidity yields another notion for modularity in formal object-oriented specifications (Extended Abstract). In Max Mühlhäuser, editor, *Special Issues in Object-Oriented Programming*. Dpunkt Verlag, 1996. Workshop Reader of the 10th European Conference on Object-Oriented Programming (ECOOP'96), Linz, Austria.

6. Hans-Dieter Ehrich, Amilcar Sernadas, and Cristina Sernadas. Objects, object types and object identity. In Hartmut Ehrig, editor, *Categorical Methods in Computer Science with Aspects from Topology*, volume 334 of *Lecture Notes in Computer Science*. Springer Verlag, 1988.

7. Hartmut Ehrig and Bernd Mahr. *Fudamentals of Algebraic Specification 1: Equations and Initial Semantics*. Springer Verlag, 1985.

8. E. Allen Emerson. Temporal and modal logic. In J. Van Leeuwen, editor, *Handbook of Theoretical Computer Science*, pages 996–1072. North Holland, 1990.

9. José Fiadeiro and Tom Maibaum. Towards object calculi. Technical report, Department of Computing, Imperial College, London, 1990.

10. José Fiadeiro and Tom Maibaum. Temporal theories as modularisation units for concurrent systems specification. *Formal Aspects of Computing*, 4(3):239–272, 1992.

11. Joseph A. Goguen and Rod M. Burstall. Institutions: Abstract model theory for specification and programming. *Journal of the ACM*, 39(1):95–146, January 1992.

12. Carl Hewitt and Henry Baker. Laws for communicating parallel processes. In *IFIP Congress*, pages 987–992, August 1977.

13. Bengt Jonsson. Compositional specification and verification of distributed systems. *ACM Transactions on Programming Languages and Systems*, 16(2):259–303, March 1994.

14. Leslie Lamport. What good is temporal logic? In R. E. A. Mason, editor, *Proc. Information Processing 83: IFIP 9th World Congress*, pages 657–668. North Holland, September 1983.

15. Tom Maibaum and Wladyslaw Tursky. On what exactly is going on when software is developed step-by-step. In *Proc. 7th International Conference on Software Engineering (ICSE'84)*, pages 525–533. IEEE Computer Society Press, March 1984.

16. Michel Raynal and Masaaki Mizzymo. How to find his way in this jungle of consistency criteria for distributed shared memories. In *Proc. 4th Workshop on Future Trends of Distributed Computing Systems*, pages 340–346. IEEE Computer Society Press, September 1993.

17. Amílcar Sernadas, Cristina Sernadas, and José Félix Costa. Object specification logic. *Journal of Logic and Computation*, 5(5):603–630, 1995.

18. A. Prashad Sistla, Emerson M. Clarke, Nissim Francez, and Albert R. Meyer. Can message buffers be axiomatized in linear temporal logic? *Information and Computation*, 63:88–112, 1984.

19. Carolyn Talcott. Interaction semantics for components of distributed systems. In Elie Najm and Jean-Bernard Stefani, editors, *Proc. 1st IFIP Workshop on Formal Methods for Open Object-Based Distributed Systems (FMOODS'96)*. Chapman and Hall, 1996.

20. Roel Wieringa, Wiebren de Jonge, and Paul Spruit. Roles and dynamic subclasses: a modal logic approach. In Mario Tokoro and Remo Pareschi, editors, *Proc. Object Oriented Programming, 8th European Conference (ECOOP'94)*, volume 821 of *Lecture Notes in Computer Science*, pages 32–59, 1994.

Nondeterministic Actions with Typical Effects: Reasoning about Scenarios

Barbara Dunin-Kęplicz[1] and Anna Radzikowska[2]

[1] Institute of Informatics, Warsaw University
Banacha 2, 02-097 Warsaw, Poland
Email: keplicz@mimuw.edu.pl

[2] Institute of Mathematics, Warsaw University of Technology
Plac Politechniki 1, 00-661 Warsaw, Poland
Email: annrad@im.pw.edu.pl

Abstract. We continue to study the problem of actions with *typical*, but not certain effects. In [3], [2] we showed how to incorporate this kind of actions into a dynamic/epistemic multi-agent system in which the knowledge, abilities and opportunities of agents are formalized together with the results of actions they perform. The novelty of the present approach is that it allows a nondeterminism in action performance. Moreover, compound actions are built both from traditionally viewed actions with certain effects and actions with typical effects. Adopting a model-theoretic approach we formalize a preferential strategy in order to reason about the results of the realizations of scenarios built over these actions.

1 Introduction

The formalization of multi-agent autonomous systems requires a rich repertoire of actions to capture a variety of agents' behaviour. The agents may be viewed as systems which continuously sense a dynamic environment they are embedded in, and which effect changes by performing actions or plans of actions (see [4]). These plans result in the planning process directed towards achieving some goals. However, independently of the method of planning, an agent's goal is usually achievable in different ways reflected in a set of plans. Plans are usually defined in terms of actions with certain effects, that is as sequences of these actions.

But there may be also another option. One may consider actions leading to some effects, being aware that these effects may be achieved in different ways, e.g. by distinguishing different types of action execution. Next, from the set of possible action performances some may be characterized as typical ones, leading to some extra - typical - effects. In other - atypical - cases there is no information about additional effects. Thus, a distinction between *typical* and *atypical* action performance results in different changes in the external world (see, for instance, [12], [13], [14]): a typical action execution leads not only to a certain effect (which always hold), but also leads to *typical* or *default* effects.

J.-J. Ch. Meyer, P.-Y. Schobbens (Eds.): Formal Methods of Agents, LNAI 1760, pp. 143-156, 1999.
© Springer-Verlag Berlin Heidelberg 1999

The application of actions with typical effects is justified in situations when either the way of achieving a goal is inessential from the agent's point of view, or is hard to predict during planning, but possible to dynamically determine during a plan execution. Let us stress that this approach essentially simplifies the planning process: particular actions with typical effects assure the achievement of partial goals in the plan without coming into details. Thus, the use of these actions maintains a rather high level of abstraction — the way of action performance has been determined by an agent "on line", i.e. during plan execution, instead of the agent deciding about it in advance. So this kind of planning is very flexible: a single plan containing actions with typical effects reflects a set of plans built from analogical actions with certain effects.

The important characteristics of these actions is their usefullness in reacting to unpredictable changes in the dynamic environment — they increase an agent's *reactivity*. For example, a particular change in the external world may definitely block a performance of an action with certain effects. However, when treating this action as the one with default effects, its atypical performance may save the realization of the plan.

In [3], [2] we model this new kind of actions by means of extending the epistemic/dynamic framework presented in [7], [8], [9]. This formal system is designed to deal with both the knowledge and the abilities of agents, and with the effects of actions they perform. Our extension provides the formalization of a deterministic version of actions with typical effects. However, the opposition of typical - atypical action performance turns out not to be subtle enough to fully characterize the variety of situations an agent may deal with. The novelty of the present approach is that it allows nondeterminism in the performance of an action.

Analogously to [3], when considering actions in isolation we assume that an agent's generic intention is to prefer a typical action performance. However, to adequately model plans of actions, the specific *preferential strategy* should be related to the characteristics (i.e. the type) of this plan. In this paper we focus on scenarios reflecting a "typical" pattern of agents' behaviour, thus we model a *nonmonotonic* preferential strategy that can be viewed as a minimization of atypical performances of actions. Within our epistemic/dynamic framework we apply this strategy to reason about scenarios, i.e. to determine a set of *desirable conclusions* which can be derived from a given scenario.

Our formal framework is designed from the perspective of a single agent, with special attention paid to different types of actions it can perform. Other aspects of multi-agent systems, including collective and social characteristics of agents' behaviour, will be the subject of a future extension of our approach.

The paper is structured in the following manner. In Section 2 and 3 we discuss notions of nondeterministic actions with typical effects and scenarios built over the traditionally viewed actions as well as those of the new type. In Section 4 we present a language defined to represent scenarios under consideration, whereas in Section 5 we provide its semantics. In Section 6 a notion of scenario realization is formalized. The paper is completed with concluding remarks and options for further research.

2   Nondeterministic Actions with Typical Effects

When defining the *result* of an action we follow the idea of [17] to identify the state of affairs resulting from the action execution with its effect. We consider an event $do_i(\alpha)$ referring to the performance of an action α by an agent i. Therefore the results of an event may be represented by a formula

$$(do_i(\alpha))\,\varphi,$$

stating that an agent i has the *opportunity* to perform an action α and that doing α leads to φ.

An opportunity of an agent to perform a certain action reflects almost wholly external, objective circumstances. Apart from agent's opportunities, we adopt a generic concept of agent's *abilities* (cf. [7]), covering physical, mental and moral capacities. Viewing abilities as a separate concept enables us to remove them as a prerequisite of an action performance. In order to formalize agents abilities an operator $\mathbf{A}$ is introduced. An expression $\mathbf{A}_i\alpha$ reflects the fact that an agent i is capable to perform an action α. A combination of both $(do_i(\alpha))\,\varphi$ and $\mathbf{A}_i\alpha$ expresses the idea that α is a *correct* $((do_i(\alpha))\,\varphi)$ and *feasible* $(\mathbf{A}_i\alpha)$ plan for agent i to achieve φ.

Now we are in a position to characterize a new kind of actions — actions with typical (default) effects which will be referred to as Δ-actions. The generic characteristics of Δ-actions is that they have different effects in typical and atypical performances: different changes in an external world can be distinguished depending on the way the action is executed.

The result of performing a Δ-action is represented by

$$(do_i(\alpha))\,\varphi,\psi$$

denoting, analogously, that an agent i has the opportunity to perform a Δ-action α and as a result of this event φ (always) holds and *typically* ψ holds. In other words, φ may be viewed as a certain and ψ as a typical effect of a Δ-action α.

Consider an example of the action Get_To_Airport. I can go there by taxi, by bus, or someone may drive me. Hiring a taxi is viewed as a typical execution of this action, but depending on circumstances I can decide differently. If I want to make up my mind at the last moment, according to my current abilities and possibilities (e.g. my friend with a car just visiting me), the use of actions with typical effects enables me to do so. The results of the example execution of this action may be represented by

$$(do_I(\text{Get\_To\_Airport}))\;\text{`}I\_am\_in\_airport\text{'},\;\text{`}I\_spend\_money\_on\_taxi\text{'}.$$

Another example is the formalization of the action Appointment_with_Cris, usually resulting in attending a concert together:

$$(do_I(\text{Meet\_Chris}))\;\text{`}I\_spend\_time\_with\_Chris\text{'},\;\text{`}I\_attend\_concert\text{'}.$$

In our approach we decided to specify only typical effects of action execution, abstracting from the actions' atypical results. This modelling decision reflects the idea that atypical effects of the performance a Δ-action α may be unpredictable.

When having a full description of the external world and of possible effects of all actions, one can also try to specify what may happen as the result of atypical action performance.

However, this characterization of the results of deterministic Δ-actions seems not to be subtle enough to describe the variety of situations an agent may face. The opposition typical - atypical action performance is not sufficiently context-sensitive when an agent has only one possibility of typical or atypical action execution (c.f. [3], [2]). So, we admit nondeterministic actions with typical effects. The nondeterminism is considered in the context of an agent's opportunities, reflecting mainly circumstantial conditions (its abilities do not depend on external circumstances) and may be considered in two respects.

First, the external (objective) nondeterminism on the level of the choice between typical and atypical action performance. Second, the internal (subjective) nondeterminism on the level of the choice between various possibilities of typical or atypical action performance. While the objective nondeterminism depends on the external circumstances, the internal one reflects an agent's (subjective) rather than objective choices.

While performing some Δ-action an agent i may proceed in a typical or atypical way but when considering an action in isolation, it usually prefers (one of) a typical execution of the action. Additionally, for Δ-actions, analogously to actions with certain effects, the characterization of correctness is applied.

3   A Scenario Realization

In this paper we focus on a rational agent (see [18]) and its activity directed to achieve some goals as a result of a plan execution. The plan, reflecting a sequence of actions, is either prepared by an agent itself or is given to it. In order to formalize an agent's plan we introduce the notion of a scenario. A *scenario* for an agent reflects a sequence of actions to be performed by this agent together with initial and final observations. An *initial observation* characterizes an initial state of affairs, including a generic precondition for execution of the scenario. A *final observation* must reflect the goals an agent wants to achieve. It may also characterize a final state of affairs.

We introduce the following notation. Let $\gamma_{pre}, \gamma_{post}$ be any formulas from the object language $\mathcal{L}$. The sequence $Sc = <\alpha_1, \ldots, \alpha_n>$ of actions to be performed by an agent i, $\alpha_k \in \mathcal{A}c$ (the set of actions), $k = 1, \ldots, n$, with the precondition γ_{pre} and the postcondition γ_{post}, is said to be a *scenario for an agent i* and denoted by $\mathrm{SCD}(i, \{\gamma_{pre}\}Sc\{\gamma_{post}\})$ or simply SCD.

In AI literature various types of scenarios have been studied (see [15], [3]). When considering a *typical character* of action performance, the situation becomes more complicated. Moreover, allowing nondeterministic action in the scenario increases the number of possiblilities to achieve the goal. A notion of a *scenario realization* (for an agent i) reflects both the execution of each action occurring in the scenario and the agent achieving its final goals. While modelling the behaviour of a rational agent we want to reflect its preferred choices. When an agent considers an action performance in isolation, it prefers (one of) typical action execution, whereas from the perspective of a scenario realization it may admit (one of) atypical courses of action performance. However, an agent's choice should always reflect a generic preferential strategy.

In the paper we focus on a typical plans, where a sequence of actions is planned in advance, in order to achieve that agent's goals become a part of the final observations after plan execution. We assume that effectiveness of an agent's behaviour usually depends on how typical execution of each element of the plan is. Possible disturbances – atypical executions of some actions – may either preclude achieving the final goals (in the worst case) or may change the way to achieve them. For this reason the applied preferential strategy amounts to a minimization of atypical performances of actions.

The realization of a given scenario based on an adequate preferential strategy, leads to certain conclusion states. As a final point of scenario realization we are in a position to determine the set of all statements that hold in all these states. We will refer to this set as the set of *desirable conclusions*.

4 The object language

In this section we show how to extend the framework defined to formalize the behaviour of rational agents in a multi-agent system. This approach, defined in [7], [8] and [9], considers epistemic aspects like agents' knowledge as well as the results of actions they perform, together with agents' opportunities and abilities to perform particular actions.

Definition 4.1 (Language $\mathcal{L}$)
The language $\mathcal{L}$ is based on the following three sets:

- a denumerable set $\mathcal{P}$ of *propositional symbols (fluents* in AI terminology);
- a finite set $\mathcal{A}$ of *agents*, denoted by numerals $1, 2, \ldots, n$;
- a finite set At of *atomic actions*, denoted by a or b; this set includes a nonempty subset At_Δ of atomic Δ-actions.

The set of formulas (the language $\mathcal{L}$) is the smallest set satisfying the following conditions:

- $p \in \mathcal{L}$, for each $p \in P$;
- if $\varphi, \phi \in \mathcal{L}$, then $\neg\varphi \in \mathcal{L}$ and $\varphi \vee \phi \in \mathcal{L}$;
- if $i \in \mathcal{A}$ and $\varphi \in \mathcal{L}$, then $\mathbf{K}_i\varphi \in \mathcal{L}$;
- if $i \in \mathcal{A}$ and $\alpha \in \mathcal{A}c$, then $\mathbf{A}_i\alpha \in \mathcal{L}$;
- if $i \in \mathcal{A}$, $\alpha \in \mathcal{A}c$ and $\varphi, \psi \in \mathcal{L}$, then $(\mathrm{do}_i(\alpha))\,\varphi \in \mathcal{L}$, $(\mathrm{do}_i(\alpha))\,\varphi, \psi \in \mathcal{L}$

The class $\mathcal{A}c$ of actions is the smallest set such that

- $At \subseteq \mathcal{A}c$;
- if $\alpha_1, \alpha_2 \in \mathcal{A}c$, then $\alpha_1; \alpha_2 \in \mathcal{A}c$;   (sequential composition)

– if $\varphi \in \mathcal{L}$ and $\alpha_1, \alpha_2 \in \mathcal{A}c$, then **if** φ **then** α_1 **else** α_2 **fi** $\in \mathcal{A}c$;

(conditional composition)

– if $\varphi \in \mathcal{L}$ and $\alpha \in \mathcal{A}c$, then **while** φ **do** α **od** $\in \mathcal{A}c$ (repetitive composition)

The constructs $True$, $False$, $\wedge$, $\rightarrow$ and $\equiv$ are defined in the usual way. Moreover, the following abbreviations are introduced:
skip $= empty\ action$; $\alpha^0 = $ **skip**; $\alpha^{k+1} = \alpha^k; \alpha$.

Remark 4.1 Intuitively the formula $\mathbf{K}_i \varphi$ states that an agent i knows about the fact represented by φ, whereas $\mathbf{A}_i \alpha$ states that the agent i is able to perform an action α. Moreover, the formulae $(\mathrm{do}_i(\alpha))\,\varphi$ and $(\mathrm{do}_i(\alpha))\,\varphi, \psi$ are explained in section 2.   □

Remark 4.2 The set of actions under consideration contains atomic actions with certain effects, atomic Δ-actions and compound actions built from any kind of actions. Sets of actions are related to agents.   □

5   Semantics for the language

In this section we define the semantics for the language $\mathcal{L}$. This semantics is based on the notion of Kripke model.

Definition 5.1 (Kripke model)
A Kripke model is a tuple $\mathcal{M} = (S, val, R, r, t, c)$ such that

1. S is a set of possible worlds, or states;

2. $val : P \times S \rightarrow \{0,1\}$ is a function that assigns truth values to fluents in states;

3. $R : \mathcal{A} \rightarrow \wp(S \times S)$ is the function that yields the accessibility relation for a given agent i, i.e. $(s_1, s_2) \in R(i)$ states that s_2 is an epistemic alternative for an agent i in a state s. Since we assume the modal system KT, $R(i)$ is reflexive for all $i \in \mathcal{A}$;

4. $r : \mathcal{A} \times \mathcal{A}t \rightarrow S \rightarrow \wp(S)$ is such that $r(i,a)(s)$ yields the result of performing an action a by an agent i in a state s;

5. $t : \mathcal{A} \times \mathcal{A}t \rightarrow S \rightarrow \wp(S)$ is such that $t(i,a)(s)$ yields the result of (typical) performing of an action a by an agent i in a state s; this function is such that

   • $\forall i \in \mathcal{A}\ \forall a \in \mathcal{A}t_\Delta\ \forall s \in S\ t(i,a)(s) \subset r(i,a)(s)$

   • $\forall i \in \mathcal{A}\ \forall s \in S\ \forall a \in \mathcal{A}t \setminus \mathcal{A}t_\Delta\ t(i,a)(s) = r(i,a)(s)$.

6. $c : \mathcal{A} \times \mathcal{A}t \rightarrow S \rightarrow \{0,1\}$ is the capability function such that $c(i,a)(s)$ indicates that an agent i is able to perform the action a in a state s.   □

Remark 5.1 It is worth noting that no demands on the interconnections between functions r and c are imposed. This leads to the formalization of agent's abilities and opportunities as separate concepts.

The function t is introduced to formalize a typical performance of a Δ-action by an agent i. Since certain effects of an action may be viewed as typical ones (clearly, not vice versa), we assume a performance of an action with certain effects to be typical.   □

The functions r, t and c can be extended for the class Ac of all actions (not only atomic). That is, the extension of r, written r^*, is defined by:[3]

$$r^* : \qquad\qquad A \times Ac \to \wp(S) \to \wp(S)$$

$$r^*(i,a)(s) \qquad\qquad = r(i,a)(s) \quad \text{for } a \in At$$

$$r^*(i,\alpha_1 ; \alpha_2)(s) \qquad\qquad = r^*(i,\alpha_2)(r^*(i,\alpha_1)(s))$$

$$r^*(i,\textbf{if } \varphi \textbf{ then } \alpha_1 \textbf{ else } \alpha_2)(s) = \begin{cases} r^*(i,\alpha_1) & \text{iff } \mathcal{M},s \models \varphi \\ r^*(i,\alpha_2) & \text{otherwise} \end{cases}$$

$$r^*(i,\textbf{while } \varphi \textbf{ do } \alpha \textbf{ od})(s) = \{s' \in S : \exists \mathcal{K} \subseteq \mathbb{N} \; \forall k \in \mathcal{K} \; \exists s_0, \dots, s_k. \; s_0 = s \; \& \\ s_k = s' \; \& \; [\forall j < k. \; s_{j+1} \in r^*(i,\alpha)(s_j) \; \& \; \mathcal{M},s_j \models \varphi] \\ \& \; \mathcal{M},s' \models \neg\varphi\}$$

$$\text{For } A \in \wp(S) : r^*(i,\alpha)(A) \quad = \bigcup_{s \in A} r^*(i,\alpha)(s)$$

$$\text{thus } r^*(i,\alpha)(\emptyset) \qquad\qquad = \emptyset$$

For atomic actions, sequential and repetitive compositions, r^* is defined in the usual way.

Obviously, for some states s an agent i has no opportunity to perform an action α, so it certainly does not have any opportunity to execute any compound action starting from α. Since for such states $r^*(i,\alpha)(s) = \emptyset$, we put $r^*(i,\alpha)(\emptyset) = \emptyset$.

Defining r^* for a repetitive composition (**while** φ **do** α **od**) we consider all possible sequences of states $< s_0, \dots, s_k >$ (of any length k) such that an agent i, starting in s_0, performs α as long as φ holds. A performance of a repetitive composition leads to *any* final state of such sequences.

$t^* : A \times Ac \to \wp(S) \to \wp(S)$ is defined analogously. While defining t^* we consider typical action performances only. Let us recall that certain effects are viewed as typical ones. Therefore, for any $i \in A$, $\alpha \in Ac$ and $s \in S$ we have

$$t^*(i,\alpha)(s) \subseteq r^*(i,\alpha)(s).$$

The extension c^* is defined as follows

$$c^* : \qquad\qquad A \times Ac \to S \to \{0,1\}$$

$$c^*(i,a)(s) \quad = c(i,a)(s) \text{ for } a \in At$$

$$c^*(i,\alpha_1 ; \alpha_2)(s) = \begin{cases} 1 & \text{iff } c^*(i,\alpha_1)(s) = 1 \; \& \\ & \quad \exists s' \in r^*(i,\alpha_1)(s). \; c^*(i,\alpha_2)(s') = 1 \\ 0 & \text{otherwise} \end{cases}$$

---

[3] Here the state $s \in S$ is identified with the singleton set $\{s\}$.

$$c^*(i, \textbf{if } \varphi \textbf{ then } \alpha_1 \textbf{ else } \alpha_2 \textbf{ fi})(s) = \begin{cases} 1 & \text{iff } c^*(i, \alpha_1)(s) = 1 \; \& \; \mathcal{M}, s \models \varphi \\ & \text{or } c^*(i, \alpha_2)(s) = 1 \; \& \; \mathcal{M}, s \models \neg\varphi \\ 0 & \text{otherwise} \end{cases}$$

$$c^*(i, \textbf{while } \varphi \textbf{ do } \alpha \textbf{ od})(s) = \begin{cases} 1 & \text{iff } \exists \mathcal{K} \subseteq \mathbb{N} \; \forall k \in \mathcal{K} \; \exists s_0, \ldots, s_k. \, s_0 = s \; \& \\ & \& \; s_k = s' \; \& \; [\forall j < k. \, c^*(i, \alpha)(s_j) = 1 \; \& \\ & \& \; \mathcal{M}, s_j \models \varphi \; \& \; s_{j+1} \in r^*(i, \alpha)(s_j)] \; \& \\ & \& \; c^*(i, \alpha)(s') = 1 \; \& \; \mathcal{M}, s' \models \neg\varphi \\ 0 & \text{otherwise} \end{cases}$$

and $c^*(i, \alpha)(\emptyset) = 0.$ □

Recall that an agent's capabilities are not related to its opportunities, viewed as circumstantial possibilities. However, from the standpoint of commonsense reasoning, it makes little sense to consider what an agent's capabilities are in unreachable states (i.e. states that it has no opportunity to reach from a given state s). It seems intuitively justified to assume that in such states an agent has no capability to perform any action at all. Thus we put $c^*(i, \alpha)(\emptyset) = 0$.

By $\mathcal{M}$ we denote the class of all Kripke models.

Definition 5.2 (Defining $\models$)
Let $\mathcal{M} = (S, val, R, r, t, c)$ be a Kripke model from $\mathcal{M}$. For any propositional formula φ, $\mathcal{M}, s \models \varphi$ is defined in the usual way.
For other formulas it is defined as follows:

$\mathcal{M}, s \models (\text{do}_i(\alpha)) \, \varphi$ iff $[\forall s' \in r^*(i, \alpha)(s) \; \mathcal{M}, s' \models \varphi] \; \&$
                                  $[\exists s' \in r^*(i, \alpha)(s) \; \mathcal{M}, s' \models \varphi]$

$\mathcal{M}, s \models (\text{do}_i(\alpha)) \, \varphi, \psi$ iff $[\forall s' \in r^*(i, \alpha)(s) \; \mathcal{M}, s' \models \varphi] \; \&$
                                  $[\forall s'' \in t^*(i, \alpha)(s) \; \mathcal{M}, s'' \models \psi] \; \&$
                                  $[\exists s'' \in t^*(i, \alpha)(s) \; \mathcal{M}, s'' \models \psi]$

$\mathcal{M}, s \models \textbf{A}_i \alpha$ iff $c^*(i, \alpha)(s) = 1$

$\mathcal{M}, s \models \textbf{K}_i \varphi$ iff $\forall s' \, [(s, s') \in R(i) \Rightarrow \mathcal{M}, s' \models \varphi]$ □

A formula φ is said to be *satisfiable in $\mathcal{M}$ in a state s* iff $\mathcal{M}, s \models \varphi$.

Remark 5.2 A formula $(\text{do}_i(\alpha)) \, \varphi$ is satisfiable in $\mathcal{M}$ in a state $s \in S$ if in all states accessible from s (by performing an action α by an agent i) φ holds, and if at least one of such states exists. On the other hand, a formula $(\text{do}_i(\alpha)) \varphi, \psi$ is satisfiable in $\mathcal{M}$ in a state $s \in S$ if in *all* states s' accessible from s (by performing the action α by an agent i) φ holds, and in *all* states s'' accessible from s by a typical performance of α (i.e. from the set $t^*(i, \alpha)(s)$) ψ is satisfied, and if at least one of such states exists. □

6   Modelling scenario realization

In this section we provide a formalization of reasoning about scenarios for a given agent. We aim to determine the set of desirable conclusions resulting from the scenario realization.

Let us recall the postulates imposed on scenarios.

S1. The scenario contains a sequence of actions of various types built from atomic actions with certain or typical effects;

S2. Each Δ-action performed by an agent introduces different changes in the external world depending on whether the agent performs it typically or atypically;

S3. The applied preferential strategy is based on the minimization of atypical performances of actions;

S4. The final goal after performing a given scenario, including an adequate preferential strategy, is to determine the set of statements characterizing the preferred concluding states.

Let us recall that a *scenario for an agent i* denoted by $\text{SCD}(i, \{\gamma_{pre}\} Sc \{\gamma_{post}\})$ reflects the sequence $Sc = <\alpha_1, \ldots, \alpha_n>$ of actions to be performed by an agent i, $\alpha_k \in Ac$, $k = 1, \ldots, n$, with a precondition γ_{pre} and a postcondition γ_{post}. Intuitively the precondition γ_{pre} and the postcondition γ_{post} indicate initial and final observations (including the agent's goals), respectively, i.e. statements which represent knowledge, abilities and/or opportunities of both the agent i and some other agents.

Definition 6.1 (Model for a scenario realization)
Let $\mathcal{M}$ be a Kripke model and $\text{SCD}(i, \{\gamma_{pre}\} Sc \{\gamma_{post}\})$ be a scenario for an agent i. We say that $\mathcal{M}$ is a *model for a scenario SCD realization* (a model of SCD, for short) iff there exist two states $s_1, s_2 \in S$ such that

- $\mathcal{M}, s_1 \models \gamma_{pre}$ and $\mathcal{M}, s_2 \models \gamma_{post}$;
- $s_2 \in r^*(i, Sc)(s_1)$ and $c^*(i, Sc)(s_1) = 1$. □

By $\text{MOD}(\text{SCD})$ we denote the class of all models of a given scenario SCD.

6.1   Preferred models of a scenario realization

Having determined the set of Kripke models of the scenario, we are in a position to choose those models which reflect a preferential strategy adequate for a considered type of scenario. As we focus on the generic scenario in this paper , the preferential strategy amounts to the minimization of atypical performances of actions from this scenario.

Note that in a given model $\mathcal{M}$ of a scenario SCD, the sequence Sc of actions may be decomposed into atomic actions (number of atomic actions differs in various scenario realizations due to nondeterminism of actions). The idea is to count atypical atomic action executions during a particular realization of a scenario. Our preferential strategy amounts to selecting models of a scenario realization with minimal numbers of atypical state transitions (i.e. those corresponding to atypical performance of a Δ-action).

To formalize these ideas we introduce some auxiliary notions.

Given a Kripke model $\mathcal{M} = (S, val, R, r, t, c)$ we define a *transition penalty function* $p : \mathcal{A} \times \mathcal{A}t \times S \times S \rightarrow \mathbb{N}$ given by

$$
p(i, \alpha, s_1, s_2) = \begin{cases} 0 & \text{iff } s_2 \in t(i, \alpha)(s_1) \text{ and } c(i, \alpha)(s_1) = 1 \\ 1 & \text{iff } s_2 \in r(i, \alpha)(s_1), \; s_2 \notin t(i, \alpha)(s_2) \text{ and } c(i, \alpha)(s_1) = 1 \\ +\infty & \text{otherwise} \end{cases}
$$

The underlying intuition is as follows. For an agent i, an atomic action α and two states s_1 and s_2, we impose zero "penalty points" whenever the agent i is capable to perform α in a state s_1 and a typical performance of α leads to the state s_2. However, if it performs α atypically resulting in a state s_2, then we impose one penalty point. In other cases infinitely many penalty points are imposed (e.g. the agent i is not capable to perform α in a state s_1 or a state s_2 is unreachable for it by execution of α).

This function can be extended for compound actions in the following manner. The function $p^* : \mathcal{A} \times \mathcal{A}c \times S \times S \rightarrow \mathbb{N}$ is defined as follows

$$
p^*(i, \alpha_1; \alpha_2, s_1, s_2) = \min_{s \in S} \{ p^*(i, \alpha_1, s_1, s) + p^*(i, \alpha_2, s, s_2) \}
$$

$$
p^*(i, \text{if } \varphi \text{ then } \alpha_1 \text{ else } \alpha_2 \text{ fi}, s_1, s_2) = \begin{cases} p^*(i, \alpha_1, s_1, s_2) & \text{iff } \mathcal{M} \models \varphi \\ p^*(i, \alpha_2, s_1, s_2) & \text{otherwise} \end{cases}
$$

$$
p^*(i, \text{while } \varphi \text{ do } \alpha \text{ od}, s_1, s_2) = \min_{\bar{\mathbf{s}}_{(k)} \in \bar{\mathbf{S}}} \sum_{j=0}^{k-1} p^*(i, \alpha, s'_j, s'_{j+1}), \text{ where } \bar{\mathbf{S}} = \bigcup_{k=0}^{\infty} \bar{\mathbf{S}}_k
$$

and $\bar{\mathbf{S}}_k$ is a set of all sequences $\bar{\mathbf{s}}_{(k)} = < s'_0, \ldots, s'_k >$ of states such that $s'_0 = s_1, s'_k = s_2, \mathcal{M}, s_2 \models \neg\varphi$, and for each $j = 0, \ldots, k-1$, $\mathcal{M}, s'_j \models \varphi$

Defining the function p^* for a sequential composition, all states in a given Kripke structure are considered as intermediate states resulting from the performance of α_1 in a state s_1 by an agent i. Then penalty points imposed on the corresponding two transitions are added. A minimal number of these points determines a global number of penalty points for a sequential composition.

For a repetitive composition a minimal number of atypical state transitions is defined in the following way. We consider every sequence of states $< s'_o, \ldots, s'_k >$ (of any length k) that ends in a state s_2, where s'_{i+1} results from a performance of α in s'_i and the condition φ holds in each state of this sequence except the last one. Adding penalty points corresponding to each intermediate transition we count a "penalty" for this sequence. A minimal penalty obtained for these sequences determines the number of penalty points for a repetitive composition.

For a model $\mathcal{M}$ of a scenario, the transition penalty function $p^*(i, \alpha, s_1, s_2)$ determines for an agent i the minimal number of atypical atomic Δ-actions which occur during performance of the action α leading from s_1 to s_2.

Given a Kripke model $\mathcal{M}$ and a scenario $\text{SCD}(i, \{\gamma_{pre}\}Sc\{\gamma_{post}\})$ we define a *penalty function* $P^{\mathcal{M}}_{\text{SCD}} : S \times S \to \mathbb{N}$ as follows

$$P^{\mathcal{M}}_{\text{SCD}}(s_1, s_2) = \begin{cases} +\infty & \text{iff } \mathcal{M}, s_1 \not\models \gamma_{pre} \text{ or } \mathcal{M}, s_2 \not\models \gamma_{post} \\ p^*(i, Sc, s_1, s_2) & \text{otherwise} \end{cases}$$

This function determines for the agent i a minimal number of atypical state transitions which occur during realization of the scenario SCD.

Given a Kripke model $\mathcal{M}$ and a scenario $\text{SCD}(i, \{\gamma_{pre}\}Sc\{\gamma_{post}\})$ for an agent i, the value

$$PV(\mathcal{M}, \text{SCD}) = \min_{s_1, s_2 \in S} P^{\mathcal{M}}_{\text{SCD}}(s_1, s_2)$$

is said to be the *penalty value for a scenario* SCD *in a model* $\mathcal{M}$.

Example 6.1 Consider the following scenario for an agent i:
$\text{SCD}(i, \{\gamma_{pre}\} A; B; C \{\gamma_{post}\})$, where A, B and C are atomic actions.

Let $\mathcal{M}$ be the Kripke model depicted in Fig.1, where typical (and certain) transitions are denoted by thickened vectors.

Suppose that the precondition γ_{pre} holds in the state s_1, but it is not satisfied in $s2$. Furthermore, assume that the postcondition γ_{post} holds in the state s_{11} but does not in states s_{10} and s_{12}.

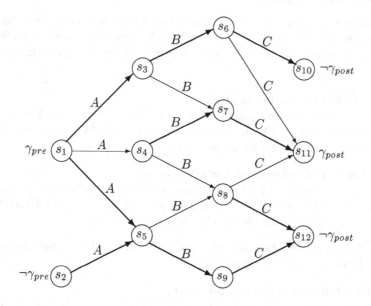

Fig.1

In order to realize the scenario and to reach the state s_{11}, the agent i has the five possibilities corresponding to the following sequences of states:

$$p_1 = <s_1, s_3, s_6, s_{11}>$$
$$p_2 = <s_1, s_3, s_7, s_{11}>$$
$$p_3 = <s_1, s_4, s_7, s_{11}>$$
$$p_4 = <s_1, s_4, s_8, s_{11}>$$
$$p_5 = <s_1, s_5, s_8, s_{11}>$$

It is easily noted that only one atypical transition occurs on the first three paths, whereas there are three such transitions on the path p_4 and two on the path p_5. Thus the penalty value for this scenario in $\mathcal{M}$ is $PV(\mathcal{M}, SCD) = 1$. $\square$

Having determined the penalty value for a scenario SCD in $\mathcal{M}$ we are in a position to prefer models of SCD.

Definition 6.2 (Preferred model)
Let SCD be a scenario and $\mathcal{M}_1, \mathcal{M}_2 \in \mathcal{M}$ be Kripke models. We say that $\mathcal{M}_1$ *is preferred over $\mathcal{M}_2$ with respect to the scenario SCD*, written $\mathcal{M}_1 \preceq_{SCD} \mathcal{M}_2$, iff $\mathcal{M}_1, \mathcal{M}_2 \in \text{MOD}(SCD)$ and $PV(\mathcal{M}_1, SCD) \leq PV(\mathcal{M}_2, SCD)$. $\square$

Given a scenario SCD for an agent i we write PMOD(SCD) to denote the class of all preferred models for SCD. Obviously, what we are actually interested in is the set of conclusions entailed by the given scenario SCD. As expected, this set is to be defined in terms of preferred models.

6.2   Scenario completion

By *scenario completion* we understand the operation of taking the scenario description, performing this scenario using the adequate nonmonotonic preferential strategy and concluding as much as possible from the resulting conclusion states.

Definition 6.3 (Conclusion states)
Let SCD be a scenario for an agent i and $\mathcal{M} \in \text{PMOD}(SCD)$ be a Kripke model. *Conclusion states* for SCD in $\mathcal{M}$, written $\text{Conc}(SCD, \mathcal{M})$, is the set $\{s \in S : P^{\mathcal{M}}_{SCD}(s', s) = PV(\mathcal{M}, SCD)$ for some $s' \in S\}$. $\square$

Definition 6.4 (Preferential Entailment $\approx$)
Let SCD be a scenario for an agent i and let $\beta \in \mathcal{L}$ be a formula. We say that SCD *preferentially entails β*, written $SCD \approx \beta$, iff for each $\mathcal{M} \in \text{PMOD}(SCD)$ and for each state $s \in \text{Conc}(SCD, \mathcal{M})$, $\mathcal{M}, s \models \beta$. $\square$

The following definition specifies the set of desirable conclusions resulting from realization of a given scenario.

Definition 6.5 (Scenario completion)
Let SCD be a scenario for an agent i. A set $\Gamma(SCD) = \{\beta : SCD \approx \beta\}$ is called a *scenario completion* for SCD. $\square$

7 Conclusions and Directions for Future Work

In this paper we semantically investigated a *nondeterminstic* actions with typical, but not necessarily certain, effects. We show how to incorporate this new kind of actions into epistemic/dynamic multi-agent system.

In the AI literature actions are usually studied in the context of scenarios. We focus on scenarios reflecting a typical pattern of behaviour of a rational agent in a multi-agent system. To capture nonmonotonic aspects of scenarios, their realizations are modelled by defining a preferential strategy which can be viewed as a minimization of atypical performances of actions. As a final step of reasoning about a scenario we determine the set of desirable conclusions to be derived from it.

In our formalization of actions and in reasoning about scenarios, the epistemic part represented by the **K** operator remain inactive. In future, the agent's knowledge may be used in the planning process, during inference about the agent's abilities and opportunities, and also when considering actions which may change the agent's mind.

There are still several topics that need to be studied. To adequately capture the variety of problems appearing during reasoning about action and change, our most important goal is to resolve the frame problem and the ramification problem in the framework presented in this paper. Next, formal properties of our formalism, as well as should be investigated. Finally, different kinds of scenarios built over Δ-actions with corresponding preferential strategies may be studied.

Another line of reserch is strictly related to multiagent systems paradigm, namely to Beliefs, Desires and Intentions - architectures. In cooperative problem solving, collective and social aspects of informational and motivational attitudes received a lot of attention lately (see [5], [1]). When considering teamwork, next step is to design actions to be performed by groups of agents. Also social and collective action with typical effects should be viewed as first class citizens in near future.

8 Acknowledgements

The authors would like to thank Rineke Verbrugge, Cristiano Castelfranchi and Pierre-Yves Schobbens for their helpful comments about this paper.

This work is supported by KBN Grant 3 P406 019 06 and KBN Grant 8T11T00111.

References

1. F. Brazier, B. Dunin-Kęplicz, J. Treur and R. Verbrugge, Modelling Internal Dynamic Behaviour of BDI Agents, In: *Proc. of MODELAGE'97*, Siena, 1997, in this volume.

2. B. Dunin-Kęplicz, A. Radzikowska: Actions with typical effects: epistemic characterization of scenarios, in *Proc. First International Conference on Multi-Agent Systems*, San Francisco, 1995.

3. B. Dunin-Kęplicz, A. Radzikowska: Epistemic approach to actions with typical effects, in *Proc. ECSQARU'95*, Fribourg, 1995, pp. 180–189.

4. B. Dunin-Kęplicz, J. Treur: Compositional formal specification of multiagent systems, in M. Wooldridge, N. Jennings (eds.), *Intelligent Agents – Proc. of the 1994 Workshop on Agent Theories, Architectures and Languages*, Springer-Verlag, 1995.

5. B. Dunin-Kęplicz, R. Verbrugge, Collective Commitments. In: *Proc. Second International Conference on MULTIAGENT SYSTEMS*, Kyoto, 1996, pp. 56-63.

6. D. W. Etherington, J. M. Crawford: Formalizing reasoning about change: A qualitative reasoning approach, in *Proc. 10th AAAI*, San Jose, CA, 1994.

7. W. van der Hoek, B. van Linder, J. -J. Ch. Meyer: A logic of capabilities, Technical Report IR-330, Vrije Universiteit Amsterdam, 1993.

8. W. van der Hoek, B. van Linder, J. -J. Ch. Meyer: Tests as epistemic updates, in *Proc. 11th ECAI*, Amsterdam, 1994.

9. W. van der Hoek, B. van Linder, J. -J. Ch. Meyer: Communicating rational agents, in *Proc. 18th German Annual Conference on Artificial Intelligence*, Saarbrücken, 1994, pp. 202–213.

10. W. van der Hoek, B. van Linder, J. -J. Ch. Meyer: The dynamics of default reasoning, in *Proc. of ECSQARU–95*, Fribourg, 1995, pp. 277–24.

11. R. Moore: A formal theory of knowledge and action, Technical Report 320, SRI International, 1984.

12. A. Radzikowska: Circumscribing features and fluents: Reasoning about actions with default effects, in *Proc. ECSQARU'95*, Fribourg, Switzerland, 1995, pp. 344–351.

13. A. Radzikowska: Reasoning about action with typical and atypical effects, in *Proc. of 19th German Annual Conference on Artificial Intelligence*, Bielefeld, 1995, pp. 197–209.

14. A. Radzikowska: Formalization of Reasoning about Default Action, in *Proc. Formal and Applied Practical Reasoning FAPR–96*, Bonn, 1996, pp. 540–554.

15. E. Sandewall: *Features and Fluents: A Systematic Approach to the Representation of Knowledge about Dynamical Systems*, Oxford University Press, 1994.

16. B. Thomas: A logic for representing actions, beliefs, capabilities and plans, in Working Notes of the AAAI Spring Symposium on *Reasoning about Mental States: Formal Theories and Applications*, 1993.

17. G. H. von Wright: *Norm and Action*. Routledge & Kegan Paul, London, 1963.

18. M. Wooldridge, N. Jennings (eds.), *Intelligent Agents – Proc. of the 1994 Workshop on Agent Theories, Architectures and Languages*, Springer-Verlag, 1995.

Agents' Dynamic Mental Attitudes

Bruno Errico

Dipartimento di Informatica e Sistemistica, Università di Roma "La Sapienza"
via Salaria 113, 00198 Roma, Italy. e-mail:errico@dis.uniroma1.it

Abstract. We present a first-order formalism for dealing with agents' cognitive attitudes in a dynamic setting. We first extend our ontology in order to represent agents' beliefs and goals. These mental attitudes are expressed in the situation calculus by means of accessibility fluents that represent accessibility relations among alternative situations. Then, we consider changes of mental attitudes in a dynamic and incompletely specified world. Changes may be caused either by the evolution of the external world or by the acquisition of new information. In particular, acquisition of information that modify agents' cognitive attitudes is expressed by cognitive actions. The effects of cognitive actions are characterized by suitable axioms, thus providing a model for the evolution of the alternative situations and the accessibility fluents. We discuss our proposal and compare our model of change with the characterization of Belief Revision postulated by Gärdenfors. We finally introduce the problem of describing agents in a dynamic environment, and briefly sketch a possible extension of the theory that copes with this problem.

1   Introduction

Most of AI problems need to cope with real domains, where the environment can dynamically change, and where the state of affairs cannot always be completely specified. For instance, theories of actions often deal with a world that evolves in a dynamic way, and that in general may be not completely known. Recently, some AI problems have been effectively analyzed within the paradigm of Intelligent Agents (see [27] for a review), viewed as autonomous entities characterized in terms of their cognitive attitudes. Thus, from one side much effort has been devoted to develop theories of actions for representing dynamic settings, and, from the other, to theories of agents accounting for cognitive attitudes. In general, much work on theories of agents can be built on top of an underlying theory of actions, where agents are seen as interacting entities within a dynamic environment.

In last years, a renewed consideration has been given to the situation calculus as a logical formalism for the definition of both a theory of actions and a theory of agents. Reiter [20], elaborating on previous accounts, provides a new solution to the frame problem. This allows the representation of a dynamic environment by axiomatizing the initial state of affairs, along with the preconditions and effects of the execution of actions. Moreover, this theory can be straightforwardly

J.-J. Ch. Meyer, P.-Y. Schobbens (Eds.): Formal Methods of Agents, LNAI 1760, pp. 157–172, 1999.
© Springer-Verlag Berlin Heidelberg 1999

translated into a logic programming language, GOLOG [11], where it is possible to specify also complex actions and programs. Finally, Scherl and Levesque [22] give an account of a knowledge attitude and of knowledge-producing actions in the situation calculus.

The aim of this paper is to further develop this research by dealing with other aspects of agents' cognitive state. We start by extending the theory of actions in order to deal with a generalized concept of situations, representing agents' alternative views of the world, and by explicitly modelling the effects of actions on the alternative situations. Next, we focus on the representation of beliefs and goals in this framework. We first consider the updates of agents' cognitive state resulting from changes, due to physical actions affecting the external environment. Then, we deal with the evolution of agents' mental attitudes. We provide a set of cognitive actions explicitly affecting agent mental attitudes and we formalize a model of belief revision that complies with principles widely accepted in the literature. Finally, we discuss the problem of describing the behaviour of agents in our framework. This is an interesting problem disregarded, in general, by most existing theories of agents that focus rather on the specification or prescription of the behaviour of agents. We start by briefly reviewing in Section 2 the situation calculus and the solution proposed by Reiter to the frame problem. Then, in Section 3 we introduce a set of mental attitudes for agents, extending our ontology in order to provide them with a semantics. In Section 4, we formalize the change of these mental attitudes, and in Section 5 we show how this model for change relates to other literature. Finally, in Section 6 we briefly tackle the problem of describing agents, and extend the ontology in order to deal with this task. In the last section we conclude this presentation with a general discussion, and a comparison with some related work.

2 The Situation Calculus

The language we consider is a reified many sorted first-order language with equality, built on the following ingredients. Five sorts: *agent*, *sit*, *action*, *fluent*, and *object*, respectively, for agents, situations, actions, fluents, and anything else. A finite number of functions and predicates including the three following ones. A ternary function $do(ag, a, s)$ from *agent* × *action* × *sit* to *sit*, denoting the situation resulting from agent ag performing action a in situation s. A ternary predicate $Poss(ag, a, s)$, defined on *agent* × *action* × *sit*, stating whether or not action a is possible for agent ag in situation s. A binary predicate $Holds(f, s)$, defined on *fluent* × *sit*, stating that a fluent f is true in a situation s. Intuitively, fluents are used to define properties changing from one situation to the future ones. A description of the state of the world in a given situation s is simply obtained by considering fluents f that *hold* in situation s, i.e., that make predicate $Holds(f, s)$ true. The evolution of the world state is thus described by new fluents holding in the new situation resulting from the action that has been performed. We start from an initial situation S_0, whose properties may be stated through fluents holding in S_0. When an action a is performed in S_0 by an agent

ag, a new situation $do(ag, a, S_0)$ is obtained, where fluents hold possibly different from those holding in S_0. As discussed by Pinto in [16], this *reified* version of the situation calculus, where fluents are introduced as terms of the language rather then as predicates, can be shown to be substantially equivalent to the non-reified version. Furthermore, in [2] we show an extension of the language that allows for a full first-order reification (with quantifying-in).

In Reiter's proposal, where a solution to the frame problem is provided, the evolution of the state of the world may be specified by defining a logical theory with two kinds of axioms: *Action precondition axioms*, specifying for each action all and only the conditions under which it can be performed; *Successor state axioms*, stating for each fluent necessary and sufficient conditions under which actions affect its truth value. For instance, the action precondition axiom for action $switchOn(c)$ that allows an agent to switch computer c on, may be of the form:[1]

$$Poss(ag, switchOn(c), s) \equiv Computer(c) \wedge Holds(functioning(c), s).$$

This axiom says that in a certain situation only computers that are functioning can be switched on. Thus, this approach requires that all the conditions or *qualifications* that define the possibility to perform an action be specified in the axiom. Hence, it ignores minor qualifications and leaves room to the well known qualification problem, as first pointed out by McCarthy in [14].

Likewise the effects of actions, under certain conditions, can be lumped together yielding a successor state axiom. For instance, the fluent *functioning* can have the following successor state axiom:

$$Poss(ag, a, s) \rightarrow$$
$$Holds(functioning(c), do(ag, a, s)) \equiv Computer(c) \wedge a = repair(c) \vee$$
$$Holds(functioning(c), s) \wedge a \neq hammer(c).$$

That is a computer will be functioning after an action if it gets repaired by that action, or it was functioning before, and the action did not consist of hammering it. This approach relies on what Reiter calls the *Causal Completeness Assumption*, which amounts to demanding that all the causal laws affecting the truth values of a fluent be specified. In this case he shows a systematic procedure to generate the parsimonious representation provided by the successor state axioms.

---

[1] We adopt the following conventions. We always assume all variables fall in the scope of a quantifier, and sometimes omit the universal quantification, with the stipulation that formulas with free variables are always implicitly universally quantified. Iterated quantification over variables $v_{t_1} \ldots v_{t_n}$, e.g., $\exists v_{t_1} \ldots \exists v_{t_n}$ can be simplified to $\exists v_{t_1} \ldots v_{t_n}$ or also $\exists \overline{v}$. Likewise, a formula $\phi(v_{t_1}, \ldots, v_{t_n})$ can also be denoted as $\phi(\overline{v})$. As for the other connectives, we sometimes drop parentheses assuming that $\wedge$ and $\vee$ bind more strongly than $\rightarrow$ and $\equiv$ (e.g., $\alpha \wedge \beta \rightarrow \gamma$ stands for $(\alpha \wedge \beta) \rightarrow \gamma$ and $\alpha \equiv \beta \vee \gamma$ stands for $\alpha \equiv (\beta \vee \gamma)$), and $\neg$ is stronger than any other connective. Finally, for the sake of readability, we generally use capitalized names to denote predicate and constant symbols, and lower case names for function symbols and variables.

In addition, it is required that unique name assumptions be postulated for fluents and actions. Furthermore, in order to have the correct semantic characterization of situations, some extra axioms are needed. In particular, a set of *foundational axioms* ensures a tree-like structure for situations. As shown by Reiter in [21], a second-order axiom that expresses induction on situations is needed to provide the intended characterization, ruling out non-standard models. Anyway, Lin and Reiter show [12] that reasoning tasks, like querying or projecting a knowledge base, can be performed in many cases by relying only on a subset of the axioms expressed at first-order.

3   Mental Attitudes in the Situation Calculus

In this work we focus on agents' beliefs and goals as basic mental notions. In a related paper [4] we show how to express a more general set of attitudes relevant to an agent-based approach that we propose for the problem of User Modelling. Mental attitudes are represented by *cognitive fluents* defined on *agent* × *situation*. The first fluent, *believes* is used to represent those facts that agents consider as true in a given state. Beliefs may be defeasible, i.e., may be withdrawn in future states, if simply more information is provided. The second fluent, *wants*, deals with agents' objectives; these represent properties of the world that agents consider as desirable ones. We do not make any assumption here on the relation between agents' objectives and the action they perform, i.e., on agents' *rationality*.

Then, we consider a possible-worlds setting for providing these cognitive fluents with a definition. The intuitive idea behind the introduction of possible worlds in the situation calculus, due originally to Moore [15] and Scherl and Levesque [22], is the following one. In order to express cognitive attitudes, instead of considering single situations, we consider sets of alternative situations representing alternative states of affairs according to agents' mental model of the world. Thus, different situations are used to represent both static and dynamic features. On the one hand they capture, in a static mode, properties of different contemporary states of affairs conceived by agents. On the other hand, in a dynamic view, properties of states evolving under the effect of actions are represented through different situations. In the sequel, in order to stress this different use of a situation, we sometimes refer to it as an *alternative* when it is used to provide alternative static properties, or as a *state* when it is used to provide dynamic properties resulting after some action gets executed.

In [2] we provide a new set of foundational axioms that extend to our alternative situations setting those proposed by Reiter [21] to provide a suitable semantic characterization of situations.

3.1   Accessibility Fluents

In our development of the possible situations setting, at a given state each agent is associated with a set of contemporary alternatives, i.e., a *cluster*. Alternatives represent agents' different views of the world that are relevant to express their mental attitudes. Clusters are expressed by an *accessibility fluent*, among situations, A, defined on *agent* $\times$ *sit*. We say that $Holds(A(ag, s'), s)$ is true iff s' is in the same cluster of s for agent ag, or, equivalently, s' is a *conceivable situation* from s for agent ag. We allow an agent to be related to the same cluster in situations corresponding to different dynamic evolutions. For instance, agents keep their cluster unchanged when an action is performed, but they are not aware of it. A given state of affairs is thus represented by a situation s, describing the actual world, and a set of clusters of alternative situations, describing agents' mental state. Intuitively, after an agent ag performs an action a in s, the state of the world changes and function do determines the new description represented by the situation resulting from ag performing a in the old starting situation. Besides, we have a new set of clusters, some of which (those relative to agents that are not aware of the action performed) are the same ones relative to the old actual situation, and some others (those relative to agents that are aware of the action occurred) are composed of situations determined by ag performing a in each of the situations belonging to the old cluster. In the next section we will give a characterization of fluent A that expresses these ideas.

Next, we introduce two more accessibility fluents, B and G, defined on sorts *agent* $\times$ *sit*, which are accessibility relations among situations. They are used to select subsets of clusters, i.e., situations accessible via relation A (or A-accessible), for characterizing the cognitive fluents. Accessibility fluent, B, holding in a situation s', expresses that, owing to suppositions or bias of agent ag, s could be a *plausible situation* when the actual situation is s'. Analogously, accessibility fluent, G, holding in a situation s', expresses that situation s is a desirable alternative, or a *desirable situation*, for agent ag in situation s'.

Relevant features of the world in a given state of affairs are expressed by fluents holding in the actual situation; relations among alternative situations relative to the same state of affairs are expressed through the accessibility fluents. Different fluents may hold when passing from a state to a successive one, and thus different relations among alternatives may hold in the new actual state. The evolution of the accessibility fluents determines an evolution of the cognitive attitudes of an agent.

Beliefs and wants about a fact can be represented by considering the truth values of that fact in the alternative situations. Thus, we state that an agent believes or wants a fact in an actual situation s if this holds in all situations that are accessible via relation B or G, respectively, from s, as stated by the following formal definitions:

$$Holds(believes(ag, p), s) \doteq \forall s' Holds(B(ag, s'), s) \rightarrow Holds(p, s')$$

$$Holds(wants(ag, p), s) \doteq \forall s' Holds(G(ag, s'), s) \rightarrow Holds(p, s').$$

We stress the fact that, as Scherl and Levesque in [22], cognitive fluents are not considered as new fluents of our ontology. Instead, they are defined as abbreviations, or macros, of formulas involving the accessibility fluents.[2] These are in fact the only fluents that need to be introduced to characterize cognitive attitudes. Anyway, in the sequel, we allow cognitive fluents to appear within formulas of the situation calculus.

4   Characterization of Mental Attitudes

In another work [4] we have discussed constraints on the accessibility fluents that determine a reasonable behaviour for the cognitive concepts built on top of them. In particular, we give the following:

Definition 1. We postulate the following properties characterizing accessibility fluents:

1. $Holds(A(ag, s_2), s_1) \wedge Holds(A(ag, s_3), s_2) \rightarrow Holds(A(ag, s_3), s_1)$;
2. $Holds(A(ag, s_2), s_1) \wedge Holds(A(ag, s_3), s_1) \rightarrow Holds(A(ag, s_3), s_2)$;
3. $Holds(B(ag, s_2), s_1) \wedge Holds(B(ag, s_3), s_2) \rightarrow Holds(B(ag, s_3), s_1)$;
4. $Holds(B(ag, s_2), s_1) \wedge Holds(B(ag, s_3), s_1) \rightarrow Holds(B(ag, s_3), s_2)$;
5. $Holds(B(ag, s_2), s_1) \rightarrow Holds(A(ag, s_2), s_1)$;
6. $Holds(G(ag, s_2), s_1) \rightarrow Holds(A(ag, s_2), s_1)$;
7. $Holds(A(ag, s_2), s_1) \wedge Holds(B(ag, s_3), s_2) \rightarrow Holds(B(ag, s_3), s_1)$;
8. $Holds(B(ag, s_2), s_1) \wedge Holds(G(ag, s_3), s_2) \rightarrow Holds(G(ag, s_3), s_1)$.

Properties characterizing conceivability relation, represented by fluent A, are transitivity and Euclidicity, expressed by formulas 1 and 2. Likewise, properties characterizing plausibility relation represented by fluent B are again transitivity and Euclidicity; they are expressed by formulas 3 and 4, and are the same properties that characterize frames of modal system K45. Sentences 5 and 6 state that two situations are accessible via fluents B or G only if they belong to a same cluster. Sentence 7 states that agents have the same plausible-accessible situations from conceivable-accessible ones, or, equivalently, that B is transitive over A and B. Likewise, sentence 8 states that agents have the same desirable-accessible situations from plausible-accessible ones, or, equivalently, that G is transitive over B and G. In [3] we show that it is actually sufficient to ensure that these constraints on accessibility fluents be met only for the initial clusters. In this case the evolution of accessibility fluents, as described in next section, does satisfy the constraints also for those clusters reached after the transition with successive actions.

As for the relationship between wants and beliefs, in general, we do not require that, in a given state, alternatives accessible by function G be a subset of those accessible by B, i.e., we drop what Cohen and Levesque call the *realism hypothesis* [1]. This simply avoids the following two problems (see, e.g., Rao and Georgeff [19]) arising in formalisms for goals and beliefs where desirable

---

[2] Anyway, in [2] we show how it is possible to introduce cognitive fluents formally *within* the full reified language.

worlds are contained in plausible ones: the *belief-goal transference problem*, i.e., the fact that any belief must be also a goal; and, the *side-effect problem*, i.e., the closure of goals under belief implication. Anyway, the choice of dropping such hypothesis does not appear here so counterintuitive as it may be when plausible or conceivable alternatives contain also the future evolutions of the current state.[3] In fact, we consider that alternatives are always contemporary. Thus, the fact that an agent desires an alternative that it does not consider plausible does not imply that it considers that situation, or better a different one where the same fluents hold, is never to be reached in the future.

As we show in the sequel, in order to express change of mental attitudes, A-accessible situations may contain, in general, alternatives that are neither plausible nor desirable. When actions are performed, the world evolves in a new state where, in general, different fluents hold. In this new state, we consider the change for two different kinds of properties: *physical* fluents describing the state of the real world, which are affected by physical actions on the real world, and accessibility fluents which are affected by informative actions, or *cognitive actions*, which determine changes on agents' mind.

4.1   Evolution of Physical Fluents

Physical actions, do not affect directly accessibility fluents, but determine changes in the real world. Now, suppose that F is a physical fluent, whose successor state axiom, according to the solution to the frame problem proposed by Reiter for the single agent case in [20], is of the form:

$$Poss(a,s) \rightarrow \{Holds(f(\overline{x}), do(a,s)) \equiv \gamma_f^+(\overline{x}, a, s) \vee (Holds(f(\overline{x}, s) \wedge \neg\gamma_f^-(\overline{x}, a, s))\}.$$

Where $\gamma_f^+(\overline{x}, a, s)$ is a formula that states the conditions that make $Holds(f)$ true, and $\gamma_f^-(\overline{x}, a, s)$ states the conditions that make $Holds(f)$ false, after action a is performed. This axiom can be easily generalized to the multi-agent case by suitably providing the extra argument of sort *agent*. Besides, in the alternative situations setting, it suffices to let it apply to all of the different alternatives, as stated by the implicit universal quantification over situations. In this case, as shown in next section, accessibility fluents allow the selection of those alternatives that are relevant to describe an agent's attitudes. Note that the evolution of physical fluents may affect the cognitive fluents relatively to agents that have some alternative that is accessible through accessibility fluents where some fluent has changed. Other changes of cognitive attitudes are described in next section.

4.2   Evolution of Accessibility Fluents

We first distinguish the case where an agent is aware of the effects of an action performed from that where it is not. In fact, in the former case we also have to

---

[3] On the contrary, a similar choice is less intuitive for frameworks where possible worlds contain all the future evolutions of the current state. For instance, the choice of weak realism of Rao and Georgeff [19] implies that agents desire or intend also worlds that they consider never to be reached.

account for a change in agent mental state. We introduce a predicate, *Aware*, defined on *agent*×*agent*×*action*×*sit*, stating that an agent is aware of the action performed by another agent in a given situation and that it is also aware of the effects that that action brings about. Thus, it becomes possible to characterize the evolution of clusters by defining a suitable successor state axiom for fluent A:

$$Poss(ag, a, s) \rightarrow \qquad (1)$$
$$\{Holds(\ A(ag_1, s_1), do(ag, a, s)) \equiv$$
$$(\neg Aware(ag_1, ag, a, s) \rightarrow Holds(A(ag_1, s_1), s)) \wedge$$
$$(Aware(ag_1, ag, a, s) \rightarrow \exists s_2. \ (s_1 = do(ag, a, s_2) \wedge Poss(ag, a, s_2) \wedge$$
$$Holds(A(ag_1, s_2), s))\}.$$

What this axiom states is that when an action is performed the new cluster associated with an agent in the resulting state is equal to the same one it was associated with in the starting situation, if it is not aware of the action performed. Otherwise, if it is aware of the action, the cluster is made of alternatives resulting from applying function *do* to those alternatives of the starting cluster where the action is possible. In [2] we prove that this successor state axiom actually captures the intuition about clusters discussed above.

Then, we provide a model of the change of the accessibility fluents, and hence of the cognitive fluents, when some cognitive action modifies mental attitudes of an agent. We extend our ontology by introducing some cognitive actions that determine the evolution of agents' attitudes. We consider actions involving only one agent and expressing atomic changes like adding, removing or revising a belief or a want. We restrict changes to *simple terms*, i.e., facts that do not contain cognitive fluents, and do not have arguments of sort *sit*.[4] This avoids complications and problems arising when revising beliefs of beliefs, as exemplified in [26]. Thus, given a simple term p, we consider the following kinds of cognitive actions: $expand_B(p)$ and $expand_G(p)$, to express that a new fact p is added to agent ag's beliefs and wants, respectively; $contract_B(p)$ and $contract_G(p)$, expressing that a fact p is to be removed from (those facts that could be inferred from) the beliefs and goals of agent ag, respectively; $revise_B(p)$ and $revise_G(p)$, to express that a new fact should be consistently added to agents ag's beliefs and goals, respectively. This means that possibly fact $\neg p$ should be removed from (those facts that could be inferred from) the beliefs and goals of agent ag, respectively, before adding fact p. In the sequel we shall characterize the effects of the expansion and contraction action only. For the revise action it is possible to rely on these solutions. In fact terms containing revise actions can be expanded by applying Levi's identity (see, for instance, [6]) expressing revision by a contraction and an expansion performed in sequence:
$$do(ag, revise(p), s) \doteq do(ag, expand(p), do(ag, contract(\neg p), s)).$$

---

[4] Elsewhere [2] we tackle the problem of dealing with cognitive actions concerning expressions that contain also cognitive attitudes.

Selection Fluents In order to characterize how cognitive actions affect agents' cognitive attitudes, two selection relations among alternative situations are introduced. Intuitively, in order to *contract* a belief (or goal) p, a new set of alternative situations where p does not hold should be added to those B-accessible or G-accessible. This expansion of the accessible situations corresponds to a contraction of the facts that are believed (or wanted). In fact, as discussed, for instance, by Gärdenfors in [6], it seems reasonable that this contraction be performed in different ways for different agents, relying on some explicit notion related to agents' characterization. Thus, recasting in the situation calculus ideas developed by van Linder et al. [26] in propositional dynamic logic (PDL), we represent this new set of alternatives through *selection fluents* S_B (or S_G), defined on *agent* $\times$ *fluent* $\times$ *situation*, expressing which situations an agent is more inclined to include as new alternatives to the plausible (or desirable) ones when a given belief (or goal) must be removed. Then, we consider constraints that can be stated for selection fluents, so that beliefs (or goals) holding after contraction meet some criteria of rationality, as will be shown in the sequel. In particular we allow only selection fluents $S_X, X \in \{B, G\}$ that meet the following restrictions:[5]

1. $Holds(S_X(ag, p, s'), s) \rightarrow Holds(A(ag, s'), s) \wedge Holds(\neg p, s')$;
2. $(\exists s'. \ Holds(X(ag, s'), s) \wedge Holds(\neg p, s')) \rightarrow (Holds(S_X(ag, p, s''), s) \rightarrow Holds(X(ag, s''), s))$;
3. $Holds(\neg S_X(ag, p, s'), s) \equiv (Holds(A(ag, s''), s) \rightarrow Holds(p, s''))$;
4. $(Holds(A(ag, s''), s) \rightarrow (Holds(p, s') \equiv Holds(q, s'))) \rightarrow (Holds(S_X(ag, p, s''), s) \equiv Holds(S_X(ag, q, s''), s))$;
5. $Holds(S_X(ag, p \wedge q, s'), s) \rightarrow (Holds(S_X(ag, p, s'), s) \vee Holds(S_X(ag, q, s'), s))$;
6. $(\exists s' Holds(S_X(ag, p \wedge q, s'), s) \wedge Holds(\neg p)) \rightarrow (Holds(S_X(ag, p, s''), s) \rightarrow Holds(S_X(ag, p \wedge q, s''), s))$.

The first axiom states that a selected situation must be one of the same cluster where $\neg p$ holds. Axiom 2 says that if there already exists some plausible situation where $\neg p$ holds, then the set of selected situations must be contained in that of plausible (resp. desirable) ones. Axiom 3 asserts that if p holds in all selected situations then it must hold in all those ones in the same cluster. Axiom 4 states that the same situations are selected for predicates that are equivalent in all situations that belong to the same cluster. Axiom 5 ensures that the situations selected when contracting a conjunction must be contained in the union of the situations selected when contracting each conjunct. Finally, Axiom 6 states that, according to a minimal change principle, if the set of situations selected when contracting a conjunction is not empty, then it must contain the situations selected when contracting one of the conjuncts.

Successor State Axioms for Accessibility Fluents The evolution of accessibility fluents through states is expressed, as usual, by defining suitable successor

---

[5] Abusing notation, we allow the logical connectives to range over terms of sort *fluent*. In [2] the corresponding term-forming operators, e.g., *and* or *not*, are formally introduced.

state axioms. We assume that only agents who perform a change of cognitive attitudes are aware of it. As for B, the axiom can be stated formally as follows:

$$Poss(ag, a, s) \rightarrow \qquad\qquad (2)$$
$$\{Holds(B(ag_1, s_1), do(ag, a, s)) \equiv$$
$$(\neg\, Aware(ag_1, ag, a, s) \rightarrow Holds(B(ag_1, s_1), s)) \wedge$$
$$[\quad Aware(ag_1, ag, a, s) \rightarrow \exists s_2 \, [s_1 = do(ag, a, s_2) \wedge Poss(ag, a, s_2) \wedge$$
$$[ag_1 \neq ag \vee (a \neq expand_B(p) \wedge a \neq contract_B(p)) \rightarrow Holds(B(ag, s_2), s)] \wedge$$
$$[a = expand_B(p) \wedge ag_1 = ag \rightarrow Holds(p, s_2) \wedge Holds(B(ag, s_2), s))] \wedge$$
$$[a = contract_B(p) \wedge ag_1 = ag \rightarrow Holds(S_B(ag, p, s_2), s))]\}.$$

Thus, it states that a situation s_1 is B-accessible to agent ag_1 from the situation resulting from agent ag performing an action a in situation s iff either we have that the agent is not aware of the action performed and s_1 is already plausible from s, or, otherwise, the agent is aware, and s_1 is the result of ag performing a possible action in a situation s_2. Moreover, one of these three conditions holds. The action is neither a contraction nor an expansion performed by ag_1 and s_2 is plausible from s. The action is an expansion of a fluent p performed by ag_1 itself and both s_2 is plausible from s and p holds in s_2. Finally, the action is a contraction of a fluent p performed by ag_1 itself and s_2 belongs to the set of situations selected by the selection function for the fluent p. Likewise, G is characterized by a similar axiom obtained by replacing B with G.

5   Analysis of the Model of Dynamic Attitudes

In this section we compare our framework dealing with dynamics of agents' cognitive attitudes with the postulates proposed by Gärdenfors in [6]. The fact that our model complies with the postulates defined for belief revision provides a rationality justification and a cognitive commitment for the model we propose.

Given an agent ag, a situation s and an accessibility fluent $X \in \{B, G\}$, we define a *belief (goal) cognitive set* $E_B(ag, s)$ ($E_G(ag, s)$) as the set of simple terms p that are believed (wanted) in situation s. From the fact that distribution holds for all accessibility fluents, it becomes evident that cognitive sets are closed under implication, and thus comply to the definition of (possibly absurd) belief sets given in [6].

In the sequel, we list a set of properties holding for cognitive sets that are the analogs of the postulates proposed by Gärdenfors for belief revision, adapted to our framework. We start with properties of cognitive sets $E_X(ag, s)$ concerning actions $expand_X(p)$ $X \in \{B, G\}$, and holding for any agent ag, situation s and simple term p.

Proposition 2. *The following relations hold:*

1. $E_X(ag, do(ag, expand_X(p), s))$ is a cognitive set;
2. $p \in E_X(ag, do(ag, expand_X(p), s))$;

3. $E_X(ag, s) \subseteq E_X(ag, do(ag, expand_X(p), s))$;
4. if $p \in E_X(ag, s)$ then $E_X(ag, s) = E_X(ag, do(ag, expand_X(p), s))$;
5. if $E_X(ag, s) \subseteq E_X(ag, s')$ then $E_X(ag, do(ag, expand_X(p), s)) \subseteq$
   $E_X(ag, do(ag, expand_X(p), s'))$;
6. $E_X(ag, do(ag, expand_X(p), s))$ is the smallest set satisfying the above properties.

Similarly, provided that axioms of Section 4.2.1 hold, we can prove properties corresponding to those defined in [6] for cognitive sets $E_X(ag, s)$ concerning actions $contract_X(p)$ $X \in \{B, G\}$, and holding for any agent ag, situation s and simple term p.

Proposition 3. *The following relations hold:*

1. $E_X(ag, do(ag, contract_X(p), s))$ is a cognitive set;
2. $E_X(ag, do(ag, contract_X(p), s)) \subseteq E_X(ag, s)$;
3. if $p \notin E_X(ag, s)$ then $E_X(ag, s) = E_X(ag, do(ag, contract_X(p), s))$;
4. if $\neg Holds(A(ag, s'), s) \rightarrow Holds(p, s')$ then $p \notin E_X(ag, do(ag, contract_X(p), s))$;
5. if $p \in E_X(ag, s)$ then $E_X(ag, s) \subseteq E_X(ag, do(ag, expand_X(p), do(ag, contract_X(p), s)))$;
6. if $Holds(A(ag, s'), s) \rightarrow (Holds(p, s) \equiv Holds(q, s))$ then
   $E_X(ag, do(ag, contract_X(p), s)) = E_X(ag, do(ag, contract_X(q), s))$;
7. $E_X(ag, do(ag, contract_X(p), s)) \cap E_X(ag, do(ag, contract_X(q), s)) \subseteq$
   $E_X(ag, do(ag, contract_X(p \wedge q), s))$;
8. if $p \notin E_X(ag, do(ag, contract_X(p \wedge q), s))$ then
   $E_X(ag, do(ag, contract_X(p \wedge q), s)) \subseteq E_X(ag, do(ag, contract_X(p), s))$.

6   Describing Agents

In general, theories of agents can be exploited for quite two different tasks. On the one hand, *designing* an agent is the task addressed by most of the existing formalisms proposed in the literature. It implies the view of an agent under an *internal* perspective, namely the standpoint of the agent itself. The main aim is to take into account agent cognitive state in order to determine how an agent ought to effect changes in the environment. Thus, designing agents can be roughly described as the problem of defining how communication affect the mental state of the agent, and how the cognitive state determine the actions performed by the agent. In this sense, the character of these theories is *prescriptive*, for they define what an agent should do, or at least should try to do.

On the other hand, the task of *modelling* an agent has been rather disregarded in the literature. In this case the perspective is *external*, namely of someone that observes agents. The aim is to describe what the content of agents' cognitive state could be, based on the observed behaviour. Thus, modelling assumes now a more *descriptive* character. This task implies as before the definition of relationships between communication and the mental state of the agent. But, the other type of relationship, i.e., between cognitive state and the actions performed, becomes less interesting. This happens because now the aim is to find out a description of the cognitive state of the agent, based on the actions observed. Thus, as also noted by Haddadi [7], unlike external theories, internal theories are *not* concerned, in general, with providing a basis for the rational formation and achievement of intentions. For instance, problems like planning may be thought of as having the aim of *designing* agents. Here what is needed is roughly to determine a behaviour, or program, that brings to a certain goal, given a specification of the current state, and a model of the hypothetical futures of a state. A different problem instead is tracking, or *executing*, agents, i.e., determining the state that has been *actually* reached after performing certain actions in some initial state. This problem is crucial to many important applications based on modelling or verifying systems where mental attitudes play some role (see, for instance [5]).

In [2] we further develop our theory of agents and present a framework for modelling agents related to the problem of User Modelling. In order to provide the ability to describe agents, we introduce there two new predicates *Actual* and *Performs*. In this limited exposition we only briefly sketch the intuition underlying the former predicate. *Actual* takes a *sit* argument and has a twofold meaning. First, a situation is actual if it represents the real world, independent of agents' biases and desires. Thus if we want to examine which features describe a given state, we have to take into account properties (fluents) holding in the corresponding actual situation. Furthermore, this predicate is also intended to single out a path of situations that have already occurred. Thus, an actual situation is meant to be the result of a sequence of actions that have been *actually* performed (by a set of agents). A similar notion, outside the context of alternative situations, has been used by Pinto in [16], where he notes that this allows the selection of a path of situation among the many branches describing the possible courses of events. Axioms for this predicate state that an actual situation can only have a predecessor that is actual as well, and that each actual situation has at most an actual successor:

$$Actual(do(ag, a, s)) \rightarrow Poss(ag, a, s) \wedge Actual(s);$$

$$Actual(do(ag, a, s)) \wedge Actual(do(ag', a', s)) \rightarrow ag = ag' \wedge a = a'.$$

An actual situation of the form $do(ag, a, s)$ expresses that ag has actually performed a in s. Besides, also the "predecessor" s must be actual and if this is still of the form $do(ag', a', s')$ we determine a sequence of actions/agents up to an initial situation. Thus it is possible to reason on the past of a given state and not only on its future. For instance it is now possible to specify formally the condition expressing that only agents who change their cognitive attitudes are aware of it, as we demanded before introducing Axiom 2, i.e.:

$$Actual(do(ag, a, s)) \wedge (a = contract_X(p) \vee a = expand_X(p))) \rightarrow$$
$$(Aware(ag, ag', a, s) \equiv ag = ag')$$

for $X \in \{B, G\}$. Moreover, by means of this predicate it is possible to single out one situation, among the many alternatives, thus describing the real state of the environment, and hence of agents' cognitive state.

7   Conclusions and Discussion

We have developed a first-order formalism for dealing with agents' beliefs and goals. In particular, we have taken into consideration the dynamics of mental attitudes, as a consequence of both changes in the external world and cognitive inputs. One of our ongoing objectives is to use the changes of the cognitive notions presented here for representing communicative acts among agents, such as those discussed by Mayfield et al. in [13]. Interesting applications could be in the area of User Modelling and Student Modelling, as we show in [4,3]. Work is in progress to provide significant applications of the framework presented for modelling the interactions between an interactive systems and users [2].

A limit of our notion of goals is that we do not consider the possibility to express temporal relations among goals. For instance, it is not possible to state that an agent has a certain goal only after another goal has been achieved. Anyway, in this case, a possible extension dealing with this aspect could be conceived by replacing alternative desirable situations with alternative paths, i.e., alternative sequences actions-situations describing possible future courses of events. Besides, as we are mainly concerned with modelling agents, where actions are already given as input to the problem, as opposed to designing agents, where actions need to be determined, no relation between goals and action has been explicitly modelled. A possible way to represent such a relation could be given by forcing some constraints between plausible and desirable situations, analogously to what is done, e.g., by Rao and Georgeff in [18].

Our work follows for many aspect the logical approach to agent programming carried on by Lespérance et al. in [10]. Anyway, that work is concerned with programming agents as opposed to our aim of modelling them. Besides, in that work only agents' knowledge is considered, and other mental attitudes are not dealt with. Lespérance et al. focus on the possibility to handle perceptual actions among agents, and discuss an application for a meeting schedule problem. On the contrary, we have considered and characterized more basic cognitive actions. In [23], Shapiro et al. introduce, under the same logical approach, a cognitive attitude accounting for one agent's goals, and express a concept of rationality that binds goals to actions. Though goals, defined as a second-order abbreviation in terms of future paths, seem to allow also for the representation of future objectives, they consider only a single agent case, and do not account for cognitive actions. Konolige and Pollack [9] refer to a definition of intentions based on minimal modal models, along with a normal modal operator for representing beliefs. Suitable relations between these operators prevent from the side effect problem. However, their framework fits only static situations where no dynamic acquisition is dealt with. Rao and Foo [17] define modal operators to represent cognitive actions in temporal modal logic and apply them in order to reason about actions. A semantical characterization of cognitive actions is given in terms of selection functions for expansions and contractions. The characterization of change due to action they give is based on revision, and does not account for the difference between revision and update pointed out by Katsuno and Mendelzon in [8]. Many ideas about how to perform revision in a possible-worlds setting have been drawn from van Linder et al. in [26]. Anyway, in their work no account is given to goals (but see van Linden et al. [25] for an account of motivational attitudes) and their aim is to define a *theorist logic* for specifying and reasoning about agents rather than modelling them. Due to the different underlying formalism, i.e., situation calculus versus PDL, other differences can be pointed out between the two approaches. First, we note that our characterization of agents' attitudes is first-order and not modal. Thus, the various methods for automated deduction developed for first-order theories can be directly exploited for reasoning in our framework. Moreover, as we highlight in [2], a main difference between situation calculus and modal approaches, is that in the former case situations are defined at the syntactic level, whereas in the latter case worlds are defined semantically. Thus in the situation calculus it is possible to state explicit (first-order) properties of situations, e.g., structural relations, even in cases where, according to the Correspondence Theory (see, e.g., van Benthem [24]), the same properties are not definable for modal accessibility relations (that belong to the semantic structures) among worlds. Another interesting aspect is that by defining situations as terms, it is possible to keep track of the history of the actions performed within the term itself. This feature, which is not straightforwardly representable for transitions among states in dynamic logic, is very appealing, especially for modelling purposes where it may be important to represent also the past history of interaction.

8   Acknowledgments

I would like to thank Luigia Carlucci Aiello who encouraged me in writing this paper. Hector Levesque, Ray Reiter and Yves Lespérance for many fruitful discussions about situation calculus. The research reported here has been partly supported by ENEA, MURST, and ASI.

References

1. P. R. Cohen and H. J. Levesque. Intention is choice with commitment. *Artificial Intelligence Journal*, 42:213–261, 1990.
2. B. Errico. *Intelligent Agents and User Modelling*. PhD thesis, Dipartimento Informatica e Sistemistica, Università degli Studi di Roma "La Sapienza", November 1996. Draft.
3. B. Errico. Student modelling in the situation calculus. In *Proc. of the European Conf. of AI in Education*, pages 305–310, 1996.
4. B. Errico and L. C. Aiello. Agents in the situation calculus: an application to user modelling. In D. M. Gabbay and H. J. Ohlbach, editors, *Practical Reasoning*, volume 1085 of *Lecture Notes in Computer Science (subseries LNAI)*, pages 126–140. Springer-Verlag, 1996.
5. M. Fisher. Representing and executing agent-based systems. In *Intelligent Agents ECAI-94 Workshop on Agent Theories, Architectures, and Languages*. Springer-Verlag, 1994.
6. P. Gärdenfors. *Knowledge in Flux*. MIT Press, 1988.

7. A. Haddadi. *Communication and Cooperation in Agent Systems*, volume 1056 of *Lecture Notes in Computer Science (subseries LNAI)*. Springer-Verlag, Berlin, Germany, 1995.

8. H. Katsuno and A. O. Mendelzon. On the difference between updating a knowledge base and revising it. In *Proceedings of the Second International Conference on the Principles of Knowledge Representation and Reasoning (KR-91)*, pages 387–394. Morgan Kaufmann, 1991.

9. K. Konolige and M. E. Pollack. A representationalist theory of intention. In *Proceedings of the Thirteenth International Joint Conference on Artificial Intelligence (IJCAI-93)*, pages 390–395. Morgan Kaufmann, 1993.

10. Y. Lespérance, H. J. Levesque, Lin F., D. Marcu, R. Reiter, and R. B. Scherl. Foundations of a logical approach to agent programming. In *IJCAI-95 Workshop on Agent Theories, Architectures, and Languages*, 1995.

11. H. J. Levesque, R. Reiter, Lin F., and R. B. Scherl. GOLOG: A logic programming language for dynamic domains. *Artificial Intelligence*, 1995. submitted.

12. F. Lin and R. Reiter. How to Progress a Database (and Why) I. Logical Foundations. In *Proceedings of the Fourth International Conference on the Principles of Knowledge Representation and Reasoning (KR-94)*, pages 425–436. Morgan Kaufmann, 1994.

13. J. Mayfield, Y Labrou, and T. Finin. Evaluation of KQML as an agent communication language. In *IJCAI-95 Workshop on Agent Theories, Architectures, and Languages*, pages 282–291, 1995.

14. J. and McCarthy. First order theories of individual concepts and propositions. In J. E. Hayes, D. Michie, and L. J. Mikulick, editors, *Machine Intelligence*, volume 9, pages 129–148. Ellis Horwood, Chichester, England, 1979.

15. R. C. Moore. A formal theory of knowledge and action. In J. R. Hobbs and R. C. Moore, editors, *Formal Theories of the Commonsense World*, pages 319–358. Norwood, 1985.

16. J. Pinto. Temporal reasoning in the situation calculus. Technical Report KRR-TR-94-1, Dept. of Computer Science, Univ. of Toronto, 1994.

17. A. S. Rao and N. Y. Foo. Minimal change and maximal coherence: A basis for belief revision and reasoning about actions. In *Proceedings of the Eleventh International Joint Conference on Artificial Intelligence (IJCAI-89)*, pages 966–971. Morgan Kaufmann, 1989.

18. A. S. Rao and M. P. Georgeff. Modelling rational agents within a BDI architecture. In *Proceedings of the Second International Conference on the Principles of Knowledge Representation and Reasoning (KR-91)*, pages 473–484. Morgan Kaufmann, 1991.

19. A. S. Rao and M. P. Georgeff. Asymmetry thesis and side-effect problems in linear-time and branching-time intention logics. In *Proceedings of the Thirteenth International Joint Conference on Artificial Intelligence (IJCAI-93)*, pages 318–324. Morgan Kaufmann, 1993.

20. R. Reiter. The frame problem in the situation calculus: A simple solution (sometimes) and a completeness result for goal regression. In V. Lifshitz, editor, *Artificial Intelligence and Mathematical Theory of Computation: Papers in Honor of John McCarthy*, pages 359–380. Academic Press, 1991.

21. R. Reiter. Proving properties of states in the situation calculus. *Artificial Intelligence Journal*, (64):337–351, 1993.

22. R. Scherl and H. J. Levesque. The frame Problem and Knowledge Producing Actions. *Artificial Intelligence*, 1994. submitted.

23. S. Shapiro, Y. Lespérance, and H. Levesque. Goals and Ractional Actions in the Situation Calculus–A Preliminary Report. In *Working Notes of AAAI Fall Symposium on Rational Agency: Concepts, Theories, Models, and Applications.* Cambridge, MA, 1995.

24. J. van Benthem. Correspondence theory. In D. M. Gabbay and F. Guenthner, editors, *Handbook of Philosophical Logic II*, pages 167–247. D. Reidel Publishing Company, 1984.

25. B. van Linder, W. van der Hoek, and J. J. Meyer. Formalising motivational attitudes of agents. In M. Wooldridge, J. P. Müller, and M. Tombe, editors, *Intelligent Agents Volume II - Agent Theories, Architectures and Languages*, pages 17–32. Springer-Verlag, 1996.

26. B. van Linder, W. van der Hoek, and J. J. Ch. Meyer. Actions that make you change your mind. Technical Report UU-CS-1994-53, Utrecht University, 1994.

27. M. Wooldridge and N. R. Jennings. Agents theories, architectures and languages: A survey. In *Intelligent Agents ECAI-94 Workshop on Agent Theories, Architectures, and Languages.* Springer-Verlag, 1994.

Diagnostic Agents for Distributed Systems

P. Fröhlich[1], I. Móra[2], W. Nejdl[1], M. Schroeder[1]

[1] Institut für Rechnergestützte Wissensverarbeitung, Lange Laube 3, D-30159 Hannover,
{froehlich,nejdl,schroeder}@kbs.uni-hannover.de
[2] Departamento de Informática, F.C.T. Universidade Nova de Lisboa,
idm@di.fct.unl.pt

Abstract. In this paper we introduce an agent–based framework for the diagnosis of spatially distributed technical systems, based on a suitable distributed diagnosis architecture. We implement the framework using the concepts of vivid agents and extended logic programming. To demonstrate the power of our approach, we solve a diagnosis example from the domain of unreliable datagram protocols.

1 Introduction

The advent of large distributed technical systems like computer and telecommunication networks has been one of the most striking developments of our time. Research in model–based diagnosis has up to now not tackled the question how to support such systems by a suitable diagnosis architecture.

We introduce an agent–based framework for the diagnosis of spatially distributed systems. The motivation for such a framework is the unnecessary complexity and communication overhead of centralized solutions. Consider a distributed system with n nodes, e.g. a computer network consisting of n machines. When using a centralized diagnosis system the size of the system description (i.e. number of ground formulas) is linear in n. Diagnosis time will usually be worse than linear in n [MH93]. Also all observations have to be transmitted to the central diagnosis machine, causing a large communication overhead.

Our agent–based approach decomposes a system into a set of subsystems. Each subsystem is diagnosed by an agent which has detailed knowledge over its subsystem and an abstract view of the neighboring subsystems. Most failures can be diagnosed locally within one subsystem. This decreases diagnosis time dramatically in large systems. In the case of the computer network most machines in a subnet can usually fail without affecting machines in other subnets. Only those computers in other subnets can be affected which have sent messages to the faulty machine. Moreover, the local computation of diagnoses avoids the communication overhead which would be needed to forward all observations to the central diagnosis engine.

Failures which affect more than one subsystem are diagnosed by the agents cooperating with each other. The cooperation process is triggered locally by an agent, when it realizes that it can not explain the observations by a failure in its own subsystem. The cooperation process is guided by a small amount of topological information.

J.-J. Ch. Meyer, P.-Y. Schobbens (Eds.): Formal Methods of Agents, LNAI 1760, pp. 173-186, 1999.

We have implemented spatially distributed diagnosis using extended logic programming [SdAMP96,SW96] and the vivid agents concept [Wag96a,Wag96b]. Vivid agents support both the declarative description of the domain by a flexible knowledge base component and the specification of the reactive behavior of agents by a set of rules, which are activated by communication events.

To demonstrate the power of our approach we formalize the domain of an unreliable protocol (like UDP) in a computer network and diagnose an example scenario.

2   Spatially Distributed Diagnosis

In [FN96] semantical and spatial distribution are identified as the relevant distribution concepts for diagnosis. Semantical distribution refers to a situation where the knowledge is distributed among the agents. Each agent is an expert for a certain problem domain. Diagnostic concepts for semantical distribution must rely on external criteria rather than cooperation among the agents because the knowledge bases of the diagnostic agents are not compatible. In this paper we describe spatially distributed diagnosis. Distributed technical systems often consist of subsystems which have the same structure. So we can describe the subsystems by a common set of axioms. The particular properties of the concrete subsystem are defined by logical facts. As we will see, the description of the subsystems by a common vocabulary allows us to resolve conflicts using cooperation among the agents. After giving a short overview of the necessary concepts of model–based diagnosis, we will describe our view of spatially distributed diagnosis in more detail. Then we will define the diagnostic conflicts between the subsystems as well as the distributed diagnosis concept formally.

2.1   Model–based Diagnosis

In model–based diagnosis [Rei87] a simulation model of the device under consideration is used to predict its normal behavior, given the observed input parameters. Diagnoses are computed by comparison of predicted vs. actual behavior. This approach uses an extendible logical model of the device, called the system description (SD), usually formalized as a set of formulas expressed in first–order logic. The system description consists of a set of axioms characterizing the behavior of system components of certain types. The topology is modeled separately by a set of facts.

We will now define the diagnostic concept mathematically. The diagnostic problem is described by system description SD, a set $COMP$ of components and a set OBS of observations (logical facts). With each component we associate a behavioral mode: $Mode(c, Ok)$ means that component c is behaving correctly, while $Mode(c, Ab)$ (abbreviated by $Ab(c)$) denotes that c is faulty. In Consistency–Based Diagnosis, the concept we are using throughout this paper, a Diagnosis D is a set of faulty components, such that the observed behavior is consistent with the assumption, that exactly the components in D are behaving abnormally. If a diagnosis contains no proper subset which is itself a diagnosis, we call it a Minimal Diagnosis.

Definition 1 (Reiter 87). A Diagnosis of $(SD, COMP, OBS)$ is a set $\Delta \subseteq COMP$, such that $SD \cup OBS \cup \{Mode(c,Ab)|c \in COMP\} \cup \{\neg Mode(c,Ab)|c \in COMP - \Delta\}$ is consistent. Δ is called a *Minimal Diagnosis*, iff it is the minimal set (wrt. $\subseteq$) with this property.

Minimal Diagnoses are a natural concept, because we do not want to assume that a component is faulty, unless this is necessary to explain the observed behavior. Since the set of minimal diagnoses can be still quite large and the ultimate goal is to identify a single diagnosis, stronger minimality criteria are used which allow stronger discrimination among the diagnoses. The most frequently used concepts are *Minimal Cardinality Diagnosis* and *Most Probable Diagnosis*. In addition to these stronger definitions of diagnosis the agents can use measurements to discriminate among competing diagnoses. For our distributed diagnosis framework we assume that every agent has identified a single diagnosis for its subsystem.

2.2 Properties of Spatial Distribution

Spatial distribution is a natural organization scheme for the distributed diagnosis of large technical systems like communication networks. With each agent we associate a certain area of the system, for which it is responsible. Consider a large distributed system, e.g. a communication network, which is divided into a set of spatially distributed subsystems (subnets), as shown in figure 1. Each square in the grid is a subsystem and has a diagnostic agent associated with it.

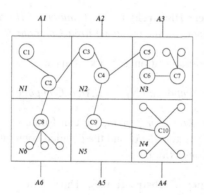

Fig. 1. A communication network

What could be the system view of agent A_1? Of course, it has detailed knowledge about its own subsystem (provided by the control component). For components in its own subsystem the agent himself is responsible and its diagnoses are reliable. Since it does not share its local observations and measurements with other agents (except for specialized information used during cooperation) it is the only agent, which can compute detailed diagnosis of its subsystem. In the decentralized structure of this network, the machine C_2 must have at least some routing information. It has to know that there are two adjacent subnets N_2 and N_6, to which it can send information. More generally we assume that each agent has some information on the neighboring subsystems, i.e. the subsystems directly connected to its own in the system structure.

Now we will describe this view by means of abstractions and simplifications: An agent A_i knows only the name of each neighboring subnet N_j (and perhaps a name of a server within N_j) but not N_j's internal structure. When A_i diagnoses an error involving subnet N_j (e.g. a lost message routed via N_j), then the diagnosis will contain $Mode(N_j, Ab)$. The abstract literal $Mode(N_j, Ab)$ implicitly implies that some particular component within N_j is faulty. In general, an agent A_i has an abstract model of the neighboring subsystems. Furthermore, A_i only knows that N_j is the first subnet on the route to the destination of the lost message. It is a simplifying assumption, that N_j is the only subnet involved in the transmission. Stated more generally, an agent A_i initially uses the simplifying assumption that all errors it cannot explain are caused by its immediate neighbors. We will see, how he can get more detailed information during the cooperation process.

2.3   Formalization

The subsystems and also the components within each subsystem have standard names. A predicate *Area_Component* denotes that component c is situated within area a of the system. We call the extension of this predicate for a given system the *Component Hierarchy*.

Definition 2 (Component Hierarchy.). The *Component Hierarchy CH* for a distributed system is a set of facts for the predicate *Area_Component*.

Example 3. For our communication network we have

$$CH : \{Area\_Component(N_1, C_1), Area\_Component(N_1, C_2), \ldots\}$$

Using the predicate *Area_Component*, we can formulate a consistency condition between the abstract subsystem–level and the detailed component level. We define the consistency of abstractions axiom:

Definition 4 (Consistency of Abstractions.). The axiom

$$\begin{aligned} CA : \forall c. \ & ((Mode(c, Ab) \wedge \exists d.Area\_Component(c, d)) \\ & \rightarrow \exists e.(Area\_Component(c, e) \wedge Mode(e, Ab))) \end{aligned}$$

requires, that each abnormality of an abstract component is caused by an abnormality of one of its subcomponents.

The axiom *Disjointness of Modes* states that a component can only be in one behavioral mode and is expressed by the following axiom:

Definition 5 (Disjointness of Modes.).

$$DM : \forall c. \forall m_1. \forall m_2.(Mode(c, m_1) \wedge Mode(c, m_2)) \rightarrow m_1 = m_2$$

2.4   Diagnosis by Cooperation

Each diagnostic agent knows only a small part of the entire system. It can compute diagnoses independently, because it maintains a set of assumptions concerning the other parts of the system. In this paper, we will assume that all locally computed diagnoses are considered as reliable. The bargain from distributed diagnosis is that a lot of problems can be solved locally so that the simplifying assumptions hold. The cooperation process is necessary when an agent cannot detect a faulty component within its subsystem. In this case, it starts a cooperation process:

Definition 6 (Need for Cooperation). Given observations *OBS*, a component hierarchy *CH*, the axiom of consistency of abstractions *CA*, and a system description *SD* such that $CH, CA \in SD$. If A_i believes that it is not abnormal, but a neighbour is , i.e.

$$SD_{N_i} \cup OBS \models \neg Mode(N_i, Ab) \text{ and } SD_{N_i} \cup OBS \cup \{Mode(N_j, Ab)\} \not\models \bot$$

then there is a *need for cooperation* to determine a global diagnosis and N_j is a possible partner for cooperation.

Example 7. In the example of the communication network the observation of a lost message (let us assume an unreliable protocol such as UDP) means that it was lost somewhere on the way from sender to recipient. But of course the agents know only their own subnet in detail and have an abstract view of the neighboring subnets. The predicate *Message_Lost* represents a reported loss of a datagram. *Message_Lost*(N_1, C_7) means that a lost message has been reported which was sent from network N_1 to a node C_7. When agent A_i transmits a message via a neighboring subnet N_j and the message is lost, A_i will assume that it was lost in N_j since this is the only point on the route it knows. We can formalize this simplifying assumption explicitly by introducing a predicate *On_Route*.

$$CLM : Message\_Lost(Sender, Recipient)$$
$$\rightarrow \exists n.(On\_Route(Sender, Recipient, n) \wedge Mode(n, Ab))$$

is called *Existence of a Cause for a Lost Message*.

Initially, each agent A_i knows the following facts about *On_Route*, if N_{r_k} is the routing table entry of *Recipient*$_k$:

$$RT : On\_Route(N_i, Recipient_1, N_i) \; On\_Route(N_i, Recipient_1, N_{r_1})$$
$$On\_Route(N_i, Recipient_2, N_i) \; On\_Route(N_i, Recipient_2, N_{r_2})...$$

Now assume a message gets lost from N_1 to C_7, i.e. *Message_Lost*(N_1, C_7) and the agent A_1 determines that it is not its fault, i.e. $\neg Mode(N_1, Ab)$ holds. Then A_1 computes a local diagnosis $Mode(N_2, Ab)$ and thus there is a need for cooperation in order to obtain a global solution.

A cooperation process is started by sending/receiving an observation. With the new observation the agent computes diagnoses which can lead to three different situations. First, it might turn out that it is abnormal itself. Then other solutions can be neglected since we assume that the agents have certain knowledge about their own state. Second, there are no diagnoses at all which means that the initial fault is intermittent. Third, there is a need for cooperation. Then the agent refines the received observation and sends it to the neighbor waiting for its reply. In any of the cases the requesting agent is informed of the final result.

Definition 8 (Diagnosis by Cooperation). Given an agent A_1 which receives a message from agent A_2 with an observation OBS such that $SD_{A_1} \cup OBS \models \bot$ then there are three cases:

1. $SD_{A_1} \cup OBS \cup \{Mode(N_1, Ab)\} \not\models \bot$, i.e. the agent's own subsystem is faulty
2. there are no D such that $SD_{A_1} \cup OBS \cup D \not\models \bot$, then there must have been an intermittent failure
3. there is a need for cooperation (see definition 6) and the observation is refined and sent to another agent which is then in charge of providing a diagnosis result

The diagnosis result is sent to A_2.

Example 9. Assume A_1 receives by a subcomponent the message that a message is lost from N_1 to C_7 and N_1 not being abnormal. A diagnosis of A_1 is that A_2 is abnormal and thus there is a need for cooperation. The initial observation $Message\_Lost(N_1, C_7)$ is refined as follows:

$$RO : Message\_Lost(Sender, Recipient) \wedge \neg Mode(Sender, Ab) \wedge$$
$$On\_Route(Sender, Recipient, Next\_Sender) \rightarrow$$
$$New\_Message\_Lost(Next\_Sender, Recipient)$$

The new observation is sent to A_2. Since a_2 is not abnormal this agent asks A_3 for help. A_3 is faulty and replies that it is responsible. A_2 passes this result to A_1. The union of all system descriptions involved is consistent with the final diagnosis of A_3.

Now we can define distributed diagnosis. A diagnosis for the union of all system descriptions is called distributed diagnosis:

Definition 10 (Distributed Diagnosis). A *Distributed Diagnosis* of $(\{SD_{A_1}, \ldots SD_{A_n}\}, COMP, OBS)$ is a set $\Delta \subseteq COMP$, such that $SD_{A_1} \cup \ldots \cup SD_{A_n} \cup OBS \cup \{Mode(c, Ab) | c \in COMP\} \cup \{\neg Mode(c, Ab) | c \in COMP - \Delta\}$ is consistent.

Example 11. $\{Mode(N_3, Ab), Mode(C_7, Ab)\}$ is a distributed diagnosis for the system description and observations in the above example.

In order to implement the scenario above we need separate diagnostic agents for each area. The agents need a knowledge base containing the description of their area and they have to be capable of reactive behavior in order to solve a problem in cooperation with other agents. The theoretical basis of the implementation is the concept of vivid agents [Wag96b] and a prototype developed for fault-tolerant diagnosis [SdAMP96,SW96]. Below we briefly review the vivid agents and extended logic programming. We proceed by showing how the axioms can be expressed as extended logic program and how the agents' reactive behavior is coded in terms of reaction rules. We round out the picture with a trace of the agents' communication after a message is lost.

3   Vivid Agents

A *vivid agent* is a software-controlled system whose state is represented by a knowledge base, and whose behavior is represented by means of *action* and *reaction rules*. Following [Sho93], the state of an agent is described in terms of mental qualities, such as beliefs and intentions. The basic functionality of a vivid agent comprises a knowledge system (including an update and an inference operation), and the capability to represent and perform actions in order to be able to generate and execute plans. Since a vivid agent is 'situated' in an environment with which it has to be able to communicate, it also needs the ability to react in response to perception events, and in response to communication events created by the communication acts of other agents. Notice that the concept of vivid agents is based on the important distinction between action and re-action: actions are first planned and then executed in order to solve a task or to achieve a goal, while reactions are triggered by perception and communication events. Reactions may be immediate and independent from the current knowledge state of the agent but they may also depend on the result of deliberation. In any case, they are triggered by events which are not controlled by the agent. A vivid agent without the capability to accept explicit tasks and to solve them by means of planning and plan execution is called *reagent*. The tasks of reagents cannot be assigned in the form of explicit ('see to it that') goals at run time, but have to be encoded in the specification of their reactive behavior at design time.

We do not assume a fixed formal language and a fixed logical system for the knowledge-base of an agent. Rather, we believe that it is more appropriate to choose a suitable knowledge system for each agent individually according to its domain and its tasks. In the case of diagnosis agents, extended logic programs proved to be an appropriate form of the knowledge base of an agent because it is essential for model-based diagnosis to be able to represent negative facts, default rules and constraints.

3.1   Specification and Execution of Reagents

Simple vivid agents whose mental state comprises only beliefs, and whose behavior is purely reactive, i.e. not based on any form of planning and plan execution, are called *reagents*. A reagent $\mathcal{A} = \langle X, EQ, RR \rangle$, on the basis of a knowledge system $\boldsymbol{K}$ consists of

1. a knowledge base $X \in L_{\text{KB}}$,
2. an event queue EQ being a list of instantiated event expressions, and
3. a set RR of *reaction rules*, consisting of epistemic and physical reaction and inter-action rules which code the reactive and communicative behavior of the agent.

A multi-reagent system is a tuple of reagents $\mathcal{S} = \langle \boldsymbol{A}_1, \ldots, \boldsymbol{A}_n \rangle$

Operational Semantics of Reaction Rules   Reaction rules encode the behavior of vivid agents in response to perception events created by the agent's perception subsystems, and to communication events created by communication acts of other agents. We distinguish between epistemic, physical and communicative reaction rules, and call the latter *interaction rules.* We use L_{PEvt} and L_{CEvt} to denote the perception and communication event languages, and $L_{Evt} = L_{PEvt} \cup L_{CEvt}$. The following table describes the different formats of epistemic, physical and communicative reaction rules:

$$Eff \leftarrow \mathsf{recvMsg}[\varepsilon(U), S],\ Cond$$
$$\mathsf{do}(\alpha(V)),\ Eff \leftarrow \mathsf{recvMsg}[\varepsilon(U), S],\ Cond$$
$$\mathsf{sendMsg}[\eta(V), R],\ Eff \leftarrow \mathsf{recvMsg}[\varepsilon(U), S],\ Cond$$

The event condition $\mathsf{recvMsg}[\varepsilon(U), S]$ is a test whether the event queue of the agent contains a message of the form $\varepsilon(U)$ sent by some perception subsystem of the agent or by another agent identified by S, where $\varepsilon \in L_{Evt}$ represents a perception or a communication event type, and U is a suitable list of parameters. The epistemic condition $Cond \in L_{Query}$ refers to the current knowledge state, and the epistemic effect $Eff \in L_{Input}$ specifies an update of the current knowledge state.

Physical Reaction: $\mathsf{do}(\alpha(V))$ calls a procedure realizing the action α with parameters V.

Communicative Reaction: $\mathsf{sendMsg}[\eta(V), R]$ sends the message $\eta \in L_{CEvt}$ with parameters V to the receiver R.

Both perception and communication events are represented by incoming messages. In general, reactions are based both on perception and on knowledge. Immediate reactions do not allow for deliberation. They are represented by rules with an empty epistemic premise, i.e. $Cond = $ true. Timely reactions can be achieved by guaranteeing fast response times for checking the precondition of a reaction rule. This will be the case, for instance, if the precondition can be checked by simple table look-up (such as in relational databases or fact bases).

Reaction rules are triggered by events. The agent interpreter continually checks the event queue of the agent. If there is a new event message, it is matched with the event condition of all reaction rules, and the epistemic conditions of those rules matching the event are evaluated. If they are satisfiable in the current knowledge base, all free variables in the rules are instantiated accordingly resulting in a set of triggered actions with associated epistemic effects. All these actions are then executed, leading to physical actions and to sending messages to other agents, and their epistemic effects are assimilated into the current knowledge base.

4   Extended Logic Programming and Diagnosis

Since Prolog became a standard in logic programming much research has been devoted to the semantics of logic programs. In particular, Prolog's unsatisfactory treatment of negation as finite failure led to many innovations. Well-founded semantics turned out to be a promising approach to cope with negation by default. Subsequent work extended well-founded semantics with a form of explicit negation and constraints [AP96] and showed that the richer language, called WFSX, is appropriate for a spate of knowledge representation and reasoning forms. In particular, the technique of contradiction removal of extended logic programs opens up many avenues in model-based diagnosis.

Definition 12 (Extended Logic Program). An extended logic program is a (possibly infinite) set of rules of the form

$$L_0 \leftarrow L_1, \ldots, L_m, notL_{m+1}, \ldots, notL_n \ (0 \leq m \leq n)$$

where each L_i is an objective literal ($0 \leq i \leq n$). An objective literal is either an atom A or its explicit negation $\neg A$.[1] Literals of the form $notL$ are called default literals. Literals are either objective or default ones.

To capture that it is contradictory for the predicted behavior to differ from the actual observations, we introduce integrity constraints:

Definition 13 (Constraint). An integrity constraint has the form

$$\bot \leftarrow L_1, \ldots, L_m, notL_{m+1}, \ldots, notL_n \ (0 \leq m \leq n)$$

where each L_i is an objective literal ($0 \leq i \leq n$), and $\bot$ stands for false.

In order to avoid a contradiction we change the beliefs that support the contradiction. The only beliefs that are subject to change concern the closed world assumption ones. From these we can define a set of revisable default literals, whose truth values may be changed to remove contradictions.

Definition 14 (Revisable). The revisables R of a program P are a subset of the default negated literals which do not have rules in P.

In general, we might remove a contradiction by partially dropping the closed world assumption about some revisable. To declaratively define the contradiction removal, we consider all subsets R' of the revisables, change the truth value of the literals in R' from false to true and check whether the revised program is still contradictory. Among those revisions that remove the contradiction we are interested in the minimal ones:

Definition 15 (Revision). Let R be the revisables of the program P. The set $R' \subseteq R$ is called a revision if it is a minimal set such that $P \cup R'$ is free of contradiction.

The revision of contradictory extended logic programs is a suitable technique to compute diagnoses for model-based diagnosis.

4.1 The Agents Knowledge Base

Using the extended logic programming formalism, the agents knowledge base contains the following logic sentences:

---

[1] Note that explicit and implicit negation are related: $\neg L$ implies $not\ L$.

Routing tables The routing information comprises facts stating to which neighbor node a message addressed to a component has to be sent. The knowledge is local since each agent only knows its neighbors. In order to keep the facts in a single knowledge base which is the same for all agents the facts hold only for the respective agent (i_am). For example, for n_1 and n_2 we get the following routing tables:

$$RT : \begin{aligned}
&on\_route(n_1, c_3, n_2) \leftarrow i\_am(n_1). &&on\_route(n_2, c_1, n_1) \leftarrow i\_am(n_2).\\
&on\_route(n_1, c_4, n_2) \leftarrow i\_am(n_1). &&on\_route(n_2, c_2, n_1) \leftarrow i\_am(n_2).\\
&on\_route(n_1, c_5, n_2) \leftarrow i\_am(n_1). &&on\_route(n_2, c_5, n_3) \leftarrow i\_am(n_2).\\
&on\_route(n_1, c_6, n_2) \leftarrow i\_am(n_1). &&on\_route(n_2, c_6, n_3) \leftarrow i\_am(n_2).\\
&on\_route(n_1, c_7, n_2) \leftarrow i\_am(n_1). &&on\_route(n_2, c_7, n_3) \leftarrow i\_am(n_2).\\
&on\_route(n_1, c_8, n_6) \leftarrow i\_am(n_1). &&on\_route(n_2, c_8, n_1) \leftarrow i\_am(n_2).\\
&on\_route(n_1, c_9, n_2) \leftarrow i\_am(n_1). &&on\_route(n_2, c_9, n_5) \leftarrow i\_am(n_2).\\
&on\_route(n_1, c_{10}, n_2) \leftarrow i\_am(n_1). &&on\_route(n_2, c_{10}, n_5) \leftarrow i\_am(n_2). \ldots
\end{aligned}$$

Component Hierarchy Additionally, each agent knows its components. Since this knowledge is local it is only derivable for the respective agent (i_am):

$$CH : \begin{aligned}
&area\_component(n_1, c_1) \leftarrow i\_am(n_1). &&area\_component(n_3, c_6) \leftarrow i\_am(n_3).\\
&area\_component(n_1, c_2) \leftarrow i\_am(n_1). &&area\_component(n_3, c_7) \leftarrow i\_am(n_3).\\
&area\_component(n_2, c_3) \leftarrow i\_am(n_2). &&area\_component(n_6, c_8) \leftarrow i\_am(n_6).\\
&area\_component(n_2, c_4) \leftarrow i\_am(n_2). &&area\_component(n_5, c_9) \leftarrow i\_am(n_5).\\
&area\_component(n_3, c_5) \leftarrow i\_am(n_3). &&area\_component(n_4, c_{10}) \leftarrow i\_am(n_4).
\end{aligned}$$

Disjointness of Modes In the implementation we model only two modes, abnormality (ab) and being ok ($not\ ab$). Therefore disjointness of modes is satisfied. The predicate ab is revisable. The default truth value of the predicate ab is false, which means that by default we assume components to be working fine. Possible contradictions to these assumption are caused by violation of consistency of abstraction and existence of a cause for a lost message.

Consistency of Abstraction An abnormal area contains at least one abnormal component. A contradiction arises if the area is detected to be abnormal but no faulty component is abduced. This constraint has only local character (i_am), since an agent cannot detect abnormal components of other areas.

$$CA : \begin{aligned}
&\bot \leftarrow i\_am(N), ab(N), not\ has\_ab\_component(N).\\
&has\_ab\_component(N) \leftarrow area\_component(N, C), ab(C).
\end{aligned}$$

Existence of a cause for a lost message The basic integrity constraint to start the diagnostic process states that it is contradictory to observe a lost message from node N to component C and not to have lost it on the route from N to C. The message is lost somewhere on this route route if at least one the involved nodes is abnormal:

$$CLM : \begin{aligned}
&\bot \leftarrow message\_lost(N, C), not\ lost\_on\_route(N, C).\\
&lost\_on\_route(N, C) \leftarrow ab(N).\\
&lost\_on\_route(N, C) \leftarrow on\_route(N, C, M), ab(M).
\end{aligned}$$

The following constraint allows us to abduce new observations. If a message is lost from N to C and M is a neighbor of N which is assumed to be abnormal by N, then N abduces the new observation that the message was lost on the way from M to C:

$$RO : \bot \leftarrow message\_lost(N, C), on\_route(N, C, M),$$
$$ab(M), not\ new\_message\_lost(M, C).$$

4.2   The Agents' Reaction Rules

The reaction rules specify how the agents behave. Since the behavior depends on their diagnostic findings they need meta predicates to revise their knowledge base in the light of new observations. Based on the revisions three results are interesting

1. There is no diagnosis to explain the observation (no_diags).
2. There is a diagnosis that the agent itself is abnormal. In this case, since an agent knows its own state, other diagnoses are not of interest.
3. There are diagnoses which do not involve the agent itself ($next$). In this case the agent abduces a new, refined observation.

With the two meta predicates $no\_diags/1$ and $next/2$ we encode the agents' reaction rules:

If an agent receives an observation and has no explanation for it, the fault must be intermittent, since neither the agent itself is faulty nor are any neighbors to accuse. This is reported to the requesting agent:

sendMsg($intermittent\_failure(B), A$) $\longleftarrow$ recvMsg($message\_lost(N, C), A$),

$no\_diags(message\_lost(N, C))$,

Def. 8.2 $i\_am(B)$.

If an agent receives an observation and is himself the cause of the problems it reports this fact back to the requesting agent:

sendMsg($responsible(B), A$) $\longleftarrow$ recvMsg($message\_lost(N, C), A$),

Def. 8.1 $i\_am(B), obs(down, B)$.

If the agents area is not abnormal and there are diagnoses suspecting the agents neighbors, the newly abduced observation is sent to the suspected neighbor:

sendMsg($message\_lost(M, C), M$) $\longleftarrow$ recvMsg($message\_lost(N, C), A$),

$i\_am(B), not\ obs(down, B)$,

Def. 8.3 $next(M, message\_lost(N, C))$.

In this case the agent has to remember to forward the final diagnosis result to the requesting agent:

$remember\_to\_reply\_to(A)$ $\longleftarrow$ recvMsg($message\_lost(N, C), A$),

$N \neq A, i\_am(B), not\ obs(down, B)$,

$not\ no\_diags(message\_lost(N, C))$.

If an agent receives a diagnosis result from one of its neighbors and has to report the result to another neighbor, it forwards it:

$$\mathsf{sendMsg}(intermittent\_failure(A), C) \longleftarrow \mathsf{recvMsg}(intermittent\_failure(A), B),$$
$$remember\_to\_reply\_to(C).$$
$$\mathsf{sendMsg}(responsible(A), C) \longleftarrow \mathsf{recvMsg}(responsible(A), B),$$
$$remember\_to\_reply\_to(C).$$

After forwarding a diagnosis result, the "bookmark" to reply is removed from the agent's knowledge base:

$$neg(remember\_to\_reply\_to(C)) \longleftarrow \mathsf{recvMsg}(intermittent\_failure(A), B),$$
$$remember\_to\_reply\_to(C).$$
$$neg(remember\_to\_reply\_to(C)) \longleftarrow \mathsf{recvMsg}(responsible(A), B),$$
$$remember\_to\_reply\_to(C).$$

4.3 Traces

To make the diagnosis process using the described knowledge base clearer, we consider the following scenario. Node n_1 sends a message to c_7, but the messages gets lost. Since n_1 does not receive an acknowledgment, a timeout mechanism informs n_1 that the message is lost and the diagnosis process starts. In the first scenario n_3 looses the message, whereas in the second one an intermittent failure occured.

Initially the creator process sends a start message to all nodes (see figure 2 lines 1,2,3,4,9,14). The timeout mechanism informs n_1 of the lost message (5,6). Node n_1 knows that it is working fine and suspects the neighbor in charge of sending messages to c_7, namely n_2. Subsequently n_1 sends the refined observation that the message is lost from n_2 to c_7 to n_2 (8,10). Similarly n_2 informs n_3 (11,12,15). Additionally it remembers that it has to report the final result to n_1 (13). Finally, n_3 turns out to be the cause of the fault and the result is sent from n_3 to n_2 (16,17) and from n_2 to n_1 (18,19). n_2 removes the fact that it has to respond to n_1 (20).

In the second trace (see figure 3) all nodes are ok at diagnosis time so the fault is intermittent. The initial phase is similar to the first trace. Only when n_3 comes up with no diagnoses (16), message of an intermittent failure is sent back.

5 Conclusion

We have defined an agent–based framework for the diagnosis of large spatially distributed technical systems. In this framework we assign an agent to every subsystem. This agent has detailed knowledge over its own subsystem and abstract knowledge over its neighbors. Using its declarative system description it can usually diagnose its own subsystem independently. Whenever it cannot detect a cause for an observed fault, it accuses a suitable neighboring subnet and starts cooperation with the responsible agent. This distributed framework leads to attractive algorithm complexity compared to a centralized solution, both concerning communication overhead and computational complexity.

1	$n_2 \longleftarrow creator$	$start$
2	$n_4 \longleftarrow creator$	$start$
3	$n_1 \longleftarrow creator$	$start$
4	$n_5 \longleftarrow creator$	$start$
5	$n_1 \longrightarrow n_1$	$message\_lost(n_1, c_7)$
6	$n_1 \longleftarrow n_1$	$message\_lost(n_1, c_7)$
7	n_1	$diag[ab(n_2), new\_message\_lost(n_2, c_7)]$
8	$n_1 \longrightarrow n_2$	$message\_lost(n_2, c_7)$
9	$n_6 \longleftarrow creator$	$start$
10	$n_2 \longleftarrow n_1$	$message\_lost(n_2, c_7)$
11	n_2	$diag[ab(n_3), new\_message\_lost(n_3, c_7)]$
12	$n_2 \longrightarrow n_3$	$message\_lost(n_3, c_7)$
13	n_2	$assimilates\ remember\_to\_reply\_to(n_1)$
14	$n_3 \longleftarrow creator$	$start$
15	$n_3 \longleftarrow n_2$	$message\_lost(n_3, c_7)$
16	$n_3 \longrightarrow n_2$	$responsible(n_3)$
17	$n_2 \longleftarrow n_3$	$responsible(n_3)$
18	$n_2 \longrightarrow n_1$	$responsible(n_3)$
19	$n_1 \longleftarrow n_2$	$responsible(n_3)$
20	n_2	$assimilates\ neg\ remember\_to\_reply\_to(n_1)$

Fig. 2. Trace for a lost message

1	$n_2 \longleftarrow creator$	$start$
2	$n_1 \longleftarrow creator$	$start$
3	$n_5 \longleftarrow creator$	$start$
4	$n_1 \longrightarrow n_1$	$message\_lost(n_1, c_7)$
5	$n_1 \longleftarrow n_1$	$message\_lost(n_1, c_7)$
6	n_1	$diag[ab(n_2), new\_message\_lost(n_2, c_7)]$
7	$n_1 \longrightarrow n_2$	$message\_lost(n_2, c_7)$
8	$n_2 \longleftarrow n_1$	$message\_lost(n_2, c_7)$
9	$n_6 \longleftarrow creator$	$start$
10	n_2	$diag[ab(n_3), new\_message\_lost(n_3, c_7)]$
11	$n_2 \longrightarrow n_3$	$message\_lost(n_3, c_7)$
12	n_2	$assimilates\ remember\_to\_reply\_to(n_1)$
13	$n_4 \longleftarrow creator$	$start$
14	$n_3 \longleftarrow creator$	$start$
15	$n_3 \longleftarrow n_2$	$message\_lost(n_3, c_7)$
16	n_3	$nodiagnoses$
17	$n_3 \longrightarrow n_2$	$intermittent\_failure(n_3)$
18	$n_2 \longleftarrow n_3$	$intermittent\_failure(n_3)$
19	$n_2 \longrightarrow n_1$	$intermittent\_failure(n_3)$
20	$n_1 \longleftarrow n_2$	$intermittent\_failure(n_3)$
21	n_2	$assimilates\ neg\ remember\_to\_reply\_to(n_1)$

Fig. 3. Trace for an intermittend failure

Our implementation is based on the concepts of vivid agents and extended logic programming. The system description as well as the axioms needed for distributed diagnosis are formulated as extended logic programs. Reaction rules allow the flexible implementation of the communication among the agents, so that the cooperation can be tailored to all kinds of applications.

Acknowledgements We would like to thank Gerd Wagner, who worked on the implementation framework during a joint project and contributed most of the work presented in section 3. Furthermore we would like to thank Lu´s Moniz Pereira for his support. Financially, the work was partially supported by ESPRIT 8319 ModelAge and the German BMBF as well as the Portuguese JNICT.

References

[AP96]   J. J. Alferes and L. M. Pereira. *Reasoning with Logic Programming.* (LNAI 1111), Springer-Verlag, 1996.

[FN96]   Peter Fröhlich and Wolfgang Nejdl. Resolving conflicts in distributed diagnosis. In *ECAI Workshop on Modelling Conflicts in AI*, 1996. To appear.

[MH93]   Igor Mozetic and Christian Holzbauer. Controlling the complexity in model–based diagnosis. *Annals of Mathematics and Artificial Intelligence*, 1993.

[Rei87]   Raymond Reiter. A theory of diagnosis from first principles. *Artificial Intelligence*, 32(1):57–96, 1987.

[SdAMP97] Michael Schroeder, Iara de Almeida Móra, and Lu´s Moniz Pereira. A deliberative and reactive diagnosis agent based on logic programming. In *Intelligent Agents III, LNAI 1193*. Springer–Verlag, 1997. As poster in Proc. of International Conference on Tools in Artificial Intelligence ICTAI96, Toulouse, 1996.

[Sho93]   Yoav Shoham. Agent-oriented programming. *Artificial Intelligence*, 60(1):51–92, 1993.

[SW97]   Michael Schroeder and Gerd Wagner. Distributed diagnosis by vivid agents. In *Proceedings of First Internationl Conference on Auonomous Agents, AA97*, pages 268–275. ACM Press, 1997.

[Wag96a]   Gerd Wagner. A logical and operational model of scalable knowledge-and perception-based agents. Proceedings of ModelAge96, Sesimbra, Portugal, 1996.

[Wag96b]   Gerd Wagner. A logical and operational model of scalable knowledge-and perception-based agents. In *Proceedings of MAAMAW96, LNAI 1038*. Springer-Verlag, 1996.

Preferential Action Semantics
(Preliminary Report)

John-Jules Ch. Meyer[1]* and Patrick Doherty[2]**

[1] Intelligent Systems Group, Dept. of Computer Science
Utrecht University, P.O. Box 80089, 3508 TB, Utrecht, The Netherlands
jj@cs.ruu.nl
[2] Dept. of Computer and Information Science
University of Linköping, S-581 83 Linköping, Sweden, patdo@ida.liu.se

Abstract. In this paper, we propose a new way of considering reasoning about action and change. Rather than placing a preferential structure onto the models of logical theories, we place such a structure directly on the semantics of the actions involved. In this way, we obtain a preferential semantics of actions by means of which we can not only deal with several of the traditional problems in this area such as the frame and ramification problems, but can generalize these solutions to a context which includes both nondeterministic and concurrent actions. In fact, the net result is an integration of semantical and verificational techniques from the paradigm of imperative and concurrent programs in particular, as known from traditional programming, with the AI perspective. In this paper, the main focus is on semantical (i.e. model theoretical) issues rather than providing a logical calculus, which would be the next step in the endeavor.

1 Introduction

Reasoning about action and change has long been of special interest to AI and issues of knowledge representation (see [15]). In particular, the issue of representing changes caused by actions in an efficient and economic way without the burden of explicitly specifying what is *not* affected by the actions involved and is left unchanged has been a major issue in this area, since typically this specification is huge and in some cases *a priori* not completely known. In a similar vein, one would also like to avoid explicitly stating all qualifications to actions and all secondary effects of actions. Most of the proposed solutions impose a so-called *law of inertia* on changes caused by actions which states that properties in the world tend to remain the same when actions occur unless this is known to be

---

* This author is partially supported by ESPRIT BRWG project No. 8319 (MODE-LAGE). This research was initiated during the author's leave to Linköping University (IDA), the hospitality of which is gratefully acknowledged. Moreover, this author wishes to dedicate this paper to the memory of his father B. John Meyer(1917-1996).
** This author is supported by the Swedish Research Council for Engineering Sciences (TFR) and the Knut and Alice Wallenberg Foundation.

J.-J. Ch. Meyer, P.-Y. Schobbens (Eds.): Formal Methods of Agents, LNAI 1760, pp. 187–201, 1999.
© Springer-Verlag Berlin Heidelberg 1999

otherwise. Formally, the inertia assumption in AI has been treated as some kind of default reasoning which in turn has triggered a host of theories about this specific application and defeasible and nonmonotonic theories in general.

The problem that tends to arise with many of the proposed solutions is that application of the inertia assumption is generally too global, or coarse, resulting in unwanted or unintended side effects. One would like to invoke a more local or fine-grained application of inertia to the scenarios at hand and recent proposals tend to support this claim. One explanation for this *coarseness* is that typically one represents an action theory as a set of axioms and then considers a subclass of the models, the preferred models, as the theories intended meaning. This means that the effects of actions are represented or obtained in a slightly roundabout way: the action theory contains axioms from which the behavior of the actions can be deduced using the preferred models of these axioms which somehow have to capture or respect the law of inertia concerning these actions. In simple situations, this approach works fine, but it is well known that in more complex situations finding the right kinds of preferences on one's models is not only very difficult, but even claimed not to be possible.

Our claim is that this is due to the fact that the instrument of considering preferred models of theories that describe complete action scenarios is too coarse because of the fact that these models employ preference relations that stem from 'global' and not action-specific frame assumptions. The specification of preferred outcomes of actions is a delicate matter depending on the actions (and the environment) at hand, and should be handled at the action semantics level rather than the global logical theory describing the whole system. So, what we will do in this paper is to put preferences at the place they should be put, viz. the semantics of actions. On this level we can more succinctly *fine-tune* these preferences incorporating the mode of inertia that is needed for a particular action given a particular context (environment). For each action occurring in a scenario one can thus state the way the variables are known/expected to be affected: are they distinctly 'set' by the action to certain values, are they expected to be not affected, or do we know nothing about this at all, so that anything could happen with them? ¿From this information one can deduce both the possible and the expected behaviour of actions in a scenario, which can be reasoned about in an action logic like dynamic logic ([7]). [1]

We call this way of assigning meaning to actions *preferential action semantics*, which may be contrasted with traditional preferential semantics, which in contrast can be referred to as preferential *theory* (or *assertion*) semantics. Our claim is that preferential action semantics provides us with a flexible framework in which the subtleties of the (expected) behaviour of actions can be expressed and handled in a straightforward and adequate manner. In this paper we will support this claim with some interesting examples which require such subtlety in representation. Interestingly, but very naturally, this view will lead us very

---

[1] To be fair, of course, it might be the case that this action-specific treatment can be encoded into one global preference relation in traditional preferential (theory) semantics, but this will inevitably lead to cumbersome and very intricate models.

close to what is studied in the area of so-called concurrency semantics, i.e. that area of computer science where models of concurrent or parallel computations are investigated. We see for instance that in this framework proposals from the AI literature dealing with action and change which use constructs such as occlusion/release ([3],[13], [8]) get a natural interpretation with respect to the aspect of concurrency.

Finally, in this introduction, we want to discuss the following possible objection to our approach of coping with the frame problem. One might think that our solution is not a solution to the frame problem at all, since the above might give the impression that one has to specify exactly what happens for each action. However, this is not exactly true. The only thing that has to be specified for each action is to which class the variables involved belong: definitely set, framed (i.e. expected to remain the same) or completely free. The semantics decides then the rest. In fact, this also holds for preferential assertion semantics, where variables must also be classified with respect to their "mode of affectedness". It is well-known by now, that this is really needed; one cannot expect to devise some kind of 'magical' preference relation to work in all cases without this kind of information about the variables involved. Hard things cannot be expected to be obtained for free! The only difference is that in preferential action semantics this needs to(or rather, put more positively, may) be done on the level of an individual action. Our point is that specifying these things at a global level might be too much to ask from a (global, assertion-based) preferential entailment relation, which is then supposed to supply the 'right' outcomes in complicated situations, in one blow, so to speak.

2 Preferential Semantics of Actions

In this section, we define a very simple language of actions[2] with which we illustrate our ideas on preferential semantics of actions. Of course, for representing *real* systems this simple language should be extended, but the current simplification will give the general idea.

We start with the set $\mathcal{FVAR}$ of feature variables and $\mathcal{FVAL}$ of feature values. Elements of $\mathcal{FVAL}$ are typically denoted by the letter d, possibly marked or subscripted.[3] Next, we define a system state σ as a function of feature variables to features values: $\sigma : \mathcal{FVAR} \rightarrow \mathcal{FVAL}$. So, for $x \in \mathcal{FVAR}$, $\sigma(x)$ yields it value. The set of states is denoted by Σ. To denote changes of states we require the concept of a variant of a state. The state $\sigma\{d/x\}$ is defined as the state such that $\sigma\{d/x\}(x) = d$ and $\sigma\{d/x\}(y) = \sigma(y)$ for $y \neq x$.

Let a set $\mathcal{A}$ of atomic actions be fixed. An atomic action $a \in \mathcal{A}$ comes with a signature indicating what variables are *framed*, which of these may nevertheless vary (are *released* from inertia) and which are definitely *set*: $a =$

---

[2] Actually, these are action expressions/descriptions rather than actions, but we will use the term rather loosely here.

[3] For convenience, we will assume that all feature variables range over the same set of feature values, mostly the booleans, but of course this restriction can be lifted.

$a(\text{set}_a, \text{frame}_a, \text{release}_a)$, where $\text{set}_a, \text{frame}_a, \text{release}_a \subseteq \mathcal{FVAR}$, such that $\text{release}_a \subseteq \text{frame}_a$ and $\text{set}_a \cap \text{frame}_a = \emptyset$. We also define $\text{inert}_a = \text{frame}_a \setminus \text{release}_a$ and $\text{var}_a = \mathcal{FVAR} \setminus (\text{set}_a \cup \text{frame}_a)$.[4] The inert variables are those subject to inertia, so that it is preferred that they retain the same value; the var variables are those not subjected to inertia and are really variables in the true sense of the word. The distinction between var and released variables is a subtle one: typically when describing an action scenario some of the framed variables (which are normally subject to inertia) are temporarily released, while some variables are considered truly variable over the whole scenario. Sandewall [14] describes the three classes of frame-released, frame-unreleased (inert), and var variables as *occluded*, *remanent*, and *dependent*. Kartha and Lifschitz [8] were probably the first to recognize this three-tiered distinction, while Sandewall [12] was the first to use the frame/occluded distinction to deal properly with nondeterministic actions and actions with duration.

Given the set of atomic actions, complex actions can be formed as follows:

$$\alpha = a \mid \text{if } b \text{ then } \alpha_1 \text{ else } \alpha_2 \text{ fi} \mid \alpha_1 \oplus \alpha_2 \mid \alpha_1 + \alpha_2 \mid \alpha_1 \parallel \alpha_2 \mid \text{fail}.$$

Here, $a \in \mathcal{A}$; if b then α_1 else α_2 fi , where b is a boolean test on feature variables, represents a conditional action with the obvious meaning; $\alpha_1 \oplus \alpha_2$ stands for *restricted choice* between actions α_1 and α_2, where the release mechanism is applied to the actions α_1 and α_2 separately; $\alpha_1 + \alpha_2$ stands for an *open* or *liberal choice* between α_1 and α_2, where the release mechanism induced by the two actions α_1 and α_2 is employed for α_1 and α_2 in a joint fashion (to be explained later on); $\alpha_1 \parallel \alpha_2$ stands for the *parallel (simultaneous) performance* of both α_1 and α_2; fail denotes the *failing* action, possessing no successor states. The class of all actions is denoted by $\mathcal{Act}$. We now introduce the class of *preferred actions* (or rather the class of preferred behaviors of actions) denoted by $\mathcal{Pref Act} = \{\alpha_\sharp \mid \alpha \in \mathcal{Act}\}$, where $\alpha_\sharp$ expresses the *preferred* behavior of α.[5]

The formal semantics of actions is given by functions which essentially describe the way actions change states. We define a semantical function $[\cdot] : \mathcal{Act} \to \Sigma \to (2^\Sigma \times 2^\Sigma)$ for $\alpha \in \mathcal{Act}$, $\sigma \in \Sigma$. $[\alpha](\sigma)$ denotes the set of states that computation of action α may result in, together with information about which of these states are preferred (or expected). So, $[\alpha](\sigma) = (S, S')$, where $S' \subseteq S \subseteq \Sigma$, and S' are the preferred (expected) outcome states of α. If $[\alpha](\sigma) = (S, S')$, we refer to S and S' by means of $([\alpha](\sigma))_\flat$ (or $[\alpha]_\flat(\sigma)$) and $([\alpha](\sigma))_\sharp$ (or $[\alpha]_\sharp(\sigma)$), respectively. If $S' = S$, this means that there is no preferred strict subset. In this case, we will just write $[\alpha](\sigma) = S$.

We allow placing constraints Φ on the set of states, so that effectively, the function $[\cdot]$ is constrained: $[\cdot] : \mathcal{Act} \to \Sigma_\Phi \to (2^\Sigma \times 2^\Sigma)$, where $\Sigma_\Phi = \{\sigma \in \Sigma \mid \sigma \models \Phi\}$.[6]

---

[4] When it is convenient, we may also specify the inert and var variables in an action, such as e.g. $a = a(\text{set}_a, \text{inert}_a, \text{var}_a)$.

[5] Note that it is senseless to talk about $(\alpha_\sharp)_\sharp$. This is not allowed by the syntax. We leave the question to future research whether nestings of preference regarding action behavior can be useful in some way.

[6] Constraints will be used to treat the ramification problem in a later section.

We are now ready to define the semantics for atomic and complex actions in terms of the functions described above.

Atomic Actions

For atomic action $a = a(\text{set}_a, \text{frame}_a, \text{release}_a)$, we define its semantics as follows. First, we determine the effect of a on the variables in set_a. We assume that this is deterministic; let us denote the (unique) state yielded by this effect by σ_a. We may e.g. write $\text{set}_a = \{+x, -y\}$ when we want to express that x is set to true and y is set to false. For instance, if σ is a state containing boolean information about the feature l ("the gun is loaded or not"), and a is the action $\text{load}(\text{set}_{\text{load}} = \{+l\})$, then $\sigma_{\text{load}} = \sigma\{T/l\}$, representing that the load action sets the variable l to true.

$$[a(\text{set}_a, \text{frame}_a, \text{release}_a)](\sigma) = (S, S')$$

where (supposing $\text{frame}_a = \{x_1, x_2, \ldots, x_m\}$, $\text{release}_a = \{x_1, x_2, \ldots, x_n\} \subseteq \text{frame}_a$, so $n \leq m$, and $\text{var}_a = \{y_1, y_2, \ldots, y_k\}$):

$$S = \{\sigma_a\{d_1/x_1, d_2/x_2, \ldots, d_m/x_m, d'_1/y_1, d'_2/y_2, \ldots, d'_k/y_k\} \in$$
$$\Sigma_\Phi \mid d_1, d_2, \ldots, d_m, d'_1, d'_2, \ldots, d'_k \in \mathcal{FVAL}\}$$
$$(= \{\sigma' \in \Sigma_\Phi \mid \sigma'(z) = \sigma_a(z) \text{ for all } z \in \text{set}_a\})$$

and

$$S' = \{\sigma_a\{d_1/x_1, d_2/x_2, \ldots, d_n/x_n, d'_1/y_1, d'_2/y_2, \ldots, d'_k/y_k\} \in$$
$$\Sigma_\Phi \mid d_1, d_2, \ldots, d_n, d'_1, d'_2, \ldots, d'_k \in \mathcal{FVAL}\}$$
$$(= \{\sigma' \in \Sigma_\Phi \mid \sigma'(z) = \sigma_a(z) \text{ for all } z \in \text{set}_a \cup \text{inert}_a\}).$$

Note that indeed $S' \subseteq S$ ($\subseteq \Sigma_\Phi$).

Although the definition looks fairly complicated, it simply states formally that the usual semantics of an action $a(\text{set}_a, \text{frame}_a, \text{release}_a)$ consists of those states that apart from the definite effect of the action on the variables in set_a, both var and frame variables may be set to any possible value, whereas the preferred semantics (capturing inertia) keeps the inert variables the same, although the var and release variables are still allowed to vary.

Let's, by way of an example, consider the action load again, now also in a context where the variable a, denoting being alive, plays a role. (You see, we are heading towards the inevitable Yale Shooting.) Suppose that $\text{load} = \text{load}(\text{set}_{\text{load}} = \{+l\}, \text{frame}_{\text{load}} = \{a\}, \text{release}_{\text{load}} = \emptyset)$. Let's consider a state σ in which a is true (I'm alive) and l is false (unloaded gun). Now the formal semantics of the load action in this state gives us: $[\text{load}](\sigma) = (S, S')$ with $S = \{\sigma\{T/l, T/a\}, \sigma\{T/l, F/a\}\}$ and $S' = \{\sigma\{T/l\}\} = \{\sigma\{T/l, T/a\}\}$, which means that apart from setting l to true (the gun becomes loaded), it is possible that both one stays alive and one dies, but that the former is preferred (expected). If one now, for some reason, would release the variable a from the frame (assumption), the expectation that a remains true is dropped.

Complex Actions

In the sequel, it will sometimes be convenient to use the notation $\alpha(\text{set}_\alpha = X, \text{frame}_\alpha = Y, \text{release}_\alpha = Z)$, or simply $\alpha(\text{set} = X, \text{frame} = Y, \text{release} = Z)$, or even $\alpha(\text{set } X, \text{frame } Y, \text{release } Z)$, for the action $\alpha(\text{set}_\alpha, \text{frame}_\alpha, \text{release}_\alpha)$, with $\text{set}_\alpha = X$, $\text{frame}_\alpha = Y$, and $\text{release}_\alpha = Z$. In addition, the set-theoretical operators are, when needed, extended to pairs in the obvious way: $(S_1, S_1') \bullet (S_2, S_2') = (S_1 \bullet S_2, S_1' \bullet S_2')$.

The conditional and fail actions are given the following meanings:

$$[\text{if } b \text{ then } \alpha_1 \text{ else } \alpha_2 \text{ fi}](\sigma) = [\alpha_1](\sigma) \text{ if } b(\sigma) = T; \text{ and } [\alpha_2](\sigma) \text{ otherwise.}$$

$$[\text{fail}](\sigma) = (\emptyset, \emptyset).$$

Let's now consider the choice operators. The difference between restricted and liberal choice is illustrated by the following example. Suppose we have the constraint that shower on (o) is equivalent to either a hot shower (h) or a cold shower (c), i.e. $o \leftrightarrow h \vee c$. Let ho stand for the action of putting the hot shower on ($h := T$), and co for the action of putting the cold shower on ($c := T$). In the case where the restricted choice action ho $\oplus$ co is performed in a state where $\neg o$ ($= \neg h \wedge \neg c$) holds, we either choose to do ho in this state resulting in a state where $h \wedge o \wedge \neg c$ holds (so inertia is applied to $\neg c$), or co is chosen resulting in a state where $c \wedge o \wedge \neg h$ holds (so inertia is applied to $\neg h$). In contrast, if the liberal choice action ho + co is performed in a state where $\neg o$, we just look at the possibilities of doing ho, co, and *possibly both*, resulting in one of the states $\{h \wedge o \wedge \neg c, \neg h \wedge o \wedge c, h \wedge o \wedge c\}$. So one may view this as if every atom o, h, or c is allowed to change value and is not subject to any inertia.

The semantics of the restricted choice operator can be stated as follows. Let the function Constrain_Φ be such that it removes all states that do not satisfy the constraints Φ: $\text{Constrain}_\Phi(S) = \{\sigma \in S \mid \sigma \models \Phi\}$. When no confusion arises, we may omit the subscript Φ.

$$[\alpha(\text{set}_\alpha, \text{frame}_\alpha, \text{release}_\alpha) \oplus \beta(\text{set}_\beta, \text{frame}_\beta, \text{release}_\beta)](\sigma) =$$
$$\text{Constrain}_\Phi([\alpha(\text{set}_\alpha, \text{frame}_\alpha, \text{release}_\alpha)](\sigma) \cup$$
$$[\beta(\text{set}_\beta, \text{frame}_\beta, \text{release}_\beta)](\sigma)).$$

The definition states that the restricted choice between α and β regards the actions α and β more or less separately. In particular, the release mechanism works separately for both actions α and β.

The semantics of the liberal choice operator can be stated as follows.

$$[\alpha(\text{set}_\alpha, \text{frame}_\alpha, \text{release}_\alpha) + \beta(\text{set}_\beta, \text{frame}_\beta, \text{release}_\beta)](\sigma) =$$
$$\text{Constrain}_\Phi([\alpha(\text{set}_\alpha, \text{frame} = (\text{frame}_\alpha \cup \text{frame}_\beta \cup \text{set}_\beta) \setminus \text{set}_\alpha,$$
$$\text{release} = (\text{release}_\alpha \cup \text{release}_\beta \cup \text{set}_\beta) \setminus \text{set}_\alpha)](\sigma) \cup$$
$$[\beta(\text{set}_\beta, \text{frame} = (\text{frame}_\alpha \cup \text{frame}_\beta \cup \text{set}_\alpha) \setminus \text{set}_\beta,$$
$$\text{release} = (\text{release}_\alpha \cup \text{release}_\beta \cup \text{set}_\alpha) \setminus \text{set}_\beta)](\sigma)).$$

In this case, the situation for the liberal choice operator is considered much more uniformly in the sense that not only the set of frame variables is taken together, but also the release mechanism works in a much more uniform manner. For both actions the sets of release and set variables is added, so that inertia is less potent and more possibility of variability (also with respect to preferred outcomes) is introduced by considering joint effects of the two actions α and β.

The semantics of the parallel operator can be stated as follows.

$$[\alpha(\text{set}_\alpha, \text{frame}_\alpha, \text{release}_\alpha) \parallel \beta(\text{set}_\beta, \text{frame}_\beta, \text{release}_\beta)](\sigma) =$$
$$\text{Constrain}_\Phi([\alpha(\text{set}_\alpha, \text{frame} = (\text{frame}_\alpha \cup \text{frame}_\beta \cup \text{set}_\beta) \setminus \text{set}_\alpha,$$
$$\text{release} = (\text{release}_\alpha \cup \text{release}_\beta \cup \text{set}_\beta) \setminus \text{set}_\alpha)](\sigma) \cap$$
$$[\beta(\text{set}_\beta, \text{frame} = (\text{frame}_\alpha \cup \text{frame}_\beta \cup \text{set}_\alpha) \setminus \text{set}_\beta,$$
$$\text{release} = (\text{release}_\alpha \cup \text{release}_\beta \cup \text{set}_\alpha) \setminus \text{set}_\beta)](\sigma)).$$

Note the similarity with the liberal choice operator. In fact, the only thing that has changed with respect to the latter is that now *only the joint* effects of both actions are taken into consideration, where the release mechanism for both actions is again taken as liberal as possible allowing for as much interaction as possible.

Finally, we consider the preferred behavior operator $\sharp$:

$$[\alpha_\sharp](\sigma) = ([\alpha](\sigma))_\sharp.$$

Example. Let us consider the shower example again. The actions ho and co can be described more precisely as $\text{ho}(\text{set}\{+h\}, \text{frame}\{o, c\}, \text{release}\{o\})$ and $\text{co}(\text{set}\{+c\}, \text{frame}\{o, h\}, \text{release}\{o\})$. Recall that we have $o \leftrightarrow h \vee c$ as a domain constraint (Φ). Let σ be such that $\sigma = \{F/h, F/c, F/o\}$. Now, $[(\text{ho} \oplus \text{co})_\sharp](\sigma)$ becomes

$$(\text{Constrain}_\Phi([\text{ho}(\text{set}\{+h\}, \text{frame}\{o, c\}, \text{release}\{o\})](\sigma) \cup$$
$$[\text{co}(\text{set}\{+c\}, \text{frame}\{o, h\}, \text{release}\{o\})](\sigma)))_\sharp =$$
$$\{\sigma\{T/h, F/c, T/o\}, \sigma\{F/h, T/c, T/o\}\}, \text{while } [(\text{ho} + \text{co})_\sharp] =$$
$$(\text{Constrain}_\Phi([\text{ho}(\text{set}\{+h\}, \text{frame} = \text{release} = \{o, c\})](\sigma) \cup$$
$$[\text{co}(\text{set}\{+c\}, \text{frame} = \text{release} = \{o, h\})](\sigma)))_\sharp =$$
$$\{\sigma\{T/h, F/c, T/o\}, \sigma\{F/h, T/c, T/o\}, \sigma\{T/h, T/c, T/o\}\},$$

as expected.

In addition, consider the action $h \parallel c$ in the same setting. Intuitively, one would expect that this action should have the effect of putting the shower on with both cold and hot water. $[(\text{ho} \parallel \text{co})_\sharp] = (\text{Constrain}_\Phi([\text{ho}(\text{set}\{+h\}, \text{frame} = \text{release} = \{o, c\})](\sigma) \cap [\text{co}(\text{set}\{+c\}, \text{frame} = \text{release} = \{o, h\})](\sigma)))_\sharp$ which is equivalent to $\{\sigma\{T/h, T/c, T/o\}\}$, as desired.

Remark on Semantical Entities

The observing reader may have noticed that in the above definitions we have abused our language slightly by mixing syntax and semantics. This is due to the fact that, although the signature of an action consisting of a specification of the set, framed and released variables has a very syntactic ring to it, it nevertheless conveys semantical information. When one is more rigorous, one should consider semantical entities of the following type: sets of tuples of the form $(S, S', (set, frame, release))$, where the S and S' with $S' \subseteq S$ are sets of states (denoting the possible resulting states and the preferred subset of these, respectively), and set, $frame$ and $release$ are sets of variables expressing the status of the variables with respect to the sets S and S'. Of course, this information is implicit in the sets S and S', but for the sake of defining the interpretation of the operators it is very convenient to have this information explicitly available in the denotations of results. Now we may define our operators on these enhanced semantical elements: on tuples they read as follows:

$$(S_1, S_1', (set_1, frame_1, release_1)) \oplus (S_2, S_2', (set_2, frame_2, release_2)) =$$
$$\{(S_1, S_1', (set_1, frame_1, release_1)), (S_2, S_2', (set_2, frame_2, release_2))\}$$

$$(S_1, S_1', (set_1, frame_1, release_1)) + (S_2, S_2', (set_2, frame_2, release_2)) =$$
$$\{(S_1, S_1', (set_1, (frame_1 \cup frame_2 \cup set_2)$$
$$\setminus set_1, release_1 \cup release_2 \cup set_2) \setminus set_1),$$
$$(S_2, S_2', (set_2, (frame_1 \cup frame_2 \cup set_1) \setminus$$
$$set_2, release_1 \cup release_2 \cup set_1) \setminus set_2)\}$$

$$(S_1, S_1', (set_1, frame_1, release_1)) \parallel (S_2, S_2', (set_2, frame_2, release_2)) =$$
$$\{(S_1 \cap S_2, S_1' \cap S_2', (set_1 \cup set_2, (frame_1 \cup frame_2) \setminus (set_1 \cup set_2),$$
$$(release_1 \cup release_2) \setminus (set_1 \cup set_2))\}$$

Finally, we extend the definition to sets of tuples T_1 and T_2 in the obvious way: $T_1 \triangle T_2 = \bigcup_{t_1 \in T_1, t_2 \in T_2} t_1 \triangle t_2$ for $\triangle = \oplus, +, \parallel$. This shows how one can do the previous definitions more formally. However, we have chosen not to do this in the remainder of the paper in order to keep things more intelligible, and to focus on the main ideas.

3   Preferential Action Dynamic Logic (PADL)

In order to define a logic for reasoning about actions which includes their preferred interpretations, we simply take the (ordinary) dynamic logic formalism which is well known from the theory of imperative programming ([7]). Formulas in the class $\mathcal{F}orm$ are of the form $[\alpha]\phi$, where $\alpha \in \mathcal{A}ct \cup \mathcal{P}ref\mathcal{A}ct$, $\phi \in \mathcal{F}orm$, closed under the usual classical connectives.

The semantics of formulas is given by the usual Kripke-style semantics. A Kripke model is a structure $M = (\Sigma, \{R_\alpha \mid \alpha \in \mathcal{A}ct \cup \mathcal{P}ref\mathcal{A}ct\})$, where the accessibility relations R_α are given by $R_\alpha(\sigma, \sigma') \Leftrightarrow_{\text{def}} \sigma' \in [\alpha]_b(\sigma)$.

Formulas of the form $[\alpha]\phi$ are now interpreted as usual: $M, \sigma \models [\alpha]\phi \Leftrightarrow$ for all $\sigma' : R_\alpha(\sigma, \sigma') \Rightarrow M, \sigma' \models \phi$. The other connectives are dealt with as usual. Note the special case involving formulas with preferred actions where $[\alpha_\sharp]\phi$ is interpreted as: $M, \sigma \models [\alpha_\sharp]\phi \Leftrightarrow$ (for all $\sigma' : R_\alpha(\sigma, \sigma') \Rightarrow M, \sigma' \models \phi$) $\Leftrightarrow$ (for all $\sigma' : \sigma' \in [\alpha_\sharp](\sigma) \Rightarrow M, \sigma' \models \phi$) $\Leftrightarrow$ (for all $\sigma' : \sigma' \in ([\alpha](\sigma))_\sharp \Rightarrow M, \sigma' \models \phi$). Validity in a model, $M \models \phi$, is defined as $M, \sigma \models \phi$ for all σ. Validity of a formula, $\models \phi$, is defined as $M \models \phi$ for all models M.

Some useful validities (here we assume the set Φ of constraints to be finite and abuse our language slightly and let Φ stand for the conjunction of its elements as well):

$\models [\alpha](\phi \rightarrow \psi) \rightarrow ([\alpha]\phi \rightarrow [\alpha]\psi)$

$\models [\text{if } b \text{ then } \alpha_1 \text{ else } \alpha_2 \text{ fi}]\phi \leftrightarrow ((b \wedge [\alpha_1]\phi) \vee (\neg b \wedge [\alpha_2]\phi))$

$\models [\alpha]\phi \rightarrow [\alpha_\sharp]\phi$

$\models [\alpha]\phi \rightarrow [\alpha \parallel \beta]\phi$

$\models ([\alpha_\sharp]\Phi \wedge [\beta_\sharp]\Phi) \rightarrow ([[(\alpha \oplus \beta)_\sharp]\phi \leftrightarrow [\alpha_\sharp]\phi \wedge [\beta_\sharp]\phi)$

$\models [(\alpha + \beta)_\sharp]\phi \rightarrow [(\alpha \oplus \beta)_\sharp]\phi$

Note, by the way, that regarding non-preferred behaviour we have that $\models [\alpha + \beta]\phi \leftrightarrow [\alpha \oplus \beta]\phi \, (\leftrightarrow [\alpha]\phi \wedge [\beta]\phi)$. Furthermore, as usual in dynamic logic we have that: $\models \phi \Rightarrow \models [\alpha]\phi$.

However, some notable non-validities are:

$\not\models [\alpha_\sharp]\phi \rightarrow [(\alpha \parallel \beta)_\sharp]\phi$

$\not\models [(\alpha \oplus \beta)_\sharp]\phi \rightarrow [(\alpha + \beta)_\sharp]\phi$

4   SKIP vs. WAIT: Concurrency

Let us now briefly examine the difference between a wait action in the AI context and a skip action in imperative programming. A strong monotonic inertia assumption is implicitly built into the state transitions of imperative programming where the meaning of the skip action for example is just the identity function; $[\text{skip}] = \lambda\sigma.\sigma$. For the wait action, it also holds that $[\text{wait}_\sharp] = \lambda\sigma.\sigma$, but in this case, the inertia assumption is weaker in the sense that the action may itself show any behavior, due to additional effects in the environment. Our approach offers the possibility of specifying this weaker notion which will even work properly in the context of unspecified concurrent actions. For example, if wait = wait(set = frame = release = $\emptyset$), load = load(set$\{+l\}$), and we consider the action wait $\parallel$ load, we obtain $[\text{wait} \parallel \text{load}](\sigma) = [\text{wait}(\text{set} = \text{frame} = \text{release} = \emptyset) \parallel \text{load}(\text{set}\{+l\})](\sigma) = [\text{wait}(\text{frame}\{l\}, \text{release}\{l\})](\sigma) \cap [\text{load}(\text{set}\{+l\})](\sigma) \, D\{\sigma\{T/l\}, \sigma\{F/l\}\} \cap \{\sigma\{T/l\}\} = \{\sigma\{T/l\}\} = [\text{load}](\sigma)$.

More interestingly, if we also consider the propositional fluent a, we see how the release and the law of inertia work together. Suppose $\mathsf{wait} = \mathsf{wait}(\mathsf{frame}\{a, l\})$, $\mathsf{load} = \mathsf{load}(\mathsf{set}\{+l\})$. $[\mathsf{wait} \parallel \mathsf{load}](\sigma) = [\mathsf{wait}(\mathsf{frame}\{a, l\}) \parallel \mathsf{load}(\mathsf{set}\{+l\})](\sigma) = [\mathsf{wait}(\mathsf{frame}\{a, l\}, \mathsf{release}\{l\})](\sigma) \cap \mathsf{load}(\mathsf{set}\{+l\}\mathsf{frame}\{a\})](\sigma)$. It follows that $\models (\neg l \wedge a) \rightarrow [\mathsf{wait} \parallel \mathsf{load}]l$, while $\models (\neg l \wedge a) \rightarrow [(\mathsf{wait} \parallel \mathsf{load})_\sharp]l \wedge a$, as would be expected.

The upshot of all this is that although preferably the wait action has the same effect as the skip action, nevertheless due to the (non-specified) *concurrent* actions that are done in parallel with the wait, and of which we do not have any control, additional effects might occur.

5   Other Examples

We will start with a number of standard examples and move towards larger and more complex examples which combine the frame and ramification problems with concurrent actions.

Yale Shooting Scenario: Initially Fred is alive, then the gun is loaded, we wait for a moment and then shoot. Of course (under reasonable conditions), it is expected that Fred is dead after shooting. In our approach, this example is represented as follows: we have the features loaded (l), alive (a), and the actions $\mathsf{load} = \mathsf{load}(\mathsf{set}\{+l\}, \mathsf{frame}\{a\})$, $\mathsf{wait} = \mathsf{wait}(\mathsf{frame}\{a, l\})$, and $\mathsf{shoot} = $ if l then $\mathsf{kill}(\mathsf{set}\{-l, -a\})$ else $\mathsf{wait}(\mathsf{frame}\{a, l\})$ fi. Now we have that $(\neg l \wedge a) \rightarrow [\mathsf{load}_\sharp](l \wedge a)$; $(l \wedge a) \rightarrow [\mathsf{wait}_\sharp](l \wedge a)$; and finally $(l \wedge a) \rightarrow [\mathsf{kill}_\sharp]\neg a$, and hence also $(l \wedge a) \rightarrow [\mathsf{shoot}_\sharp]\neg a$, so that $\models (\neg l \wedge a) \rightarrow [\mathsf{load}_\sharp][\mathsf{wait}_\sharp][\mathsf{shoot}_\sharp]\neg a$.

Russian Turkey Shoot: The scenario is more or less as before, but now the wait action is replaced by a spin action: $\mathsf{spin} = \mathsf{spin}(\mathsf{frame}\{a\})$, leaving the variable l out of the frame, which may then vary arbitrarily. Clearly, $\not\models (\neg l \wedge a) \rightarrow [\mathsf{load}_\sharp][\mathsf{spin}_\sharp][\mathsf{shoot}_\sharp]\neg a$, since $\not\models (l \wedge a) \rightarrow [\mathsf{spin}_\sharp]l$, although it is the case that $\models (l \wedge a) \rightarrow [\mathsf{spin}_\sharp]a$,

The Walking Turkey Shoot (Ramification): Similar to the Yale Shooting Scenario, but now we also consider the feature walking (w) and the constraint that walking implies alive: $\Phi = \{w \rightarrow a\}$. So now we consider the action $\mathsf{shoot} = $ if l then $\mathsf{kill}(\mathsf{set}\{-l, -a\}, \mathsf{release}\{w\})$ else $\mathsf{wait}(\mathsf{frame}\{a, l\})$ fi, and obtain $\models (l \wedge a) \rightarrow [\mathsf{shoot}_\sharp](\neg a \wedge \neg w)$. In this case, inertia on w is not applied.

We now proceed to some more complicated scenarios.

Jumping into the Lake Example ([1], [5]): Consider the situation in which one jumps into a lake, wearing a hat. Being in the lake (l) implies being wet (w). So we have as a constraint $\Phi = \{l \rightarrow w\}$. If one is initially not in the lake, not wet and wearing a hat, the preferred result using inertia would be that after jumping into the lake, one is in the lake and wet, but no conclusions concerning wearing a hat after the jump can be derived. We do not want to apply inertia to the feature of wearing a hat , since it is conceivable that while jumping, one could lose one's hat. So technically, this means that the feature variable hat-on (h) is left out of the frame. (Another way of representing this, which one might prefer and which will give the same result, is viewing the frame constant over the whole scenario, including h, and then releasing h in the present situation.)

If one is in the lake and wet, we would expect that after getting out of the lake, one is not in the lake, but *still wet* in the resulting state. So, inertia would be applied to the feature wet. Furthermore, we may assume that getting out of the lake is much less violent than jumping into it, so that we may also put h in the frame. Finally, if one is out of the lake and wet, then putting on a hat would typically result in a state where one has a hat on, while remaining out of the lake and wet.

Formally, we can treat this relatively complicated scenario by means of our semantics as follows. Consider the feature variables l (being in the lake), w (being wet), h (wearing a hat), and the constraint $\Phi = \{l \rightarrow w\}$. In addition, we would need three actions.

- jump-into-lake = jil(set$\{+l\}$, frame$\{w\}$, release$\{w\}$), where w must be released in view of the constraint $l \rightarrow w$.
- get-outof-lake = gol(set$\{-l\}$, frame$\{w, h\}$); although l is set, w is not released, since l is set to false and this does not enforce anything in view of the constraint $l \rightarrow w$.
- put-on-hat = poh(set$\{+h\}$, frame$\{l, w\}$,).

Now, applying the logic gives the desired results: $(\neg l \wedge \neg w \wedge h) \rightarrow [\text{jil}_\sharp](l \wedge w)$, and $(\neg l \wedge \neg w \wedge h) \rightarrow [\text{jil}](l \wedge w)$; $(l \wedge w) \rightarrow [\text{gol}_\sharp](\neg l \wedge w)$, (even $(l \wedge w \wedge h) \rightarrow [\text{gol}_\sharp](\neg l \wedge w \wedge h)$), and $(l \wedge w) \rightarrow [\text{gol}]\neg l$; $(\neg l \wedge w) \rightarrow [\text{poh}_\sharp](\neg l \wedge w \wedge h)$, and $(\neg l \wedge w) \rightarrow [\text{poh}]h$.

What this example shows is that one still has to choose the signature of actions: what is put in the frame and what is not. This is not done automatically by the framework. We claim this to be an advantage because it provides enormous flexibility in its use, while at the same time it calls for exactness, so that the specifying of agents forces one to specify per action how things should be handled. The law of inertia (applied on non-released frame variables) takes care of the rest, so to speak.

It is important to emphasize that some of the newer approaches for dealing with directed ramification which introduce explicit causal axioms ([9],[16]) essentially encode the same types of behavior, but at the same time rule out similar flexibility in specification of actions. Thielscher [16] for example, claims that the frame/released approaches are limited and provides the extended circuit example as a counterexample. One should rather view frame/released approaches as the result of a compilation process which compiles causal dependencies of one form or another [6]. The distinction to keep in mind is whether one's formalism is capable of specifying frame/released constraints differently from state to state. This deserves further analysis in the context of this approach.

Lifting a Bucket of Water. One can also use preferential action semantics in cases where one has certain default behavior of actions *on other grounds than the law of inertia* . Consider the lifting of a bucket filled with water with a left and right handle by means of a robot with two arms. Let lift-left (ll) be the action of the robot's lifting the left handle of the bucket with its left arm and lift-right (lr) be the analogous action of the robot's right arm. Obviously, when only one of the two actions are performed separately, water will be spilled. On the other hand, when the two actions are done concurrently, things go alright and no water is spilled. We place a constraint on the scenario that $\neg s \leftrightarrow (l \leftrightarrow r)$.

Now, we can say that normally when lift-right is performed, water gets spilled. However, in the extraordinary case when lift-right is performed in a context where (coincidentally) lift-left is also performed, water is not spilled. This example can be represented clearly and succinctly with our semantics. We assume that initially, in state σ, neither arm is lifted, and no water is spilled (yet), i.e. the variables l, r and s are all false. One can associate with lift-right the semantics:

$$[\mathsf{lr}(\mathsf{set}\{r\}, \mathsf{frame}\{l\})](\sigma) = (\{\sigma\{T/r\}\{T/s\}, \sigma\{T/r\}\{F/s\}\}, \{\sigma\{T/r\}\{T/s\}\}),$$

expressing that performance of lift-right leads to a state where the right arm is raised (r) and either water gets spilled or not, but that the former is preferred (on other grounds than inertia: note that s is not framed). Analogously, we can define this for lift-left, where instead of the variable r, a variable l is set to indicate the left arm is raised. So, in our dynamic logic, the result is $\models [\mathsf{lr}]r$ and $\models [\mathsf{ll}]l$, but $\not\models [\mathsf{lr}]s$ and $\not\models [\mathsf{ll}]s$. On the other hand, we do have $\models [\mathsf{lr}_\sharp]s$ and $\models [\mathsf{ll}_\sharp]s$. Furthermore, since $[\mathsf{ll} \parallel \mathsf{lr}](\sigma) =$

$$[\mathsf{ll}(\mathsf{set}\{+l\}, \mathsf{frame}=\mathsf{release}=\{r\})](\sigma) \cap [\mathsf{lr}(\mathsf{set}\{+r\}, \mathsf{frame}=\mathsf{release}=\{l\})](\sigma) =$$
$$\{\sigma\{T/l\}\{T/r\}\{F/s\}, \sigma\{T/l\}\{F/r\}\{T/s\}\} \cap$$
$$\{\sigma\{T/r\}\{T/l\}\{F/s\}, \sigma\{T/r\}\{F/l\}\{T/s\}\} = \{\sigma\{T/r\}\{T/l\}\{F/s\}),$$

we also obtain that $\models [\mathsf{ll} \parallel \mathsf{lr}](r \wedge l \wedge \neg s)$, as desired.

6   Directions for Future Work

We would like to investigate the possibility of introducing sequences of actions by considering the class *ActSeq* given by $\beta = \alpha \mid \beta_1; \beta_2$. This would allow one to write down the outcome of a scenario such as the Yale Shooting problem as: $(\neg l \wedge a) \rightarrow [\mathsf{load}_\sharp; \mathsf{wait}_\sharp; \mathsf{shoot}_\sharp]\neg a$, instead of having to resort to the (equivalent) slightly roundabout representation $(\neg l \wedge a) \rightarrow [\mathsf{load}_\sharp][\mathsf{wait}_\sharp][\mathsf{shoot}_\sharp]\neg a$, as we did earlier. Note that by this way of defining action sequences, we (purposely) prohibit considering preferred sequences. Thus, something like $(\beta_1; \beta_2)_\sharp$ would now be ill-formed in our syntax, while $\alpha_{1\sharp}; \alpha_{2\sharp}$ is allowed. It remains subject to further research whether something like $(\beta_1; \beta_2)_\sharp$ could be given a clear-cut semantics and whether it would be a useful construct to have.

Surprises ([12], [13]) can also be expressed in preferential action semantics. A surprise is some outcome of an action which was not expected, so formally we can express this as follows: ϕ is a surprise with respect to action α (denoted surprise(α, ϕ)) iff it holds that $[\alpha_\sharp]\neg\phi \wedge \langle\alpha\rangle\phi$. This states that although it is expected that $\neg\phi$ will hold after performing α, ϕ is nevertheless (an implausible but possible) outcome of α. For instance, in a state where Fred is alive (a), it would come as a surprise that after a wait action, he would be *not* alive: $a \rightarrow ([\text{wait}(\text{frame}\{a\})_\sharp]a \wedge \langle\text{wait}(\text{frame}\{a\})\rangle\neg a)$ is indeed true with respect to our semantics.

An interesting question, raised by one of the anonymous referees, is whether for some applications it would be useful or even required to extend the 'two-level' semantics (viz. possible and expected behaviour) into a more fine-grained one with multiple levels. We do not see the need for this at the moment. It might be possible that our approach is already sufficiently fine-grained due to the fact that we consider these two levels for any action in the scenario, which in total yields an enormous flexibility.

Other interesting issues to be studied are delayed effects of actions and prediction. It will be interesting to see whether modeling delay by using a wait action with a specific duration *in parallel* with other actions would give adequate results, while prediction seems to be very much related to considering expected results of (longer) chains of actions as compared to chains of preferred actions (as briefly indicated above). Perhaps a notion of *graded typicality* of behavior might be useful in this context. We surmise that by the very nature of the $[\alpha]$ modality (related to weakest preconditions) the framework so far seems to fit for prediction but is not very suitable for postdiction or explanation of scenarios ([13]). Perhaps extending it with the notion of strongest postconditions ([2], [11], [10]) would be helpful here.

Finally, although we made a plea for using preferential *action* semantics rather than preferential *assertion* semantics to describe action scenarios, it would, of course, be interesting to investigate the relation between the two, hopefully substantiating our claim that the former is more flexible or easier to use than the latter. We expect that systematic studies of relations between underlying (ontological and epistemological) assumptions of action/agent systems and (assertion) preferential models such as ([13]) will be useful guidelines in this investigation.

7   Related Work

We were much inspired by work by ([11], [10]). In this work the authors also attempted to employ proven verification and correctness methods and logics from imperative programming for reasoning about action and change in AI. In particular Dijkstra's wp-formalism is used. This formalism is based on the notion of weakest preconditions (and strongest postconditions) of actions and is in fact very close to the dynamic logic framework: formulas of the form $[\alpha]\phi$ are actually the same as the wlp (weakest liberal precondition) of action α with respect to postcondition ϕ. In ([11], [10]) a central role is played by the following theorem from Dijkstra and Scholten ([2]) which says that a state $\sigma \models \alpha \wedge \neg wlp(S, \neg\beta)$ iff there is a computation c under control of S starting in a state satisfying α and terminating in a state satisfying β such that σ is the initial state of c.

What all this amounts to is that when in [11], weakest (liberal) preconditions and the above theorem are used, something is stated of the form that after execution of an action α ϕ may possibly be true, which in dynamic logic is expressed as $\langle\alpha\rangle\phi(=\neg[\alpha]\neg\phi)$. Typically, this leads to too weak statements: one does not want to say that there is *some* execution of α that leads to ϕ, but that the set of *all expected* (but of course not *all*) output states satisfy some property. This is exactly what we intend to capture by means of our preferential action semantics. Another aspect that we disagree with, as the reader might suspect from the above, is that [11] uses the skip statement to express the wait action. In our view this is equating *a priori* the action of waiting with its preferred behavior (in view of the law of inertia).

Finally, we mention that the work reported in [4] is similar in spirit to ours. Here also, a distinction between typical (preferred) and possible behavior of actions is made within a dynamic logic setting. Our approach is more concrete in the sense that we directly incorporate aspects of inertia into the semantics, and, moreover, have an explicit preference operator (applied to actions) in the language. This implies that we can also speak about preferred versus possible behavior in the object language. On the other hand, we have not (yet) considered preferred paths of executions of actions as in [4]

Acknowledgement. The authors are grateful for the very useful suggestions of the anonymous referees to improve the paper. Also the comments of the attendants of Modelage'97 on the presentation of this paper are greatly appreciated.

References

1. J. Crawford. Three issues in action. Unpublished note for the 5th Int. Workshop on Nonmonotonic Reasoning, 1994.
2. E. W. Dijkstra and C. S. Scholten. Predicate Calculus and Program Semantics Springer-Verlag, 1990.
3. P. Doherty. Reasoning about action and change using occlusion. In Proc. of the 11th European Conference on Artificial Intelligence, Amsterdam , pages 401–405, 1994.
4. B. Dunin-Keplicz and A. Radzikowska. Epistemic approach to actions with typical effects. In Chr. Froideveaux and J. Kohlas, editors, Symbolic and Quantitative Approaches to Reasoning and Uncertainty, Proc. ECSQARU'95 , Lecture Notes in Artificial Intelligence, pages 180–188. Springer-Verlag, 1995.
5. E. Giunchiglia and V. Lifschitz. Dependent fluents. In Proc. IJCAI-95, Montreal , pages 1964–1969, 1995.
6. J. Gustafsson and P. Doherty. Embracing occlusion in specifying the indirect effects of actions. In Proc. of the 5th Int'l Conf. on Principles of Knowledge Representation and Reasoning, (KR-96) , 1996.
7. D. Harel. Dynamic logic. In D. M. Gabbay and F. Guenthner, editors, Handbook of Philosophical Logic , volume 2, pages 496–604. Reidel, Dordrecht, 1984.

8. G. N. Kartha and V. Lifschitz. Actions with indirect effects (preliminary report). In Proc. of the 4th Int'l Conf. on Principles of Knowledge Representation and Reasoning, (KR-94) , pages 341–350, 1994.

9. F. Lin. Embracing causality in specifying the indirect effects of actions. In Proc. IJCAI-95, Montreal , 1995.

10. W. Łukaszewicz and E. Madalińska-Bugaj. Reasoning about action and change : Actions with abnormal effects. In I. Wachsmuth, C.-R Rollinger, and W. Brauer, editors, Proc. KI-95: Advances in Artificial Intelligence , volume 981 of Lecture Notes in Artificial Intelligence , pages 209–220. Springer-Verlag, Berlin, 1995.

11. W. Łukaszewicz and E. Madalińska-Bugaj. Reasoning about action and change using Dijkstra's semantics for programming languages: Preliminary report. In Proc. IJCAI-95, Montreal , pages 1950–1955, 1995.

12. E. Sandewall. Features and fluents. Technical Report LITH-IDA-R-91-29, Department of Computer and Information Science, Linköping University, 1991.

13. E. Sandewall. Features and Fluents: A Systematic Approach to the Representation of Knowledge about Dynamical Systems . Oxford University Press, 1994.

14. E. Sandewall. Systematic comparison of approaches to ramification using restricted minimization of change. Technical Report LiTH-IDA-R-95-15, Dept. of Computer and Information Science, Linköping University, May 1995.

15. E. Sandewall and Y. Shoham. Nonmonotonic temporal reasoning. In D. M. Gabbay, C. J. Hogger, and J. A. Robinson, editors, Epistemic and Temporal Reasoning , volume 4 of Handbook of Artificial Intelligence and Logic Programming . Oxford University Press, 1994.

16. M. Thielscher. Computing ramifications by postprocessing. In Proc. IJCAI-95, Montreal , pages 1994–2000, 1995.

Dialectical proof theory for defeasible argumentation with defeasible priorities (preliminary report)

Henry Prakken*

Hoptille 46, 1102 PN Amsterdam
email: henry@rechten.vu.nl

Abstract. In this paper a dialectical proof theory is proposed for logical systems for defeasible argumentation that fit a certain format. This format is the abstract theory developed by Dung, Kowalski and others. A main feature of the proof theory is that it also applies to systems in which reasoning about the standards for comparing arguments is possible. The proof theory could serve as the 'logical core' of protocols for dispute in multi-agent decision making processes.

1 Introduction

Recent nonmonotonic logics often have the form of a system for defeasible argumentation (e.g. [Pollock 87, Simari & Loui 92, Vreeswijk 93a, Dung 95] and [Prakken & Sartor 96a]). In such systems nonmonotonic reasoning is analyzed in terms of the interactions between arguments for alternative conclusions. Nonmonotonicity arises since arguments can be defeated by stronger counterarguments. In this paper a dialectical proof theory is proposed for systems of this kind that fit a certain abstract format, viz. the one defined by [Dung 95]. The use of dialectical proof theories for defeasible reasoning was earlier studied by [Dung94] and, inspired by [Rescher 1977], by [Loui 93, Vreeswijk 93b, Brewka 94b], while also [Royakkers & Dignum 1996] contains ideas that can be regarded as a dialectical proof theory. The general idea is based on game-theoretic notions of logical consequence developed in dialogue logic (for an overview see [Barth & Krabbe 82]). Here a proof of a formula takes the form of a dialogue game between a proponent and an opponent of the formula. Both players have certain ways available of attacking and defending a statement. A formula is provable iff it can be successfully defended against every possible attack.

In this paper first the general framework of [Dung 95] will be described (Section 2), after which in section 3 the dialectical proof theory is presented. Then in Section 4 Dung's framework and the proof theory will be adapted in such a

---

* The research reported in this paper was made possible by a research fellowship of the Royal Netherlands Academy of Arts and Sciences, and by Esprit WG 8319 'Modelage'.

J.-J. Ch. Meyer, P.-Y. Schobbens (Eds.): Formal Methods of Agents, LNAI 1760, pp. 202–215, 1999.

way that the standards used for comparing conflicting arguments are themselves (defeasible) consequences of the premises.

The ideas of this paper were originally developed in [Prakken & Sartor 96b], for a logic-programming system presented in [Prakken & Sartor 96a], which in turn extended and revised [Dung 93b]'s application of his semantics to extended logic programming. In [Prakken & Sartor 96b] the system is applied to legal reasoning. The main purpose of the present paper is to show that the proof-theoretical ideas apply to any system of the format defined by [Dung 95]. For this reason the present paper does not express arguments in a formal language; it just assumes that this can be done.

2   An abstract framework for defeasible argumentation

Inspired by earlier work of Bondarenko, Kakas, Kowalski and Toni, [Dung 95] has proposed a very abstract and general argument-based framework. An up-to-date technical survey of this approach is [Bondarenko et al. 95]. The two basic notions of the framework are a set of arguments, and a binary relation of defeat among arguments. In terms of these notions, various notions of argument extensions are defined, which aim to capture various types of defeasible consequence. Then it is shown that many existing nonmonotonic logics can be reformulated as instances of the abstract framework.

The following version of this framework is kept in the abstract style of [Dung 95], with some adjustments proposed in [Prakken & Sartor 96a]. Important differences will be indicated when relevant.

Definition 1. An argument-based theory (AT) is a pair $(Args_{AT}, defeat_{AT})$,[2] where $Args_{AT}$ is a set of arguments, and $defeat_{AT}$ a binary relation on $Args_{AT}$.

- An AT is *finitary* iff each argument in $Args_{AT}$ is defeated by at most a finite number of arguments in $Args_{AT}$.
- An argument A *strictly defeats* an argument B iff A defeats B and B does not defeat A.
- A set of arguments is *conflict-free* iff no argument in the set is defeated by another argument in the set.

This definition abstracts from both the internal structure of an argument and the origin of the set of arguments. The idea is that an AT is defined by some nonmonotonic logic or system for defeasible argumentation. Usually the set $Args$ will be all arguments that can be constructed in these logics from a given set of premises, but this set might also just contain all arguments that a reasoner has actually constructed. In this paper I will (almost) completely abstract from the source of an AT. Moreover, unless stated otherwise, I will below implicitly assume an arbitrary but fixed AT.

The relation of *defeat* is intended to be a weak notion: intuitively 'A defeats B' means that A and B are in conflict and that A is not worse than B. This

---

[2] Below the subscripts will usually be left implicit.

means that two arguments can defeat each other. A typical example is the Nixon Diamond, with two arguments 'Nixon is a pacifist because he is a Quaker' and 'Nixon is not a pacifist because he is a Republican'. If there are no grounds for preferring one argument over the other, they defeat each other.

A stronger notion is captured by strict defeat (not used in Dung's work), which by definition is asymmetric. A standard example is the Tweety Triangle, where (if arguments are compared with specificity) the argument that Tweety flies because it is a bird is strictly defeated by the argument that Tweety doesn't fly since it is a penguin.

A central notion of Dung's framework is acceptability. Intuitively, it defines how an argument that cannot defend itself, can be protected from attacks by a set of arguments. Since [Prakken & Sartor 96a, Prakken & Sartor 97], on which this paper's proof theory is based, use a slightly different notion of acceptability, I will tag Dung's version with a d.

Definition 2. An argument A is *d-acceptable* with respect to a set S of arguments iff each argument defeating A is defeated by some argument in S.

The variant of Prakken & Sartor will just be called 'acceptability'.

Definition 3. An argument A is *acceptable* with respect to a set S of arguments iff each argument defeating A is strictly defeated by some argument in S.

So the only difference is that Dung uses 'defeat' where Prakken & Sartor use 'strict defeat'. In Section 4.1 I will comment on the significance of this difference.

To illustrate acceptability, consider the Tweety Triangle with A = 'Tweety is a bird, so Tweety flies', B = 'Tweety is a penguin, so Tweety does not fly' and C = 'Tweety is not a penguin', and assume that B strictly defeats A and C strictly defeats B. Then A is acceptable with respect to $\{C\}$, $\{A, C\}$, $\{B, C\}$ and $\{A, B, C\}$, but not with respect to $\emptyset$ and $\{B\}$.

Another central notion of Dung's framework is that of an admissible set.

Definition 4. A conflict-free set of arguments S is *admissible* iff each argument in S is d-acceptable with respect to S.

In the Tweety Triangle the sets $\emptyset$, $\{C\}$ and $\{A, C\}$ are admissible but all other subsets of $\{A, B, C\}$ are not admissible.

On the basis of these definitions several notions of 'argument extensions' can be defined. These notions are purely declarative, in that they just declare a set of arguments to be 'OK', without defining how such a set can be constructed. For instance, Dung defines the following credulous notions.

Definition 5. A conflict-free set S is a *stable extension* iff every argument that is not in S, is defeated by some argument in S.

Consider an AT called TT (the Tweety Triangle) where $Args_{TT} = \{A, B, C\}$ and $defeats_{TT} = \{(B, A), (C, B)\}$. TT has only one stable extension, viz. $\{A, C\}$. Consider next an AT called ND (the Nixon Diamond), with $Args_{ND} = \{A, B\}$, where A = 'Nixon is a quaker, so he is a pacifist', B = 'Nixon is a republican, so he is not a pacifist', and $defeats_{ND} = \{(A, B), (B, A)\}$. ND has two stable extensions, $\{A\}$ and $\{B\}$.

Since a stable extension is conflict-free, it reflects in some sense a coherent point of view. Moreover, it is a maximal point of view, in the sense that every possible argument is either accepted or rejected. The maximality requirement makes that not all AT's have stable extensions. Consider, for example, an AT with three arguments A, B and C, and such that A defeats B, B defeats C and C defeats A (such circular defeat relations can occur, for instance, in logic programming because of negation as failure, and in default logic because of the justification part of defaults.) To give also such AT's a credulous semantics, Dung defines the notion of a preferred extension.

Definition 6. A conflict-free set is a *preferred extension* iff it is a maximal (with respect to set inclusion) admissible set.

Clearly all stable extensions are preferred extensions, so in the Nixon Diamond and the Tweety Triangle the two semantics coincide. However, not all preferred extensions are stable: in the above example with circular defeat relations the empty set is a (unique) preferred extension, which is not stable.

Preferred and stable semantics clearly capture a credulous notion of defeasible consequence: in cases of an irresolvable conflict as in the Nixon diamond, two, mutually conflicting extensions are obtained. Dung also defines a notion of sceptical consequence, and this is for which I will define the dialectical proof theory. Application of the proof theory to the credulous semantics will be briefly discussed in Section 5. Dung defines the sceptical semantics with a monotonic operator, which for each set S of arguments returns the set of all arguments d-acceptable to S. Its least fixpoint captures the smallest set which contains every argument that is acceptable to it. I will use the variant with plain acceptability.

Definition 7. Let $AT = (Args, defeat)$ be an argument-based theory and S any subset of $Args$. The *characteristic function* of AT is:

- $F_{AT} : Pow(Args) \longrightarrow Pow(Args)$
- $F_{AT}(S) = \{A \in Args | A$ is acceptable with respect to $S\}$

I now give the, perhaps more intuitive, definition of [Prakken & Sartor 96a], which by a result of [Dung 95] for finitary AT's is equivalent to the fixpoint version (which is also used in [Prakken & Sartor 97]). The formal results on the proof theory hold for both formulations, although for the fixpoint formulation completeness holds under the condition that the AT is finitary; cf. [Dung 95, Prakken & Sartor 97].

Definition 8. For any $AT = (Args, defeat)$ we define the following sequence of subsets of $Args$.

- $F_{AT}^0 = \emptyset$
- $F_{AT}^{i+1} = \{A \in Args \mid A$ is acceptable with respect to $F_{AT}^i\}$.

Then the set $JustArgs_{AT}$ of arguments that are justified on the basis of AT is $\cup_{i=0}^{\infty}(F_{AT}^i)$.

In this definition the notion of acceptability captures reinstatement of arguments: if all arguments that defeat A are themselves defeated by an argument in F^i, then A is in F^{i+1}. To illustrate this with the Tweety Triangle: $F_{TT}^1 = \{C\}$, $F_{TT}^2 = \{A, C\}$, $F_{TT}^3 = F_{TT}^2$, so A is reinstated at F^2 by C.

That this semantics is sceptical is illustrated by the Nixon Diamond: $F_{ND}^1 = F_{ND}^0 = \emptyset$.

3   A dialectical proof theory

3.1   General idea and illustrations

In this section a dialectical proof theory will be defined for the just-presented sceptical semantics. Essentially it is a notational variant of [Dung94]'s dialogue game version of his sceptical semantics of extended logic programs. A proof of a formula takes the form of a dialogue tree, where each branch is a dialogue, and the root of the tree is an argument for the formula. The idea is that every move in a dialogue consists of an argument based on an implicitly assumed AT, and that each move attacks the last move of the opponent in a way that meets the player's burden of proof. That a move consists of a complete argument means that the search for an individual argument is conducted in a 'monological' fashion, determined by the nature of the underlying logic; only the process of considering counterarguments is modelled dialectically. The required force of a move depends on who states it, and is motivated by the definition of acceptability. Since the proponent wants a conclusion to be justified, a proponent's move has to be strictly defeating, while since the opponent only wants to prevent the conclusion from being justified, an opponent's move may be just defeating.

Let us illustrate this with an informal example of a dialogue (recall that it implicitly assumes a given AT). Let us denote the arguments stated by the proponent by P_i and those of the opponent by O_i. The proponent starts the dispute by asserting that P_1 is a justified argument.

> P_1: Assuming the evidence concerning the glove was not forged,
> it proves guilt of OJ.

(Many nonmonotonic logics allow the formalization of assumptions, e.g. logic programming with negation as failure and default logic with the justification part of a default.)

The opponent must defeat this argument. Suppose O can do so in only one way.

> O_1: I know that the evidence concerning the glove was forged,
> so your assumption is not warranted.

The proponent now has to counterattack with an argument that strictly defeats O_1. Consider the following argument

> P_2: The evidence concerning the glove was not forged, since it was found by a police officer, and police officers don't forge evidence.

and suppose (for the sake of illustration) that defeat is determined by specificity considerations. Then P_2 strictly defeats O_1, so P_2 is a possible move. If the opponent has no new moves available from $Args_{AT}$, s/he loses, and the conclusion that OJ is guilty has been proved.

In dialectical proof systems a 'loop checker' can be implemented in a very natural way: no two moves of the proponent in the same branch of the dialogue may have the same content. It is easy to see that this rule will not harm P; if O had a move the first time P stated the argument, it will also have a move the second time, so no repetition by P can make P win a dialogue.

Assume for illustration that the arguments in $Args$ are those that can be made by chaining one or more of the following premises:

(1) Mr. F forged the glove-evidence
(2) Someone who forges evidence is not honest
(3) Mr. F is a police officer
(4) Police officers are honest
(5) Someone who is honest, does not forge evidence.

Assume again that defeat is determined by specificity, in the obvious way. Now the proponent argues that Mr. F did not forge the glove-evidence.

> P_1: Mr. F is a police officer, so he is honest and therefore does not forge evidence.

O attacks this argument on its 'subconclusion' that Mr. F is honest; and since the counterargument is more specific, this is a defeating argument.

> P_1: I know that F forged evidence, and this shows that he is not honest.

P now wants to attack O's argument in the same way as O attacked P's argument: by launching a more specific attack on O's 'subconclusion' that F forged the glove-evidence. However, P has already stated that argument at the beginning of the dispute, so the move is not allowed. And no other strictly defeating argument is available, so it is not provable that Mr. F did not forge the glove-evidence, not even that he is honest. However, by a completely symmetric line of reasoning we obtain that also the contrary conclusions are not provable. So no conclusion about whether Mr. F is honest or not, and forged evidence or not, is provably justified.

3.2   The proof theory

Now the dialectical proof theory will be formally defined. Again the definitions assume an arbitrary but fixed AT.

Definition 9. A *dialogue* is a finite nonempty sequence of moves $move_i = (Player_i, Arg_i)$ $(i > 0)$, such that

1. $Player_i = P$ iff i is odd; and $Player_i = O$ iff i is even;
2. If $Player_i = Player_j = P$ and $i \neq j$, then $Arg_i \neq Arg_j$;
3. If $Player_i = P$, then Arg_i strictly defeats Arg_{i-1};
4. If $Player_i = O$, then Arg_i defeats Arg_{i-1}.

The first condition says that the proponent begins and then the players take turns, while the second condition prevents the proponent from repeating its attacks. The last two conditions form the heart of the definition: they state the burdens of proof for P and O.

Definition 10. A *dialogue tree* is a tree of dialogues such that if $Player_i = P$ then $move_1$'s children of are all defeaters of Arg_i.

It is this definition that makes dialogue trees candidates for being proofs: it says that the tree should consider all possible ways in which O can attack an argument of P.

Definition 11. A player *wins a dialogue* iff the other player cannot move. And a player *wins a dialogue tree* iff it wins all branches of the tree.

The idea of this definition is that if P's last argument is undefeated, it reinstates all previous arguments of P that occur in the same branch of a tree, in particular the root of the tree.

Definition 12. An argument A is *provably justified* iff there is a dialogue tree with A as its root, and won by the proponent.

In [Prakken & Sartor 97] it is shown that this proof theory is sound and for finitary AT's also complete with respect to the sceptical fixpoint semantics. This is not surprising, since what the proof theory does is, basically, traversing the sequence defined by Definition 8 in the reverse direction. Note that it implies that an argument A is justified iff there is a sequence $F^1, \ldots, F^n$ such that A occurs for the first time in F^n (in the explicit fixpoint definition of [Dung 95, Prakken & Sartor 97] this only holds for finitary AT's; in the general case only the 'if' part holds). We start with A, and then for any argument B defeating A we find an argument C in F^{n-1} that strictly defeats B and so indirectly supports A. Then any argument defeating C is met with a strict defeater from F^{n-2}, and so on. Since the sequence is finite, we end with an argument indirectly supporting A that cannot be defeated.

It should be noted that completeness here does not imply semi- decidability: if the logic for constructing individual arguments is not decidable, then the search for counterarguments is, as is well-known, not even semi-decidable.

4 Defeasible priorities

In several argumentation frameworks, as in many other nonmonotonic logics, the defeat relation is partly defined with the help of priority relations, usually defined on the premises, but sometimes directly on arguments. In most systems these priorities are undisputable and assumed consistent. However, as discussed in e.g. [Gordon 95, Prakken & Sartor 96b, Hage 97], these features are often unrealistic. In several domains of practical reasoning, such as legal reasoning, the priorities are themselves subject to debate, and therefore a full theory of defeasible argumentation should also be able to formalise arguments about priorities, and to adjudicate between such arguments.

This section presents a formalisation of this feature, which forms the main technical addition to [Dung 93b, Dung94]. As the previous section, also this section is based on [Prakken & Sartor 96a], in which the semantics of [Dung 93b] is revised, and on [Prakken & Sartor 97], in which the same is done with the proof theory of [Dung94]. The present section generalises these revisions to any system fitting the format of [Dung 95].

However the generalisation is only well-defined if the logic generating an AT satisfies some additional assumptions. Firstly, I assume that for each AT a set O is defined of objects to be ordered. For most AT's the set O will contain the premises from which the arguments of the AT can be constructed; however, since some AT's instead define the priorities between sets of premises or even directly between arguments (as [Vreeswijk 93a]), I will leave the content of O undefined.

Next I assume that the defeat relation of an AT is determined by a strict partial ordering of O. In fact, this assumption transforms the defeat relation of an AT into a *set* of defeat relations $<$-*defeat*, where $<$ is any strict partial ordering of O.

On the basis of these assumptions I now define the notion of a prioritised argument-based theory.

Definition 13. A prioritised argument-based theory (PAT for short) is a triple $(Args_{PAT}, O_{PAT}, defeat_{PAT})$,[3] where $Args_{PAT}$ is a set of arguments, and where $defeat_{PAT}$ is a set of binary relations $<$-*defeat* on $Args_{PAT}$, $<$ being any strict partial order on O_{PAT}.

- A PAT is *finitary* iff for all $<$ each argument in $Args_{PAT}$ is $<$-defeated by at most a finite number of arguments in $Args_{PAT}$.
- An argument A *strictly* $<$-*defeats* an argument B iff A $<$-defeats B and B does not $<$-defeat A.
- A set of arguments is $<$-*conflict-free* iff no argument in the set is $<$-defeated by another argument in the set.

Finally, I assume that the argument language of a PAT is sufficiently expressive to express partial orderings on O; i.e. I assume that this language contains a distinguished twoplace predicate symbol $\prec$, intended to denote the relation $<$,

---

[3] Below the subscripts will usually be left implicit.

and that there is a naming function $N : O \longrightarrow Names$, where $Names$ is a set of terms. N is not assumed to be a bijection, since it might be handy to assign the same name to more than one object.

4.1   Changing the semantics

Now how can we make the priorities that are needed to determine defeat, defeasible consequences of the AT, according to Definition 8? The idea is that in determining whether an argument is acceptable with respect to F^i_{PAT}, we look at those priority statements that are conclusions of arguments in F^i_{PAT}. To this end I first define the notion of an ordering expressed by a set of arguments.

Definition 14. For any set S of arguments

$$<_S = \{o < o' \mid N(o) \prec N(o') \text{ is a conclusion of some } A \in S\}$$

Below I will abbreviate '$<_S$-defeat' as 'S-defeat'; and for singleton sets $\{C\}$ I will write '$\{C\}$-defeat' as 'C-defeat'.

For arbitrary sets S it is not guaranteed that $<_S$ is a strict partial order. However, it is sufficient that the properties hold for each $<_{F^i_{AT}}$. In virtually any nonmonotonic logic this can be assured by including the axioms of a strict partial order for $\prec$ in the undebatable part of the premises (see [Prakken & Sartor 97] for an illustration in argument-based extended logic programming).

I now redefine the notion of acceptability as follows (d-acceptability can be changed in the same way).

Definition 15. An argument A is *acceptable* with respect to a set S of arguments iff all arguments S-defeating A are strictly S-defeated by some argument in S.

Note that with this definition Dung's original definition is not only changed (by using strict defeat), but also refined: this is since Dung does not consider defeasible priorities and therefore does not make defeat relative to sets of arguments.

Definition 8 can now be applied with Definition 15. However, to make this application well-behaved, the notion of S-defeat should have the following two properties, which are crucial in proving that each F^i is contained in F^{i+1}; this in turn guarantees that each set of justified arguments is conflict-free. The properties are also crucial in proving that the explicit-fixpoint definition of [Prakken & Sartor 97] is monotonic. Note that they does not follow from the above definitions but must instead be enforced by a proper definition of the notion of defeat.

Property 4.1 *For any two conflict-free sets of arguments S and S' such that $S \subseteq S'$, and any two arguments A and B we have that*

1. If A S'-defeats B, then A S-defeats B.
2. If A strictly S-defeats B, then A strictly S'-defeats B.

Given our weak interpretation of the defeat notion, this property can easily be enforced: the idea is to define 'A S-defeats B' in terms of the absence of priorities in $<_S$ that would make A worse than B; then adding more priorities cannot create new defeat relations, while the only defeat relations that go away are one side of a mutual defeat relation.

Property 4.2 *For any conflict-free set of arguments S and arguments $A \in S$ and B: if A strictly S-defeats B, then some $C \in S$ strictly C-defeats B.*

Also this property seems very natural. The intuition behind it is that C is the combination of A with the priority arguments in S that make A strictly S-defeat B; and C can then be used in a dialectical proof as a reply to B.

I can now comment on the use of strict defeat in Definitions 3 and 15: Property 4.1(2) will usually not hold for defeat, while yet it is essential to make Definition 8 well-behaved when combined with Definition 15.

4.2   Changing the proof theory

I now discuss how the proof theory must be changed. The main problem here is on the basis of which priorities the defeating force of the moves should be determined. What is to be avoided is that we have to generate all priority arguments before we can determine the defeating force of a move. The pleasant surprise is that, to achieve this, a few very simple conditions suffice. For O it is sufficient that its move $\emptyset$-defeats P's previous move. This is so since Property 4.1 implies that if A is for some S an S-defeater of P's previous move, it is also an $\emptyset$-defeater of that move. So O does not have to take priorities into account. Let us illustrate this by modifying our informal glove dialogue as follows (we again leave it to the readers to formalise the arguments in their favourite formalism). Again the proponent starts with

> P_1: Assuming the evidence concerning the glove was not forged,
>   it proves guilt of OJ.

Suppose the opponent now replies with

> O_1: I know that the evidence concerning the glove was forged,
>   since I was told so, so your assumption is not warranted.

In agreement with most nonmonotonic logics, I assume that an attack on an assumption succeeds if no priority relations hold: i.e. O_1 $\emptyset$-defeats P_1.

P, on the other hand, should take some priorities into account, since strict defeat usually requires 'better than' relations between rules. However, it suffices to apply only those priorities that are stated by P's move; more priorities are not needed, since Property 4.1 also implies that if P's argument Arg_i strictly $Args_i$-defeats O's previous move, it will also do so whatever more priorities will be derived. So P can reply to O_1 with

P_2: The evidence concerning the glove was not forged, since it was found
  by a police officer, and as a general rule police officers
  don't forge evidence. This rule is more reliable than your
  rule that what you are told is true.

Because of the priority statement at the end, P_2 strictly P_2-defeats O_1.

However, this is not the only type of move that the proponent should be
allowed to make. To see this, note that O can respond with repeating O_1 as
O_2, at least assuming that O_1 $\emptyset$-defeats P_2, which in many systems it will do
(e.g. in [Prakken & Sartor 96a]). And because of the nonrepetition rule P cannot
respond to O_2 with $P_3 = P_2$. Therefore P must be allowed to state a priority
argument that neutralises the defeating force of O_2, i.e. to state an argument P_3
such that O_2 does not P_3-defeat P_1. If P is allowed to make such a move, it can
in our example repeat the priority part of P_2:

P_3: The rule that police officers don't forge evidence is more reliable
  than your rule that what you are told is true.

Of course, O might challenge P's priority argument, for instance, by saying that
instead the 'what I am told is true' rule is more reliable since O only listens
to very reliable people. However, I will end the discussion of our example and
describe the changes of the proof theory. All we have to change is the burdens
of proof in Definition 9:

(3) If $Player_i = P$ then

 - Arg_i *strictly* Arg_i-defeats Arg_{i-1}; or
 - Arg_{i-1} *does not* Arg_i-defeat A_{i-2}.

(4) If $Player_i = O$ then Arg_i $\emptyset$-defeats Arg_{i-1}.

The other definitions stay the same.

In [Prakken & Sartor 97] it is shown that the proof theory is, with respect
to the fixpoint semantics, sound in the general case and complete for finitary
AT's. The corresponding results for the system with fixed priorities are proven
as a special case. Although these results are proven for a particular system, the
proofs are based on only the definitions and properties presented in this paper.

4.3   A clash of intuitions

In some cases the semantics of this section gives results that seem debatable.
Consider an AT with $Args_{AT} = \{A, B, C, D\}$ where $A = $ 'John is an adult, so
John is employed', $B = $ 'John is a student, so John is unemployed', $C = $ 'John is
imprisoned, so John is unemployed' and D is a priority argument with conclusion
$A \prec B \lor A \prec C$. Assume that this induces an ordering $<_{JustArgs_{AT}} = \emptyset$, so that
none of the arguments is justified. Assume now that if this ordering were instead
$\{A < B\}$ or $\{A < C\}$, then B and C would be justified and A overruled. It

might be argued that then this should also be the outcome in the original case. However, intuitions seem to differ here: from a constructive point of view the outcome of the present definitions seems acceptable.

Yet it is worthwhile investigating how the alternative, non-constructive intuition can be formalized. Probably techniques from [Brewka 94a] and [Prakken 95] can be used, which formalize the non-constructive intuition for extension-based systems, but this has to be left for future research, as well as the corresponding proof theory. Alternatively, syntactic restrictions will do; practically this seems a feasible option, since in practical applications disjunctive priority information seems very rare.

5   Proof theory for credulous semantics

In this section I sketch how a dialectical proof theory can be developed for the credulous semantics discussed in Section 2. I will first focus on the case with fixed priorities. Defining a proof theory for stable semantics will not be easy, since we always have to prove that a stable extension exists. Therefore I concentrate on preferred semantics. This is also relevant for stable semantics, since [Dung 95] identifies conditions under which preferred and stable semantics coincide.

Note first that the existence of a proof means that the argument is in *some* preferred extension. Now the idea is to reverse the burden of proof of P and O. P now only has to defeat O's arguments, while O now must strictly defeat P's moves. Moreover, the non-repetition rule now holds for O instead of for P, while the children of P's moves are now all its *strict* defeaters. Finally, since preferred extensions are conflict-free, we must require that in each dialogue the set of all moves of the proponent is conflict-free.

With respect to soundness and completeness, it is relevant that by definition every admissible set is contained in some preferred extension. Then soundness follows since it is easy to see that the union of all P's arguments in a dialogue tree is an admissible set. Completeness can be proven for the finite case, by showing that each finite admissible set corresponds to a proof for each of its members. For the infinite case there are obvious counterexamples. Consider e.g. an infinite set of arguments $\{A_1, \ldots, A_n, \ldots\}$, where each $A_i (i > 1)$ strictly defeats A_{i-1}: both the set of all 'odd', and that of all 'even' arguments are preferred extensions, but any 'proof' has to be infinite.

Extending these ideas to the case with defeasible priorities is still to be investigated.

6   Formal models of agents and protocols for dispute

With respect to formal models of agents this paper is relevant as follows. As noted earlier by [Vreeswijk 96], the dialectical proof theory can serve as the 'logical core' of protocols for disputes in multi-agent decision and negotiation processes (where the agents can be humans, computers or a combination of both). Such protocols define possible, allowed or obligatory dialogue moves of the agents involved in the dispute, and they define criteria for termination and evaluation of a dispute. Such protocols can be studied as to their degree of rationality (cf. e.g. [Loui 93, Gordon 95, Vreeswijk 96]). The leading idea here is that rationality has a procedural side: an argument is acceptable if it has been successfully defended in a properly conducted dispute. The main aim of this line of research is to find out what makes a dispute proper, i.e. what makes it fair and effective.

A key feature of realistic disputes is that the body of information from which arguments can be constructed is not given in advance, but is constructed dynamically in the course of a debate. Although our dialectical proof theory is relative to a given set of arguments, it can still be embedded in such protocols for dispute (cf. also [Loui & Norman 95, Vreeswijk 96]). The set $Args_{AT}$ is then defined as the arguments that are constructible on the basis of the premises that are introduced and not withdrawn at a give stage. Thus our definitions also apply to disputes where the set of premises is dynamically constructed. Moreover, the soundness and completeness results are thus part of the criteria for fair and effective disputation. This is at least how [Vreeswijk 96] defines fairness and effectiveness: a protocol is fair if every argument that can be successfully defended against every attack is justified, and it is effective if every justified argument can be successfully defended against every attack.

7   Concluding remarks

In this paper I have discussed three contributions to the formalisation of defeasible argumentation. Firstly, I have, by generalising work of [Prakken & Sartor 96a], discussed how the abstract framework of [Dung 95, Bondarenko et al. 95] can be extended with defeasible priorities. Secondly, I have, by generalising work of [Dung94] and [Prakken & Sartor 97], discussed how dialectical proof theories can be defined for this framework and its extension. Finally, I have given an impression of the research questions that arise in the dialectical approach to the proof theory of defeasible argumentation, and I have indicated how this approach is relevant to formal protocols for disputation in multi-agent environments.

As for future research, first of all the preliminary contributions of this paper should, of course, be further developed. Moreover, it would be interesting to investigate in more detail the relation between dialectical proof theories and dialectical protocols for disputation.

References

[Barth & Krabbe 82] E.M. Barth and E.C.W. Krabbe. *From Axiom to Dialogue: a Philosophical Study of Logic and Argumentation.* Walter de Gruyter, New York, 1982.

[Bondarenko et al. 95] A. Bondarenko, P.M. Dung, R.A. Kowalski and F. Toni. An abstract argumentation-theoretic approach to default reasoning. Technical Report Department of Computing, Imperial College London, 1995. Also to appear in *Artificial Intelligence.*

[Brewka 94a] G. Brewka. Reasoning about priorities in default logic. *Proceedings AAAI-94*, 247–260.

[Brewka 94b] G. Brewka. A reconstruction of Rescher's theory of formal disputation based on default logic. *Proceedings of the 11th European Conference on Artificial Intelligence*, 366-370.

[Dung 93b] P.M. Dung. An argumentation semantics for logic programming with explicit negation. *Proceedings of the Tenth Logic Programming Conference*, MIT Press 1993, 616–630.

[Dung94] P.M. Dung. Logic programming as dialogue game. Unpublished paper.

[Dung 95] P.M. Dung. On the acceptability of arguments and its fundamental role in nonmonotonic reasoning, logic programming, and n-person games. *Artificial Intelligence* 77 (1995), 321–357.

[Gordon 95] T.F. Gordon. *The Pleadings Game. An Artificial Intelligence Model of Procedural Justice.* Kluwer, Dordrecht, 1995.

[Hage 97] J.C. Hage. *Reasoning With Rules. An Essay on Legal Reasoning and Its Underlying Logic.* Kluwer Law and Philosophy Library, Dordrecht etc. 1997.

[Loui 93] R.P. Loui. Process and policy: resource-bounded non-demonstrative reasoning. Report WUCS–92–43, Washington-University-in-St-Louis, 1993. To appear in *Computational Intelligence*.

[Loui & Norman 95] R.P. Loui and J. Norman. Rationales and argument moves. *Artificial Intelligence and Law* 3: 159–189, 1995.

[Pollock 87] J.L. Pollock. Defeasible reasoning. *Cognitive Science* 11 (1987), 481–518.

[Prakken 95] H. Prakken. A semantic view on reasoning about priorities (extended abstract). *Proceedings of the Second Dutch/German Workshop on Nonmonotonic Reasoning*, Utrecht 1995, 152–159.

[Prakken & Sartor 96a] H. Prakken and G. Sartor. A system for defeasible argumentation, with defeasible priorities. *Proceedings of the International Conference on Formal and Applied Practical Reasoning (FAPR'96)*, Bonn 1996. Springer Lecture Notes in AI 1085, Springer Verlag, 1996, 510–524.

[Prakken & Sartor 96b] H. Prakken and G. Sartor. A dialectical model of assessing conflicting arguments in legal reasoning. *Artificial Intelligence and Law* 4 (1996), 331–368.

[Prakken & Sartor 97] H. Prakken and G. Sartor. Argument-based extended logic programming with defeasible priorities. To appear in *Journal of Applied Non-classical Logics*, 1997.

[Rescher 1977] N. Rescher. *Dialectics: a controversy-oriented approach to the theory of knowledge.* State University of New York Press, Albany, 1977.

[Royakkers & Dignum 1996] L. Royakkers and F. Dignum. Defeasible reasoning with legal rules. In M.A. Brown and J. Carmo (eds.) *Deontic Logic, Agency and Normative Systems.* Springer, Workshops in Computing, London etc. 1996, 174–193.

[Simari & Loui 92] G.R. Simari and R.P. Loui. A mathematical treatment of defeasible argumentation and its implementation. *Artificial Intelligence* 53 (1992), 125–157.

[Vreeswijk 93a] G. Vreeswijk. *Studies in defeasible argumentation.* Doctoral dissertation Free University Amsterdam, 1993.

[Vreeswijk 93b] G. Vreeswijk. Defeasible dialectics: a controversy-oriented approach towards defeasible argumentation. *Journal of Logic and Computation*, 1993, Vol. 3, No. 3., 317–334.

[Vreeswijk 96] G. Vreeswijk. Representation of formal dispute with a standing order. *Research Report MATRIX, University of Limburg, 1996.* Also presented at the **Workshop Computational Dialectics** of the International Conference on Formal and Applied Practical Reasoning (FAPR'96), Bonn 1996.

The Role of Diagnosis and Decision Theory in Normative Reasoning

Leendert W.N. van der Torre[1], Pedro Ramos[2], José Luiz Fiadeiro[3], and Yao-Hua Tan[4]

[1] Max-Planck-Institute for Computer Science
Im StadWald, D-66123 Saarbrücken, Germany
torre@mpi-sb.mpg.de
[2] Department of Informatics, ISCTE
Av. das Forcas Armadas Edifícío ISCTE, 1600 Lisboa
Pedro.Ramos@iscte.pt
[3] Department of Informatics, Faculty of Sciences - University of Lisbon
Campo Grande 1700 Lisboa
llf@di.fc.ul.pt
[4] EURIDIS, Erasmus University Rotterdam
P.O. Box 1738, 3000 DR Rotterdam, The Netherlands
tel (+31)10-4082601 fax (+31)10-4526134
ytan@euridis.fbk.eur.nl

Abstract. A theory of diagnosis and qualitative decision theory are able to formalize reasoning *with* norms. They are thus different from deontic logic, that formalizes reasoning *about* norms. In this paper, we compare two theories of diagnosis for normative systems: Ramos and Fiadeiro's theory of diagnosis developed for organizational process design and Tan and Van der Torre's theory of diagnosis extended with notions of qualitative decision theory. We observe several similarities.

1 Introduction

In this paper we argue that normative reasoning is more than deontic logic. Deontic logic tells you which obligations can be derived from a set of other obligations. In particular, it characterizes the logical relations between obligations. For example, in most deontic logics the conjunction $p \wedge q$ is obliged, if both p and q are obliged. However, it does not explain how norms effect the behavior of rational agents. From Op you cannot infer whether somebody will actually perform p. This is no critique on deontic logic, it is just an observation. Deontic logic was never intended to explain this effect of norms on behavior. However, If we want to explain all the different aspects of normative reasoning, then we need more formalisms than just deontic logic. In this paper we discuss two formalisms that can be used to analyze two different types of aspects of how norms effect behavior, namely the theory of diagnosis and qualitative decision theory.

Two theories that are able to formalize reasoning with norms are represented in Figure 1. A *theory of diagnosis* reasons about violations. In particular, it reasons about the past with incomplete knowledge (if everything is known than a diagnosis is completely known). Diagnostic theories have a modest purpose, because they do not support the

J.-J. Ch. Meyer, P.-Y. Schobbens (Eds.): LNAI 1760, pp. 216–239, 1999.

decision-making process of the user. They do not derive decisions, they only check systems against given principles. A more expressive framework is qualitative decision theory. *Qualitative decision theory* describes how norms influence behavior. It is based on the concept of agent rationality. For example, in a normative system usually sanctions and rewards correspond with norms, and a rational agent tries to evade penalties and achieve rewards. In contrast to diagnostic theories, a (qualitative) decision theory reasons about the future. The main characteristic of qualitative decision theory is that it is goal oriented reasoning, usually for planning problems. Moreover, it combines reasoning about goals with uncertainty. This reasoning is based on the application of strategies, which can be considered as qualitative versions of the 'maximum utility' criterion.

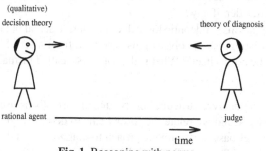

Fig. 1. Reasoning with norms

Logical relations between obligations are an essential component of any formalism that explains the effect of norms on behavior. Hence, in this paper we also argue that deontic logic can be used as a component in the theory of diagnosis as well as qualitative decision theory. Actually, we even argue for the stronger claim that the theory of diagnosis as well as qualitative decision theory can be viewed as extensions of deontic logic. In both cases the formalism contains extra principles that are added to a deontic logic basis. For example, in the case of the theory of diagnosis one of the principles that can be added to deontic logic is the parsimony principle, i.e. the assumption that as few as possible obligations are violated. There is nothing contradictory in the claim that on the one hand these formalisms explain aspects of normative behavior that deontic logic does not, whereas deontic logic is still an essential component of these theories. In the same sense physics can explain phenomena that mathematics cannot, whereas mathematics is still an essential component of physics. There are several structural similarities between preference-based deontic logic and the logics developed for diagnosis and qualitative decision theory, see e.g. [Bou94,Lan96]. The distinction between the different perspectives and deontic logic raises several important questions.

Norms and dedicated theories. The diagnosis of a normative system can use a formalism to represent norms and additional assumptions or principles to do the diagnosis. For example, Reiter's diagnosis is basically a minimization principle (called the principle of parsimony). Similarly, qualitative decision theory has a formalism for representing norms (or goals) and additional assumptions or principles to reason with them. Is such a special purpose formalism a deontic logic? How do they stand the test against the Chisholm paradox, the paradox of the gentle murderer, the problem of how to represent permissions, the problem of conflicting obligations? What are the structural similarities and distinctions between the different formalisms?

Norms and preferences [Lan96]. Qualitative decision theory is based upon the concept of preference. This preference is a kind of desire, i.e. it is an endogenously motivating mechanism (coming from the agent itself). Therefore, it is not a natural candidate for dealing with normative decision-making, since a norm is by definition exogenous, in the sense that it is something the agent would not spontaneously want. How do agents work out norms in terms of gains and losses? What are the gains of observing norms? How do they learn the effects of norms and how do they reason about these effects? Which rules are implied, which ingredients enable agents to make normative decisions? In which way does a normative decider differ from an ordinary decider, if any?

Norms and obligations. A deontic logic does not derive actual but ideal behaviors. Do we have to distinguish the obligations derivable from a set of norms and a set of facts, from the norms itself? What is the role of so-called factual detachment in deontic logic?

In this paper we analyze structural properties of formalisms used in two dedicated theories of diagnosis, and we relate the formalisms to deontic logic. Reiter formalized in [Rei87] the model-based reasoning approach to diagnosis, and that theory is adapted to deontic systems in [TvdT94a,TvdT94b,RF96b,RF96a] by using obligations to represent the ideal behavior of a system. In Reiter's theory of diagnosis, a violation is represented by a predicate expression $Ab(c)$, where c is a component of a system to be diagnosed and Ab an abnormality predicate. For example, this violation can be derived from the system description that p is the correct behavior of a component $\neg Ab(c) \rightarrow p$ and the observation $\neg p$. In a modal deontic logic, a violation can be represented by the sentence $\neg p \wedge Op$, where the modal sentence Op is read as 'it is obligatory that p.' The typical diagnostic reasoning with normative systems is performed by a judge, who has to determine whether a suspect is guilty or not. Diagnostic reasoning has to deal with incomplete knowledge, not formalized in a deontic logic. For example, a popular additional assumption of theories of diagnosis is the so-called principle of parsimony: 'you are innocent until proven guilty.' Such a principle about incomplete knowledge is not made in deontic logic; it is an extra-logical assumption about the legal domain.

The DIagnostic framework for DEontic reasoning DIODE [TvdT94b,TvdT94a] is Reiter's theory of diagnosis [Rei87] applied to normative systems. In this paper we compare two extensions of DIODE. The first extension is DDD, Ramos and Fiadeiro's Deontic framework for DIagnosis of process Design [RF96b,RF96a]. They make a distinction between benevolent and exigent diagnoses, respectively minimal and maximal violated-norm sets (comparable to sets of broken components in Reiter's theory). Moreover, they make a distinction between structural concepts and design actions. Their deontics-based diagnosis is based on a minimal deontic logic LDD. The second extension of DIODE is Tan and Van der Torre's DIagnostic and DEcision-theoretic framework for DEontic reasoning $\text{DIO}(\text{DE})^2$. The most important element of (qualitative) decision theory incorporated in $\text{DIO}(\text{DE})^2$ is – besides the violation-oriented reasoning of DIODE – also goal-oriented reasoning. Deontic-based diagnosis is based on the two-phase preference-based deontic logic 2DL. Two-phase reasoning illustrates the distinction between reasoning about violated-norm sets and reasoning about diagnoses, i.e. *minimal* violated-norm sets.

We identify several similarities between the two approaches DDD and DIO(DE)[2]. DIODE defines minimal violated-norm sets, based on the basic distinction between violated and non-violated norms. DDD defines also maximal violated-norm sets, based on the distinction between fulfilled and non-fulfilled norms. The exigent diagnosis corresponds to qualitative decision theory in the sense that exigent diagnosis not only reasons about the past (about incomplete knowledge) but also reasons about the future (design actions). For example, the distinction between structural concepts and design actions in DDD corresponds to the distinction between parameters and decision variables in qualitative decision theory. The theory DDD is not only used for diagnosis, but for more general decision support. Moreover, we also observe several similarities in the logics LDD and 2DL like a contingency clause (the use of consistency checks) and lack of weakening of the consequent.

The layout of this paper is as follows. In Section 2 we discuss Reiter's theory of diagnosis, the adaptation of that theory to deontic systems by using obligations to represent the ideal behavior of a system, and qualitative decision theory. In Section 3 we discuss the framework of Ramos and Fiadeiro, in Section 4 the framework of Tan and Van der Torre and in Section 5 we compare them.

2 The role of deontic logic in diagnosis and qualitative decision theory

Deontic logic formalizes reasoning *about* norms. Two important extensions of deontic logic that reason *with* norms are theory of diagnosis and qualitative decision theory. They are extensions in the sense that reasoning with norms uses a formalization of norms (although several aspects of norms may not be represented in a particular formalization of the norms). In this section we discuss the two theories that formalize reasoning with norms, and we observe a distinction in deontic logic analogous to the distinction between diagnosis and decisions.

2.1 Reiter's theory of diagnosis and DIODE

The model based reasoning approach has been studied for several years (for a survey of the topic see [DW88]). Numerous applications have been built, most of all for diagnosis of physical devices. The basic paradigm is the interaction of prediction and observation. Predictions are expected outputs given the assumption that all the components are working properly (i.e. are working according to the model of the structure and behavior of the system). If a discrepancy between the output of the system (given a particular input) and the prediction is found, the diagnosis procedure will search for defects in the components of the system (the correctness of the model is assumed).

The contribution of Reiter to the theory of diagnosis is widely accepted. His *consistency based approach* [Rei87] is the first one to model the model based reasoning approach to diagnosis. The main goal is to eliminate system inconsistency, identifying the minimal set of abnormal components that is responsible for the inconsistency. That is, reasoning about diagnosis is based on the following assumption of diagnostic reasoning.

Principle of parsimony Diagnostic reasoning is based on the conjecture that the set of faulty components is minimal (with respect to set inclusion).

Related to a diagnosis is a set of measurements. Finally, a conflict set is a minimal set of components of which at least one is broken (such sets are used in efficient diagnostic algorithms).

Definition 1. (Diagnosis) A *system* is a pair (COMP, SD) where COMP, the *system components*, is a finite set of constants denoting the components of the system, and SD, the *system description*, is a set of first-order sentences. An *observation* of a system is a finite set of first-order sentences. A system to be diagnosed, written as (COMP, SD, OBS), is a system (COMP, SD) with observation OBS. A *diagnosis* for (COMP, SD, OBS) is a minimal (with respect to set inclusion) set $\Delta \subseteq$ COMP such that

$$\text{CONTEXT}_\Delta = \text{SD} \cup \text{OBS} \cup \{Ab(c) \mid c \in \Delta\} \cup \{\neg Ab(c) \mid c \in \text{COMP} - \Delta\}$$

is consistent. A diagnosis Δ for (COMP, SD, OBS) *predicts* a *measurement* Π iff

$$\text{CONTEXT}_\Delta \models \Pi$$

A *conflict set* for a system to be diagnosed (COMP, SD, OBS) is a minimal (with respect to set inclusion) set $\Delta \subseteq$ COMP such that CONTEXT$_\Delta$ is inconsistent.

The DIagnostic framework for DEontic reasoning DIODE formalizes deontic reasoning as a kind of diagnostic reasoning. Notice that DIODE is not a deontic logic (it does not describe which obligations follow from a set of obligations) and it should not be considered as such. On the other hand, since diagnosis is about violations and deontic logic is exactly for situations where violations are important [JS92], it makes sense to have a deontic framework for diagnosis like DIODE. The framework treats norms as components of a system to be diagnosed; hence the system description becomes a norms description ND. We refer to the base logic of DIODE as $\mathcal{L}_V$, and the fragment of $\mathcal{L}_V$ without violation constants as $\mathcal{L}$. We write $\models$ for entailment in $\mathcal{L}_V$. The definition of minimal violated-norm set is analogous to the definition of diagnosis. Just as we can have multiple diagnoses with respect to the same (COMP, SD, OBS), we can have multiple minimal violated-norm sets Δ with respect to (NORMS, ND, FACTS). The fact that we can have more than one minimal violation state reflects that we can have different situations that are optimal, i.e. as ideal as possible. In Section 3 we present an example that illustrates deontic diagnosis in organization scenarios.

Definition 2. (DIODE) A *normative system* is a tuple NS = (NORMS, ND) with:

1. NORMS, a finite set of constants denoting *norms* $\{n_1, \ldots, n_k\}$,
2. ND, the *norms description*, a set of first-order $\mathcal{L}_V$ sentences denoting *obligations* $\neg V(n_i) \rightarrow (\beta \rightarrow \alpha)$.

A *normative system to be diagnosed* is a tuple NSD = (NORMS, ND, FACTS) with:

1. NS = (NORMS, ND), a normative system, and
2. FACTS, a set of first-order $\mathcal{L}$ sentences that describe the facts.

Let NSD = (NORMS, ND, FACTS) be a normative system to be diagnosed. A *minimal violated-norm set* Δ of NSD is a minimal (with respect to set inclusion) subset of NORMS such that

$$\text{CONTEXT}_\Delta = \text{ND} \cup \text{FACTS} \cup \{V(n_i) \mid n_i \in \Delta\} \cup \{\neg V(n_i) \mid n_i \in \text{NORMS} - \Delta\}$$

is consistent. The set of *contextual obligations* of a minimal violated-norm set Δ of a normative system to be diagnosed NSD is $\text{CO}_\Delta = \{\alpha \mid \alpha \in \mathcal{L}, \text{CONTEXT}_\Delta \models \alpha\}$.

Obligations are represented in DIODE analogously to the way they are represented in Anderson's reduction of so-called Standard Deontic Logic (SDL) to alethic modal logic. SDL is a normal modal system of type KD according to the Chellas classification [Che80]. It satisfies, besides the propositional tautologies modus ponens and necessitation, axiom **K**: $O(\alpha \rightarrow \beta) \rightarrow (O\alpha \rightarrow O\beta)$, which states that modus ponens holds within the scope of the modal operator, and axiom **D**: $\neg(O\alpha \wedge O\neg\alpha)$, which states that dilemmas are inconsistent. Anderson [And58] showed that SDL can be expressed in alethic modal logic by the translation $O\alpha =_{def} \Box(\neg V \rightarrow \alpha)$, in which V is the so-called violation constant (not a propositional variable!), together with the axiom **D**: $\Diamond\neg V$ (as usual, $\Diamond\alpha =_{def} \neg\Box\neg\alpha$). In SDL, a conditional obligation can be represented by $\beta \rightarrow O\alpha$ or by $O(\beta \rightarrow \alpha)$. The latter is according to the Anderson schema similar to $O(\beta \rightarrow \alpha) =_{def} \Box(\neg V \rightarrow (\beta \rightarrow \alpha))$. In spite of the analogy in the way obligations are represented, there are also two important distinctions between the representation of obligations in DIODE and Anderson's reduction. First, in Anderson's reduction every deontic formula is preceded by a box $\Box$. Semantically, in the theory of diagnosis distinct *models* represent distinct situations, whereas in a modal system distinct *worlds* within a model represent distinct situations. Second, in Anderson's reduction there is only one violation constant. For a further discussion see [TvdT94a]. In spite of the analogy in the representation of obligations in DIODE and Anderson's reduction, DIODE is quite different from a deontic logic. On the one hand DIODE is more than a deontic logic, because the parsimony principle adds the assumption that the set of violations of obligations is minimal. This assumption is based on the idea that people tend to comply with norms, which is an empirical assumption about the behavior of people, and which has clearly nothing to do with the logic of norms itself. On the other hand one could argue that DIODE is less than a deontic logic, because, if ND would be a deductively closed set of sentences, then the DIODE counterpart of the formula $p \rightarrow Op$ would be contained in every ND. Clearly, $p \rightarrow Op$ is not an intuitive deontic theorem, and the counterpart of this formula is also not valid in Anderson's reduction due to his box operator. Although these counter-intuitive theorems do not occur in DIODE, because ND is not deductively closed, we give another formulation at the end of this paper of DIODE in the logic 2DL, which gives a better representation of the deontic logic component in DIODE.

2.2 Qualitative decision theory

Boutilier [Bou94] develops a logic of qualitative decision theory in which the basic concept of interest is the notion of *conditional preference*. Boutilier writes $I(\alpha \mid \beta)$, read "ideally α given β," to indicate that the truth of α is preferred, given β. This holds exactly when α is true at each of the most preferred of those worlds satisfying β. Boutilier remarks that from a practical point of view, $I(\alpha|\beta)$ means that if the agent (only) knows α, and the truth of β is fixed (beyond his control), then the agent ought to ensure α. Otherwise, should $\neg\alpha$ come to pass, the agent will end up in a less than desirable β-world. Boutilier mentions that the statement can be *roughly* interpreted as "if β, do α." Moreover, Boutilier observes that the conditional logic of preferences he proposed is similar to the (purely semantic) proposal put forth by Hansson [Han71]. He concludes that 'one may simply think of $I(\alpha \mid \beta)$ as expressing a conditional obligation to see to it that α holds if β does.' Thomason and Horty [TH96] and Lang [Lan96] also observe the link with deontic logic when they develop the foundations for qualitative decision theory.

Boutilier [Bou94] introduces a simple model of action and ability. The atomic propositions are partitioned into *controllable* propositions, atoms over which the agent has direct influence, and *uncontrollable* propositions. He ignores the complexities required to deal with effects, preconditions and such, in order to focus attention on the structure and interaction of ability and goal determination. The consequence of this lack of an action model is that 'we should think of a rule as an *evidential rule* rather than a *causal rule*.' Moreover, Boutilier observes 'the implicit temporal aspect here; propositions should be thought of as *fluents*. We can avoid an explicit temporal representation by assuming that preference is solely a function of the truth values of fluents.' Lang [Lan96] calls controllable and uncontrollable propositions respectively decision variables and parameters. Moreover, he argues that it is necessary to distinguish not only between desires (goals) and knowledge as in [Bou94] but also between background factual knowledge (which tells which worlds are physically impossible) and contingent knowledge (which tells which of the physically possible worlds can be the actual states of affairs). This last distinction was introduced in [vdT94].

The simplest definition of goals is in accordance with the general maxim 'do the best thing possible consistent with your knowledge.' Boutilier [Bou94] dubbed such goals CK goals because they seem correct when an agent has *Complete Knowledge* of the world (or at least of uncontrollable atoms). But Boutilier also shows that CK-goals do not always determine the best course of action if an agent's knowledge is *incomplete*. For example, Wald's criterion is a pessimistic strategy: maximize the minimum return (see e.g. [DP95,Lan96]).

2.3   Context of justification versus context of deliberation

The distinction between the perspective of a rational agent (qualitative decision theory) and a judge (theory of diagnosis) corresponds to Thomason's distinction between the context of deliberation and the context of justification [Tho81]. Thomason distinguishes between two ways in which the truth values of deontic sentences are time-dependent. First, these values are time-dependent in the same, familiar way that the truth values of all tensed sentences are time-dependent. Second, their truth values are dependent of a set of choices or future options that varies as a function of time. If you think of deontic operators as analogous to quantifiers ranging over options, this dependency on context is a familiar phenomenon. Thus, the context of deliberation is the set of choices when you are looking for practical advice, whereas the context of justification is the set of choices for someone who is judging you.[1] The following example discussed in [Han71] illustrates that it is important to discriminate between these two contexts, because a sentence can sometimes be interpreted differently in each of them.

Example 3. Consider the obligation 'you should not smoke if you smoke.' In the context of justification the obligation is interpreted as the identification of the fact that you are violating a rule, whereas in the context of deliberation, it is interpreted as the obligation to stop smoking. When the context is not known, it is also not known which of these two interpretations (or probably both) is meant. The two perspectives are represented in Figure 2. At the present moment in time, smoking (s) is true. The context of justification considers the moment before the truth value of s was settled, and considers whether at that moment in the past, $\neg s$ was preferred over s. The context of deliberation considers the moment the truth value of s can be changed, and considers whether at that moment in the future, $\neg s$ will be preferred over s.

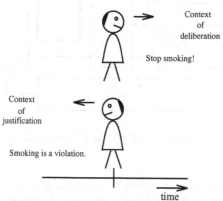

Fig. 2. Contexts of normative reasoning

The distinction between the two interpretations of the obligation 'you should not smoke if you smoke' is as important as the distinction between Alchourrón-Gärdenfors-Makinson belief revision (or theory revision) [AGM85] and Katsuno-Mendelzon belief update [KM92] in the area of logics of belief. There is a strong analogy, because belief revision is reasoning about a non-changing world and update is reasoning about a changing world. It follows directly from Figure 2 that a similar distinction is made between respectively the context of justification and the context of deliberation, because the past is fixed, whereas the future is wide open.

---

[1] Thomason defines the context of justification in terms of the context of deliberation: at a certain point in time p is justification-obligatory iff at some earlier point in time p was deliberation-obligatory (in both cases p has the same time index). This is in our opinion too simple. We should make a distinction analogous to the distinction between revision and update to formalize it.

3   Diagnostic framework for process design

The work of Ramos and Fiadeiro should be understood as a contribution to the more general purpose to build a formal framework to support organizational process design diagnosis according to predefined process design principles. By principles they mean general rules that characterize the ideal behavior of an organization. They are interested in forms of diagnoses that report violations of such principles. The architecture of their intended framework is represented in Figure 3 (taken from [RF96b]).

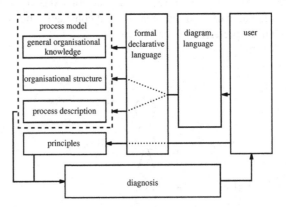

Fig. 3. Architecture of Ramos and Fiadeiro's framework

The user in Figure 3 represents both the designer and the person responsible for defining general principles. As represented in Figure 3, the user (supported by a diagrammatic language) can describe the structure of the organization and design the process (process description). The diagnosis procedure uses that information, together with general organizational knowledge, to detect violations of the principles indicated by the organization (user). The translation from a diagrammatic language to a declarative formal language is necessary, because Ramos and Fiadeiro want to use logical deduction in the diagnosis procedure. The components of the process model are the following ones:

Organizational structure. The set of structural concepts that characterize an organization, e.g. *agents, tasks, hierarchies*. These concepts are independent of the processes. They describe the fixed components over which the processes should 'flow'. The structural concepts represent what is fixed in the organization in the sense that it cannot be changed as a consequence of a process (re)design.

Process description. The description of the process design, made with typical primitives used in organizational process like *assign-task, output-to-task* etc. Variable concepts are concepts that can be manipulated by the person that designs the process. They can be understood as 'design actions'.

General organizational knowledge. Definitions (e.g. *available, informed*) and rules common to all organizations (e.g. *if a task is assigned to a collective agent, all the members of the collective agent are assigned to that task*).

Principles. General rules that characterize the ideal behavior of an organization. Each organization decides which rules should be used. Usually the rules that guide the design are general rules. For example, *'no employee can be assigned to a control task if the decision to control is assigned to an agent up in the hierarchy.'*

The following example of [RF96b] illustrates the design of an order delivering process, and is adapted from [CL92]. In Chen and Lee's framework for the evaluation of internal accounting control procedures, the idea of having general principles guiding organizational diagnosis is already present. However, this framework is not supported by a theory of diagnosis. For instance, it does not deal with either alternative or minimal diagnoses.

Example 4. (**Delivering order**) To avoid frauds in organizational accounting procedures, some control rules are often used. In Figure 4, the process is designed in order to (partially) fulfill those rules (principles). The process is as follows. The stock manager receives an order (from a salesman, for example), fills up an internal delivery order (IDO) and sends the IDO to agent 1, assigned to the task of verifying the IDO. After receiving the same order the accounting department fills up the invoice and also sends it to agent 1. Agent 1 checks if the values of the IDO and the invoice are the same, stores the invoice in the invoice file and sends the IDO to agent 2, assigned to the task of filling up the outgoing delivery order (ODO). After filling up the ODO agent 2 sends it to the client together with the goods.

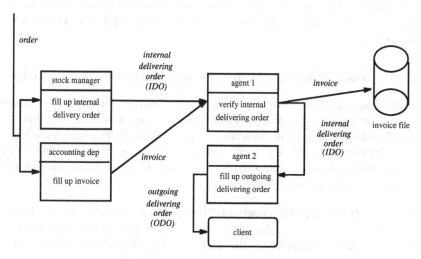

Fig. 4. Ideal order delivering process

Agent 1 is involved in the process in order to avoid a potential fraud between the stock manager and the client, because agent 1 checks if the goods in the IDO matches the values in the invoice. In the process design in Figure 4 one general rule, to ensure that the document is not manipulated by other agents, is fulfilled: *'all documents must go straight to the control agent after they are created.'* Two other rules that apply to the process are *'an agent should not control a superior in the hierarchy'* and *'socially-close agents should not control each other.'* For example, the stock manager should not be a superior of agent 1 and agent 2 should not be socially-close to the stock manager.

We give a simple formalization of this example in a propositional language, which suffices for our purpose of illustrating DDD. Instead of formalizing the three generic rules as first-order obligations, we formalize several consequences (instances) of these generic rules as propositional obligations. Let us assume the following organization structure: John, Ann and Phil are agents of the organization, Phil is socially-close to John and the stock manager is hierarchical superior than John. The obligations are (a) the output of the task verify-IDO must go to the task fill-up-ODO, (b) we must not assign Phil to the task fill-up-ODO, because socially close agents should not be involved in this process, (c) we must not assign John to the task verify-IDO, because one agent should not control a superior in the hierarchy, and (d) the output of the task fill-up-invoice must go to the task verify-IDO. Using the violation constants of DIODE, we represent the four obligations by $\neg V_1 \to a$, $\neg V_2 \to b$, $\neg V_3 \to c$ and $\neg V_4 \to d$, respectively. An instance of the general organisational knowledge is that if the output of task verify-IDO goes to fill-up-ODO and Phil is not assigned to fill-up-ODO, then Phil does not receive the ODO, which is represented by $a \wedge b \to e$. Finally, facts (design) are that Ann is agent 1, Phil is agent 2, John is not assigned to the task verify-IDO and that Phil receives the ODO, i.e., $c \wedge \neg e$. Notice that one of the first or second obligation is violated, the third obligation is fulfilled, and nothing is know about the fourth obligation.

In the following section we show how we can reason about this delivering order example in the deontic framework for diagnosis of process design, based on Reiter's theory of diagnosis.

3.1   DDD **Deontic framework for diagnosis of (organizational) process design**

Minimal diagnoses have proven to be adequate for detecting violations of obligations. However, for the purpose of process design diagnosis, it is not sufficient to capture cases of unfulfilled obligations. This particularity of process design lead Ramos and Fiadeiro in [RF96b] to propose a more general diagnosis, one that distinguishes between potential, benevolent and exigent diagnosis. The following example criticizes the principle of parsimony for organizational process design.

Example 5. (**Delivering order, continued**) If it is important that the invoice goes straight to the task verify-IDO, then a design that does not commit itself with the output of the invoice must be avoided. Indeed, if the principle is not enforced, it is possible that, during the implementation of the process in the organization, the invoice goes straight to the invoice file. To avoid this undesired situation, the diagnosis should alert to the 'incompleteness' of the design. When it is important to ensure that all obligations are fulfilled, and not only detect violations of obligations, the principle of parsimony is much too *benevolent* (it is like the assumption of the fulfillment of obligations in the absence of information). In that case an approach based only on minimal diagnosis is not adequate and an *exigent* diagnosis (where unfulfilled obligations are detected) is more suitable.

In order to deal with diagnoses that are not minimal, Ramos and Fiadeiro extend the representation of obligations by assuming that norms are completely described. With this new approach, more useful information can be obtained for process design, keeping at the same time all the results of model based reasoning. When a set of norms is translated to DDD, the following two assumptions are made to incorporate fault knowledge. The underlying assumption of 'innocent until proven guilty' is not always the right one; sometimes 'guilty until proven innocent' is preferred. So-called fault knowledge (see e.g. [dKMR90]) describes the consequences of broken components, in general represented by $\beta \wedge Ab(c) \rightarrow \gamma$. Hence, with fault knowledge from the abnormality of a component new information can be derived. If the rules from the system description SD are represented by $\beta \wedge \neg Ab(c) \rightarrow \alpha$, then there is no fault knowledge. In that case, the maximal diagnosis is simply the set of all components. Obviously, for any reasonable definition of a maximal diagnosis, fault knowledge has to be added.

- **Assumption 1** As a rule, each (conditional) obligation of a premise set corresponds to a separate norm. A set of obligations is translated to a set of norms.
- **Assumption 2** Every norm description completely describes an obligation. Thus, a conditional obligation 'α should be the case if β is the case' is represented in DDD by the norm description $\neg V(n_i) \leftrightarrow (\beta \rightarrow \alpha)$. The conditional obligation can be read in DDD as 'if the norm n_i is not violated, then and only then if β is the case then α is the case.' The sentence is logically equivalent with $V(n_i) \leftrightarrow (\neg \alpha \wedge \beta)$, which explains why $V(n_i)$ is called a *violation constant*.

Ramos and Fiadeiro propose the following deontic framework for diagnosis of (organizational) process design DDD. They discriminate between minimal and maximal violated-norm sets.

Definition 6. (DDD) A *normative system* is a DIODE tuple NS = (NORMS, ND) where ND, the *norms description*, is a set of obligations $\neg V(n_i) \leftrightarrow (\beta \rightarrow \alpha)$. Let NSD = (NORMS, ND, FACTS) be a normative system to be diagnosed and CONTEXT$_\Delta$ the context of a set of norms $\Delta \subseteq$ NORMS. A *potential diagnosis* Δ of NSD is a subset of NORMS such that CONTEXT$_\Delta$ is consistent. A *benevolent (exigent) diagnosis* Δ is a minimal (maximal) subset (with respect to set inclusion) of NORMS such that CONTEXT$_\Delta$ is consistent. The *implicit violation set* Δ of NSD is a minimal subset (with respect to set inclusion) of NORMS such that CONTEXT$_\Delta$ is inconsistent.

The set of potential diagnosis can be ordered by set inclusion, of which the benevolent and exigent diagnosis are respectively the lower and upper bounds. Diagnostic reasoning is not restricted to the minimal elements of the graph, but to all elements. Moreover, for the benevolent diagnosis we have the additional information supplied by the implicit obligation sets and the contextual obligations. This is illustrated by the example of the delivering order in DDD, see [RF96b] for a full discussion of this example in DDD.[2]

---

[2] As remarked in [dKMR90], with the representation of fault knowledge it is no longer possible to compute all consistent sets of normal and abnormal components based on minimal diagno-

Example 7. (**Delivering order, continued**) Consider the following normative system:

1. NORMS $= \{n_1, n_2, n_3, n_4\}$, and
2. ND $= \{\neg V(n_1) \leftrightarrow a, \neg V(n_2) \leftrightarrow b, \neg V(n_3) \leftrightarrow c, \neg V(n_4) \leftrightarrow d\}$.

The set of potential diagnoses of FACTS $= \{a \wedge b \rightarrow e, c \wedge \neg e\}$ is represented in Figure 5. We have FACTS $\models \neg a \vee \neg b$ and FACTS $\cup$ ND $\models V(n_1) \vee V(n_2)$. Moreover, we have FACTS $\cup$ ND $\models \neg V(n_3)$. There is one exigent diagnosis, $\{V(n_1), V(n_2), V(n_4)\}$, and two benevolent diagnoses, $\{V(n_1)\}$ and $\{V(n_2)\}$. The implicit violation set is the set $\{V(n_1), V(n_2)\}$, which means that either the first or the second norm has to be violated.

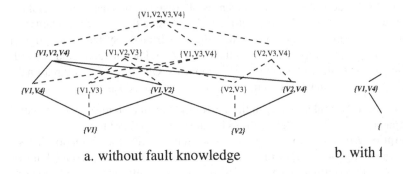

a. without fault knowledge   b. with 1

Fig. 5. Consistent sets of violations

3.2 DDD² **Deontic framework for Diagnosis for process Design based on Deontic logic**

In [RF96a] Ramos and Fiadeiro show how a theory of diagnosis can use deontic logic. Ramos and Fiadeiro use dyadic deontic logic to represent conditional obligations.[3] With the dyadic operator, Chisholm's paradox for conditional obligations does not occur. The obligations $O(\alpha | \beta)$ are read as 'α is obligatory in the context β.' They have the following desiderata for the dyadic logic.

1. Conditional obligation, thus not $O(\alpha | \beta) \leftrightarrow O(\beta \rightarrow \alpha)$. For example, if there is a rule '*if an order form is send to a supplier, then a copy of the order form should be send to the department store*' $O(c|o)$ and neither c and o nor their negations can be derived, then an exigent diagnosis should not contain the violation of the obligation. The situation is avoided if we only consider violations of *actual* obligations

---

sis: not all supersets of minimal sets are consistent. In Reiter's minimal diagnosis that property holds. Indeed, in Figure 5.a, only the sets in italics are consistent if we adopt the complete description of norms.

[3] A deontic logic describes besides obligations also permissions. However, the 'organization' does not say : you are permitted to do ... ! That makes no sense in design. The diagnosis is not going to check if the permissions are 'fulfilled', because it is a designer problem. The designer is permitted to do anything except violating the rules.

in a diagnosis, because with actual obligations, if o cannot be derived, then the violation will never appear in a diagnosis. Thus a normal modal system like SDL and Anderson's reduction to alethic modal logic is insufficient.

2. Contraposition $O(\alpha \mid \beta) \leftrightarrow O(\neg\beta \mid \neg\alpha)$. For example, if there is the rule $O(c \mid o)$ and $\neg c$ can be derived and $\neg o$ cannot be derived, then an exigent diagnosis should contain the violation of the obligation.

3. No weakening of the consequent. Consider the rule of inference RM : if $\vdash \beta \rightarrow \alpha$ then $O\beta \rightarrow O\alpha$. Assume the following rule: *if one agent sends a document to other, then the second receives the document.'* Notice that A sending a document to B is more specific than B receiving it because it can be send by anyone. Furthermore, assume the obligation *'Ann is obliged to send a budget to John'* and the fact *'Ann does not send the budget'* (thus John does not receive it). Given rule RM, the diagnosis will report two violations. However only one violation really occurs. Thus a normal modal system like SDL and a non-normal modal system like Chellas minimal deontic logic are insufficient.

4. Design action and context. Dyadic obligations $O(\alpha \mid \beta)$ have two components. First, the *design action* (α) that indicates what the designer should do. Second, *the context* (β) that describes the situation in which the design action should be done.

5. No structural variables in the scope of the modal operator. It is assumed that it makes no sense to have obligations that oblige a process designer to act in the structure of the organisation. This is formalized by the contingency clause $\neg struct(\alpha)$, as explained below. It follows from that assumption that, whatever the context, any obligation where the action is represented by a structural concept is not valid. For example, the following rule *'if the task approve-budget is assigned to John, then John must be the Head of Department (HD)'* $O(h \mid a)$ is not valid because John being or not being the HD is not an design action (it is a part of the structure of the organisation). The rule should be: *'if John is not the HD, then he cannot be assigned to the task approve-budget'* $O(\neg a \mid \neg h)$.

Ramos and Fiadeiro make a distinction between structural and action variables (4). The basic idea is the following, inspired by Castañeda's distinction between assertions and actions [Cas81]. The modal language of deontic logic gives us the opportunity – not present in Reiter's first order theory of diagnosis – to distinguish between structural variables which are fixed *within a model*, and variables which are allowed to vary within the model. For a structural variable p, we have $\Box p \vee \Box\neg p$. Hence, we have $p \rightarrow \Box p$: if the structural variable is true in the actual world, it is true in all worlds. Notice that $\Box p$ should be read as p is a structural concept, not as p is necessarily true (as in Anderson's proposal). Moreover, they restrict the scope of the deontic operator to action variables (5). Hence, we add the clause $\neg struct(\alpha)$ to an obligation for α. This is a formalization of von Wright's contingency principle, because we have $Op \rightarrow \Diamond\neg p$ and $Op \rightarrow \Diamond p$. The contingency clause $\neg struct(\alpha)$ is a kind of consistency check. Von Wright remarks that 'the last may be regarded as a version of the principle, commonly associated with the name of Kant, that 'Ought implies (entails) Can' [vW71, p.163].

In [RF96a] the following logic LDD is proposed. It is defined in terms of a monadic minimal modal logic, and thereby we have trivially soundness and completeness of the logic. The modal operator I is a technical trick to avoid the problems of Chellas' standard modal operators. The interested reader is referred to [RF96a] for further details.[4]

Definition 8. (LDD) Consider a bimodal logic with $\Box$ and I. The logic is the smallest set of formula that contains the propositional tautologies and the following axioms and is closed under the following rules of inference.

> **MP:** $\frac{\alpha \to \beta, \alpha}{\beta}$
> **Nes:** $\frac{\vdash \alpha}{\vdash \Box \alpha}$
> **RE:** $\frac{\alpha_1 \leftrightarrow \alpha_2}{I\alpha_1 \leftrightarrow I\alpha_2}$
> **K:** $\Box(\beta \to \alpha) \to (\Box \beta \to \Box \alpha)$
> **T:** $\Box \alpha \to \alpha$
> $\quad \neg I \bot$
> $\quad \neg I \top$
> $\quad \Box \alpha \to I\alpha$

The logic LDD is extension of the bimodal logic with the following definitions.

$$struct(\alpha) =_{def} \Box \alpha \vee \Box \neg \alpha$$
$$O(\alpha|\beta) =_{def} I(\beta \leftrightarrow \alpha) \wedge \neg I(\neg \alpha \wedge \beta) \wedge \neg struct(\alpha)$$

Definition 9. (Semantics LDD) Kripke models $M = \langle W, R_1, R_2, V \rangle$ for LDD consist of W a set of worlds, $R_1(w, w')$ a binary reflexive accessibility relation, $R_2(w, W')$ an accessibility relation that gives a nonempty set of sets of worlds ($\neq W$) for each world (we write either $R_1(w, w')$ and $R_2(w, W')$, or $w' \in R_1(w)$ and $W' \in R_2(w)$), such that for all $W' \in R_2(w)$ we have $W' \subset R_1(w)$, and V a valuation function for the propositions in the worlds. We have:

$M, w \models \Box p$ iff for all w' such that $R_1(w, w')$ we have $M, w' \models p$
$M, w \models Ip$ iff $\exists W'$ such that $R_2(w, W')$ and $W' = \{w' \in R_1(w) \mid M, w' \models p\}$.

The logic is not closed under conjunction, weakening of the consequent, etc. The following proposition shows that LDD has the desired properties.

Proposition 10. *The logic* LDD *validates the following theorems.*

$\neg O(\top|\beta)$
$\neg O(\bot|\beta)$
$(\beta \wedge struct(\beta) \wedge O(\alpha|\beta)) \to O(\alpha|\top)$
$(struct(\alpha_2) \wedge O(\alpha_1 \wedge \alpha_2|\beta)) \to O(\alpha_1|\beta)$
$(\neg struct(\beta) \wedge O(\alpha|\beta)) \to O(\neg\beta|\neg\alpha)$

The logic LDD *does not validate the following theorem (the first desideratum of the list at the beginning of this section).*

---

[4] In this paper, we have simplified the formalization. In [RF96a], the dyadic operator is defined directly in the semantics: $O(\alpha \mid \beta)$ is true iff in all ideal designs $\alpha \leftrightarrow \beta$ and in ideal designs it is not the case that $\beta \wedge \neg \alpha$.

$$(\neg struct(\beta \to \alpha) \wedge O(\alpha|\beta)) \to O(\beta \to \alpha|\top)$$

Proof *The two theorems* $\neg O(\top \mid \beta)$ *and* $\neg O(\bot \mid \beta)$ *follow directly from* $\neg struct(\alpha)$. $(\beta \wedge struct(\beta) \wedge O(\alpha|\beta)) \to O(\alpha|\top)$ *and* $(struct(\alpha_2) \wedge O(\alpha_1 \wedge \alpha_2|\beta)) \to O(\alpha_1|\beta)$ *follow from* $\alpha \wedge struct(\alpha) \to \Box\alpha$. *The theorem* $(\neg struct(\beta) \wedge O(\alpha|\beta)) \to O(\neg\beta|\neg\alpha)$ *follows from* $(I(\beta \leftrightarrow \alpha) \wedge \neg I(\neg\alpha \wedge \beta)) \to (I(\neg\alpha \leftrightarrow \neg\beta) \wedge \neg I(\neg\neg\beta \wedge \neg\alpha))$. *For a countermodel of* $(\neg struct(\beta \to \alpha) \wedge O(\alpha|\beta)) \to O(\beta \to \alpha \mid \top)$, *consider the set* $W = \{w_0, w_1, w_2, w_3, w_4\}$ *with* $w_1 = \{\neg a, \neg b\}$; $w_2 = \{a, b\}$; $w_3 = \{\neg a, b\}$; $w_4 = \{a, \neg b\}$, $R_1(w_0, w_1)$; $R_1(w_0, w_2)$; $R_1(w_0, w_3)$; $R_1(w_0, w_4)$; $R_2(w_0, \{w_1, w_2\})$. *Given the set* W *we have* $M, w_0 \models I(a \leftrightarrow b)$ *because* $W' = \{w_1, w_2\}$, *we have* $M, w_0 \not\models I(\neg a \wedge b)$ *because we do not have* $R_2(w_0, \{w_3\})$, *and we have* $M, w_0 \not\models I((b \to a) \leftrightarrow \top)$ *because we do not have* $R_2(w_0, \{w_1, w_2, w_4\})$.

The logic LDD is used for deontics-based diagnosis.[5]

Definition 11. (Deontics-based diagnosis) An obligation system is given by a tuple OS = (OBL, STRUCT) with:

1. OBL, a finite set of modal sentences denoting conditional obligations $O(\alpha|\beta)$,
2. STRUCT, a set of expressions denoting which variables are structural $\Box p \vee \Box \neg p$.

An obligation system to be diagnosed is a tuple OSD = (OBL, STRUCT, FACTS) with:

1. OS = (OBL, STRUCT), an obligation system, and
2. FACTS, a finite set of propositional sentences.

The *actual obligation set* AO is the set of obligations (without logical equivalents):

$$\text{AO} = \{O_a\alpha \mid \text{OBL} \cup \text{FACTS} \cup \text{STRUCT} \models O(\alpha|\beta) \wedge \beta\}$$

A potential diagnosis Δ is a subset of the actual obligation set AO such that

$$\text{CONTEXT}_\Delta = \text{OBL} \cup \text{FACTS} \cup \text{STRUCT} \cup \{\neg\alpha \mid O_a\alpha \in \Delta\} \cup \{\alpha \mid O_a\alpha \in \text{AO} - \Delta\}$$

is consistent.

Deontics-based diagnosis is illustrated by the following example.

Example 12. **(Delivering order, continued)** Consider the following additional rule to the initial example in Example 4: 'if an ODO is sent to a client, a copy of the ODO should be sent to the department store' ($O(g \mid f)$). Since the condition of the obligation does not hold (it is not 'designed' yet), there is no actual obligation of g (send a copy of ODO to the department store). Consider the following obligation system to be diagnosed OSD=(OBL, STRUCT, FACTS) with

1. OBL = $\{O(a|\top), O(b|\top), O(c|\top), O(d|\top), O(g|f)\}$,
2. STRUCT = $\emptyset$,
3. FACTS = $\{a \wedge b \to e, c \wedge \neg e\}$.

The actual obligation set is AO = $\{O_a a, O_a b, O_a c, O_a d\}$ and the set of potential diagnoses is similar to the previous representation in DDD in Example 7.

---

[5] We have simplified the deontics-based diagnosis a bit. The obligation system that consists of the single obligation $O(a|b)$ and facts $b \wedge \neg a$ will report that a is a violation. But in [RF96a] the user is informed that if he changes b to $\neg b$, then the violation will disappear.

4   Diagnostic and decision-theoretic framework

The work of Tan and Van der Torre should be understood as a contribution to a more general purpose to build a formal framework to support drafting of bureaucratic procedures, in particular international trade procedures [BLWW95]. For example, in [RTvdT96] it is shown how to extend the Petri net formalism to represent different types of behavior, in particular normative behavior. This extension is motivated by the use of Petri nets to model bureaucratic procedures, which contain normative aspects like obligations and permissions. It is important that violations of obligations, i.e. sub-ideal states, are represented explicitly in the modeling of procedures, because in most procedures it is described explicitly what is considered as ill-behavior, and how this will be punished (the corresponding sanction). However, the representation of violations and sub-ideal behavior in Petri nets is not very satisfactory, see [RTvdT96]. The modeling of violations of bureaucratic procedures explains Tan and Van der Torre's interest in theories of diagnosis.

4.1   DIODE with applicable norms

In DIODE, there is no distinction between fulfilling a dyadic obligation, and inapplicability of a dyadic obligation. For example, for $O(\alpha|\beta)$ we have $\neg V(n) \leftrightarrow (\beta \to \alpha)$, which is logically equivalent with $\neg V(n) \leftrightarrow (\neg\beta \vee (\beta \wedge \alpha))$. A solution is to add applicability information. For example, for $O(\alpha|\beta)$ we have $\neg V(n) \leftrightarrow (\beta \to \alpha) \wedge A(n) \leftrightarrow \beta$. Thus, the underlying logic is extended with an applicability predicate similar to the violation predicate. Now, first we determine the applicable obligations by minimizing the $A(n)$. Secondly, for applicable obligations we can have minimal or maximal sets.

Definition 13. (DIODE **with applicable norms**) A *normative system* is a DIODE tuple NS = (NORMS, ND) where ND, the *norms description*, is a set of *conditional obligations*

$$\neg V(n_i) \leftrightarrow (\beta \to \alpha) \wedge A(n) \leftrightarrow \beta$$

Let NSD = (NORMS, ND, FACTS) be a normative system to be diagnosed. The *active norms* Δ_a of NSD is a minimal subset of NORMS such that

$$\text{ND} \cup \text{FACTS} \cup \{A(n_i) \mid n_i \in \Delta_a\} \cup \{\neg A(n_i) \mid n_i \in \text{NORMS} - \Delta_a\}$$

is consistent. A *potential diagnosis* Δ of NSD is a subset of some Δ_a of NSD such that

$$\text{CONTEXT}_\Delta = \text{ND} \cup \text{FACTS} \cup \{V(n_i) \mid n_i \in \Delta_a\} \cup \{\neg V(n_i) \mid n_i \in \Delta_a - \Delta\}$$

is consistent.

The following example illustrates the adaptation of DIODE.

Example 14. Consider the normative system of the obligation $O(c|o)$.

1. NORMS = $\{n_1\}$,
2. ND = $\{((\neg V(n_1) \leftrightarrow (o \to c)) \wedge (A(n_1) \leftrightarrow o))\}$.

The set of active norms Δ_a is empty for FACTS $= \emptyset$, thus there is no potential diagnosis which contains the norm n_1. In particular, the only exigent diagnosis is the empty set. Moreover, consider the following normative system of the two obligations $O(p_1|q)$ and $O(p_2|\neg q)$.

1. NORMS $= \{n_1, n_2\}$,
2. ND $= \left\{ \begin{array}{l} (\neg V(n_1) \leftrightarrow (q \to p_1)) \wedge (A(n_1) \leftrightarrow q), \\ (\neg V(n_2) \leftrightarrow (\neg q \to p_2)) \wedge (A(n_2) \leftrightarrow \neg q) \end{array} \right\}$.

Given the tautology $q \vee \neg q$, we have for FACTS $= \emptyset$ two minimal active sets $\Delta_a = \{n_1\}$ and $\Delta_a = \{n_2\}$. Finally, consider the following normative system of the two obligations $O(p|q)$ and $O(q|\top)$.

1. NORMS $= \{n_1, n_2\}$,
2. ND $= \{ (\neg V(n_1) \leftrightarrow (q \to p)) \wedge (A(n_1) \leftrightarrow q), (\neg V(n_2) \leftrightarrow q) \wedge (A(n_2) \leftrightarrow \top) \}$.

The minimal active set for FACTS $= \{\neg p\}$ is $\Delta_a = \{n_2\}$.

4.2 DIO(DE)^2

A theory of diagnosis like DIODE is based on the distinction between violated and non-violated, and a (qualitative) decision theory is based on the distinction between fulfilled and non-fulfilled. DIO(DE)^2 is short for the DIagnostic and DEcision-theoretic framework for DEontic reasoning. It combines reasoning about violated and fulfilled norms. Hence, it combines reasoning about the past (violated versus non-violated) with reasoning about the future (already fulfilled versus not yet fulfilled). As illustrated in Figure 1, DIO(DE)^2 combines the reasoning of a judge with reasoning of a rational agent. DIO(DE)^2 is the extension of DIODE with (1) goal oriented reasoning, (2) distinction between parameters and decision variables and (3) addition of uncertainty and strategies. Here, we restrict ourselves to the first item. Technically, it has fulfilled-norm constants (F). In the following definition of DIO(DE)^2, for an obligation $O(\alpha|\beta)$ we have besides $\neg V(n) \leftrightarrow (\beta \to \alpha)$ also $F(n) \leftrightarrow (\beta \wedge \alpha)$. We minimize the applicable norms by minimizing the relation $(\Delta_f, \Delta_v) \leq (\Delta'_f, \Delta'_v)$.

Definition 15. (DIO(DE)^2) A *normative system* is a DIODE tuple NS $=$ (NORMS, ND) where ND, the *norms description*, is a set of *conditional obligations* represented by the formula $\neg V(n_i) \leftrightarrow (\beta \to \alpha) \wedge F(n) \leftrightarrow (\beta \wedge \alpha)$. Let NSD $=$ (NORMS, ND, FACTS) be a normative system to be diagnosed. A *fulfilled-violated set* (Δ_f, Δ_v) of NSD is a pair of subsets of *norms* such that

$$\text{CONTEXT}_\Delta = \text{ND} \cup \text{FACTS} \cup \{V(n_i) \mid n_i \in \Delta_v\} \cup \{\neg V(n_i) \mid n_i \in \text{NORMS} - \Delta_v\}$$
$$\cup \{F(n_i) \mid n_i \in \Delta_f\} \cup \{\neg F(n_i) \mid n_i \in \text{NORMS} - \Delta_f\}$$

is consistent. Let $\leq$ be the ordering on fulfilled-violated sets $(\Delta_f, \Delta_v) \leq (\Delta'_f, \Delta'_v)$ iff $\Delta_f \subseteq \Delta'_f$ and $\Delta_v \subseteq \Delta'_v$. A *potential diagnosis* (Δ_f, Δ_v) of NSD is a pair of subsets of NORMS that is minimal in the ordering $\leq$.

The following example illustrates the adaptation of DIO(DE)^2 and compares it with DIODE with applicable norms.

Example 16. Consider the following normative system of the obligation $O(c|o)$.

1. NORMS = $\{n_1\}$,
2. ND = $\{(\neg V(n_1) \leftrightarrow (o \rightarrow c)) \wedge (F(n_1) \leftrightarrow (c \wedge o))\}$

The unique potential diagnosis for FACTS = $\emptyset$ is $(\Delta_f, \Delta_v) = (\emptyset, \emptyset)$. In DIODE with applicable norms, the set of active norms Δ_a is empty for FACTS = $\emptyset$. Hence, the two systems behave similarly. Moreover, consider the following normative system of the two obligations $O(p_1|q)$ and $O(p_2|\neg q)$.

1. NORMS = $\{n_1, n_2\}$,
2. ND = $\{ \begin{matrix} (\neg V(n_1) \leftrightarrow (q \rightarrow p_1)) \wedge (F(n_1) \leftrightarrow (p_1 \wedge q)), \\ (\neg V(n_2) \leftrightarrow (\neg q \rightarrow p_2)) \wedge (F(n_2) \leftrightarrow (p_2 \wedge \neg q)) \end{matrix} \}$.

The potential diagnoses (Δ_f, Δ_v) for FACTS = $\emptyset$ are $(\{n_1\}, \emptyset), (\{n_2\}, \emptyset), (\emptyset, \{n_1\})$ and $(\emptyset, \{n_2\})$. In DIODE with applicable norms, we have for FACTS = $\emptyset$ two minimal active sets $\Delta_a = \{n_1\}$ and $\Delta_a = \{n_2\}$. Hence, the two systems behave again similarly. Finally, consider the following normative system of the two obligations $O(p \mid q)$ and $O(q|\top)$.

1. NORMS = $\{n_1, n_2\}$,
2. ND = $\{ (\neg V(n_1) \leftrightarrow (q \rightarrow p)) \wedge (F(n_1) \leftrightarrow (p \wedge q)), (\neg V(n_2) \leftrightarrow q) \wedge (F(n_2) \leftrightarrow q) \}$

The potential diagnoses for FACTS = $\{\neg p\}$ are $(\Delta_f, \Delta_v) = (\emptyset, \{n_2\})$ and $(\Delta_f, \Delta_v) = (\{n_2\}, \{n_1\})$. In DIODE with applicable norms, the minimal active set for FACTS = $\{\neg p\}$ is $\Delta_a = \{n_2\}$. The two systems do not behave similarly, because in DIO(DE)^2 it is possible that the first obligation is violated.

There is an interesting connection between the latter set of obligations of Example 16 and deontic detachment (or transitivity) $O(\alpha \mid \beta) \wedge O(\beta \mid \gamma) \rightarrow O(\alpha \mid \gamma)$. With deontic detachment we can derive the obligation $O(p \mid \top)$ from the two premises $O(p \mid q)$ and $O(q \mid \top)$. Thus, if deontic detachment is valid, then the fact $\neg p$ is a violation. In DIODE, there is only one active set, that contains the second obligation. It is possible that this obligation is fulfilled, and there are therefore no violations. On the other hand, in DIO(DE)^2 every potential diagnosis contains violations.

4.3   The two-phase deontic logic 2DL

The two-phase preference-based deontic logic 2DL [TvdT96,vdTT97b] can be used to make the comparison between DIO(DE)^2 and classical deontic logics. In the modal preference semantics of 2DL, the accessibility relation is interpreted as a preference relation. For example, $w_1 \leq w_2$ has to be read as 'world w_1 is at least as preferable as world w_2.' It is a well-known problem from preference logics that we cannot define an obligation Op as a strict preference of p over $\neg p$, because two obligations Op_1 and Op_2 would conflict for $p_1 \wedge \neg p_2$ and $\neg p_1 \wedge p_2$. This motivates the following weaker definition: an obligation p is the absence of a preference of $\neg p$ over p, see [TvdT96,vdTT97b].

Definition 17. (2DL) A Kripke model $M = \langle W, \leq, V \rangle$ consists of W, a set of worlds, $\leq$ a binary transitive and reflexive accessibility relation interpreted as a preference relation, and V, a valuation of the propositions at the worlds. We have $M \models O(\alpha|\beta)$ iff

1. for all w and w' such that $M, w \models \alpha \wedge \beta$ and $M, w' \models \neg\alpha \wedge \beta$, we have $w' \not\leq w$, and

2. there are such worlds w and w'.

DIO(DE)^2 corresponds to deontics-based diagnosis based on the modal logic 2DL. That is, DIO(DE)^2 corresponds to deontics-based diagnosis in Definition 11 in the previous section, where the logic LDD is replaced by 2DL. The correspondence follows directly from the preference-based semantics. An obligation $O(\alpha \mid \beta)$ in DIO(DE)^2 is a preference of $\alpha \wedge \beta$ (fulfilled norm) over $\neg\alpha \wedge \beta$ (violated norm). This preference is defined in two steps: in the base language the fulfilled and violated norm constants are defined, and in the definition of potential diagnosis the set of applicable norms is minimized. In 2DL, the preference is not represented by fulfilled and violated norm constants, but defined directly in the preferential semantics. With other words, DIO(DE)^2 is the deontic logic 2DL in which certain aspects (fulfillments and violations) are made explicit with the use of a naming convention, i.e. to use names n_i to denote norms.

5   Comparison

The similarity between the two approaches DDD and DIO(DE)^2 presented in this paper is that exigent diagnosis is like reasoning about goals. Moreover, there are several technical similarities between the logics LDD and 2DL like the use of a contingency clause (consistency checks) and lack of weakening of the consequent.

5.1   Exigent diagnosis and goal oriented reasoning

The main similarity between DDD and DIO(DE)^2 is that both are extensions of DIODE with concepts of qualitative decision theory. The extended diagnostic framework DDD can be considered as a kind of qualitative decision framework for the following reason. The exigent diagnosis of DDD reports norms not yet fulfilled. Hence, it reports norms that should be fulfilled in the future. These norms are the goals in decision theory, which are represented by F predicates in DIO(DE)^2.

We can discriminate two phases in DDD and DIO(DE)^2. The first phase reasons about all potential diagnosis and the second phase only about benevolent or exigent diagnoses. This is in accordance with the argumentation in [TvdT96] about the two-phase treatment of violated obligations. Moreover, Lang [Lan96] observes that his methodology in an alternative approach to qualitative decision theory contains two phases. First generate the preference relation from a set of desires, and then find the optimal feasible worlds, and thus the optimal decision.

5.2   Properties of the logics LDD and 2DL

There are two important similarities between the logics LDD and 2DL, contingency clause (consistency checks in the definition of obligation) and most importantly the lack of weakening of the consequent. In this paper, we argued that these properties are essential for diagnosis. In [TvdT96] it is shown that these properties are essential to solve the notorious contrary-to-duty paradoxes of deontic logic.

Contingency clause Von Wright introduced the contingency clause, because he wanted to formalize a deontic logic based on a theory of conditions: 'to say that something ought to be, or ought to be done, is to state that the being or doing of this thing is a necessary condition (requirement) of something else' [vW71]. In DDD the contingency clause is introduced, because the consequent is restricted to design actions. In 2DL we have the theorems $O(\alpha|\beta) \rightarrow \Diamond(\alpha \wedge \beta)$ and $O(\alpha|\beta) \rightarrow \Diamond(\neg\alpha \wedge \beta)$. These consistency checks were introduced, because they are necessary to solve the notorious contrary-to-duty paradoxes like the Forrester and Chisholm paradoxes.

A distinction is that in 2DL we have $O(\alpha|\beta) \rightarrow \Diamond(\alpha \wedge \beta)$ whereas in LDD we only have $O(\alpha|\beta) \rightarrow \Diamond\alpha$. Notice that in LDD obligations of type $O(p|\bot)$ can be valid. Even if an obligation can never be violated in a model (the condition never holds), there are situations where the obligation should hold. Consider the following example: *all salesman responsible for at least one region must participate in the preparation of the annual budget*. It could be the case that, in a particular moment (i.e., in a model, if we consider that been responsible for a region is a structural concept), there are no salesmen responsible for regions (due, for example, to a ungoing reorganisation), i.e., the obligation is always fulfilled. However, since this is a temporary situation, the organization could be interested in keeping the rule (in order to avoid the necessity to change the normative systems when the structure changes).

Lack of weakening of the consequent Lack of weakening of LDD is a desirable property in DDD[2], because it avoids too many violations as discussed in Section 3.2. Lack of weakening is used in 2DL because of the ctd paradoxes. Lack of weakening of the consequent is a well-known theme in deontic logic. Ross, who gave the following counterintuitive example of weakening of the consequent, called the Ross paradox: 'if you should mail the letter, then you should mail or burn the letter' [Ros41]. A similar SDL theorem has been questioned by Von Wright. He observed that 'in a deontic logic which rejects the implication from left to right in the equivalence $O(p \wedge q) \leftrightarrow (Op \wedge Oq)$ while retaining the implication from right to left, the paradoxes would not appear' [vW81, p.7]. Beatty [Bea73] suggests that 'descriptive sentences' do not have closure under logical implication. Jennings [Jen85] observes that 'It has been suggested that a unary operator O capable of bearing a deontic interpretation might be defined in a logic of preference by $O\alpha =_{def} \alpha P \neg\alpha$', and that 'if the preference logic has the natural distributive properties as von Wright advocates, the defined deontic necessity will be nonmonotonic' (i.e. does not have weakening).

Fulfilled goals and violations in LDD Reconsider the definition of obligation in LDD $O(\alpha|\beta) =_{def} I(\beta \leftrightarrow \alpha) \wedge \neg I(\neg\alpha \wedge \beta) \wedge \neg struct(\alpha)$. The following definition discriminates between violations and fulfillments of this definition of obligations in the deontic logic LDD.

Definition 18. (LDD) The logic LDD is a minimal deontic logic as defined in Definition 9, extended with the following definitions.

$$struct(\alpha) =_{def} \Box\alpha \vee \Box\neg\alpha$$
$$F(\alpha|\beta) =_{def} I(\alpha \leftrightarrow \beta)$$
$$V(\alpha|\beta) =_{def} \neg I\neg(\beta \to \alpha)$$
$$O(\alpha|\beta) =_{def} F(\alpha|\beta) \wedge V(\alpha|\beta) \wedge \neg struct(\alpha)$$

Observe that $(\alpha \leftrightarrow \beta) \leftrightarrow ((\alpha\wedge\beta)\vee(\neg\alpha\wedge\neg\beta))$. In DIO(DE)[2] only $\alpha\wedge\beta$ corresponds to a fulfilled goal, in LDD also $\neg\alpha \wedge \neg\beta$. The intuition of the bi-implication in LDD is as follows. In conditional obligations, ideally, if the condition is true, the action must be performed (and the condition cannot be true if the action is not performed). A situation where the condition is true and the action is not performed, is not an ideal one. Situations where the condition is false, and the action is performed, are not in the scope of truth in conditional obligations. We can analyze properties of the logic LDD by analyzing the properties of the definitions F and V. For example:

$$F(\alpha|\beta) \leftrightarrow F(\neg\beta|\neg\alpha) \quad V(\alpha|\beta) \leftrightarrow V(\neg\beta|\neg\alpha)$$
$$F(\alpha|\beta) \leftrightarrow F(\beta|\alpha) \quad V(\alpha|\beta) \leftrightarrow V(\beta \to \alpha|\top)$$
$$F(\alpha|\beta) \leftrightarrow F(\neg\alpha|\beta)$$
$$F(\alpha|\beta) \leftrightarrow F(\beta \leftrightarrow \alpha|\top)$$

6 Conclusions

Classical approaches to a theory of diagnosis are based only on minimal diagnoses, and as a consequence they are not suitable to support decision-making processes. That limitation of classical approaches becomes more relevant when diagnosis is used in the context of a design support framework. In this paper two distinct non-classical diagnosis approaches have been presented, DDD and DIO(DE)[2], both supporting the design of procedures/ process in organizations. Both are extensions of DIODE, a deontic version of classical diagnoses.

LDD and 2DL are two deontic logics that have been introduced in a theory of diagnosis. Both languages presented are based on propositional logic. We are aware that this is a simplification of the real process/ procedures diagnosis. Usually the rules that guide designs are generic ones, which have to be expressed in first-order logic. It is necessary to extend the languages in order to capture those generic rules (see also [CL92]). Conflicting obligations is also a subject that it is important to consider in a framework that aims to help a designer. Not only because conflicting sometimes occur in organizations, but also due to alternative diagnoses. It is important to find a useful way to help the designer to deal with alternative choices. Conflict resolution strategies from defeasible deontic logic could be a possible answer, see [vdTT95,vdTT97a]. Castañeda's proposal [Cas81] for handling conflicting obligations is another possible approach.

References

[AGM85]   C.E. Alchourrón, P. Gärdenfors, and D. Makinson. On the logic of theory change: partial meet contraction and revision functions. *Journal of Symbolic Logic*, pages 510–530, 1985.

[And58]   A.R. Anderson. A reduction of deontic logic to alethic modal logic. *Mind*, 67:100–103, 1958.

[Bea73]   H. Beatty. On evaluating deontic logics. In *Exact philosophy*, pages 173–178. Reidel, 1973.

[BLWW95]   R.W.H. Bons, R.M. Lee, R.W. Wagenaar, and C.D. Wrigley.   Modeling inter-organizational trade procedures using documentary Petri nets. In *Proceedings of the 27th Hawaii International Conference on System Sciences (HICSS'95)*, Hawaii, 1995.

[Bou94]   C. Boutilier.   Toward a logic for qualitative decision theory.   In *Proceedings of the Fourth International Conference on Principles of Knowledge Representation and Reasoning (KR'94)*, pages 75–86, 1994.

[Cas81]   H. Castañeda. The paradoxes of deontic logic: the simplest solution to all of them in one fell swoop. In *New Studies in Deontic Logic*. D. Reidel, 1981.

[Che80]   B.F. Chellas. *Modal Logic: An Introduction*. Cambridge University Press, 1980.

[CL92]   K.-T. Chen and R.M. Lee. Schematic evaluation of internal accounting control systems. Technical Report Research Monograph RM-1992-08-01, Euridis, Erasmus University Rotterdam, 1992.

[dKMR90]   J. de Kleer, A.K. Mackwort, and R. Reiter. Characterizing diagnosis. In *Proceedings AAAI'90*, pages 324–330, Boston, MA, 1990.

[DP95]   D. Dubois and H. Prade. Qualitative decision theory. In *Proceedings IJCAI'95*, pages 1924–1930. Morgan Kaufmann, 1995.

[DW88]   R Davis and H. Walter. Model based reasoning: troubleshouting. In *Exploring Artificial Intelligence: Survey talks from the National Conferences on Artificial Intelligence*, pages 297–346, San Mateo, California, 1988. Morgan Kaufmann.

[Han71]   B. Hansson. An analysis of some deontic logics. In *Deontic Logic: Introductionary and Systematic Readings*, pages 121–147. D. Reidel Publishing Company, Dordrecht, Holland, 1971.

[Hor93]   J.F. Horty. Deontic logic as founded in nonmonotonic logic. *Annals of Mathematics and Artificial Intelligence*, 9:69–91, 1993.

[Jen85]   R.E. Jennings. Can there be a natural logic? *Synthese*, 65:257–274, 1985.

[JS92]   A.J.I. Jones and M. Sergot. Deontic logic in the representation of law: Towards a methodology. *Artificial Intelligence and Law*, 1:45–64, 1992.

[KM92]   H. Katsuno and A.O. Mendelzon. On the difference between updating a belief base and revising it. In P. Gärdenfors, editor, *Belief Revision*, pages 183–203. Cambridge University Press, 1992.

[Lan96]   J. Lang. Conditional desires and utilities - an alternative approach to qualitative decision theory. In *Proceedings of the ECAI'96*, pages 318–322, 1996.

[Rei87]   R. Reiter. A theory of diagnosis from first principles. *Artificial Intelligence*, 32:57–95, 1987.

[RF96a]   P. Ramos and J.L. Fiadeiro. A deontic logic for diagnosis of organisational process design. Technical report, Department of Informatics, Faculty of Sciences – University of Lisbon, 1996.

[RF96b]   P. Ramos and J.L. Fiadeiro. Diagnosis in organisational process design. Technical report, Department of Informatics, Faculty of Sciences – University of Lisbon, 1996.

[Ros41]   A. Ross. Imperatives and logic. *Theoria*, 7:53–71, 1941.

[RTvdT96]   J.-F. Raskin, Y.-H. Tan, and L.W.N. van der Torre. How to model normative behavior in Petri nets. In *Proceedings of the Modelage'96*, Sesimbra, 1996.

[TH96]   R. Thomason and R. Horty. Nondeterministic action and dominance: foundations for planning and qualitative decision. In *Proceedings of the Sixth Conference on Theoretical Aspects of Rationality and Knowledge (TARK'96)*, pages 229–250. Morgan Kaufmann, 1996.

[Tho81]   R. Thomason. Deontic logic as founded on tense logic. In R. Hilpinen, editor, *New Studies in Deontic Logic*, pages 165–176. D. Reidel, 1981.

[TvdT94a] Y.-H. Tan and L.W.N. van der Torre. DIODE: Deontic logic based on diagnosis from first principles. In *Proceedings of the Workshop 'Artificial normative reasoning' of the Eleventh European Conference on Artificial Intelligence (ECAI'94)*, Amsterdam, 1994.

[TvdT94b] Y.-H. Tan and L.W.N. van der Torre. Representing deontic reasoning in a diagnostic framework. In *Proceedings of the Workshop on Legal Applications of Logic Programming of the Eleventh International Conference on Logic Programming (ICLP'94)*, Genoa, Italy, 1994.

[TvdT96]   Y.-H. Tan and L.W.N. van der Torre. How to combine ordering and minimizing in a deontic logic based on preferences. In *Deontic Logic, Agency and Normative Systems. Proceedings of the Δeon'96. Workshops in Computing*, pages 216–232. Springer Verlag, 1996.

[vdT94]   L.W.N. van der Torre. Violated obligations in a defeasible deontic logic. In *Proceedings of the Eleventh European Conference on Artificial Intelligence (ECAI'94)*, pages 371–375. John Wiley & Sons, 1994.

[vdTT95]   L.W.N. van der Torre and Y.H. Tan. Cancelling and overshadowing: two types of defeasibility in defeasible deontic logic. In *Proceedings of the Fourteenth International Joint Conference on Artificial Intelligence (IJCAI'95)*. Morgan Kaufman, 1995.

[vdTT97a] L.W.N. van der Torre and Y.H. Tan. The many faces of defeasibility in defeasible deontic logic. In D. Nute, editor, *Defeasible Deontic Logic*. Kluwer, 1997. To appear.

[vdTT97b] L.W.N. van der Torre and Y.H. Tan. Prohairetic deontic logic (PDL). In *Proceedings of AAAI spring symposium on qualitative preferences in deliberation and practical reasoning*, 1997. To appear.

[vF73]   B.C. van Fraassen. Values and the heart command. *Journal of Philosophy*, 70:5–19, 1973.

[vW71]   G.H. von Wright. Deontic logic and the theory of conditions. In *Deontic Logic: Introductory and Systematic Readings*, pages 159–177. D.Reidel, Dordrecht, 1971.

[vW81]   G.H. von Wright. On the logic of norms and actions. In *New Studies of Deontic Logic*. D.Reidel, Dordrecht, 1981.

Contextual Deontic Logic

Leendert W.N. van der Torre[1] and Yao-Hua Tan[2]

[1] Max-Planck-Institute for Computer Science
Im StadWald, D-66123 Saarbrücken, Germany
torre@mpi-sb.mpg.de
[2] EURIDIS, Erasmus University Rotterdam
P.O. Box 1738, 3000 DR Rotterdam, The Netherlands
ytan@euridis.fbk.eur.nl

Abstract. In this article we propose contextual deontic logic. Contextual obligations are written as $O(\alpha \mid \beta \setminus \gamma)$, and are to be read as 'α should be the case if β is the case, unless γ is the case'. The unless clause is analogous to the justification in Reiter's default rules. We show how contextual obligations can be used to solve certain aspects of contrary-to-duty paradoxes of dyadic deontic logic.

1   Contrary-to-Duty Reasoning

In recent years several researchers have argued that deontic logic is a useful tool to model reasoning in (legal) knowledge-based systems [JS92,RL92,Smi94,Roy96]. The problem, however, is that deontic logic is hampered by the so-called deontic paradoxes. The contrary-to-duty paradoxes like the notorious Chisholm paradox are the classic benchmark problems of deontic logics, which have initiated developments of monadic deontic logics [Chi63,For84], dyadic deontic logics [Tom81] and temporal deontic logics [vE82]. In this article we analyze certain aspects of the paradoxes in dyadic deontic logics, in which an obligation $O(\alpha|\beta)$ is read as 'α should be the case if β is the case.' An obligation $O(\alpha \mid \beta)$ is a *contrary-to-duty* obligation of the *primary* obligation $O(\alpha_1 \mid \beta_1)$ if and only if $\beta \wedge \alpha_1$ is inconsistent, as represented in Figure 1.

$$O(\alpha_1|\beta_1)$$

inconsistent

$$O(\alpha|\beta)$$

Fig. 1. $O(\alpha|\beta)$ is a contrary-to-duty obligation of $O(\alpha_1|\beta_1)$

The following example illustrates that the derivation of the dyadic obligation $O(\alpha_1|\neg\alpha_2)$ from the obligation $O(\alpha_1 \wedge \alpha_2|\top)$ is a fundamental problem underlying several contrary-to-duty paradoxes. Hence, the underlying problem of the contrary-to-duty paradoxes is that a contrary-to-duty obligation can be derived from its primary obligation.

J.-J. Ch. Meyer, P.-Y. Schobbens (Eds.): Formal Methods of Agents, LNAI 1760, pp. 240–251, 1999.

Example 1. (**Contrary-to-Duty Paradoxes**) Assume a dyadic deontic logic that validates at least substitution of logical equivalents and the following (intuitively[1] valid) inference patterns *Restricted Strengthening of the Antecedent* (RSA), *Weakening of the Consequent* (WC), *Conjunction* (AND) and a version of *Deontic Detachment* (DD′), in which $\overset{\leftrightarrow}{\Diamond}$ is a modal operator (that will be explained later) and $\overset{\leftrightarrow}{\Diamond}\phi$ is true for all consistent propositional formulas ϕ.

$$\text{RSA}: \frac{O(\alpha|\beta_1), \overset{\leftrightarrow}{\Diamond}(\alpha \wedge \beta_1 \wedge \beta_2)}{O(\alpha|\beta_1 \wedge \beta_2)} \qquad \text{WC}: \frac{O(\alpha_1|\beta)}{O(\alpha_1 \vee \alpha_2|\beta)}$$

$$\text{AND}: \frac{O(\alpha_1|\beta), O(\alpha_2|\beta)}{O(\alpha_1 \wedge \alpha_2|\beta)} \qquad \text{DD}': \frac{O(\alpha|\beta), O(\beta|\gamma)}{O(\alpha \wedge \beta|\gamma)}$$

Furthermore, consider the sets

$$S = \{O(\neg k|\top), O(g \wedge k|k)\}$$

$$S' = \{O(a|\top), O(t|a), O(\neg t|\neg a)\}$$

$$S'' = \{O(\neg a|\top), O(a \vee p|\top), O(\neg p|a)\}$$

where $\top$ stands for any tautology. S formalizes the Forrester paradox [For84] when k is read as 'killing someone' and $g \wedge k$ as 'killing someone gently,' S' formalizes the Chisholm paradox [Chi63] when a is read as 'a certain man going to the assistance of his neighbors' and t as 'the man telling his neighbors that he will come,'[2] and finally, S'' formalizes the apples-and-pears example [TvdT96] when a is read as 'buying apples' and p as 'buying pears.' The last obligation of each premise set is a contrary-to-duty obligation of the first obligation of the set, because its antecedent is contradictory with the consequent of the latter. The paradoxical consequences of the sets of obligations are represented in Figure 2. The underlying problem of the counterintuitive derivations is the derivation of the obligation $O(\alpha_1|\neg\alpha_2)$ from $O(\alpha_1 \wedge \alpha_2|\top)$ by WC and RSA: respectively the derivation of $O(\neg(g \wedge k)|k)$ from $O(\neg k|\top)$, $O(t|\neg a)$ from $O(a \wedge t|\top)$, and $O(p|a)$ from $O(\neg a \wedge p|\top)$.

---

[1] For example, we would like to use strengthening of the antecedent to derive 'you should not kill in the morning' from 'you should not kill,' and weakening of the consequent to derive 'you should not kill' from 'you should not kill and drive on the right side of the street.' However, besides problems created by contrary-to-duty reasoning there are also problems related to dilemma reasoning. For example, one may argue that the derivation of $O(p|\neg(p \wedge q))$ from the set $\{O(p|\top), O(q|\top)\}$ is counterintuitive. This could be an argument saying that strengthening of the antecedent is counterintuitive. We argued in [TvdT96,vdTT97b] that these dilemma problems should be analyzed separately from contrary-to-duty problems. In this paper, we only analyze so-called minimal deontic logics in which dilemmas are consistent. For the formalization of the no-dilemma assumption, see [TvdT96,vdTT97b].

[2] The original Chisholm set also contains the fact that the man does not go to the assistance. However, the addition of this fact does not have any consequences, because we do not derive monadic obligations from dyadic ones (so-called factual detachment). We do not accept factual detachment, because it results in so-called pragmatic oddities, see [PS94].

$$\frac{\dfrac{\dfrac{O(\neg k|\top)}{O(\neg(g \wedge k)|\top)}\ \text{WC}}{O(\neg(g \wedge k)|k)}\ \text{RSA} \qquad O(g \wedge k|k)}{O(\neg(g \wedge k) \wedge (g \wedge k)|k)}\ \text{AND}$$

$$\frac{\dfrac{\dfrac{\dfrac{O(t|a) \quad O(a|\top)}{O(a \wedge t|\top)}\ \text{DD}'}{O(t|\top)}\ \text{WC}}{O(t|\neg a)}\ \text{RSA} \qquad O(\neg t|\neg a)}{O(t \wedge \neg t|\neg a)}\ \text{AND} \qquad\qquad \frac{\dfrac{\dfrac{\dfrac{O(\neg a|\top) \quad O(a \vee p|\top)}{O(\neg a \wedge p|\top)}\ \text{AND}}{O(p|\top)}\ \text{WC}}{O(p|a)}\ \text{RSA} \qquad O(\neg p|a)}{O(p \wedge \neg p|a)}\ \text{AND}$$

Fig. 2. Three contrary-to-duty paradoxes

There are two types of dyadic deontic logics, dependent on how the antecedent is interpreted. The first type, as advocated by Chellas [Che74,Alc93], defines a dyadic obligation in terms of a monadic obligation by $O(\alpha|\beta) =_{def} \beta > O\alpha$, where '$>$' is a strict implication. These dyadic deontic logics have strengthening of the antecedent, but they cannot represent the contrary-to-duty paradoxes in a consistent way. Dyadic deontic logics of the second type, as introduced by Hansson [Han71] and further investigated by Lewis [Lew74], do not have strengthening of the antecedent and therefore they can represent the paradoxes. Intuitively, the solution of these logics is that the antecedent of the dyadic obligations is interpreted as a kind of 'context'. For example, in the Forrester paradox the derivation of the obligation $O(\neg(g \wedge k)|k)$ from $O(\neg k|\top)$ is counterintuitive, because in the context where you kill, it is not obligatory not to kill gently (whereas this is obligatory in the most general context). Because there are many different problems related to the Forrester and Chisholm paradoxes, we restrict our analysis to the apples-and-pears example. In the contextual interpretation of the apples-and-pears example, the derivation of the obligation $O(p|a)$ from $O(\neg a|\top)$ and $O(a \vee p|\top)$ is counterintuitive, because in the context where apples are bought, it is not obligatory to buy pears (whereas this is obligatory in the most general context).

In this paper, we propose a solution for the paradoxes based on contextual obligations. A contextual obligation, written as $O(\alpha|\beta \backslash \gamma)$, is an extension of a dyadic obligation $O(\alpha|\beta)$ with an unless clause γ. The unless clause can be compared to the justification in a Reiter default 'α is normally the case if β is the case unless γ is the case,' written as $\beta : \neg\gamma/\alpha$ [Rei80]. For example, 'birds fly unless they are penguins' can be represented by $b : \neg p/f$, and 'penguins do not fly' by $(b \wedge p) : \top/\neg f$. Hence, the unless clause is analogous to the justification of a Reiter default, which means that it formalizes a kind of consistency check.

This paper is organized as follows. In Section 2 we give the solution of the apples-and-pears problem in labeled deontic logic LDL. In Section 3 we introduce contextual obligations $O(\alpha|\beta \backslash \gamma)$, and we show how they solve the apples-and-pears problem. Finally, in Section 4 we mention some interesting connections with logics of defeasible reasoning and qualitative decision theory.

2   Labeled Obligations

In [vdTT95] we introduced labeled deontic logic LDL, a logic inspired by contextual logic [BT96]. Labeled obligations $O(\alpha|\beta)_L$ can *roughly* be read as 'α ought to be the case, if β is the case, because of L.'

2.1   Implicit and Explicit Obligations

To illustrate the distinction between implicit and explicit obligations, we recall the well-known distinction between implicit and explicit knowledge. The latter distinction originates in the logical omniscience problem: in principle, an agent cannot know all logical consequences of his knowledge. The benchmark example is that knowledge of the laws of mathematics does not imply knowledge of the theorem of Fermat. That is, an agent does not explicitly know the theorem of Fermat, she only implicitly knows it. Analogously, explicit obligations are not deductively closed, in contrast to implicit obligations.

Several researchers make a distinction between imperatives and obligations, although many researchers hold them as essentially the same. Explicit obligation can be used to formalize imperatives, and implicit obligations can be used to formalize the 'usual' type of obligations. The idea behind labeled obligations is to represent the explicit obligation, of which the implicit obligation is derived, in the label. The label is the reason for the obligation. If we make the distinction between imperatives and obligations, then the label L of the obligation $O(\alpha|\beta)_L$ represents the imperatives from which the obligation is derived. This explains our reading of the label obligation $O(\alpha|\beta)_L$: 'α ought to be the case if β is the case, because of the imperatives L.'

We can use labeled deontic logic to solve the contrary-to-duty paradoxes, because we use the label to check that a derived obligation is not a contrary-to-duty obligation of its premises. Remember that we can test for CTD with a consistency check, see Figure 1. The label of an obligation represents the consequents of the premises from which the obligation is derived. In labeled deontic logic we use a consistency check of the label of the obligation with its antecedent. If the label and the antecedent are consistent, then the derived obligation is not a contrary-to-duty of its premises.

2.2   Labeled Obligations

In this section we introduce a deontic version of a labeled deductive system as it was introduced by Gabbay in [Gab91]. The language of dyadic deontic logic is enriched by allowing labels in the dyadic obligations. Roughly speaking, the label L is a record of the consequents of all the premises that are used in the derivation of $O(\alpha|\beta)$.

Definition 2. (Language of LDL**)** *The language of labeled deontic logic is a propositional base logic* $\mathcal{L}$ *and labeled dyadic conditional obligations* $O(\alpha \mid \beta)_L$, *with* α *and* β *sentences of* $\mathcal{L}$, *and* L *a set of sentences of* $\mathcal{L}$.

Each labeled obligation occurring as a premise has its own consequent in its label. This represents that the premises are explicit obligations, because it is derived 'from itself.'

Definition 3. (Premises of LDL**)** *A labeled obligation which has its own consequent as its label is called a premise.*

We assume that the antecedent and the label of an obligation are always consistent. The label of an obligation derived by an inference rule is the union of the labels of the premises used in this inference rule. Below are some labeled versions of inference schemes. We write $\overset{\leftrightarrow}{\Diamond} L$ for a consistency check of a set of formulas.

$$\text{RSA}_V : \frac{O(\alpha \mid \beta_1)_L, \overset{\leftrightarrow}{\Diamond}(L \cup \{\beta_1 \wedge \beta_2\})}{O(\alpha \mid \beta_1 \wedge \beta_2)_L}$$

$$\text{WC}_V : \frac{O(\alpha_1 \mid \beta)_L}{O(\alpha_1 \vee \alpha_2 \mid \beta)_L}$$

$$\text{RDD}'_V : \frac{O(\alpha \mid \beta)_{L_1}, O(\beta \mid \gamma)_{L_2}, \overset{\leftrightarrow}{\Diamond}(L_1 \cup L_2 \cup \{\gamma\})}{O(\alpha \wedge \beta \mid \gamma)_{L_1 \cup L_2}}$$

$$\text{RAND}_V : \frac{O(\alpha_1 \mid \beta)_{L_1}, O(\alpha_2 \mid \beta)_{L_2}, \overset{\leftrightarrow}{\Diamond}(L_1 \cup L_2 \cup \{\beta\})}{O(\alpha_1 \wedge \alpha_2 \mid \beta)_{L_1 \cup L_2}}$$

Informally, the premises used in the derivation tree are not violated by the antecedent of the derived obligation, or, alternatively, the derived obligation is not a contrary-to-duty obligation of these premises. We say that the labels formalize the assumptions on which an obligation is derived, and the consistency check $\overset{\leftrightarrow}{\Diamond}$ checks whether the assumptions are violated. The following example illustrates that the labeled deductive system gives the intuitive reading of the Apples-and-Pears example.

Example 4. **(Apples-and-Pears, continued)** Assume a labeled deductive system that validates at least the inference patterns RSA$_V$, RAND$_V$ and WC$_V$. Consider the premise set of labeled obligations $S = \{O(a \vee p \mid \top)_{a \vee p}, O(\neg a \mid \top)_{\neg a}\}$ as premise, where a can be read as 'buying apples' and p as 'buying pears'. In Figure 3 below it is shown how the derivation in Figure 2 is blocked.

The apples-and-pears example in labeled deontic logic showed an important property of dyadic deontic logics with a contextual interpretation of the antecedent, namely that the context is restricted to non-violations of premises. If the antecedent is a violation, i.e. if the derived obligation would be a contrary-to-duty obligation, then the derivation is blocked. Obviously, as a logic the labeled deductive system is quite limited, if only because it lacks a semantics. In the following section, we consider contextual deontic logic, which has an intuitive preference-based semantics.

$$\frac{O(a \vee p | \top)_{\{a \vee p\}} \quad O(\neg a | \top)_{\{\neg a\}}}{O(\neg a \wedge p | \top)_{\{a \vee p, \neg a\}}} \text{ AND}$$
$$- - - - - - - - - \text{ (SA/RSA)}$$
$$\frac{O(\neg a \wedge p | a)_{\{a \vee p, \neg a\}}}{O(p | a)_{\{a \vee p, \neg a\}}} \text{ WC}$$

$$\frac{O(a \vee p | \top)_{\{a \vee p\}} \quad O(\neg a | \top)_{\{\neg a\}}}{O(\neg a \wedge p | \top)_{\{a \vee p, \neg a\}}} \text{ AND}$$
$$\frac{}{O(p | \top)_{\{a \vee p, \neg a\}}} \text{ WC}$$
$$- - - - - - - \text{ (SA/RSA)}$$
$$O(p | a)_{\{a \vee p, \neg a\}}$$

Fig. 3. The apples-and-pears example

3   Contextual Obligations

Contextual obligations are formalized in Boutilier's modal preference[3] logic CT4O, a bimodal propositional logic of inaccessible worlds. For the details and completeness proof of this logic see [Bou94a]. In the logic we abstract from actions, time and individuals.

Definition 5. (CT4O) *The logic CT4O is a propositional bimodal system with the two normal modal connectives $\Box$ and $\overline{\Box}$. Dual 'possibility' connectives $\Diamond$ and $\overline{\Diamond}$ are defined as usual and two additional modal connectives $\overleftrightarrow{\Box}$ and $\overleftrightarrow{\Diamond}$ are defined as follows.*

$$\Diamond \alpha =_{def} \neg \Box \neg \alpha \qquad \overleftrightarrow{\Box} \alpha =_{def} \Box \alpha \wedge \overline{\Box} \alpha$$
$$\overline{\Diamond} \alpha =_{def} \neg \overline{\Box} \neg \alpha \qquad \overleftrightarrow{\Diamond} \alpha =_{def} \Diamond \alpha \vee \overline{\Diamond} \alpha$$

CT4O is axiomatized by the following axioms and inference rules.

K $\Box(\alpha \to \beta) \to (\Box \alpha \to \Box \beta)$ **Nes** *From* α *infer* $\overline{\Box} \alpha$
K′ $\overline{\Box}(\alpha \to \beta) \to (\overline{\Box} \alpha \to \overline{\Box} \beta)$ **MP** *From* $\alpha \to \beta$ *and* α *infer* β
T $\Box \alpha \to \alpha$
4 $\Box \alpha \to \Box \Box \alpha$
H $\overleftrightarrow{\Diamond}(\Box \alpha \wedge \overline{\Box} \beta) \to \overleftrightarrow{\Box}(\alpha \vee \beta)$

Kripke models $M = \langle W, \leq, V \rangle$ *for CT4O consist of* W, *a set of worlds,* $\leq$, *a binary transitive and reflexive accessibility relation, and* V, *a valuation of the propositional atoms in the worlds. The partial pre-ordering* $\leq$ *expresses preferences:* $w_1 \leq w_2$ *i* w_1 *is as preferable as* w_2. *The modal connective* $\Box$ *refers to accessible worlds and the modal connective* $\overline{\Box}$ *to inaccessible worlds.*

$$M, w \models \Box \alpha \ i \quad \forall w' \in W \text{ if } w' \leq w, \text{ then } M, w' \models \alpha$$

---

[3] The use of preferences follows from the fact that an obligation $O\alpha$ is interpreted as some kind of choice between α and $\neg\alpha$. This idea of deontic choice results in utilitarian (preference-based) semantics [Jen74]. It should be noted that preference-based semantics are closely related to semantics based on choice functions and other classical semantics [Lew74].

$$M, w \models \overline{\square} \alpha \ i \quad \forall w' \in W \ if \ w' \not\leq w, \ then \ M, w' \models \alpha$$

Contextual obligations are defined in CT4O as follows. In this paper, we do not discuss the properties of $>_s$ but we focus on the properties of the contextual obligations.[4]

Definition 6. (CDL) *The logic* CDL *is the logic CT4O extended with the following definitions of contextual obligations. The contextual obligation ' α should be the case if β is the case unless γ is the case', written as $O(\alpha|\beta\backslash\gamma)$, is defined as a strong preference of $\alpha \wedge \beta \wedge \neg\gamma$ over $\neg\alpha \wedge \beta$.*

$$\alpha_1 >_s \alpha_2 \quad =_{def} \overline{\square}(\alpha_1 \to \square\neg\alpha_2)$$
$$O(\alpha|\beta\backslash\gamma) \quad =_{def} (\alpha \wedge \beta \wedge \neg\gamma) >_s (\neg\alpha \wedge \beta)$$
$$= \quad \overline{\square}((\alpha \wedge \beta \wedge \neg\gamma) \to \square(\beta \to \alpha))$$
$$O^c(\alpha|\beta\backslash\gamma) \quad =_{def} (\alpha \wedge \beta \wedge \neg\gamma) >_s (\neg\alpha \wedge \beta) \wedge \overleftrightarrow{\diamond}(\alpha \wedge \beta \wedge \neg\gamma)$$
$$O^{cc}(\alpha|\beta\backslash\gamma) =_{def} (\alpha \wedge \beta \wedge \neg\gamma) >_s (\neg\alpha \wedge \beta) \wedge \overleftrightarrow{\diamond}(\alpha \wedge \beta \wedge \neg\gamma) \wedge \overleftrightarrow{\diamond}(\neg\alpha \wedge \beta)$$

From the definitions follows immediately the following satisfiability conditions for the modal connectives $\overleftrightarrow{\square}$: $M, w \models \overleftrightarrow{\square} \alpha$ iff $\forall w' \in W \ M, w' \models \alpha$ and $\overleftrightarrow{\diamond}$: $M, w \models \overleftrightarrow{\diamond} \alpha$ iff $\exists w' \in W \ M, w' \models \alpha$. As a consequence, the truth value of a contextual obligation does not depend on the world in which the obligation is evaluated. For a model $M = \langle W, \leq, V \rangle$ we have $M \models O(\alpha|\beta\backslash\gamma)$ (i.e. for all worlds $w \in W$ we have $M, w \models O(\alpha|\beta\backslash\gamma)$) iff there is a world $w \in W$ such that $M, w \models O(\alpha|\beta\backslash\gamma)$.

The following proposition shows the truth conditions of contextual obligations.

Proposition 7. (Contextual Obligation) *Let* $M = \langle W, \leq, V \rangle$ *be a CT4O model and let* $|\alpha|$ *be the set of worlds that satisfy* α. *For a world* $w \in W$, *we have* $M, w \models O(\alpha|\beta\backslash\gamma)$ *i for all* $w_1 \in |\alpha \wedge \beta \wedge \neg\gamma|$ *and all* $w_2 \in |\neg\alpha \wedge \beta|$ *we have* $w_2 \not\leq w_1$.

Proof *Follows directly from the definition of* $>_s$.

The following proposition shows several properties of contextual obligations.

Proposition 8. (Theorems of CDL**)** *The logic CT4O validates the following theorems.*

---

[4] The preference relation $>_s$ is quite weak. For example, it is not anti-symmetric (we cannot derive $\neg(\alpha_2 >_s \alpha_1)$ from $\alpha_1 >_s \alpha_2$) and it is not transitive (we cannot derive $\alpha_1 >_s \alpha_3$ from $\alpha_1 >_s \alpha_2$ and $\alpha_2 >_s \alpha_3$). The lack of these properties is the result of the fact that we do not have connected orderings. Moreover, this a-connectedness is crucial for our preference-based deontic logics, see [TvdT96,vdTT97b].

SA: $O(\alpha|\beta_1\backslash\gamma) \rightarrow O(\alpha|\beta_1 \wedge \beta_2\backslash\gamma)$
WC: $O(\alpha_1 \wedge \alpha_2|\beta\backslash\gamma) \rightarrow O(\alpha_1|\beta\backslash\gamma \vee \neg\alpha_2)$
WT: $O(\alpha|\beta\backslash\gamma_1) \rightarrow O(\alpha|\beta\backslash\gamma_1 \vee \gamma_2)$
AND: $(O(\alpha_1|\beta\backslash\gamma) \wedge O(\alpha_2|\beta\backslash\gamma)) \rightarrow O(\alpha_1 \wedge \alpha_2|\beta\backslash\gamma)$
RSA: $(O^c(\alpha|\beta_1\backslash\gamma)\wedge \overset{\leftrightarrow}{\Diamond}(\alpha \wedge \beta_1 \wedge \beta_2 \wedge \neg\gamma)) \rightarrow O^c(\alpha|\beta_1 \wedge \beta_2\backslash\gamma)$
RAND: $(O^c(\alpha_1|\beta\backslash\gamma) \wedge O^c(\alpha_2|\beta\backslash\gamma)\wedge \overset{\leftrightarrow}{\Diamond}(\alpha_1 \wedge \alpha_2 \wedge \beta \wedge \neg\gamma)) \rightarrow O^c(\alpha_1 \wedge \alpha_2|\beta\backslash\gamma)$

Proof *The theorems are proven in the preferential semantics. Consider* **WC.**
Assume $M \models O(\alpha_1\wedge\alpha_2|\beta\backslash\gamma)$. *Let* $W_1 = |\alpha_1\wedge\alpha_2\wedge\beta\wedge\neg\gamma|$ *and* $W_2 = |\neg(\alpha_1\wedge\alpha_2)\wedge\beta|$, *and* $w_2 \not\leq w_1$ *for* $w_1 \in W_1$ *and* $w_2 \in W_2$. *Moreover, let* $W_1' = |\alpha_1\wedge\beta\wedge\neg(\gamma\vee\neg\alpha_2)|$ *and* $W_2' = |\neg\alpha_1 \wedge \beta|$. *We have* $w_2 \not\leq w_1$ *for* $w_1 \in W_1'$ *and* $w_2 \in W_2'$, *because* $W_1 = W_1'$ *and* $W_2' \subseteq W_2$. *Thus,* $M \models O(\alpha_1|\beta\backslash\gamma \vee \neg\alpha_2)$. *Verification of the other theorems is left to the reader.* [5]

To illustrate the properties of CDL, we compare it with Bengt Hansson's mini-mizing dyadic deontic logic. First we recall some well-known definitions and prop-erties of this logic. In Bengt Hansson's classical preference semantics [Han71], as studied by Lewis [Lew74], a dyadic obligation, which we denote by $O_{HL}(\alpha|\beta)$, is true in a model iff 'the minimal (or preferred) β worlds satisfy α'. A weaker version of this definition, which allows for moral dilemmas, is that $O_{HL}^w(\alpha|\beta)$ is true in a model iff there is an *equivalence class* of minimal (or preferred) β worlds that satisfy α.

Definition 9. (Minimizing Obligation) *Let* $M = \langle W, \leq, V\rangle$ *be a Kripke model and* $|\alpha|$ *be the set of all worlds of* W *that satisfy* α. *The weak Hansson-Lewis obligation 'α should be the case if β is the case', written as* $O_{HL}^w(\alpha|\beta)$, *is defined as follows.*

$$O_{HL}^w(\alpha|\beta) =_{def} \overset{\leftrightarrow}{\Diamond}(\beta \wedge \Box(\beta \rightarrow \alpha))$$

The model M satisfies the weak Hansson-Lewis obligation 'α should be the case if β is the case', written as $M \models O_{HL}^w(\alpha|\beta)$, iff there is a world $w_1 \in |\alpha \wedge \beta|$ such that for all $w_2 \in |\neg\alpha \wedge \beta|$ we have $w_2 \not\leq w_1$. The following proposition shows that the expression $O_{HL}^w(\alpha|\beta)$ corresponds to a weak Hansson-Lewis minimizing obligation. For simplicity, we assume that there are no infinite descending chains.

Proposition 10. *Let* $M = \langle W, \leq, V\rangle$ *be a CT4O model, such that there are no infinite descending chains. As usual, we write* $w_1 < w_2$ *for* $w_1 \leq w_2$ *and not* $w_2 \leq w_1$, *and* $w_1 \sim w_2$ *for* $w_1 \leq w_2$ *and* $w_2 \leq w_1$. *A world* w *is a minimal* β-*world, written as* $M, w \models_\leq \beta$, *i* $M, w \models \beta$ *and for all* $w' < w$ *holds* $M, w' \not\models \beta$. *A set of worlds is an equivalence class of minimal* β-*worlds, written as* E_β, *i there is a* w *such that* $M, w \models_\leq \beta$ *and* $E_\beta = \{w' \mid M, w' \models \beta \text{ and } w \sim w'\}$. *We have* $M \models O_{HL}^w(\alpha|\beta)$ *i there is an* E_β *such that* $E_\beta \subseteq |\alpha|$.

---

[5] This proposition also shows an important advantage of the axiomatisation of the deontic logic in a underlying preference logic: the properties of our dyadic obligations can simply be proven by proving (un)derivability in CT4O.

Proof $\Leftarrow$ *Follows directly from the definitions. Assume there is a w such that* $M, w \models_\leq \beta$ *and* $E_\beta = \{w' \mid M, w' \models \beta$ *and* $w \sim w'\}$ *and* $E_\beta \subseteq |\alpha|$. *For all* $w_2 \in |\neg\alpha \wedge \beta|$ *we have* $w_2 \not\leq w$.

  $\Rightarrow$ *Assume that there is a world $w_1 \in |\alpha \wedge \beta|$ such that for all $w_2 \in |\neg\alpha \wedge \beta|$ we have* $w_2 \not\leq w_1$. *Let* w *be a minimal* β-world *such that* $M, w \models_\leq \beta$ *and* $w \leq w_1$ *(that exists because there are no i nfinite descending chains), and let* $E_\beta = \{w' \mid M, w' \models \beta$ *and* $w \sim w'\}$.

Now we are ready to compare contextual deontic logic with Bengt Hansson's dyadic deontic logic. The following proposition shows that under a certain condition, the contextual obligation $O(\alpha|\beta\backslash\gamma)$ is true in a model if and only if a set of the weak Hansson-Lewis minimizing obligations $O^w_{HL}(\alpha|\beta')$ is true in the model.

Proposition 11. *Let* $M = \langle W, \leq, V \rangle$ *be a CT4O model, that has no worlds that satisfy the same propositional sentences. Hence, we identify the set of worlds with a set of propositional interpretations, such that there are no duplicate worlds. We have* $M \models O^{cc}(\alpha|\beta\backslash\gamma)$ *i there are $\alpha \wedge \beta \wedge \neg\gamma$ and $\neg\alpha \wedge \beta$ worlds, and for all propositional* β' *such that* $M \models^{\overleftrightarrow{\square}} (\beta' \rightarrow \beta)$ *and* $M \not\models^{\overleftrightarrow{\square}} (\beta' \rightarrow \gamma)$, *we have* $M \models O^w_{HL}(\alpha|\beta')$.

Proof $\Rightarrow$ *Follows directly from the semantic definitions. $\Leftarrow$ Every world is characterized by a unique propositional sentence. Let $\overline{w}$ denote the sentence that uniquely characterizes world w. Proof by contraposition. If $M \not\models O^{cc}(\alpha|\beta\backslash\gamma)$, then there are w_1, w_2 such that $M, w_1 \models \alpha \wedge \beta \wedge \neg\gamma$ and $M, w_2 \models \neg\alpha \wedge \beta$ and $w_2 \leq w_1$. Choose $\beta' = \overline{w_1} \vee \overline{w_2}$. The world w_2 is an element of the preferred β' worlds, because there are no duplicate worlds. (If duplicate worlds are allowed, then there could be a β' world w_3 which is a duplicate of w_1, and which is strictly preferred to w_1 and w_2.) We have $M, w_2 \not\models \alpha$ and therefore $M \not\models O^w_{HL}(\alpha|\beta')$,*

The following example illustrates that contextual deontic logic solves the contrary-to-duty paradoxes.

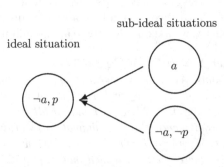

sub-ideal situations

ideal situation

Fig. 4. Semantic solution in contextual deontic logic

Example 12. (**Apples-and-Pears, continued**) Consider the premise set of contextual obligations $S = \{O^c(a \vee p | \top \backslash \bot), O^c(\neg a | \top \backslash \bot)\}$. The crucial observation is that we do not have $O^{cc}(p | a \backslash \gamma)$ for any γ, and a typical countermodel is the model in Figure 4. This figure should be read as follows. Each circle represents an equivalence class of worlds, that satisfy the propositions written in the circle. The arrows represent strict preferences for all worlds in the circle. We have $S \models O^c(p | \top \backslash a)$, as is shown in Figure 5, which expresses that pears should be bought, unless apples are bought. From the contextual obligation $O^c(p | \top \backslash a)$ we cannot derive $O(p | a \backslash a)$ due to the unless clause.

$$
\frac{\dfrac{O^c(a \vee p | \top \backslash \bot) \quad O^c(\neg a | \top \backslash \bot)}{O^c(\neg a \wedge p | \top \backslash \bot)} \text{ AND}}{\dfrac{}{O^c(p | \top \backslash a)} \text{ WC}}
$$

$$
- - - - - - \text{ NO (RSA)}
$$

$$
O^c(p | a \backslash a)
$$

Fig. 5. Proof-theoretic solution in contextual deontic logic

It is easily verified that the contextual obligations also solve the other contrary-to-duty paradoxes in Example 1.

4   Conclusions

Recently, several researchers have noticed a remarkable resemblance between logics of qualitative decision theory, logics of desires and deontic logic, see for example [Bou94b,Lan96]. In future research, we will investigate whether contextual deontic logic proposed here can be applied to model qualitative decision theory, and which extensions are needed (see [TvdT96] for possible extensions).

In the introduction, we already observed that we can also define contextual defaults 'α is usually the case if β is the case unless γ is the case,' written as $\beta : \neg \gamma / \alpha$. The main distinction between CDL and Reiter's default logic is that contextual obligations are not used as inference rules. In CDL, we derive contextual obligations from contextual obligations, which can be compared to the derivation of defaults from defaults. A set of defaults Δ derives a default δ iff the set of extensions of $\langle \Delta, F \rangle$ is the same as the set of extensions of $\langle \Delta \cup \{\delta\}, F \rangle$ for every set of facts F. In Reiter's default logic, defaults are used to generate extensions. A similarity between CDL and default logic is that contextual obligations as well as defaults express preferences. Reiter's defaults express preferences on assumptions. We can view the default $\frac{\beta : \neg \gamma}{\alpha}$ as expressing the preference that models which make $\alpha \wedge \beta$ true are more preferred than models that make $\neg \alpha \wedge \beta$ true, and this preference is cancelled for models that make γ true.

Contextual obligations give rise to a kind of defeasibility, in the sense that the obligations lack unrestricted strengthening of the antecedent (the typical property of defeasible conditionals [Alc93]). A non-monotonic (defeasible) aspect is necessary for a satisfactory analysis of the contrary-to-duty paradoxes. However, it is important to notice that this defeasibility related to contextual reasoning is in fundamentally different from the defeasibility related to specificity or prima facie obligations, see [vdTT95,vdTT97a]. An important inference pattern in our analysis of the contrary-to-duty paradoxes is weakening of the consequent. Weakening of the consequent plays an important role in default logic too, as shown by the normally-presumably logic of Veltman [Vel96]. The normally defaults do not have weakening of the consequent, whereas the presumably defaults do.

References

Alc93.   C. E. Alchourrón. Philosophical foundations of deontic logic and the logic of defeasible conditionals. In Deontic Logic in Computer Science: Normative System Specification , pages 43–84. John Wiley & Sons, 1993.

Bou94a.   C. Boutilier. Conditional logics of normality: a modal approach. Artificial Intelligence , 68:87–154, 1994.

Bou94b.   C. Boutilier. Toward a logic for qualitative decision theory. In Proceedings of the Fourth International Conference on Principles of Knowledge Representation and Reasoning (KR'94)   , pages 75–86, 1994.

BT96.   Philippe Besnard and Yao-Hua Tan. A modal logic with context-dependent inference for non-monotonic reasoning. In Proceedings of ECAI96 , 1996.

Che74.   B.F. Chellas. Conditional obligation. In Logical Theory and Semantical Analysis , pages 23–33. D. Reidel Publishing Company, Dordrecht, Holland, 1974.

Chi63.   R.M. Chisholm. Contrary-to-duty imperatives and deontic logic. Analysis , 24:33–36, 1963.

For84.   J.W. Forrester. Gentle murder, or the adverbial Samaritan. Journal of Philosophy , 81:193–197, 1984.

Gab91.   D. Gabbay. Labelled deductive systems. Technical report, Centrum fur Informations und Sprachverarbeitung, Universitat Munchen, 1991.

Han71.   B. Hansson. An analysis of some deontic logics. In Deontic Logic: Introductionary and Systematic Readings   , pages 121–147. D. Reidel Publishing Company, Dordrecht, Holland, 1971.

Jen74.   R.E. Jennings. A utilitarian semantics for deontic logic. Journal of PHhilisophical Logic , 3:445–465, 1974.

JS92.   A.J.I. Jones and M. Sergot. Deontic logic in the representation of law: Towards a methodology. Artificial Intelligence and Law , 1:45–64, 1992.

Lan96.   J. Lang. Conditional desires and utilities - an alternative approach to qualitative decision theory. In Proceedings of the ECAI'96 , 1996.

Lew74.   D. Lewis. Semantic analysis for dyadic deontic logic. In Logical Theory and Semantical Analysis , pages 1–14. D. Reidel Publishing Company, Dordrecht, Holland, 1974.

PS94.   H. Prakken and M.J. Sergot. Contrary-to-duty imperatives, defeasibility and violability. In Proceedings of the Second Workshop on Deontic Logic in Computer Science (Deon'94)   , Oslo, 1994. To appear in: Studia Logica .

Rei80.   R. Reiter. A logic for default reasoning. Artificial Intelligence , 13:81–132, 1980.

RL92.   Y.U. Ryu and R.M. Lee. Defeasible deontic reasoning and its applications to normative systems. Technical report, EURIDIS, 1992.

Roy96.   L. Royakkers. Representing Legal Rules in Deontic Logic . PhD thesis, University of Brabant, 1996.

Smi94.   T. Smith. Legal Expert Systems: Discussion of Theoretical Assumptions   . PhD thesis, University of Utrecht, 1994.

Tom81.   J.E. Tomberlin. Contrary-to-duty imperatives and conditional obligation. Noûs, 16:357–375, 1981.

TvdT96.   Y.-H. Tan and L.W.N. van der Torre. How to combine ordering and minimizing in a deontic logic based on preferences. In Deontic Logic, Agency and Normative Systems, Proceedings of the third workshop on deontic logic in computer science (ΔEON'96) , pages 216–232. Springer Verlag, Workshops in Computer Science, 1996.

vdTT95.   L.W.N. van der Torre and Y.H. Tan. Cancelling and overshadowing: two types of defeasibility in defeasible deontic logic. In Proceedings of the Fourteenth International Joint Conference on Artificial Intelligence (IJCAI'95)   , pages 1525–1532. Morgan Kaufman, 1995.

vdTT97a.   L.W.N. van der Torre and Y.H. Tan. The different faces of defeasibility in defeasible deontic logic. In D. Nute, editor, Defeasible Deontic Logic . Kluwer, 1997. To appear.

vdTT97b.   L.W.N. van der Torre and Y.H. Tan. Prohairetic deontic logic and qualitative decision theory. In Proceedings of AAAI spring symposium , 1997. To appear.

vE82.   J. van Eck. A system of temporally relative modal and deontic predicate logic and its philosophical applications. Logique et Analyse , 99,100, 1982.

Vel96.   F. Veltman. Defaults in update semantics. Journal of Philosophical Logic , 25:221–261, 1996.

Author Index

Lecture Notes in Artificial Intelligence (LNAI)

Lecture Notes in Computer Science